The Quarantined Culture

Studies in Australian History

Series editors:
Alan Gilbert, Patricia Grimshaw and Peter Spearritt

The Quarantined Culture

Australian Reactions to Modernism 1913–1939

John F. Williams

CAMBRIDGE
UNIVERSITY PRESS

CAMBRIDGE UNIVERSITY PRESS
Cambridge, New York, Melbourne, Madrid, Cape Town, Singapore,
São Paulo, Delhi, Dubai, Tokyo

Cambridge University Press
The Edinburgh Building, Cambridge CB2 8RU, UK

Published in the United States of America by Cambridge University Press, New York

www.cambridge.org
Information on this title: www.cambridge.org/9780521477130

First published 1995
Re-issued in this digitally printed version 2010

A catalogue record for this publication is available from the British Library

National Library of Australia Cataloguing in Publication data

Williams, John F. (John Frank).
The quarantined culture: Australian reactions to
modernism 1913–1939.
Bibliography.
Includes index.
1. Art, Modern – 20th century – History. 2. Art,
Australian – History – 20th century. 3. Art and society –
Australia. 4. Australia – History – 1901–1945.
5. Australia – Civilization – 1901–1945. I. Title. (Series:
Studies in Australian history (Cambridge, England)).
306.470994

Library of Congress Cataloguing in Publication data

Williams, John Frank
The quarantined culture: Australian reactions to modernism,
1913–1939 / John F. Williams.
p.   cm.–(Studies in Australian history)
Includes bibliographical references and index.
1. Art, Australian. 2. Modernism (Art) – Public opinion.
3. Public opinion – Australia. I. Title. II. Series.
N7400.W553   1995
709'.94'09041–dc20   95–11772

ISBN 978-0-521-47139-8 Hardback
ISBN 978-0-521-47713-0 Paperback

Contents

Illustrations

Plates

Figures

Acknowledgments

Without an Australia Council Visual Arts Board Fellowship in 1988 this work would not have taken the form it did, and could not have been finished in 1994. It began life as a PhD thesis, commenced in 1988 in a studio at the Cité des Arts in Paris, and without Duncan Waterson's enthusiasm, knowledge, and forbearance, for what was an inter-disciplinary plunge into the unknown, I doubt it would have got this far.

More recently Jeanette Hoorn, Phillipa McGuinness and Roderic Campbell have provided, from quite different standpoints, supportive, critical and thoughtful editorial assistance. Jeanette Hoorn's reading of the draft material brought forth a string of new ideas and attitudes that introduced new insights which countered and transformed some of the assertions of the original thesis. To her my debt is incalculable. To Kate Blackmore, Bridget Foley-Griffin, Harry Knowles, Debra Phillips, Heather Johnson, Avenel Mitchell, Peter Henderson, Ingeborg Tyssen, Paul Ashton, and Maureen Burns, who passed on material from their own researches, goes my gratitude.

As it does to Colin Doxford, George Parsons, Dennis Phillips, Heather Jamieson, and the late Steven Shortus, for whom the subject was always of interest and from whom pertinent advice was always forthcoming. Ulrike Levy guided me through some sticky passages in German, Victoria Andrieu helped in Spanish and Jean Levy kept talking French to me. No less knowledgeable and generous in advice and time were Ursula Prunstler, Sandra Byron, Terence Maloon and Barry Pearce at the Art Gallery of New South Wales; Isobel Crombie at the National Gallery of Victoria, and Gael Newton at the Australian National Gallery. At the Australian War Memorial Peter Stanley was supportive and enthusiastic, while the help of Bet Dracoulis and the research staff there was quite simply indispensable.

My wife Ingeborg Tyssen is a professional artist and writer with a full-time creative life of her own. It would be hard to count the number of discoveries she made in the process of her own not-altogether related researches that she simply passed on to me. At the right moment she provided the right support: to her I dedicate this book.

Introduction

Visions of a new world

By 1913 Australia had experienced, along with other developing and developed nations, more than a quarter of a century of unparalleled change. The first multi-storied buildings of steel and concrete—in large part made possible by the recent development of the electric, cable-winched elevator—had appeared in cities where electric lighting was becoming the principle source of illumination, where lorries, motor cars and motor omnibuses were no longer novelties, and where electric-powered tramways had almost completely displaced horse-drawn and cable-driven systems. Evidence of 'new society' modernity was not restricted to cities. Aided by the wonders of science and with the help of improved transportation means, modern farming techniques would, it was almost universally believed, allow the fringes of viable settlement to be pressed outwards to absorb a manifoldly increased population, for whom even the deserts would finally bloom.

But it was in the cities where evidence of the process of 'becoming modern' was most readily perceivable. The major Australian cities were casting off the lingering vestiges of a provincial backwater past and turning into medium-sized, modern metropolises by world standards, and impressively large ones by the yardsticks prevailing (London alone excepted) in the white British Empire. As well as bearing witness to most of the technological innovations of the modern age, the citizens of these cities might, if they cared to, begin to come to terms with many of the ideas of the modern age as well. In newspapers carrying an impressive

1

quota of world news, they could, for example, read articles extolling modernity, make contact with the ideas of Nietzsche, see examples of futurist and cubist art reproduced (though not in colour), and learn how these movements, futurism particularly, were now about to take over in the realm of high art.

In 1913 the art and writing of the 'golden' 1890s were often looked back on as summing up the previous century; its works offered Australians a solid cultural achievement to build on rather than being the rigid exemplars of a national school. Indeed, the local cultural scene was fluid, and the idea that an art which was not expressive of the nation's soul was of intrinsic inferiority, or even somehow unpatriotic, was far from universally accepted. There was no great consensus so far as to whether there was a national soul, or even a national 'type'; the debate was still being waged about what being an Australian meant, and even whether white Australians were as yet other than transplanted Britons. And where the bush had previously seemed to symbolise Australian cultural values, its continued iconographic relevance to the most urbanised society on earth was under scrutiny. Now, voices could be heard calling for a national theatre hosting plays that dealt with the 'real' Australia of the cities rather than melodramas treating the clichés of imaginary bush life; and calling for painting that went beyond the depiction of gum trees and pastorales, for an art which encouraged painters to examine the 'ordinary', or the commonplace experience of Australians in a critical manner.

In an environment that was becoming supportive of innovation and showed few signs of being afraid of it, it is not surprising that some Australian artists had begun to examine, and work with, some of the recent ideas that had revolutionised the world of art, first in Europe and now, in 1913, in the United States. This experimentation continued, in isolated pockets, throughout the Great War—appearing most notably perhaps in the work of Grace Cossington Smith—and in a sense climaxed in the first full postwar year, 1919, with Roland Wakelin and Roi de Mestre's joint exhibition in Sydney. Although nothing as radical as this show would be seen in Australia again for two decades, it was received by critics, for the most part with bewilderment, but also with a degree of tolerance that would soon be hard to find. But at this moment the eyes of the art-world Establishment were hardly turned towards the music-inspired, abstract paintings of those two young men.

Harbingers of reaction

The main focus of the art world's attention in 1919 was on the extensive monograph on Arthur Streeton, published as a special number of *Art in*

Australia. By that time, at least one English critic had long believed that Streeton had 'become in his art an Englishman', while as far back as 1913 an Australian critic was already carping that Streeton seemed 'to specialise in castles with wide, stretching domains. Is it to prove to Australians he is still abroad?'. But if Streeton, too, felt of his years of exile that he had fallen into a rut, his time spent painting with the Australian Corps in the rolling downs of Picardy had been to his benefit; or at least he thought so, later describing *Amiens, the key of the west*, 'for its fine art qualities,' as 'one of the most important pictures I have painted'. But it was not this work or similar recent examples that drew the critical attention of Lionel Lindsay and Julian Ashton in Sydney in 1919, rather it was Streeton's Australian paintings of the 1880s and 1890s. Ashton saw these as unresolved. Streeton's quarter-century of exile had done him no good: 'On that foreign soil [England] so saturated with formulae, Streeton's true purpose could not be fulfilled'. But Lionel Lindsay positively gushed. In these 'pictures of the Hawkesbury, sleeping in the sun amidst its fat pastures, the essential genius of our birthplace is revealed'. Ashton and Lindsay did seem to hold opposing views on Streeton, but on what was important they were in accord: what really mattered was how well these outer-urban landscapes of the Victorian *fin de siècle* appeared to capture an expression of the national soul.[1]

Their little dispute about artistic blood-and-soil worthiness was then, and now seems, mild enough, but it was actually a harbinger for the more general mood of reaction that came to prevail in the interwar years. Australia, of course, would not be alone in having a patriotically inspired version of an ageing landscape-tradition pressed into service—in the way that Streeton's work was—as part of a bulwark against an allegedly 'cosmopolitan' threat. Nor, as elsewhere, were reactions against modernity confined to art. Indeed, in all national societies where such responses occurred, the prevailing attitudes in respect of the need to 'protect' high art were invariably indicative of an underlying mood of disaffection with the modern age, of which hostility to modern art was merely a manifestation. Art was easily shown up for its alleged decadence and all-too-readily brought into the orbit of special-interest groups acting as custodians of a national and supposedly racially inspired culture.

It was one thing to 'expose' the decadent atrocities of modernist art, but in doing so it was necessary to have a ready-made institutionalised counter-product to serve as an alternative: usually this was genre and landscape art from the previous century. In Australia the art of Streeton, the nation's most famous living painter, served admirably, not least because he had once been thought of as a radical. In addition, he had been confirmed as a presence, albeit minor, in the capital of the British race—at that time the only race which seemed to count. Nor did the fact that his best work was probably behind him count against his re-invention as a cultural precursor. What mattered was that his work was celebrated, and that it depicted what was now presented as an ideal Australian civilisation basking in an exemplary golden age. This work became, thus, a kind of propaganda fodder to be exploited in the name of the spirit of the times; for, in the 1920s and 1930s the trick for cultural reactionaries, and not only in Australia, was to encourage artists to spurn modernity and recapture, in paint as in essence, the spirit of an imagined lost Arcadia. Streeton's old art was to provide the nostalgic model for future generations of Australian painters.

Nevertheless, the interwar years seemed to begin promisingly enough. In 1919 and 1920 much of Australia, despite a drought and some unpalatable, economic home truths to face, was in a mood of celebratory optimism. The nation was now sorting out how it should respond to peace; in that interregnum, while Streeton's art was discussed and Wakelin and de Mestre enjoyed what would be their last relatively pleasant reviews for almost two decades, there was also a flurry of local films. Of these, *On Our Selection* was praised in the press for its 'general Australianness', but already had Vance and Nettie Palmer bemoaning this 'nostalgia for an Australia that has ceased to be'. An association between 'Australianness' and nostalgia had already been made. It was an alliance that would dominate 1920s high culture. Thus, in the first full year of peace there were already hints that Australia was about to head down an isolationist path—a cultural isolationism which could only be made viable with some kind of quarantine in place.[2]

Quarantined culture

Nostalgia is a sign of longing that expresses a sense of being out-of-tune with one's present time and place. The idea that the past is always better—based upon what Marshall Berman calls 'nostalgic myths of a pre-modern'—is centred upon the beliefs that in the past issues had been plainer and simpler, the air had been purer, people kinder, and life more decent. In these largely imaginary times—before industrialisation had ruined the landscape and turned workers into machines, and before mass education had made people discontented with their lot—life's race had been run at a more sedate pace. So leisurely was this pace, in fact, that one had time to take in the trees and the landscape, which was just as well, considering that the pre-modern environment to which anti-modern quarantiners wished to return was invariably agrarian. Such nostalgic overviews did not take into account the dreadful poverty that abounded in pre-industrial rural societies, nor the minimal educational opportunities village and country life presented for the poor, nor the chronic in-breeding rampant in what were later idealised as 'close-knit' societies.

The agrarian nostalgia that manifested itself in 'back-to-the-land' movements was not something new to emerge from the Great War, for it had been present in the folkloric revival of north-western Europe in the late-nineteenth century, and it had waxed and waned in 'new society' cultures for generations. But in the disenchantment that followed the war these movements received vital shots in the arm, as the power élites in many societies claimed to seek—albeit often half-heartedly and mostly as a propaganda fantasy—a return to the racial and simple values of that imaginary past. The intensity, duration and synchrony of these reactions varied from society to society: in some—like France, where there were then fewer illusions about peasant existence—they were hardly manifest at all. But wherever Arcadian nostalgia was turned into cultural ideology, this presented a need to deny and decry all that was seen as confronting and potentially contagious, whether within or outside the frontiers of the nation state. Where possible, this meant the exclusion of the offending idea or object lest it contaminate or even seduce elements in the local population; but where exclusion was not possible, it meant marginalising, ridiculing or otherwise demeaning those who had the effrontery to entertain unsound ideas or produce decadent works. In fascist Italy, Nazi Germany or Franco's Spain—where rosy nostalgia for a never-never past underpinned much that passed for ideology—exclusion and complete repression could be achieved by the command or nod of a Duce, Führer or Caudillo. In democratic societies, fortunately, it was never so simple.[3]

By about 1921, nonetheless, an improvised, unstated but de facto cultural quarantine existed in Australia. It was propagated by an inchoate grouping of racial supremacists, anti-Semites, anti-bolshevists, protectionists, anti-industrialisers and the leaders of an élitist and conservative art-world Establishment—men, mostly, who as individuals often manifested many or all of the foregoing traits. The quarantine they endorsed was fortuitously, but not surprisingly, augmented by a range of political actions or inactions, from the draconian Anti-Alien Laws of 1920 to the failure to repeal the much-criticised duty on imported works of art. On the proposition that isolation was better than contagion, Australian high culture was being 'protected': from decadence, from modernism, from almost anything that was unfamiliar—implying, given the imperial spirit of nationalism prevailing, almost all that was not British, and some things that were British as well. Keeping out the 'other' meant ensuring that Australian racial purity, and the purity of the ideas and characteristics that were supposedly borne by the race, could be safeguarded—and safeguarded they were, with a devotion, according to Stuart Macintyre, that 'verged on the pathological' during the interwar years.[4]

Compared with the full-blooded and institutionalised versions that became features in some European societies, the Australian cultural quarantine was ad hoc; a sometimes inadvertent by-product of the widespread self-congratulation, complacency and apathy then current. This quarantine could hardly have been other than improvised, for Australia's cultural custodians did not have the means either to physically prohibit or to legislate for a future physical prohibition. But because they held influential positions and represented, for the 1920s at least, the cultural mainstream, their task was made easy for them. They needed do little else but attack modernism at every opportunity, or ridicule—sometimes in vile and scatological terms—those they saw as infected with the modernist virus and, where possible, brand them with what were for cultural custodians the undesirable contagions of bolshevism and Judaism, or whatever else came to mind. Even among less apathetic Australians who actually cared about culture, there were those who saw little wrong in this; for the nation was in fact passing through what can now be seen as a disturbingly isolationist phase.

Directly abetting the cause of these cultural protectors and quarantiners, who by age and inclination were almost invariably Edwardians, was the disquieting fact that young Australian men appeared to lose interest in the making of music, art and literature during the war; it was as though these activities had become effete and feminised, ill-befitting the rugged image of the hard-faced digger that had now become the Australian beau ideal. Clearly, something happened during the war years that made painting, writing or composing unattractive or unrewarding activities to young males; this strange near-absence is sometimes blamed on a 'lost generation', but it seems more directly related to the near-total disappearance of young men, after 1913, from institutions like art schools. For their young, female contemporaries, who were bound to stand outside the conforming influence of the Anzac legend, the same apparent strictures did not apply. Young women, accordingly, made a disproportionate contribution to progressive interwar art; however, while they had the talent and ideas, the men of an older generation had control. And with little pressure from a rising generation of radical young males, this dominant Edwardian clique—conservative, imperial-minded and almost to a man anti-modern—for almost two decades was able to control the levers of power on a machine only they had keys for.

Provincial culture in 'a rotted world'

In the interwar years Australian high culture—which by default seems to have become almost synonymous with visual art—existed on a plane of its own. Rarely could the gulf between mass and élite culture have seemed wider: while it was not difficult to discourage people from taking modern art and 'alien' thought seriously, it was impossible to convince them to 'Buy British' and nothing but, or to turn their backs on comic books, Coca Cola, Model T Fords and Hollywood movies. A British exhibition made up of modernistic-looking art actually made it to Australian shores in 1923, but even its organiser was apologetic, admitting that it 'included examples that showed the depths of degradation and disillusion to which art had been brought in certain quarters in the old world'. The culture born of the hardy, irreverent and iconoclastic nationalism of the 1880s was beginning to bear only superficial resemblance to that spawned by the imperial-centred, ambiguous nationalism of the 1920s. Indeed, the nation was becoming a cultural desert, as was amply demonstrated in the 1923 exhibition of Australian paintings held in London. Their old-fashioned provincialism was praised as a virtue by Lionel Lindsay—proof for him that Australians had preserved themselves 'from all the revolutionary manias of a rotted world'. But the English hosts were unimpressed with familiar paintings in the Salon styles of the *fin de siècle*, and even less with the work of the exhibition's star turn, Norman Lindsay—though in Australia he was compared favourably with Goya or Rembrandt, he was criticised in London for vulgarity and poor drawing.[5]

The isolationist thinking that underwrote that exhibition came naturally enough to a nation remote from world centres; one whose most potent visual and verbal images often centred upon notions of the virtue of isolation, and where country life was often eulogised for its remoteness from the vice that city-based civilisation seemed to represent. Protectionism, the flip-side of the isolationist coin, was also rampant, Australians being obsessed, Richard White argues, with the 'idea that Australia was young, white, happy and wholesome, and in constant need of protection'. But protection was not only needed from alien influences. Australians who lived in cities seemed to need protection from themselves; no longer could proletarians be trusted in public with alcohol after dusk, or at any time in groups of more than a handful. And while the measures that enforced such attitudes may have helped keep crime out of city centres, they did so at the cost of emptying streets of the life that may have helped stimulate a vital and living culture. In the spirit of the time and place, it seemed only natural that an agrarian political party, based on an organisation which saw the votes of country people being worth more than those of their city cousins, should achieve government in coalition. To the men of the Country Party, the city was no centre of cultural vitality from which the life of the nation might take a lead; rather, it was a place which, according to Manning Clark, they saw as filled with 'bludgers, street loungers and gas pipe loafers', sponging on 'the "hard yakka" of the farmers'. Lionel Lindsay and the influential gallery director and critic, J. S. MacDonald, would have hardly disagreed.[6]

Imperialism, war and national identity

The idea that there could be such a thing as a unique and, at the same time, vulnerable national culture—in which all that was good came from the racial heritage of the national folk, and their agrarian values acquired over generations, centuries, or even millennia—accorded neatly with then-prevailing, imperial-conservative political assumptions, whose strongest and most vocal upholders were to be found in the British dominions. Joseph Chamberlain's dream of a federated, and isolated, white empire—self-sufficient, self-protecting and literally able to ignore the rest of the world—while anathema to the anti-imperial wing of the British Labour Party, enjoyed a considerable postwar vogue, especially among what was still called the 'new school' of imperialists. Australia's place in this schema was to remain fundamentally agrarian; for it was not in the imperial interest for dominions to elaborate or intensify the rudimentary industrialisation that already existed. What was the point of giving primary exports from the dominions preferential entry into the Motherland if those dominions began to manufacture for themselves the products that could be, and were made at 'Home'?

Although S. M. Bruce seems at times to have recognised the folly of too narrow an export base, his government did little to encourage diversification; the agrarian-conservative governments that ruled Australia during the 1920s largely accepted the idea that Australia's future lay as a dependent mining and farming satellite of the United Kingdom. Prodded by his Country Party coalitionists, Bruce presided over a situation which saw public indebtedness raised to dizzy heights for infrastructure and other government spending, much of it being frittered away in trying to aid and even prop up over-optimistic soldier and closer settlement schemes. Measures were neglected that might have aided diversification—such as were taken in hand by Canada at that time—and which might have helped wean Australia from a risk-laden dependence on primary production. Narrow imperial and farming interests dictated Australia's future, as though C. E. W. Bean's agrarian and under-industrialised nation of *In Your Hands, Australians* was no longer the sketchy vision of a city bushman tutored in a Patersonian version of the Australian legend, but a real blueprint for the nation reborn at Gallipoli on 25 April 1915.

In 1913 few Australians, only close followers of the Balkan War, had even heard of Gallipoli. And, although visiting British imperialists had a vested interest in saying otherwise, on the eve of the war Australia had a perceptible national identity. Even though a national 'type' had not delineated itself and while Australians still often regarded themselves as 'oversea' Britons, Australia by 1913 was already an important, world trading-nation and identified, no longer as a collection of British colonies nor even as just a British appendage, but as one of the world's up-and-coming new societies. Indeed, the nation's per capita traded income already exceeded Britain's by 50 per cent and was more than double that of Germany or France. It is true that over half this trade was with Britain, for there were still strong 'commercial and sentimental, preferences in favour of the Mother Country'; but it is also important to note that Australia, on the eve of the Great War, was fifth among nations from which Germany imported—a relative position of influence and importance which it would never again attain.[7]

The Act of Federation that brought the colonies together into the new Commonwealth of Australia on 1 January 1901 was nothing if not the political act that designated nationhood, and for the first new nation of the twentieth century. So, the idea that the nation should need a new birth, or rebirth, on 25 April 1915 might seem perplexing, or superfluous. It might also suggest, and this is perhaps closest to the point, that at least some Australians thought there was something inadequate about a nationhood that lacked a baptism of fire. In Australia the pressure to take as gospel this bloody 'right' was propelled by perceptions of a less than adequate, sometimes unmentionable, national history which even the civilised act of federation had been unable to annul. The war, thus, suggested to Australians that they had finally proven themselves, allowing them sole occupational rights to the only island continent, and at the same time permitting them to brush a long-standing chip off a collective shoulder. The convict stain had been wiped away. Australians had now proven their blood rights to a racial military history dating from antiquity.

In the extraordinary mood of national self-congratulation that followed the Armistice, Australians were told that their reputation as the people of a fighting nation excelled all others. Indeed, Australia's five divisions, on a western front involving hundreds, had provided the British army with some of its best shock-troops. But, though the French and, occasionally, the Germans had mentioned Australians between 1914 and 1918, the world was hardly now in awe of 'the motherland of a race of incomparable fighters and athletes'. Indeed, most of the words of praise appearing about them in the foreign (British) press were written by an Australian, C. E. W. Bean, who himself had often complained—once directly to the British prime minister, Lloyd George—how the work of the Australian Imperial Force (AIF) was credited, in official communiqués, to the British Army. As Bean well knew, British and, hence,

dominion press coverage of the war was dictated by imperial considerations; these determined when it was in the imperial interest to praise
the work of 'oversea' Britons, and when the blanket use of the term
'British Army' was required. In fact, dominion troops, their commanders
and their correspondents had been but cogs in an imperial machine and
the war, rather than giving rise to a fresh, vigorous and independent
Australian sense of nationality, had merely confirmed the nation's
dependent status in the empire.[8]

The idea that Australians had become universally recognised as the
fighting élite of the race that stood at the head of the other races—
rammed home through the organs of the imperialist press during 1919—
would have profound effects on Australian society and culture. There
had been great changes afoot in Australia, between ca. 1890 and 1913,
and again between 1913 and 1919; the idea that the war simply caused
'the prolongation of the Victorian era in Australia' surely misses the point.
This is not to say that, by about 1921, what Manning Clark called 'Old
Australia' had not made a comeback, for Old Australia was now becoming
synonymous with future Australia—a land 'covered with farms' and offering prosperous work for fifty, one hundred, two hundred million people.
The sky seemed no limit to fanciful projections. But it was a land, too,
that could only be contemplated if somebody elsewhere within the imperial family did the dirty manufacturing work and, as a quid pro quo,
offered a guaranteed market for the nation's primary products. With Australia's future seeming to lie in shearing, harvesting and digging, the back-
to-the-land movement of 1919 came to focus on diggers who, often
maimed, sick or psychologically damaged, were invested with the qualities of the pioneers of yore and promoted as ideal yeoman-farmer material. Now that many acceptable sources of immigrant rural labour had
dried up, these diggers surely would provide the national lead that could
make come true Bean's dream of an up-country civilisation to outweigh,
in terms of its population as well as its culture, the decadent city.

The realisation that the Australian continent was mostly unsuited to
intense European-style cultivation had hardly begun to dawn in 1918.
The diggers did not actually conform to their bushman-type image; many
of them probably knew less about rural Australia than they did about
rural northern France, for most came from labouring or trade backgrounds that reflected the highly urbanised nature of Australian society.
And although these citizen soldiers had been depicted as colourful
bushwhackers by the wartime correspondents, it was clear to some
British observers on the western front that they were anything but: what
struck C. E. Montague was the fascination young Australians showed for
the machinery of war, a fascination he considered to be far greater than
that demonstrated by the British Tommy. The diggers of 1918 were

mechanically adroit, the products of a society in which adaptability and the skill at 'making do' that might keep a machine running were much valued; they were, therefore, well-suited to the open and (at its onset) mechanised warfare that was the feature of their last battles against the resourceful troops of the Reich. Unsurprisingly, when the AIF set up an educational training scheme, most of these young men elected not to train as yeoman-farmers, but opted instead for careers as mechanics, or in the skilled trades.[9]

The end of the agrarian dreamtime

It was no coincidence that a landscape and neo-classical art became the anti-modern ideal to illustrate a kind of 'post-modern' agrarian civilisation, nor was it a coincidence that some of the foremost advocates of this new-old civilisation should be found in the white British Empire. The vision of a federated empire made the agrarian dreamtime seem possible. But to achieve this new imperial interdependence—in which in each imperial component part dug, grew, harvested or manufactured according to its environment and abilities and drew from the others according to its needs—dominion statesmen, supported by 'new school' imperialists at Home, had to reverse the thrust of the prewar British 'policy of laissez-faire'. This policy was now condemned by the likes of W. M. Hughes for having 'left our citadels open to the enemy', even giving the enemy 'control of the keys of national and economic life and death'. To avoid a recurrence of this state of affairs, an already insular and inward-looking empire was encouraged to put kith and kin first and let the rest of the world manage as best it might.[10]

Insularity went hand in glove with complacency born of racial superiority: 'It was a fact often observed, that in a ship-wreck or a bush-fire one man of British stock could compass the work of several Germans', Bean later wrote in all seriousness, adding that 'this capacity the Australian possessed in an extreme degree'. Its alleged superiority notwithstanding, the white empire declined as a world force in the interwar years, in about inverse proportion to the rise of another, more-or-less Anglo-Saxon society. Throughout the 1920s and 1930s, the United States of America proved a more formidable economic threat to the British Empire as an exclusive white-man's trading club than prewar Germany had ever been; it was, by virtue of its highly exportable mass-produced popular culture, a cultural imperialist the likes of which the world had never seen. By the late 1920s the dominions were flooding with cheap and efficient goods of American manufacture, and soaking up the products of American popular culture.[11]

By the mid-to-late 1920s, too, the sentimental ties of empire that once bound England and Australia had begun to fray. Accusations and counter-accusations of wartime cowardice or incompetence had quickly flared up in 1927, and just as quickly subsided, but the decision of the British Labour government in 1929 to phase out imperial preferences was an unmistakable signal to the dominion rural lobby that there was no such thing as an eternally guaranteed overseas market for foodstuffs. This was a signal they chose to ignore or dismiss for many decades. But the most dramatic fraying of ties, one that apparently almost caused a rupture, was due neither to economic realities nor to ill-remembered events in the war; it flared-up in the grim, depression summer of 1932–33, during the infamous bodyline cricket series. Sport, always in the forefront when Australians considered national identity, thus provided the catalyst for an explosion that was probably overdue and dated back even beyond Gallipoli, Fromelles and Bullecourt, into murky origins in colonial times.[12]

The federated vision of empire crumbled in the face of national self-interest and its own impracticality, but the conservative cultural ties between England and Australia actually seemed to strengthen for a time. London's Royal Academy was the unchallenged Home of Art. Indeed, many conservatives carried on as though nothing had changed in the imperial relationship; even the depression failed to wake the influential gallery director and critic, J. S. MacDonald, from his agrarian dreamtime. In 1931—despite the near-collapse of the soldier settlement schemes and the abundant evidence that yeoman farming was unsuited to the Australian environment—MacDonald used Streeton's 1890s landscapes as the excuse for a colourised piece of imperial and racist propaganda. Streeton's paintings, he felt, showed Australians how 'life should be lived in Australia, with the maximum of flocks and the minimum of factories'. MacDonald's rhetoric presaged by some years other calls for a racial and national art, most notably from Germany, where the calls were noisily voiced as befitted the *Weltanschauung* dictating a state-controlled art form. A high Tory, MacDonald assuredly would have bristled at Nazi appropriation of ideas that then held fair currency in much of the Anglo-Teutonic world; anyhow, unlike the Nazi cultural ideologues to come, he was writing for a minute audience. In Australia art and literature had long been marginal to the greater expression of a nationality centred, as Bean suggested, as much on 'test matches, and on the quality of their sheep and racehorses, as on their achievements in art, poetry, politics or social progress'.[13]

Mixed signals for the future

Britain had always been the link of kith and kin that told Australians they were not alone; the friendly enforcer that on their behalf told the world

Plate 1 Max Dupain (Australia 1911–92) *Pyrmont silos through windscreen* 1933
gelatin silver photograph 25.2 × 19.2 cm National Gallery of Australia, Canberra.
  In the 1930s photographers such as Dupain were exploring new forms that cubism
had presaged, and working within the modernist idiom.

they had powerful friends. What bound Australians and Britons could not
in the longer term—or at least for another generation—be damaged by
unflattering cross-references to each other's soldiers, or even unfair sporting practices. By about 1935, with the depression fading 'John Bull and
Coy.' was back in business, if on a reduced scale. In Australia it was as
though that depression had brought forth a new mood of tolerance, for
the old 1920s hostility to Europe and modernity seemed on the wane
and there were mounting criticisms of the petty isolationism of the past
decade-and-a-half. But while the mass *Woman's Weekly* now devoted
occasional columns in praise to young women artists and even praised
their modernity, this new-found spirit of tolerance did not extend to
foreigners, like Egon Kisch, the Czech-born and anti-Nazi 'objective
reporter', or others whose politics veered to the left. For them the quarantine was as solid as ever.[14]

The 1930s was a time of mixed cultural signals from abroad. Germany,
Italy, Soviet Russia and finally Spain—nations about which large volumes

of European cultural history had once been written—were now ruled by totalitarian regimes, where repressive and old-fashioned ideas about culture were enforced by ferocious quarantines. By the time of the Spanish Civil War it was possible to either believe that European decadence had reached its abyss in communist and fascist societies alike, or accept that fascism was the lesser of two evils and a means of containing the menace from the East. But whether in democracies or totalitarian societies, the art and architecture of 1930s power—vacillating between neo-classicism and art deco—reflected more similarities than differences. And with more-or-less representational art conscripted on two continents across the widest political spectrum into the service of the State, it could be read by those who wanted to that abstract or expressionist modernist forms had already enjoyed their very brief heyday.

Unlike the Lindsays and MacDonalds, many younger Australian artists by the mid-1930s were ignoring the apparent approaching demise of modernist art, and by the late 1930s J. S. MacDonald's star was on the wane. In 1939, almost over his dead body, the first exhibition for sixteen years of international modern art was held in Australia. Twenty-five years after Grace Cossington Smith and Norah Simpson had pioneered local post-impressionism and Wakelin first made what he called 'severe cubistic sketches', a new if very belated Australian 'cubist' artist was noted, without malice, as though this was something terribly new. With the world poised on the brink of another war, Australians were tearing down the last metaphorical bricks from the wall of a quarantine that had held out the strange or dangerous, but had also held back the cultural life of a generation.[15]

CHAPTER ONE

The mad *kermesse*

> *Historians will regard it, I think, as a mad kermesse; a cosmopolitan*
> *confusion of white and nigger charlatans; a babel of theory and*
> *malpractice . . .*
> Lionel Lindsay ('Modernism in Art', *The New Triad* 11 January 1927)

Becoming modern in Australia

The word '*moderniste*' possibly dates from classical times, but towards
the end of the eighteenth century Jean-Jacques Rousseau, fearing European society was 'at the edge of the abyss', may have been the first to
use it in a pejorative sense. Rousseau was pleading for a spiritual union
with nature against the enemy—the city. Specifically he meant Paris with
its mobs, modernists, and its intellectual and commercial fervour—a parasitic appendage, unable to survive without a steady inflow of life-giving
products from the countryside. The political abyss Rousseau anticipated
was reached in the French Revolution, but a more all-embracing *mod-
ernité* would not manifest itself for generations. By the mid-nineteenth
century Europe was still, in Robert Hughes's words, so 'over-whelmingly
rural', that most 'Englishmen, Frenchmen and Germans, let alone Italians,
Poles or Spaniards, lived in the country or in small villages'. A century
after Rousseau's edict:

> the machine, with its imperative centralizing of process and product, had
> tipped the balance of population towards the towns. Baudelaire's *fourmil-*
> *lante cité* of alienated souls . . . began to displace the pastoral images of
> nature whose last efflorescence was in the work of Monet and Renoir. The
> master image of painting was no longer landscape but the metropolis.[1]

15

By then the Eiffel Tower, erected to celebrate the centenary of 1789, was already the edifice that symbolised the advent of modern times; indeed, the years about 1889 saw an unparalleled burst of technological creativity, including the first practical internal-combustion powered auto-mobiles, recognisably modern men-of-war, hand-held roll-film cameras and electric elevators. Early cable tramcars now contested city streets with horse-drawn cabs and buses and underground railway systems offered fast, punctual and weatherproof, urban public transportation. Modernism was not, however, just a question of technology. Those years saw the death of van Gogh, the incarceration of Nietzsche and the births of de Gaulle, Nehru and Adolf Hitler.

Marshall Berman's description of modernism as 'any attempt by modern men and women to become subjects as well as objects of mod-ernization, to get a grip on the modern world and make themselves at home in it', suggests the difficulty faced by many in coming to terms with what they had taken for granted in pre-modern times—a pre-ordained place in the world. Indeed, on the eve of the century's first apocalypse the terms 'modernism' and 'modernity' described in Western societies a perplexing multitude of unparalleled changes across a broad spectrum of endeavour. In post-colonial societies remote from the centres of change the first hints were customarily conveyed by news-papers—the standard of Australian newspapers being, according to Sir Charles Lucas in 1914, 'as high as anywhere in the world'.[2]

Australia was, by 1914, passing from a typical boom into a no-less typical bust; with the bust, paradoxically, it was also entering a fruitful cultural age. But the term 'golden nineties' is a misnomer for a decade in which, by the time it was half way, many of its celebrated figures had fled seeking richer pastures. Nor was the depression that precipitated their flight confined to the pre-federation era, for Australians had to wait until Edwardian times for market confidence to return. But by the eve of the Great War they had, belatedly at first and then vigorously, shared in the technological and cultural explosion which caused Charles Péguy to announce in 1913 that the world had 'changed less since the time of Jesus Christ than it has in the last thirty years'.[3]

Péguy's view was Euro-centric, for true global activity was limited; the great modernist conceptualisers were restricted to western Europe and the United States. Australia at that time shared with other 'new societies' like Argentina and Canada the claim to sobriquets like 'Young Hercules', but in 1913 had a natural client-relationship to modernity, importing up-to-datedness in exchange for raw materials and foodstuffs. To be other than an exporter of primary products implied increased urban manufac-turing and to many Australians and virtually all members of the school of Chamberlainian Imperialists, the mention of dominion city growth was like waving a red flag at a bull. Was not Australia already one of the most urbanised nations on earth? And was it not the backblocks where population was wanted?—men 'who would do the pioneer work of the country, of which', according to Sir George Reid, 'there was still much to be done'. This idea of an ongoing and virtually endless pioneer era was but one element in an economically flawed fantasy. Not only was the technology of modernity increasing farming and mining productivity and thereby reducing the absolute need for rural muscle, but Australia could only absorb a dramatically increased inland population if rivers could magically appear in places where none existed and the desert was then made to bloom. Only then could such a population be sustained, provided the rest of the world stopped producing and permitted Australia, unhindered, to become the planet's breadbasket.[4]

With a population of less than 5 million Australia was already a major world exporter of rural products; considering what about 500,000 Australians were already doing, it can only be imagined what a glut tens of millions employed on fantasy farms might have generated on world markets. Reflecting, not fantasy, but twentieth century reality, the early decades show a sharp rise in the numbers of workers employed in industry, a response not only to increases in opportunities offered by urban factories and workshops, but to improved rural productivity. Indeed, the numbers engaged in agriculture grew comparatively slowly after 1900— at times hardly at all (figure 1).[5]

While comparatively few people were needed to produce Australia's national wealth, it was still tied up in what could be grown on the land or dug up from under the land. With a small market-base and protected by high tariffs, a low-productivity manufacturing sector was inevitable. In general, though, local manufacturing—much of it still geared to the trades of the Victorian era—had little choice but to concern itself with jobbing, repair, limited-scale production or simple unit design and construction. Still, it is not necessary to design or build a machine to understand it, make it work profitably, repair it, modify it, admire it, or thrill to it. And Australians between the *Exhibition of 9 by 5 Impressions* in 1889 and the realisation that they were at war in 1914 had grappled with more than just the fascinating technology of the New Age; some saw Australasia at that time as the socio-political laboratory of the Western world.

Heyday of the print media

For sheer inventiveness, the first quarter-century of the Modern Age— since the construction of the Eiffel Tower—may never be equalled;

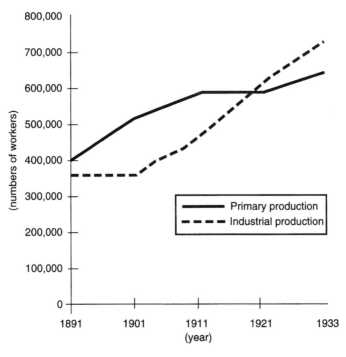

Figure 1 Workers in primary production and in industrial production, Australia: 1891–1933
SOURCE: *Census of the Commonwealth of Australia 1933*, p. 28.

nothing like it occurred during either of the World Wars. The First World War provided a mixed base to develop machines with potential peace-time applications. Consequently, production engineering and tool design became the real beneficiaries of the need to produce millions of easily assembled weapons for the mass conscript armies. Aviation perhaps excepted, the explosive innovation that marked this period had flattened out by 1914; the war came rather as a breather, for the developed world probably could not sustain the 1889–1913 tempo. Time was needed to assimilate, improve and find practical uses for new processes and tech-nologies: violent uses, as it transpired, in a monstrous interlude that offered the Western world the chance, for better or worse, to reorder societies that had become modern in all but their institutional structures.

   Modernism was not just motor cars, aeroplanes, electric lighting and power, skyscrapers, tanks, howitzers, town-planning or advances in social hygiene, any more than it was just social responses to the ideas of Darwin, Marx, Nietzsche, Marinetti, and Freud. By 1914 many might have heard of these soothsayers of modernity, but few knew or cared what they had written. People in general may or may not have been aware, supportive, or critical of the increasing agitation for social change—of the demands for equality by women, for instance, or pleas for another new order of justice and equality—ideas they may have weighed in the balance against change's potential to disrupt the apparent political and international status quo. But if they did know and care it was because they could read: since the 1870s there had been such a marked growth in literacy rates that, now, most adults—often unlike their parents and almost certainly unlike their grandparents—were able to read with some degree of facility. The Modern Age was also the Age of Mass Literacy.

In 1914 there was no such thing as 'the media': the medium was the printed page. For the press the last phase of the Belle Époque was *belle* indeed; never again would it enjoy such credibility or claim such exclusivity. Not that it was confined to news. In 1914, as today, high circulation tabloids thrived on converting trivia and gossip into mass entertainment. Australia had its yellow press just as it had serious journals of record like the *Argus* and the *Sydney Morning Herald*; the serious journals closely resembling their London equivalents and sharing British cable sources and articles or essays, but not always with due acknowledgment. Australians had a chance hardly excelled elsewhere, or since, to be as well-informed as they wanted, with the foreign news coverage of the best journals of record now appearing admirably broad, even if the editorials were sometimes not. Being ten hours ahead of Greenwich, Australians would generally read of events the day after the news became available to Britons: the idea of a tyranny of distance, in media terms at least, can be overstated. Modernity, by 1913, had shrunk the world to the point where information, criss-crossing the globe at the speed of electricity, was available for the use of those in editorial offices who had access to the means of decoding it.[6]

To suggest that the press played anything less than the crucial role in the rapid spread of the ideas and imagery of modernity is to drastically underestimate its prewar power. For inhabitants of old, new or antipodean worlds, newspapers provided information about not only what they needed to know but how they should dress, act, and play out their roles in life. Critics advised them on the plays worth seeing, the books worth reading and the art which merited attention. The cultural power of the press was almost total—almost because many of modernity's revolutionary advances were being made by those who refused to kow-tow to a press that either scorned them or failed to treat their efforts seriously. It would later be realised that some artists by 1913 had already been making art that resonated to the pulse of the New Age for half-a-dozen years, but at that time few readers anywhere would have been aware of what that art was, or its potential importance, or much beyond the fact that it existed—often as the object of journalistic ridicule.

Culture wars

The year 1913 was when the première of Stravinsky's *Rite of Spring* took place; it was also the year that Americans—otherwise at the forefront of the modernist experience—had their first large-scale involvement with the new art. It was not a particularly comfortable contact, for high art had become an institutionalised and conservative Western experience, dominated by taste and values that reflected past epochs. Nor was contemporary art aided by the fact that many who had come to grips with modernisation in other areas of life preferred their art to be comfortable and comforting. Much new art seemed crude or primitive, and lacked the qualities to which they had become accustomed from the works in their own galleries, or from illustrations of what was being hung at the annual Paris Salons. While the idea of the dealer-gallery had taken hold by 1913, most high-profile artists still sold from the Salons. Although nowadays they have an image of being stuffy, Salons catered for a spectrum of taste from the Salon des Artistes Français—derided by contemporary-spirited souls as the *Salon-des-gens-sans-goût* (Salon of people without taste)—to the radical Salon des Indépendants. It was at the Indépendants, a 'laboratory of modern art', that the young D. H. Kahnweiler discovered post-impressionism and cubism. This Salon 'by painters for painters . . . open to research and strong enough to affront the mocking crowds', as described by Fernand Léger, was where one went to seek cubistic paintings in 1913, although many went to mock, for opposition to art that was still regarded as crazy was widespread.[7]

In 1913 few Australians—apart from London or Paris expatriates and, more recently, Norman Lindsay—had actually seen an original cubist painting. This does not mean that similarly negative reactions to those in Europe were not to be found in Australia, although not all responses were negative. Coloured post-impressionist reproductions had come to the attention of some younger artists, who seem to have greeted them enthusiastically. Australians generally were becoming fairly well-informed of recent European cultural developments. In 1913 Marinetti's Futurist Manifestos could be found in the weekly *Sydney Mail*, Duchamp's *Nude Descending a Staircase* was reproduced in the *Sydney Sun*, and the *Bulletin* told its

Plate 2 The Sydney press reveals 'Duchamp's Masterpiece' (*Sydney Sun* 4 May 1913, courtesy of State Library of NSW).
   Duchamp's *Nude Descending a Staircase No. 2* (1912) seems to have been frequently reproduced in Sydney papers in 1913, perhaps because of the scandals surrounding it that year at the Armory Show in New York and in 1912 at the Salon des Indépendants in Paris. By September, at any rate, the *Sydney Mail* thought it was familiar enough to be discussed without the need to be reproduced yet again (*see plate 5*).

CUBISM IN LIFE.

ARTISTS FOLLOW MUSICIANS.

Applicability to All Callings.

Futurism Old in Everything but Art.

> Henry Malone argues that the Cubists, the Futurists, and the Post Impressionists have brought home to the public by means of art what great things may be accomplished by the application of the same principles to the various phases of human endeavor.

It is only a year or two since the proto-Post-Impressionist startled the world by throwing a mass of color into a frame and exhibiting it. Many Philistines arose to scoff, but a new school was founded, and the Post-Impressionists became a power in the artistic land, selling their pictures where the old conventional colorists, who painted

DUCHAMP'S MASTERPIECE.

The Cubist painting, "Nude Descending a Staircase," which excited the admiration of the school and the derision of the Philistines.

objects resembling things on the earth, in the heavens above, and in the waters beneath, were forced to turn their masterpieces into fascia boards for restaurants, or backgrounds for incidents connected with the efficacy of Purple Pills.

ART MADE PAYABLE.

The Post-Impressionist had found the way to make Art a payable proposition—a matter which had troubled Art since the day that Ung, the maker of pictures, fashioned an image of snow. This wonderful discovery

Futurists, who are the only persons who understand Futurism, hail Mr. Duchamps and Mr. Brancusi as the greatest of their kind, and we must be content to accept the views of experts.

THE PART OF FUTURISM.

The aim of Art is to conceal art, and certainly no artists have ever yet existed who can so effectually conceal art as the Futurists; but after all there is nothing new about Futurism. It was only in painting and sculpture that it was unknown until recent years. Certainly it is something new to have pictures and statues without form, but it is centuries since we have had music without tune. What is the composer of grand opera but a Futurist of the most advanced type? Those of us who have had to suffer in silence through the enormities of sound devised by emancipists from the oyster shop, can face the works of the Futurist artist with the equanimity of the seasoned veteran. It is easy to close the eyes; but nothing can prevent the percolations of harrowing sound to the inflamed ear-drum. I knew a man who had made boilers at Mort's Dock for 17 years, only to be decoyed into sitting out a performance of "Madame Butterfly." That man, a strong, lusty athlete, was taken home a physical wreck, knocked out by Futurist music, and to-day he draws his invalid pension.

FUTURIST ORATORS.

In oratory Futurism has always held a leading position. Backward as they are in Art, people are more appreciative as listeners. While they scoff at a picture which they cannot understand, they are more respectful towards a speech, and the less comprehensible it is the more important and learned they regard it. During the next month many speeches strongly reminiscent of Mr. Duchamps's picture will be delivered all over Australia. A great many politicians —and leading politicians at that—are addicted to the Futurist speech. Mr. Deakin, in fact, might be regarded as a very Post-Futurist, while Mr. Wade is distinctly a Cubist. It is the custom of people who attend political meetings to read the speeches they heard delivered the previous night in the morning papers in order that they may gain a glimmering of what they are about. Yet at the time they are listening they punctuate the remarks of the Futurist orator with the disturbances described by a grateful reporter as: (Cheers.) (Cheers.) (Loud and prolonged cheers.).

IN POETRY.

For very many years Futurism has taken a leading part in poetry, under the name of Symbolism. As an example we may consider the following symbolic poem, penned by a notable poet of this city over 10 years ago:—

> I was alone, yet not alone;
> I saw a spectral band
> That did a cold blue music make
> Upon a scarlet strand;
> While on a high asylum roof
> A widowed crayfish mourned aloof.

LAW AND LIFE.

In law Futurism is as old as the first definition of a place. Mr. Duchamps's picture is strongly reminiscent of many happy days in the Equity Court, while it would serve admirably to illustrate almost any judgment delivered by the High Court or the Supreme Courts of the States. It has its replica in politics, for a very large number of those who attended the New South Wales Assembly during the bright debates of last session carried away with them impressions of the proceedings which are very like the masterpiece illustrated here. In sport Futurism is so prevalent that if this picture, instead of being called "The Nude Descending a Staircase," were renamed "The Reason Bullawool Ran Second," it would be perfect-

readers that Arnold Schönberg was the leader of a new school of Viennese music, that cubism was 'at present painting itself' (with monochrome reproductions to illustrate the point), and that Futurism was 'breathing life into art that is long since dead, but won't believe it'.[8]

The *Bulletin*'s editorial approval of cubism was based on reproductions and foreign press reports. It was also tongue-in-cheek, as much a rejection of the fashionable high art of the time as an appreciation of this facet of modernity. But futurism's endorsement of war, its contempt for women and its outright modernity struck an openly sympathetic chord. It named—in an unlikely group—Richard Strauss, Rodin and H. G. Wells as adherents of a movement which 'promises to be interesting'. But the *Bulletin* was exceptional. Cautionary notes warning that the 'wanton eccentricity' of the 'so-called "futurists" and "cubists" ' should not be 'mistaken for legitimate development, and that the school of "originality at all cost" is invariably fatal to nobility and sincerity in art', prevailed in mainstream journals.[9]

Still, there was no shortage of Australian recognition that something important had been stirring in the studios of painters in Paris, Vienna, Berlin, and Saint Petersburg. This is perhaps striking in itself, given present-day perceptions of early-Georgian Australia as a sleepy cultural backwater that had dozed off at some point before federation. Nor was the conservative press implacably opposed to modernity per se. W. E. Rayner's futuristic 'Romance of Modern Life' appeared in the *Sydney Morning Herald*, the same paper which also praised Nietzsche for his 'his long-sighted vision': the day seemed nigh when this 'apostle of individualism' would 'come down from his mountain, his eagle over his head, his serpent at his feet, and in the market places those who see him will bow the head'.[10]

By late 1914 Nietzsche was accused of having 'combined intellectual eminence and moral cynicism to an extraordinary degree'. Had he not provided German warmongering with its 'historical and philosophical vindication'? The accusation was ludicrous, but good propaganda; and in a war where commanders and correspondents on opposing sides customarily claimed victory from the same battle, it was hardly remarkable. Similar misrepresentations became validations for what was portrayed in the press of all belligerents as a war in which normal rules no longer applied.[11]

The Germans were waging 'a war of extermination,' screamed the *Figaro* in October 1914, 'a kulturkrieg [*sic*] whose success would mean a regression to Barbary'. This was hardly atypical; for, from the outbreak of war all nations portrayed culture—defined in the simplest of nationalistic terms—as being under dire threat. In the British Empire this rarely led to great introspection, but a Franco-German culture war was

meanwhile raging in the columns of stately journals of record on both sides
of the Rhine, embroiling academics, philosophers, writers, artists and musi-
cians. Edition after edition of the *Berliner Tageblatt* or the *Figaro* carried
treatises and counter-treatises appearing over long lists of signatories,
which were attacked and justified, then counter-attacked and re-justified
in Paris and Berlin, then revised, rewritten and reformulated with still more
countersignatures, ad nauseam it seemed, or at least for the duration. For
the sake of French culture at least, it now appeared that August 1914 had
come in the nick of time. The 'intellectual promiscuity of Germany' was
already beginning 'to corrupt French imagination'.

> In writing their plays, some authors preoccupied themselves with the German
> public; our artists commenced to submit to the grossnesses of the far side of
> the Rhine, comprising simultaneously clumsiness and violence, and which is
> nothing if not Prussian. Our architecture, under the same influence, was
> becoming heavy and baroque.[12]

To disagree was to risk being accused of unpatriotic behaviour: the fallout
produced some sad casualties. Close relations that had gradually built up,
after 1870, between many German and French writers, philosophers and
artists were now affected; among those most vulnerable in this new situation were French composers who had written in the Germanic symphonic
form. Such composers included Camille Saint-Saëns, a man who been given
the keys of German towns and feted by German princes, but who was now
obliged to repudiate his German admirers and former close colleagues and
friends by formally asserting his patriotism in a letter devoted to 'The
Abominable Germany' published in the *Figaro*.

> I have not forgotten that German artists often played my works, that German
> theatres have presented my opera *Samson*, that I have received German dec-
> orations; of all that I am fully aware. So what? A river of blood and mud
> henceforth separates us. I can no longer have sympathy for a people . . . that
> massacres women and children, that is returning civilisation to the most bar-
> barian times, which has the effrontery to notify its intention to avail itself of
> three-quarters of Europe.[13]

The French were entreated, for the sake of *civilisation*, to maintain
'hatred for the hideous race that has thrown itself upon us' while the
Germans, with little of their territory under threat, proclaimed they had
'nothing against the French'; indeed, the 'union of the German and
French cultural element' promised 'a strong furtherance of mankind's
purpose'. French and Germans were of 'the same spirit, of the same
fineness and yet so different, that they are endlessly able to give each
other so much'. German vituperation was reserved for the 'English' of

the British Isles and the white dominions, a 'fish-blooded . . . island people', in whom all 'warm-blooded virtues are allowed to perish with hypocritical equanimity'.[14]

The culture war of 1914–18 was fought on a pre-modern battlefield, for proof of national superiority seemed to lie in the number of great names from past cultural eras that could be marshalled in the national cause. Goethe, Voltaire, Rousseau, Dürer, Beethoven, Victor Hugo, Kant—all were given a celebrity status that among the living was only accorded to a Hindenburg, a Haig or a Joffre. On one thing French and Germans agreed. Unless it was Shakespeare no Englishman merited mention. The English devotion to 'mercantilism' meant that England had 'not produced one single musician even of the second rank, no painter quite of the first rank, no sculptor of importance, no significant architects'. Its philosophers were 'deficient of the sense of what is higher than all reason'. In the one activity where pre-eminence might be claimed, England had 'badly treated' its 'few great poets'.[15]

The art of war

Reciting the great names of long-passed cultural history to score propaganda points is not one of the signs of a vital living culture. Nor is war an appropriate time to search for them. Where modernist artists had been ridiculed before the war, from 1914 unless they were in uniform they now faced accusations of unpatriotic behaviour. Modern art was now portrayed by most critics as an alien disease which some local practitioners had caught from the enemy. Good art was old art and that was patriotic art; so, Frenchmen were told to ask for 'kubisme'—'demand the k like soup, for it isn't French art', while Wyndham Lewis, C. R. W. Nevinson, Paul Nash and Jacob Epstein stood accused by a *Times* critic of 'Junkerism in Art'. 'Perhaps if the Junkers could be induced to take to art, instead of disturbing the peace of Europe, they would paint so and enjoy it.'[16]

As it became clearer that traditional battle-painting was irrelevant—even compared to doctored and carefully censored photographs—so modernist art began to claim an audience. By 1917 three of the four British 'Junkerists' had become official war painters, and Nevinson was credited by P. G. Konody, who despised that 'species of enlarged coloured newspaper illustration that continues to represent the art of the battle painter', with breaking the mould of war art.

> [The] ordinary representational manner of painting is wholly inadequate for the interpretation of this tremendous conflict . . . A more synthetic method

is needed to express the essential character of this cataclysmic war, in which the very earth itself is disembowelled and rocky mountain summits are blown sky-high to bury all life under the falling debris.[17]

In choosing to employ moderns as war artists, Britain and Canada were the exceptions. The more open Canadian (compared to the Australian) response to modern art in the early 1920s owes much to the respectability accorded modernist painters in the war. This was no question of 'modern art for art's sake', rather that Lord Beaverbrook sensed it could generate publicity and open an audience to other propaganda possibilities. Under his guidance, according to Philip Gibbs, the Canadians:

> organized their publicity side in [a] masterful way, and were determined that what Canada did the world should know—and damn all censorship. They bought up English artists, photographers, and writing men to record their exploits. With Lord Beaverbrook in England they engineered Canadian propaganda with immense energy, and Canada believed her men made up the British Army and did all the fighting.[18]

Beaverbrook was happy to ask anyone of talent to work for the Canadian propaganda cause, Australians such as Streeton and the splendid war photographer Frank Hurley if needs be. Bean was able to block these moves, was hostile to the manoeuvrings and generally unimpressed with the Canadian war painting, comparing it unfavourably with the much less costly, if hardly noticed Australian effort. They 'got English artists of the fashionable sort to paint their national pictures—we have employed Australian artists only'. They produced 'a very interesting exhibit of curious styles of contemporary art, [but] the Australian pictures are a far more interesting set . . . of what the artists actually saw at the front'. For Bean, only Australians could adequately depict the Australian experience of the war, even if they were expatriates like Streeton. His faith in the relevance of artists painstakingly drafting what they saw did not necessarily mean an accurate or meaningful record, for painters were constrained in what they were allowed to see or paint. Paul Nash, a modernist of that 'fashionable sort', revealed that he was 'not allowed to put dead men into my pictures because apparently they don't exist'.[19]

Traditionally based artists were ill-suited to a war that had so little in common with old battle-paintings. 'There is to be no Salon this year', a *Times* correspondent lamented in 1915, the 'world of art in Paris' was 'very void of life'. Of official painters 'doing their service', even Georges Scott, 'the artist of the French Army':

> seems to have failed to find in the trench any inspiration. His sketches and canvases deal . . . with moral rather than actual facts of war . . . The artist

lamented the changes that had come over war, changes which had robbed it
of its beauty. The trench is the enemy of military art.[20]

With most young artists at the front, '*La vie artistique*' was understand-
ably depressed. But older artists were still able to keep at their easels
and the Salons returned later in the war, if on a reduced scale. When
they did, sentimental—if imagined—refugee scenes and images of
reported heroics studded the walls of the *Salon-des-gens-sans-goût* and
provided pictorial endorsement for editorial leaders in *L'Echo de Paris*.
For artists who continued to make prewar-looking pictures, all was not
lost. A clever title could convert a painting of cavorting nudes into an
allegory loaded with patriotic meaning. In the meantime a gradual awakening to the real, if unreported, horror of the Great War—impossible to
address in paintings treating moral content—was creating an audience
for the fragmented and often violent images of futurism and cubism.

The Bolshevik revolution provided the Allies—in their worst year of
the war—with yet another enemy, perhaps more threatening than the
one they were still trying to defeat. Futurism, the art of extreme Italian
nationalists, was now condemned as a malignant disease spread by the
dreaded internationalists. By summer 1918 it had become 'almost the
academic Bolshevik art'. The seeds of the Jewish–Bolshevist–Modernist
conspiracy were planted. As early as 1920 Lionel Lindsay was making
most of the appropriate connections. The futurist was a 'Bolshevist in
Art . . . [who] flings his stupid dynamite with the tolerance of a madman
and would immolate them all'.[21]

Learning from history

The Bolshevik became the new 1919 enemy, but Australians were barely
allowed to forget the old one. No one 'could ever assail the blessed
memory of the noble dead or seek to diminish the glory of their achievements, the brilliance of their daring gallantry, or the splendid fibre of
their Character'. Gallipoli had shown for all time and to all nations 'the
standard of Australian character'. Few living Australians could have
doubted that the landing at Gallipoli was anything but a feat of arms
unparalleled in history. As an imaginative but flawed attempt at amphib-
ious warfare it probably was; but, what Australians were encouraged to
celebrate was the fortitude shown by the Anzacs on landing and scaling
the cliffs, climaxing, in Ashmead Bartlett's words, when 'the first
Ottoman Turk since the last Crusade received an Anglo-Saxon bayonet
in him at 5 minutes after 5 a.m. on April 25'. Wars, as this prose celebrated, were still fought and won as they always had been, by courage,

moral and racial superiority, and cold steel. But Ashmead Bartlett did not invent the now celebrated Birth of the Nation: Australians did that. From now on Australians had a history *as Australians*, but they could believe they had also earned the right to one stretching back to antiquity; together, these histories could for all time displace an unpalatable convict past.[22]

Ashmead Bartlett's May 1915 dispatch was close to the verbal equivalent of a Georges Scott illustration. It could be said of both that their intention was to boost morale and that neither required much first-hand evidence. As Scott's drawings resolutely depicted a Western front largely devoid of modernist technology, so too did Ashmead Bartlett treat the landing in reassuring pre-modern terms. Far better a clean war in which a vigorous charge was followed by bayonets plunging into soft flesh than a war of trenches, mud, mines, grenades, gas, shells—where death was likely to be an anonymous encounter with a machine-propelled missile. Similar pre-modern depictions were enjoying a heyday in British reporting; in the *Times* its 'Own Correspondent', a few months before Gallipoli, was offering the assurance that 'a machine, no matter how powerful or complex, remains but an insecure buttress against the two hands of a man'. The cowardly Germans would, therefore, 'so far as possible, conduct this battle with artillery. The man hides himself behind the machine!':

> 'Every battle,' an officer told me the other day, 'is won by the bayonet in the last issue.' It is a truism, but the truth of it is only now dawning upon the minds of those who constructed the great war machine and forgot that the world still belongs to the brave and the daring. Our British soldiers have put the doctrine of the machine to great shame.[23]

It was indeed a truism; it was also dangerous nonsense for which men died needlessly. But the Anzacs by May 1915 belonged to that same mythical, recruiting-inspired world of the brave and the daring; a world which existed in the press of the British Empire until universal conscription, Australia excepted, made it no longer necessary.

The need to encourage recruitment for the duration meant that the nation's correspondents had little choice but to write up war as the greatest game of all and highlight the digger's nonchalant recklessness. This was notwithstanding the fact that after 1916 the Australian Imperial Force (AIF) was evolving into an efficient and highly trained team, armed-to-the-teeth with, and trained to use and work with technology and encouraged by Monash to fight for attainable objectives with minimum losses. Indeed the Australian Corps may well be seen as a primitive forerunner of a Second World War Panzer Korps, even if this was beyond

Bean's understanding of what war was meant to be. He carried the myth-making pre-modern prose of wartime dispatches into his official histories, and his willingness to account for the AIF's success in terms of physical and moral superiority drew a rebuke from General Sir James Edmonds, the British official historian, in 1927.

> Anything tending to demonstrate that war can be entered on without prepa-ration or training (especially of the Staff and regimental officers) by a number of individuals simply because they are brave, have natural fighting instincts and are fine specimens of manhood is to be deprecated. The lesson of the war, to my mind, is that men of a much lower type—as the Germans were—can by system and discipline be trained so as to stand up to a first-class nation.[24]

Edmonds had known command and recognised that a soldier was made by nurture not nature. But Bean continued in succeeding volumes to stress natural fighting instincts and physical superiority, attempting to delineate a distinct Australian type to fit the image of new nationhood.

In asserting that there was something special and unique in the Aus-tralian mixing of the blood of the British Isles baked under the sun of the Australian countryside, Bean was inventing nothing; the idea had been around for generations. In the early postwar years Australians were constantly made aware of the country-bred Australian's uniqueness. Sol-dierly qualities resided in the blood of the 'Briton re-born', inherited from pioneers who were, according to the *Sydney Morning Herald*, 'selected stock—it was a case of natural selection'. Given a history of transporta-tion 'selected stock' was not the happiest phrase. But the message was clear.

> We did not breed the original strain here; that came from our forefathers of the British peoples at home . . . Drake Frobisher, Raleigh, Cook, were, in the best sense, adventurers, not men of war. The Australian spirit and stamina are no new-bred qualities; they came to us in the blood of our British ancestry. What we may congratulate ourselves upon is that we have kept the qualities of the stock good and pure.[25]

Like so much that appeared in the Fairfax press that year, this was a lead-up to a piece of agrarian propaganda. Paraphrasing *In Your Hands, Australians*, it warned that efforts to preserve the quality of the breeding stock would be to no avail if the 'Toll of the City' was not reversed. Australians were 'already far too fond of swelling the already swollen ranks of the town'. What was needed was 'a large agricultural population to reinforce our nerves and sinews throughout the ensuing centuries'. Citizens who had been invited to draw comparisons between their men and those warriors at Troy were now asked to learn from other ancient examples. 'One of the chief causes of the fall of the Roman Empire was the tendency of the sturdy yeomanry to flock to Rome in pursuit of Government doles, Government jobs, and free Government amusements. History has an unpleasant habit of repeating itself.'[26]

Keeping Coca Cola and modern art at bay

Learning from history is one thing, creating serviceable modern truisms from antiquity is another. A society drawing lessons for its future from a hazy, mythical past was unlikely to be sympathetic to modernism's claim to remake the world. Australians were not alone in finding that prospect daunting. Their reaction was to elect the Bruce-Page government, whose vision of the future was borrowed, firmly agrarian, and had at heart the barely disguised idea that the urban working-classes represented the rural backbone's natural enemy. It should be no surprise that the Bruce-Page years marked the institutionalisation of the landscape tradition of the 1890s and a reinforcement of cultural ties with Great Britain. The year of the formation of that government, in 1923, marked the last inflow of modern-ish art to Australia until the eve of the Second World War. Following closely on the 1923 exhibition of Australian painting in London, another backward-looking collection appeared at the British Empire Exhibition at Wembley of 1924. This exhibition 'for the first time':

> made possible the assembling under one roof of the paintings of today, not only from the United Kingdom, but from every Dominion of the Crown. Now first can be seen in one place how the Daughter Nations have developed their art from the English School which is represented so splendidly in the Retrospective Galleries.[27]

By the time of this Wembley exhibition Canadian artists were already divided into academics and moderns, but Wembley was the watershed for the Canadian modern school. 'At a time when Canada was declaring its diplomatic and economic independence, the Group of Seven presented to the art world a school and style of painting that was truly Canadian.' If nothing else this might have suggested to Australians that it was possible to have a national school—as had existed in Australia in the 1880s and 1890s—that was not necessarily backward-looking.

> As a result of the Wembley art show and the very favourable critical response to the northern landscapes of Tom Thompson and the colourful canvasses of the group artists, the academicians lost a decisive battle . . . British opinion

confirmed that which a divided art world could not: the Group of Seven carried the day.[28]

By 1924, Roi de Mestre, Roland Wakelin, Grace Cossington Smith and Lionel Lindsay were all abroad seeking enlightenment and in London to find it. Lindsay stayed over, and in the following years enjoyed perhaps as much success as a colonial artist could hope for. He repaid his London admirers in full, telling how 'extraordinarily keen' he was 'about the painting being done in England, which he ranked as "the best to be seen on this side of the world" '. He was now a confirmed anglophile.[29]

Lindsay was delighted to find that Australia was 'too far away to be influenced to any extent by these rapidly-changing fashions in art', but it was not so far away as to miss out altogether on the cultural ramifications of the Jazz Age. By the critical year of 1929 Australians who could afford to, read books the censor considered befitting, printed in typefaces designed at the Bauhaus, watched Hollywood's first sound offerings at picture palaces now built in art-deco styles, drove a locally assembled but North-American made Chevrolet or Ford A, and lived in California bungalows. They could listen to Americanised radio programs and respond to advertisements that used sleek New Objectivity photographs or graphics while their children pored over American-style comics. American-style mass consumerism had all but overwhelmed the local popular culture.[30]

In the twentieth century in capitalist nations any attempt to quarantine chewing gum, Coca Cola, popular movies and the Hollywood value-system, jazz, comics, packaged food and the technologically advanced, reliable and comparatively inexpensive products of American interwar modernity was bound to fail. So, those who saw themselves as upholders of a culture defined by the parameters of a nation state might protest at the vulgar Americanisation of their national life but, if they wished to hold modernity at bay, had little choice save to focus their attention on that which they could quarantine—the nation's high culture. It was not America itself that was the threat here; rather, it was a sinister, oriental-based contagion threatening cultural values in America as much as elsewhere.

The total exclusion of high-cultural modernism from an advanced society's national life was only possible in a totalitarian state. Where draconian interdictions could be used in a fascist nation, in the Australian democracy marginalisation and discouragement was all there was to achieve similar ends. By failing to review the exhibitions of modernist artists, or questioning the sanity of those who supported or indulged in such supposedly anti-social or unpatriotic pastimes, a wall of discouragement could be constructed. Modernism and madness went hand in glove to the small élite who held positions of power in national galleries, served as critics and influenced opinion on major newspapers, or edited influential cultural magazines. Thus, an effective isolationist power bloc reigned for much of the 1920s and while its influence was strongest, the chance of new work entering into country or young artists being encouraged to pursue less conformist directions was slim indeed.

Nevertheless, there were signs by 1929 that the Australian quarantine was crumbling. *Art in Australia*, by default the country's premier cultural journal, had been moving towards a more tolerant position since 1923, and now appeared as an honest broker between the powerful faction that favoured isolationism and the emerging one which believed in opening up the culture. Lionel Lindsay's 1923 idea that 'stunt' art could be contained was proving premature. Indeed, 1929 was a year of mixed cultural signals in Australia. The fall of the Bruce-Page government, on the one hand, was a defeat for vested agrarian interests and a sign that the notion of the man-on-the-land being the only upholder of true Australian values might again be losing cultural potency. The banning of *All Quiet on the Western Front* suggested, on the other hand, that pacifism was not an activity suitable for patriotic Australians. The cultural guardians of the nation were still not prepared to relax their vigilance, even if it meant presenting an image of the nation that was repressively militaristic.[31]

The flickering spark of change that appeared in 1929 was snuffed out by the depression. J. S. MacDonald, director of the NSW National Gallery, continued to write panegyrics dedicated to artists he admired while confiding to his colleagues and notebooks a curious obsession with modernism as a simile for putrefaction. A disillusioned Basil Burdett—who was MacDonald's confirmed enemy and had contested his directorship of the gallery—quit the scene for Europe in 1931. That year, a depressed Lionel Lindsay, now back in the fold, seemed about to do the same. 'We had a wonderful time in Europe and really feel more at home there than in this so-far-away country from tradition. But for old friends, I don't feel much in touch with the present Australia, which has no ideas and has long disliked thinking.' In the depression years, while MacDonald publicly pretended modernism wasn't there, Lindsay responded to it with sniping letters to newspapers aimed at anyone who had the temerity to endorse any aspect of it.

Did not Picasso acclaim a hideous Negro god more beautiful than the Venus of Milo? The true modernist exalts ignorance as holy naivete. He trusts to his instincts so that he may evade all study, all technical accomplishment, or, he follows the theory of a cult . . . In the five years I spent recently in Europe I saw very little except the abominations of German Expressionismus.[32]

By 1935, with the worst of the depression passed, it was by now clear that the unreconstructed Edwardians whose taste and prejudice had been such a force for repression in the 1920s were losing their battle to keep Australia innocent. As it had in 1913, modernist art once more became the subject of articles in the popular press. Perhaps responding to the disproportionate number of women artists now associating with the ideas of what was generally called the 'Modern Movement', the mass-circulation *Australian Woman's Weekly* typified the mood of change, asking its readers to visit an exhibition of the 'youngsters on view at Julian Ashton's. You will be amused at first, but you will be vastly impressed in fine.' The *Weekly* included illustrations, of which 'an oil, "Intermediate French" by Mary Alice Evatt' was considered 'typical' of the work that could be seen. Evatt's painting showed a generic resemblance to portraits by Norah Simpson and Grace Cossington Smith from 1913, suggesting a new generation was catching up with some neglected unfinished business from the past.[33]

Though the article gushed with fashionable lightweight journalese, this kind of popular attention must have been disturbing to those who guarded the faith that what art must show was their interpretation of what 'technical accomplishment' was. And with many post-depression-generation artists now identifying with the modern movement, the counterweight of something like an Australian Academy of Art was always likely to be on the cards, even if it was a reactionary last hand: R. G. Menzies, friend of both Lionel Lindsay and MacDonald, threw his political weight behind its establishment. Again Streeton was to be the nonpareil and the Heidelberg School, the model; a second coming of landscape painters whose heyday dated from the 1890s or before was not, however, unique to Australia in the interwar years. Nor was the idea unusual of highlighting their work as the true racial expression to be contrasted against that of cosmopolitan modernists. A few years after MacDonald's 1931 Streeton panegyric, one notable continental connoisseur put it thus:

> So today there is not a German or a French art, but a 'modern art.' This is to reduce art to the level of fashion in dress, with the motto 'Every year something fresh'—Impressionism, Futurism, Cubism, perhaps also Dadaism. These newly created art phrases would be comic if they were not tragic . . .
>
> But true art is and remains eternal, it does not follow the law of the season's fashions: its effect is that of a revelation arising from the depths of the essential character of a people which successive generations can inherit . . . These facile daubers in art are but the products of a day: yesterday, nonexistent: tomorrow, out of date. The Jewish discovery that art was just the affair of the period was for them a godsend: theirs could be the art of the present time.[34]

Thus spake Adolf Hitler in 1937. There is a familiar ring to this: the idea that modernist art was a fad inspired by Jews, and that true art was eternal and sprang from the national soul was held dear by prominent traditionalists in many other societies. But it is unlikely that those in democratic societies who found themselves sharing ideological common ground with National Socialist art dicta would have endorsed Hitler's final solution. For those who failed to toe the official line and persisted with abstraction or expressionism Hitler offered 'only two possibilities'.

> either these 'artists' do really see things in this way and believe in that which they represent—then one has to ask how the defect in vision arose, and if it is hereditary the Minister of the Interior will have to see to it that so ghastly a defect of vision shall not be allowed to perpetuate itself—or if they do *not* believe in the reality of such impressions but seek on other grounds to impose upon the nation by this humbug, then it is a matter for a criminal court.[35]

This illustrates why a totalitarian cultural quarantine not only is bound to be more rigorous and complete but why it is more obvious than in a democracy. In a totalitarian society the quarantine will proudly proclaim itself through associated measures like the forbidding of overseas travel, prohibitions against listening to foreign broadcasts or reading foreign periodicals, or the public burning of unwelcome books. In a democracy there may be no shortage of those who would endorse extreme measures to keep out 'filth' or 'decadence', but even if their efforts do come under some scrutiny, cultural quarantines in democratic societies are as much the consequence of public apathy as of personal will.

Hitler knew what he liked, which for the most part was central European genre art of the late-nineteenth century. His taste broadly accorded with that of the 'class of people' who elsewhere, according to R. G. Menzies, would 'in the next 100 years, determine the permanent place to be occupied in the world of art by those painting today'. Menzies, too, shared Hitler's view of art having a useful role in promoting certain self-images of nationality and cultural wellbeing. But he was light years away from the Nazi leader in his methods for dealing with those who might have offended his sensibilities. In 1937, with castration or imprisonment hardly viable options, the most Menzies could threaten a modernist artist with was non-membership of an Academy of Art few outside of New South Wales wanted to join. The Academy, for which he was 'the prime mover', provided government support for the arts at the cost of cultural conformity: it would not only 'set standards for the work' but also 'raise the standards of public taste by directing attention to good work'. Australian modernist artists still had something to fear from the Menzies proposal. Much of modernity, in his opinion, 'consisted of doing all the things that Rembrandt would not have done, and to be really original the artists had to paint a face in the form of a cabbage and vice versa'.

> I find nothing but absurdity in much so-called 'modern art', with its evasion of real problems and its cross-eyed drawing . . . I think that in art beauty is the condition of immortality—a conclusion strengthened by an examination of the works of the great European Masters—and that the language of beauty ought to be understood by reasonably cultivated people who are not them-selves artists.[36]

While these pronouncements probably did him no harm in his constit-uency, artists who objected to them did something that would be unthinkable in a totalitarian state: they formed their own society.

It is not always easy to comprehend why politicians in the 1930s, in democracies and totalitarian states alike, who might otherwise have endorsed much of modernism's brief, took time out to actively repress the art made as a response to living in the modern era. Paintings on their own threaten nothing; but paintings that can be associated—no matter how tenuously—with international Jewry, bolshevism or a general sense of alien decadence were interpreted as a threat to civilisation itself, their continued existence attesting to the presence and influence of the 'cos-mopolitan'. For those who believed isolation could provide the distanc-ing from modernity that might lead to a cultural reawakening, the visual arts were the simplest of cultural expressions to treat and control. The presence of an abstract or expressionist work on a gallery wall can be taken in at a glance; 'subversive' literature, on the other hand, needs to be read and understood and may escape for a time the notice of censors not always blessed with sensitivity or intelligence. Yet the art of even the most barrenly conformist epochs still provides a resource to be valued beyond mere commercial or aesthetic criteria, since it provides insights into the mind-frame of the culture that endorsed it. Thus, the *idées fixes* of National Socialist quasi-ideology reveal themselves more clearly in German paintings and photography of 1933 to 1945 than they ever could in the ramblings of a Rosenberg or a Darré.

A similar observation could be made of Australia, and indeed the fash-ionable art practice of many national societies carried on in the 1920s and 1930s as though the century's first two decades had never happened. In Australia in the 1920s and Germany in the 1930s—to name just two nations where the ideal of Aryan exclusivity played a prominent role— idealised pastorales enshrining the nobility of agrarian ways of life har-monised seamlessly with depictions of the tranquil and clean-limbed superiority of blue-eyed blondes. In this context the female was passive, the warrior grand or a spirit, and all themes blended into metaphorical connections with ancient civilisations. Rarely in these cultures, except among photographers and female painters, was the city acknowledged as having aesthetic potential, and that romanticised idealisation of the machine as a thing-in-itself—so typical of modernist responses—was mostly off-limits. To look at the Establishment art of such interwar societies is to look at an art of reaction signifying a deeper, more fundamental fear of modernity. Yet these societies could no more formally reject modernity per se than they could invoke an immediate postmodern future sourced in the past. Even those who believed, like Lionel Lindsay, that the 'machine destroys all culture' had become dependent upon the modernity they scorned: they travelled abroad in ships or even aeroplanes, communicated through the telephone, drove to studios or offices in automobiles, scanned newspapers and journals and listened to radios. Many, like Lindsay, a printmaker, depended upon machinery for the production of their art. Although they would have hated the idea, they had actually made the 'reconciliation of technology and unreason' which Jeffrey Herf terms 'reactionary modernism'.[37]

CHAPTER TWO

1913: A year of golden plums

We must populate this continent or perish.
Joseph Cook (*Sydney Morning Herald* 14 February 1913)

At times the written and visual record seems to imply there may have been two 1913s: one in which everyone was young, beautiful and upper-middle class, wore white and lived in eternal innocence and sunshine; in another, more neurotic 1913 the frolicking was hectic and accompanied by furtive over-the-shoulder glances at the looming apocalypse. The latter seems closer to Modris Eksteins's 1913, in which the première performance of Stravinsky's *Rite of Spring* was not so much the opening of a ballet season, but 'perhaps the emblematic *oeuvre* of a twentieth-century world that, in its pursuit of life, has killed off millions of its best human beings'. Perhaps, but there are other reasons for considering as culturally pivotal a year in which so much that was new occurred, or was first brought to public consciousness.[1]

The year 1913 was also the one in which Australian artists made some of their first serious forays in response to a new-found awareness of what their European contemporaries had been dealing with. Culture was higher on the political agenda than it would again be for decades; not only had the nation's future capital been named, but the foundation stone had been laid for a city that Prime Minister Fisher foresaw as a 'home of art'. This was the year that Alfred Deakin retired from politics and W. M. Hughes toyed with retirement. Australians changed a federal government, welcomed the arrival of their 'tin-pot navy' and the first of their newly trained cadets, worried about the future of the empire should the United States and Japan decide to make war, and looked with increasingly furrowed brows at the entanglements that seemed about to drag the

European empires into war. But the Germans were racial cousins, and mutual distrust couldn't stop many Australians from raising glasses and shouting *Hoch*! on Wilhelm II's twenty-fifth anniversary as German emperor.[2]

Australians on the eve of the apocalypse seem to have been a peaceable lot, content that their country was evolving towards a greater destiny and that the act of federation on 1 January 1901 was a reasonable starting point. Most were probably more interested in the future than in the past, too much of which—as visiting Britishers were fond of reminding them—was less than palatable. Of the national and imperial celebrations then observed, the attention paid to Empire Day at the expense of Australia Day seems to signify the ambiguity of Australian nationhood, and also to explain why clear links with the Motherland were so much more desirable than murky pre-1850 connections with a dubious local ancestry that few wished to know about.

There was no blanket consensus on this greater destiny's shape. Traditional city versus country antagonisms and prejudices bedevilled debate but most agreed that Australia's future lay with the 'man on the land'. Whether to a small-scale manufacturer producing for the domestic market or to a pastoralist for whom the city was a blight, the land symbolised the same: a treasure trove for exploitation. Where manufacturer and pastoralist may have differed was over what was to be done with the resource after its extraction or harvest. Was it to be sent as a raw material solely—primarily to the British Isles—which would permit Australians to avoid the vice, slums, mobs and unrest that supposedly went hand-in-hand with larger-scale urban industrialisation? Or was it to be exported 'as the manufactured article rather than the raw material', in which case Australians should turn 'our wool into woollen goods and eat the sheep here!'.[3]

As the nation entered that last full year of peace, the mainstream press encouraged qualified optimism. Although the country had been 'living at a rather fast pace lately', if a man was 'not prosperous it is not for lack of Nature's bounty'. The country was 'all right'. As testimony the *Sydney Mail* pointed to 'the growth in local manufactures', as well as 'the habit of buying locally-made goods where they merit custom', developments its prestigious stablemate, the *Herald*, viewed with less equanimity. An expanding local industrial base, according to the *Sydney Morning Herald*, could be achieved only at the cost of 'burdening the land'.

The high wages and comfortable conditions of Australian city workers may be sustained by passing tariff laws and arbitration Acts. But the farmer who produces those golden plums is exposed to the full competition of the world.

No acts of Australian Parliament can help him in that market. And if he goes—
with him departs the wealth and the main strength of this nation.[4]

The *Herald* was worried that Australia was now 'heavily indebted abroad,
both publicly and privately'. If Australians were to 'continue to import
goods from abroad to a greater value than our surplus wool and our
hides, our butter and our metals', then 'the inevitable day of reckoning
must sooner or later be faced'. As far as the *Argus* was concerned this
day had already arrived. Blame lay with Labor governments who in office
were always 'spendthrift and ne'er-do-well'.[5]

By 1913 the *Bulletin* had come a long way from Bushman's Bible days.
A radically nationalist and even modernistic weekly, it crusaded for an
independent and decentralised Australian manufacturing sector in new
industrial cities and towns. It too bemoaned the fact that this 'maddened
country is still following the downward track as regards its finances, and
though the Jew at the other end of deal is steadily putting up interest
rates on the spendthrift at this end, there is no sign of returning sanity'.
It had a point, for with a 'living wage' of £2 14s weekly and a population

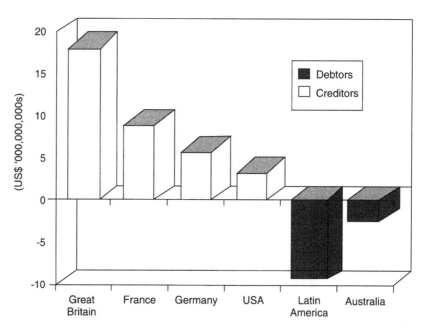

Figure 2 Foreign investment: 1913–1914 (in US$ '000,000,000)
SOURCE: Based on figures in Hardach, *The Pelican History of World Economy in the
Twentieth Century; The First World War 1914–1918*, table 3, p. 6.

of less than 5 million, Australians bore the highest per capita debt on earth (figure 2).[6]

Perhaps their prosperity was a little too dependent upon other people's money but the better-off were enjoying the last full year of an antipodean version of what later would be called the Belle Époque. For the majority of inhabitants of the nations of the Entente and their satellites, the blessings of modernity were abundant. Four decades of continental peace, increases in knowledge and improvements in hygiene had seen life expectancy soar. Modern transportation made travelling vacations an expectation: even to foreign climes. The age of tourism—of the tour or of the cure—had become almost a 'mass' one as far as the middle class was concerned. With taxation low, never again would the upper classes enjoy such a rarefied comparative affluence, often at the expense of a vast under-class. True, Australia lacked the obvious and caste-like class distinctions of the Motherland, but middle-class laments about overpaid 'mechanics in Australian city industries' who 'received higher wages than those in any country', and burdened the country's backbone, were common enough. Nor were all workers 'average'. For those who weren't, the condition of inner-city housing was often perceived as a disgrace. 'We have our slums', acknowledged the *Sydney Morning Herald*, and— as if there was an irrefutable connection between poverty and sin—'we have our degenerate women'.[7]

Not all Australians lived in decent housing, enjoyed three square meals or mixed with supposed degenerates, but most were at least spared the ravages of northern climates. The continent, compared to Europe and much of North America, offered a less demanding winter climate in which to subsist. In those days when there was little after rent, food, clothes and rudimentary entertainments for most to spend money on, an index of comparative national prosperity might revolve around the quantity of quality food consumed. At least the *Age* thought so. In the consumption of what one eminent dietitian deemed most desirable foodstuff, 'meat—and a great deal of it—three times a day', Australians led the world (figure 3).[8]

Finding the right immigrant type

Another indicator of prosperity, or at least middle-class prosperity, might have been the number of households with servants and the number of servants per household, if they were to be found. 'The problem of securing domestic servants is a tense one', one commentator overstated, 'vitally affecting Australian women'. After a male agricultural labourer, the most sought after immigrant in 1913 was a female domestic. 'Every

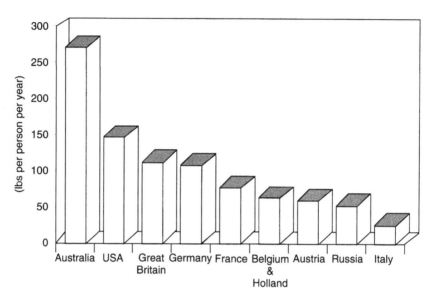

Figure 3 Meat consumption, per capita, per annum: 1912 (in pounds avoirdupois)
SOURCE: *Age*, 5 August 1913.

young woman who comes to Australia to domestic service not only provides the State with a potential mother, but fills a gap in the ranks of
our industrial workers.' Marriage to a qualified female could help an
immigrant male find work, it being often preferable 'that the woman
should be a good domestic help than that the man should be a good
farm labourer'.[9]

Immigration was perceived as the most pressing Australian problem;
for, without a suitable inflow of human material, how would the nation
state ever justify its unique occupancy of a whole continent and satisfac-
torily assert its right to a place in the sun? It was customarily assumed
that the Commonwealth could maintain a population equalling or
exceeding that of the United States, estimates varying from Sir Rider Haggard's '40 or 50 millions of white people', through C. E. W. Bean's 1907
estimate of New South Wales alone that it might 'by cooperative irrigation and mixed farming,' bear 'a population of at least 40,000,000', to
Foster Fraser's 'restrained calculation' of 1910, that 'Australia is able to
support at least 200,000,000 people'. A hundred million was the happy
medium for one defence expert, who asked Australians to imagine what
their country 'as a world power will be like' when carrying such a
population.

There is no fear of starvation with such a rich soil, capable of producing every commodity that the world requires, and with magnificent rivers in suitable places to give the soil, by irrigation, the nourishment it requires. Do we not possess, too, a climate second to none, which permits work to be carried out without cessation? There is no fear of invasion provided our sea-girth[?] is protected by a strong modern navy, capable of protecting our interstate and oversea commerce.[10]

But how long would it take to reach a hundred million? Immigration over the previous decade had not been a spectacular success. The States, in uncoordinated programs, had spent vast sums to attract the desired British or northern European migrants; while there had been improvements since Foster Fraser noted 'a startling result—72,208 immigrants arrived in Australia in 1908, and 59,058 people emigrated from Australia that year!', a disquieting tendency was again emerging. The 'healthy stream of British immigration' that had marked 1912, and for which Sir George Reid, then High Commissioner in London, took credit, had become a trickle.

[There] has been practically no emigrant traffic to Australia for some months past, and . . . the present empty state of the vessels is a remarkable contrast to the crush during the rush of last year. They attribute the falling off to the present high level of wages among skilled labourers in this country [England].[11]

There were good reasons why 'fresh blood' was said to be needed. Perhaps the 'new species' that Francis Adams had found 'absolutely defined after two generations' in the 1880s was not necessarily an improvement upon the old, for by 1913 Australians had already been dealing for decades with allegations 'that persons born in the colonies lose something of the physical strength of Europe, as well as of the stamina by which it is conserved'. When Foster Fraser took up this theme in 1909–10, asking 'what will be the characteristics of the third and subsequent generations?', this slur on the local-born was met with hostility. But the barbs flung by patronising Britons still stung, especially given a disproportionate domination of British-born in positions of power in political, religious and commercial life. While Australians by 1913 were about 80 per cent Australian-born, they shared with other Anglo-Saxons a birthrate that was 'low as compared with the Slav and the German, the yellow man and the black man'. To boost Australia's population to the levels envisaged by the likes of Foster Fraser might require waiting until the day when 'countless millions of the British race' would be 'pushed out of the already over-crowded islands known as Great Britain'. Few believed Australia could wait that long.[12]

Australia's image was not too glowing, either, as a welcoming and attractive land in which to settle. One immigrant, confronted by 'the antipathy of the Australians' for the English newcomer, 'an antipathy which is reciprocated', encountered a recently coined pejorative term— ' "Pommy," which is the diminutive of pomegranate'. The 'curt treatment' accorded to many desirable immigrants had made 'them turn their eyes to Canada, where immigrants are welcomed with open arms instead of being given the cold shoulder'. Potentially useful British would-be immigrants were also discriminated against at the highest level. 'I do not encourage the city dwellers to come and live here', Sir George Reid admitted. 'The man I try to get hold of is the agricultural labourer, and the tiller of the soil'. Reid's over-simplistic assertions brought on the ire of even the conservative Sydney *Daily Telegraph*, which saw the flaws in his version of a back-to-the-land movement.

> People do not leave remunerative work in the country and come into the cities to starve. 'The current' referred to by Sir George Reid as flowing from the country to the metropolis, and the strength of which alarms him, simply means that industrial affairs are finding their own level . . .
> This impetus to city growth is not a condition peculiar to New South Wales or to Australia; it exists throughout the whole world. It is the result of modern changes in industrial methods, due to the increasing use of mind for doing what was in more primitive times done by muscle.[13]

Neither were the farm labourers Reid sought what the imperial government wanted the dominions to take, as Sir Rider Haggard, the celebrated novelist, travelling with the Empire Trade Commission, quickly spelled out. Agreeing that a much greater population was 'vitally needed to develop the illimitable wealth with which Nature had endowed Australia', he pointed out that there was 'no plentiful supply which could be drawn upon in the rural districts of England', suggesting instead that 'the surplus people of the English cities should be given a chance upon the land'. The problem was that 'Australians had come a little late into the market'. While they had 'been contemplating the riches in this land', other dominions and colonies had 'been taking the surplus population'.

> 'I have often heard it said, "Send us out your best; nothing second rate for us." (Laughter.) When you inquire . . . you will find that in nine cases out of 10 it means young agricultural laborers who have been taught their craft at Home, and young women in the first flush of youth . . . are these to be sent in any great numbers? I think not.'[14]

In Britain during the previous sixty years 'the number of agricultural laborers has fallen from 2,088,400 to about the minimum possible;

869,800'. Some Australians recognised, like Victoria's minister for Lands, that it was 'out of the question for Britain to furnish the settlers that Australia needed'. No other country had been 'so "combed" for settlers' and 'no other country had a smaller surplus of the kind of settlers Australia needed'. Already the 'feeling in Scotland and Ireland', as it was in England, 'was strong against the further emigration of farmers or farm labourers'. Canada already recognised this, and had accordingly 'shifted much of its activity from Britain to the Continent'.[15]

No less concerned about dominion immigration priorities, the editor of the London *Morning Post* called the dominions to task for 'seeking to attract our agricultural laborers'. The best type for Australia, 'surely', was 'the healthy lad who has not had his courage beaten down by a losing fight in one of our cities, but has all his youth and all his hopes before him, and his keen, plucky British character as his capital to face the new conditions of your land with its boundless opportunities'. Now that the 'theory that town boys were no good for the country had been disproved', Australia might take British slum lads who, on a State farm, 'would produce good, wholesome food for themselves' and 'produce a good class for our soldiers and sailors'.[16]

To promote the idea that British city types could successfully undertake Australian rural work, Sir Rider Haggard led Empire Trade Commission witnesses to explore the theme that knowledge or skill was not needed for Australian farming. One 'expert' told of 'people who knew nothing about farming' who had 'taken up land . . . and done very well'. Asked by Haggard, 'How do you account for that?', he replied:

[Witness]—Well, they were not hampered with old ideas, and were willing to take the experience of good men.
[Haggard] Therefore, the less experience they have of agriculture at the other end, the better for their success here?
[Witness]—Very often.[17]

The arguments posed by the commissioners were one-sided: at no point was the idea canvassed that surplus British urban labourers or tradespeople might find employment in Australian cities. Debate centred upon conversion; on how readily the British urban under-class might adapt to the needs of an endless pioneer era. But by 1913 the virgin plains and tablelands the nineteenth century pioneers had found—where hard work, pluck and ignorance could still reap rewards—were in the past. It was now acknowledged in farming columns that those 'who come later will get land not quite so good in its virgin state'. This was nonetheless 'capable of being transformed by the new methods that science is constantly inventing. Irrigation and dry farming will throw open enormous areas that are at present lying waste.'[18]

The wonders of modernity now meant that the 'days of the small farm in Australia' were 'beginning in earnest'. All that was needed was irrigation and time 'before the new order of things can be regarded as an established fact'. Hard-pressed farmer-settlers were not so sanguine. A Victorian Commission on Closer Settlement was told that:

> While most settlers were fully satisfied with the quality of the land they contended that the holdings were far too small . . . The present holdings were so small that very little land could be fallowed, and it was next to impossible to run any sheep, without which a settler was handicapped in managing his block.[19]

Adding to the problem, many blocks fell short of being 'not quite so good'. While Victorian settlers seemed happy with the quality of land on offer, one 'would-be settler' in New South Wales had already lost all illusions.

> If N.S.W. wants immigrant of the right kind—viz. British yeomanry . . . she must . . . be able to offer suitable Crown lands within the wheat belt, in living areas, and not the rock-strewn, waterless, mountainous, dingo-haunted, rabbit infested, useless country that is being doled out in slices about the size of a stockyard. No wonder your population drifts into the metropolitan area.[20]

'Fortunately', added the writer, suggesting that farming experience was after all indispensable, 'my knowledge of wool has enabled me to earn a living'.

Fantasies about subterranean seas—comparable to those of the surface, inland seas once sought by nineteenth century explorers—were rebuffed by the New South Wales Labor government's representative at the National Irrigation Congress at Chicago. Niels Nielsen was 'struck at once by the miserably small amount of water available for irrigation' in Australia. It was 'ridiculous in the extreme, to suggest that its population is ever likely to compare . . . with countries that are blessed with a much greater rainfall'. Of the continent, 36 per cent had to be 'classed as arid and another 36 per cent as semi-arid'. These indisputable, 'even if not very encouraging, facts every Australian should know'. But Sir Rider Haggard offered Australians more reassuring platitudes. He'd 'been taught that there was a fertile ring round the coast of Australia, and that the rest of the country was desert', but now, after a few weeks in Australia, knew that to be wrong. What Haggard described as the 'water terror' would be seen to 'vanish or to be lessened under examination. If the

ON A YANCO ORCHARD : SCIENTIFIC USE OF WATER.

Plate 3 The 'scientific use of water' transforms the land (*Sydney Mail* 26 March 1913, courtesy of State Library of NSW).

Water was the key to imperialist dreams of making deserts bloom to support vast populations and cultivate foodstuffs for the imperial larder.

water that fell and the water beneath the surface were conserved, ines-
timable fields of wealth would be created.' Australia's problems could be
solved by a few scientific wonders backed by millions of men of the right
type and muscle to chop, plough, dig, plant and carry—a formulation
Australians mostly agreed with. The immigration program that was
adding wealth and cultural diversity to the United States, and making
American cities potentially explosive, but exciting cultural melting pots,
was anathema to most Australians.[21]

> Homer Lee expresses the opinion that 'the heterogeneous racial elements con-
> stitute America's greatest national weakness.' A writer in the 'Atlantic Monthly'
> remarked recently: 'We have reached a point where the congestion of tens of
> thousands of foreigners . . . in our industrial cities is preparing a very dark
> problem for the future.'[22]

Canada was also becoming an example of what not to do. It was 'doubtful whether English will be the language of more than half the population
of Canada in another quarter of a century'. Worse, 'the difficulty of converting the foreign elements into British Canadians is daily becoming
more serious' now that 'all hope of assimilating this element in the large
Canadian cities' had 'gone forever'.[23]

Britain aside, only Germany in the Old World possessed racially desirable types in sufficient numbers. If British farm labourers were becoming
unprocurable, then perhaps Sir George Reid could attract them from a
Reich which he considered had 'one of the finest peoples in the world.
She deserves the place she has got.' He tried, but in doing so ran foul of
German law; in Germany it was now 'an offence to do anything calcu-
lated to unsettle the mind of any German' in order 'to dispose him to
leave his country'. Reid ought to have known better; months previously
the German consul-general in Sydney had publicly announced 'that he
did not think his country could spare many emigrants'.[24]

Australia's immigration wants bore relationship to imaginary needs.
Many attachments to immigration ideals were emotional, comforting and
politically expedient rather than economically viable. Farm hands and
domestics, at the low ends of prevailing social orders, presented little
threat to established interests. Middle-class aspirations to lifestyles imi-
tating those at Home could be partially sated by domestic help; the fears
of job losses among urban workers could be mollified by suggesting priorities that rested with the importation of rural muscle. In the background lurked an assumption indebted to the agrarian myth: a man's
place was on the land. This was a truism even the urban bourgeoisie
accepted.

Much as he admired his hosts in this 'magnificent city of Sydney', Sir

George Reid believed the city was 'living on the wealth of the country districts'; he therefore 'admired the men who went pioneering in the backblocks a thousand times more than he admired them [that is, his hosts]. (Cheers.)' Sir Rider Haggard, too, speaking 'as a practical farmer, and one who knows the agricultural conditions throughout the world', warned that if the cities grew unchecked, 'the country must decay, as other nations have decayed'. Preaching to the converted, he claimed 'the towns in Australia were already too big ... (Cheers.)'. It was the 'Australia of the land that urgently needed developing. (Cheers.)'. If Australians wanted farms 'to spring up everywhere', then they would have to 'have more people to own and work them'.[25]

Australia was not England, nor even Kenya. Soil, distance, water and climate made impossible the dream of a continent cut up into yeoman-farm blocks, and the economic realities of 'becoming modern' were demanding the growth of cities. While dominion industrialisation might be viewed with distaste in the corridors of power at Whitehall, among large landholding interests and in conservative editorial offices, it could be discouraged but not avoided. Threaten imperial tidiness it might, but some mechanically skilled urban tradesmen were bound to successfully seek money-making manufacturing possibilities and in time compete with manufacturers based in the Motherland. The *Sydney Morning Herald* seemed to recognise it had a fight on its hands. In a leader entitled 'Burdening the Land', it implied that almost all domestic manufacturing was more trouble than it was worth.

> There is scarcely a single Australian manufacturing industry which pays its way apart from the tariff that forces Australians to pour money into it. And practically the whole of money by which these city wages are sustained, and on which these manufacturing industries live, is the surplus which comes from those Australians who do pay their way in the world—the farmers and pastoralists of Australia.[26]

And, as loyal Britons, should not Australians be concerned that British manufacturers were already facing enough industrial competition from foreigners without the dominions and colonies joining in? Sir Rider Haggard had already been told that the 'goods supplied by the German traders were equal to, if not better, than those supplied by British merchants'; given that the Germans were more obliging, therefore, 'the natural tendency was for trade to go to Germany'.[27]

Britain's vested interests lay in the development and exploitation of the Australian backblocks. As far as Australia itself was concerned, pastoralist truisms provided a poor base from which to develop a diversified national economy—though, what can be seen in hindsight does not

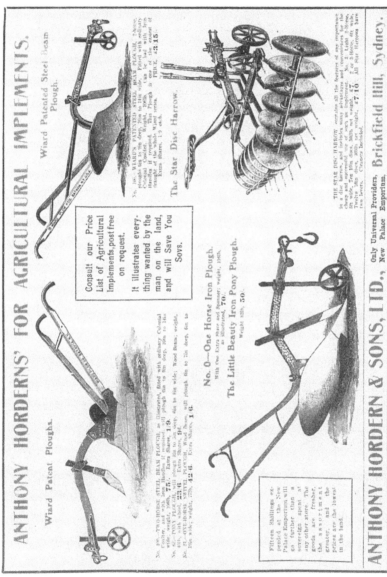

Plate 4 Modern implements to develop the backblocks (Hordern's advertisement, *Sydney Mail* 12 March 1913, courtesy of State Library of NSW).
But they also symbolise the dilemmas of the industrialisation debate, since by 1913 Australia already had its own booming and innovative agricultural implements industry.

account for what seemed real in 1913. Australia's future was integrated with Greater Britain's; Australians, and what they dug up, sheared or planted, were partners with, and dependent upon a 'John Bull and Coy.' that already had its manufacturing sector, not in Sydney, Geelong, Newcastle or Melbourne, but in Birmingham, Coventry and Leeds.[28]

Not all Australians viewed this with equanimity; some doubted the invincibility of an empire at whose head was a nation seen as showing signs of decadence. 'We must so order our great democracy in Australia', Alderman J. D. Fitzgerald warned, 'that we shall never have it said of us as was said of England—that millions of our fellow countrymen and women are ill-clothed, ill-housed, and ill-fed; that 12,000,000 out of 50,000,000 are on the verge of subsidence, or that our children die because the mothers are sweated and the fathers ill-paid'. From a differing political and social standpoint, the general manager of the Australian Mutual Provident Society, who had made 'six visits to England in the last 38 years' was also less than impressed, though he confined his criticism to the behaviour of the 'respectable' classes.

> Home life has largely disappeared, and the spirit of hedonism is abroad. One was always somewhat surprised to see women of the respectable class drinking in public bars, but to witness . . . restaurants of first-class hotels full at all hours . . . young girls drinking cocktails, smoking cigarettes, and hugging and mugging dogs, makes one anxious about the future of the race.[29]

Sir George Reid was quick to offer rebuttals. The 'mother country was no decadent', he insisted. He had found 'a new England, a new Scotland, and a new Ireland growing up, showing no signs of decay'. And when asked his opinion 'as to the condition of things in the old country', the representative of the 'meat freezing companies of New Zealand and Australia' stated that British 'business was never better and never sounder'. Any suggestion of British decadence impinged directly on the Australian self-image; most Australians considered themselves Britons and any criticism of the British race was a criticism of them, too. Only Britons could or should populate the Australian continent, whose development was now seen in the light of greatest urgency: 'populate or perish' in 1913 was the expression of genuine fear.[30]

A 'ruined and down-trodden' people and 'the others'

The *Bulletin* wanted the population numbers but not if it meant a land covered with the farms and quarries of one of John Bull & Coy's agricultural and mining rumps. It despaired that poets—in an age when poets still spoke to the population at large—'had little to say, except a bland approval, to the policy of the Government of introducing agricultural labourers from overseas'. What the country 'badly' needed instead was 'the people who make these imported goods—it wants them as citizens, as taxpayers, as customers to the local farmer, and as defenders'. But what added urgency to these considerations and distinguished Australia from other new societies was its continental situation. No other people on earth, of one language and one ethnic clan, could claim to be 'sole' occupants of a continent. Fulfilling 'our larger hopes of a White Man's continent' barely considered an indigenous people who had not died out and whose presence had a tendency to generate unwelcome attention. In 1913 settlers 'in the far north-west of Western Australia' were finding 'the aborigines to be more than usually troublesome. Some time ago the dead body of a man was found at Wyndham, and particulars have just been received in Perth from a Wyndham letter of the finding of the body.'[31]

Unhelpful to the cause of this 'ruined and down-trodden' people—of which it was sometimes 'solemnly declared' that they 'were barely one degree higher than the anthropoid apes'—was the decision 'to republish in book form a collection of "yarns" reprinted from the "Aboriginalities" column of the "Bulletin" ', something the Sydney *Daily Telegraph* thought was 'a capital idea'. Lionel Lindsay, 'a draughtsman with a fine humor of his own, and his drawings hit the bulls-eye every time', was responsible for the illustrations. Of the bulls-eye in question there was no doubt. Aborigines, while useful as trackers, were depicted as at best harmless unhygienic dolts, and at worst stupid, shifty, physical degenerates fit to only act as a target for the white man's jokes or drawings. In a practical demonstration of related sentiments, the people of Wingham attempted to invoke a localised apartheid to protect cattle. The Upper Manning dairymen 'resented the idea of placing a large number of blacks, who have dangerous ideas of sanitation, on the banks of a creek from which their dairy cows get water'. But it was still possible to learn from the experience of this 'dying race'—albeit negatively. Just as they 'failed' to develop the land and gave way to 'superior' white people, so might Australians 'fail' the challenge posed by the immensity of the continent and be forced to cede possession. A 'visiting American press-man' was among those to endorse this theory: ' "Take it from me . . . if you don't develop this fair land of Australia, it will be swamped by Indians, Malays, Japanese and Chinese" '.[32]

Australia's continental nationality incurred responsibilities and problems of which sub-continental new societies had no perception. So long as the shared western coastline of Canada and the United States seemed vulnerable to action by a hostile Japanese navy, Canada's national interest was inseparable from that of her great southern neighbour. Nor was Argentina under threat, certainly not from a Japan whose interests lay 'in the partition of Great Britain and her colonies. By the establishment of an alliance between Germany and Japan the latter may take possession of Australia, while the former may establish a protectorate over the various countries and islands of the South Pacific.' A Japanese invasion of the Australian continent through the open northern door would, according to one expert, have 'as its objective' the cluster of tents and prefabricated buildings that was Canberra in 1913. Fear of imminent Japanese invasion was in the air at the *Bulletin*, where the idea of the yellow plague from the north, viral and human, had a long tradition.[33]

> And those who were laughing cease and peer,
> Through the sea's darkness that holds the Fear.
> *Shadow of Asia is here—is here!*[34]

The Germans argued that Japan's interests, despite the Anglo-Japanese treaty, were the same as the Reich's: by the year '1916 the Japanese fleet will be strong enough to land a Japanese army in Australia, and to deprive England forever of that immeasurably rich colony'. But not everyone in Australia was screaming about yellow hordes, nor accepting the inevitability of an occupation attempt that 'would require some 200,000 men, and many years, during which time long lines of communication on sea and land would have to be kept open'. Japan really wanted Australia 'to maintain a White Australia with its high standard of living, so that her trade may be maintained and increased. The Dutch East Indies and the Philippines are infinitely more valuable, and will satisfy Japan's ambitions and her capital for half a century.'[35]

If, to Australians, Dutch and American possessions to the north seemed expendable, then the idea of an open, unguarded northern door provoked thought on who might most usefully be asked to live in the Northern Territory and close that door. The climate was perceived as the greatest problem for white people; the excessive humidity and 'trying heat brings on insomnia', making it 'very hard to keep going'. Others believed the Territory was the 'the finest tropical country in the world', and its climate 'conducive to longevity. But you do not want cotton-wool or artificial men there. What is required is the strong, healthy, hopeful man, men who have made Australia what it is.' If it could have been populated by imperialist rhetoric, it would have long since been full. In such vein the minister for External Affairs promised the coming of a time, 'and not in the dim and distant future, when in that Territory . . . there will be a vast population, a great multitude, speaking our language, swearing allegiance to the flag we love'.[36]

Argentina does it

As a solution to the problems facing whites in the tropics, in 1909 Foster Fraser suggested that Italians 'under the supervision of Australians' might do field work. In time 'with Italian settlers no doubt inter-marrying with those of British race, there might grow up a people acclimatised to the conditions of the north'. In the meantime a solution could lie in 'the utilisation of Indian native labour'. This idea was not welcome. While Indians were imperial subjects, why populate the place with people you sought to exclude? Dr Gilruth, the Northern Territory Administrator, also thought agriculturalists from the northern Mediterranean would 'be better suited to cultivate and develop the Northern Territory than would British people, who are used to the colder latitudes'.[37]

The war adjourned this discourse, but its intensity and breadth are testimony to the importance and urgency being attached to populating the Commonwealth. Most Australians believed they were a 'mighty people in the infant days of its greatness', but Australia was not the only new society to have a future seen in rosy terms. Indeed, the country was embroiled in competition in a human resources market with two others, Argentina and Canada—a competition in which Australia had no choice but to enter with vigour even if it was losing the battle for numbers. Argentina and Canada had less restrictive policies in respect of ethnicity and occupation and were able, therefore, to draw potential immigrants from a much larger pool than was Australia with its preference for British farm labourers. Nor could imperial rhetoric disguise the fact that Australia's elder-sister dominion, Canada, was its prime competitor for people and markets, and had been for some time. 'Australia needs every Briton whom it can get', C. E. W. Bean wrote in 1907. 'It is life and death to us.' His was a hymn of praise for Australia, aimed at Britons 'trooping into Canada at an almost fabulous rate'. By 1913 Australia's sibling was still admired for its 'spirited immigration campaign'. In ten years 'immigrants into Canada introduced over 100 millions sterling into that Dominion', offering Australia an example to follow. But were Australians 'afraid of new men lest they should divide instead of adding to the strength of the country'? In Canada and the United States, claimed Sydney University's Professor Irvine, 'they realise that the newcomer is an acquisition, and welcome him accordingly'.[38]

Argentina was having no trouble finding all the farm hands and domestic servants needed—as well as skilled artisans and professionals—in Spain and Italy. By 1913 about 90 per cent of the population had originated in Latin countries. The millions that had migrated since 1850 went to a country largely 'cleansed' of its indigenous Indian population;

because slavery had only touched the region, there were few blacks, either. A minority of Argentines were mestizo or had African origins; but, if racial conflict was minor, class conflict was ferocious—between the landed gentry, the emerging middle-class and the great mass of the *descamisados* (who later became Evita Perón's constituency). What helped unite Argentines, irrespective of class, was a belief in themselves as Europeans surrounded by racial inferiors. 'Every Argentine knows,' John Gunther later wrote, 'that his country has a great imperial destiny. Every Argentine knows that Buenos Aires is the finest city in the world.' Decades before Gunther, this idea of an imperial destiny had given rise to fanciful predictions.

> The Pacific will become the theatre of mighty movements, and South America will wax strong and wealthy. The British Empire will disintegrate: the Slavs and the Teutons will dominate Europe, and expel the Latins, who will find a welcome under southern skies. 'The torch which bears the ideal of Latin Civilisation would pass from Paris to Buenos Aires'.[39]

In the meantime the British Empire—or rather Great Britain—was ensuring its slice of the Argentine cake: for decades British capital had poured in. The railroads were almost wholly British-owned and, to the chagrin of patriotic *argentinos*, their *Patria* was sometimes called the 'Sixth Dominion'. 'You may take Canada from us', an Englishman told Gunther, 'but never Argentina'. By 1913 Argentina was already one of the world's largest exporters of agricultural products, and the globe-trotting Foster Fraser contrasted *The Amazing Argentine* with an Australia held back by the native-born's lack of interest in the vast untouched plains 'which ought to be doing much more in food production'. Some Australians agreed with him that Argentina was a 'Marvellous Place' where private enterprise was encouraged and, as one grazier said, 'great development' had resulted: 'If they had all their land in use, and knew how to farm properly . . . it would be a bad outlook for us, for they could almost keep the whole world going'.[40]

Argentina also might provide an example of how better Australia could run its immigration policy. 'The admixture of Spaniards and Indians had produced a fine race', stated one Australian businessman. If 'some of our legislators went to the Argentine they would have their eyes opened' and even 'change their ideas about some things', now that filling-up 'the empty spaces was becoming more and more imperative every day'. The *Bulletin* agreed about filling the spaces but was otherwise unimpressed. A new society's calibre was measured by the quality of the racial stock it could attract. Despite all its 'encouragement to Private Enterprise and the consequent "great development" ', Argentina had 'not attracted the Britisher in quantities. It has only managed to acquire 2,000,000 Italians and a large number of Russians'.[41]

As far as Australian immigration priorities were concerned, Italians, Russians and 'Spanish Farm Hands from Argentina' might or might not pass through the immigration net; people whose skin was darker than olive, or whose eyes lacked Caucasian fullness had no chance, however. Little had changed since 1907 when C. E. W. Bean warned of the evils of 'mixing the East with the West', and of a racial war 'so ghastly and gruesome that if you want only sleep to-night you had better not try to imagine it'. In 1913 racist arguments still prevailed.

> From the southern extremity of the Malay peninsula, right through the Dutch possessions and the other islands lying to the north of Australia, Chinese and Japanese are to be found in considerable number . . . and wherever Chinese or Japanese or Indian come into contact with Polynesian there is not the least doubt as to which will survive and which will perish.[42]

With Social Darwinism then at the height of its credibility, it was assumed that contact between races would lead to conflict in which the fitter would survive while the 'lesser' race submerged or perished. That nations or societies of different ethnic origins could live in proximity without wiping each other out, either by economic or military means, did not fit with such a dictum—notions that were, after forty years of continental peace, providing war with an almost attractive aura.

'A breezy, buoyant, Imperial spirit'

The *Bulletin* endorsed both futurism's claim that war was 'the only hygiene of the world' and von Bernhardi's faith in 'combat as a biological necessity'. Not all Social Darwinists were in Potsdam. In 1908 W. M. Hughes wondered why men 'speak of war as though it were the greatest curse on earth', when it was only the 'Nemesis which overtakes nations, just as diseases and casualties, and death, overtake the individual'. When a man was diseased, it was 'in consequence of a violation of nature's laws'. Likewise, when a nation was sick 'she' became 'an easy prey to a conqueror' and met 'a doom she has invited and deserved'. It was easy for middle-aged politicians to proclaim these so-called natural laws. It was other, younger men who would have to die for them. Among those who accepted war's inevitability, J. H. M. Abbott, who had fought in the Boer War, saw war from the standpoint of the youths likely to be caught up in it. In the Sydney *Daily Telegraph*, on the eve of a march of cadets through Sydney, he wrote with an almost Delphic wisdom, in view of Fromelles and Bullecourt only a few years away:

> These lads, these fresh faced, athletic boys will probably have to starve and remain wet for days, and sleep in the mud, and swarm with vermin, and die in ditches, and rot with dysentery, and get lung complaints and fever, and be torn with bits of shell, and get bullets through their stomachs, and have the fear of God in their souls, and suffer exceedingly . . . They will learn in a variety of ways . . . that war is exactly what General Sherman said it was— Hell.[43]

Abbott knew death in battle was not the sweetest of all. It could be a ghastly affair 'in a muddy trench under shrapnel, and with no tucker in [one's] haversack'.

This was not the stuff to quicken the pulse and bring forth stirring deeds. C. E. W. Bean, who the *Bulletin* thought should be 'appointed Patriotic Writer-in-Ordinary to the Commonwealth', was the man for that. For the *Sydney Mail Naval Number* of October 1913 Bean had *carte blanche* to write text for an issue filled with photographs, diagrams and charts, and addressed to spectators expected to line the Sydney harbour foreshores at the arrival of Australia's navy. Bean asked them to see, not a 'tin-pot' navy, but a 'complete British fleet in miniature'—the forerunner of a fleet-to-be; in twenty years, he said, Sydneysiders would be 'looking down' upon 'a score of battleships and cruisers and a flotilla of 30 torpedo craft moored in that same silver expanse—a fleet to be reckoned with all over the world'. The spectator of 1913 would have to use some imagination.

> The great battle squadron will be there—only three ships instead of a line of them. The light, fast, scouting cruisers will be there—only three ships instead of a number. The low, lean torpedo-boat-destroyers will be there—only three ships instead of a flotilla. But the Australian who has never left his own State will, for the first time in history, be able to inspect all classes of ships in a complete fleet just as surely as if he were watching a naval revue at Spithead.[44]

In response, the people of Sydney gave this 'British fleet in miniature' the thumbs down; but it was poor timing to allow the 'welcome of the Australian fleet to coincide with the opening of the Spring race meeting'. The *Age* gloated at the 'Melancholy Festival' Sydney had bungled, boasting that if 'the new fleet had sailed into Hobson's Bay and had its first official reception in Melbourne, instead of Port Jackson, the occasion would have been marked by more warmth'. If nothing else, this beggar-thy-neighbour reaction was indicative of the level of inter-state and inter-city jealousies still prevailing more than a decade after federation.

Australia often still gave the impression of being six quite separate and distinct little Britains.[45]

What seemed to unite the Australians of the various States—as Britons were fond of telling them—was not so much their Australianness as their British heritage. In 1909 Foster Fraser sensed a 'breezy, buoyant Imperial spirit', but cautioned that 'the national spirit, as it is understood elsewhere, is practically non-existent'. Many Australians saw little wrong in that, and there was none better than the *Argus* to articulate their imperial sentiments.

> When [men] . . . spoke of Imperialism [they] had in their minds the power, the wealth, and the influence of the great empire of which the United Kingdom was the centre, and of which Australia was so important a part . . . [The] British Empire was the greatest civilising force under Providence that the world had ever seen. If they stood, as they did, determined to defend their heritage, they none the less stood for peace, for ordered progress, for good and stable government, and for civilisation.[46]

Imperialism also signified Australia's safeguard. The knowledge that survival supposedly depended upon the guns of the world's greatest navy may have played some part in the passivity of the welcome to an Australian fleet able to protect but a few miles of shore. Australians knew they lived in dangerous times; on the eve of the war broadsheets such as the *Argus* or *Sydney Morning Herald* provided readers with extensive coverage of a continuously changing worldview of heightening uncertainty—war seemed as much a question of 'where' and 'when' as of 'if'. The wretched, bewildering and outwardly interminable Balkan War seemed constantly at the point of embroiling the major powers. It would take little to have Austria and Russia, caught up by treaty in opposing camps, at each other's throats, and then the dominos would tumble. If not the Balkan War—and its daily progress or lack thereof lurched through the news pages of 1913 as a kind of background obbligato—then something, almost anything could bring about the final showdown between Germany and the British Empire, which seemed inevitable. It was a prospect in 1913 that most Australians must have viewed with dismay, especially as the most likely enemy was their racial 'cousins'.

With shared origins in 'Teutonic stock', the Anglo-Saxons and Germans were placed, some said, 'at the head of all other races'. While no consolation to the British Empire, it was admirable nonetheless that during 'the last ten years Germany's steel industries have increased 100 per cent., those of America 29 per cent., while England's have increased a bare 7 per cent.'. The Germans were not only admired for their efficiency

and industrial might. Few world figures received more Australian attention, at least in the conservative press, than the Kaiser did. On his twenty-
fifth anniversary as emperor, the Sydney *Daily Telegraph* claimed he had
'qualified himself as King Edward's successor to the title "Prince of
Peace" '.

> It has been his dream since youth that England and Germany should march
> shoulder to shoulder for their common good in the field of international pol-
> itics. Joining in that happy sentiment, Australians could yesterday have joined
> in the toast to the Kaiser with a 'Hoch! Noch ein Mal!—Hoch!! Zum dritte
> Mal—Hoch!!!'[47]

If war was inevitable, not everyone in Whitehall accepted that it must
be with Germany. Leo Amery, described as one of the 'younger school
of Imperialist', regarded 'American interests as being more likely to clash
with our own'. The idea of war with a nation—Germany—it admired
caused the *Bulletin* to dismiss the threat it didn't want to believe, in
favour of one it did. 'There is no fear that the helmeted frown, with its
brushed-up moustache is going to Teutonize or Prussianize the world. It
is the browny-yellow grin in a smooth, slant-eyed face that we must
watch.'[48]

Australian attitude to the empire's ally, France, was ambivalent. Paris
remained the City of Art and the Home of Fashion, but the Entente Cor-
diale had far from effaced centuries of Anglo-French distrust. To the
French, the British often seemed cold and lacking in *joie de vivre*, as
might be expected from a nation/empire boasting such an abominable
cuisine. To Britons, the French were not Gallicised Celts upholding the
civilisation that was Rome; rather, they were excitable Mediterraneans
lacking—in what still required a French phrase in the better circles—
sang froid. About the French there was an aura of vicarious excitement,
stimulated through stories of liberal, even enviable sexual habits and attitudes, somewhat deflated by exaggerated stories about the supposedly
less than enviable sanitary appointments of French hotels.

The arrangements of the Entente envisaged Australians fighting alongside Englishmen and Frenchmen against Germans. But during this last
phase of the Belle Époque, in addition to the Balkan powder-keg, an
outbreak of war seemed possible between the United States on one side,
and either—or both—Japan and Mexico on the other. While the battlefield alignments of a future European—or even trans-Atlantic—war were
open to dispute, there was consensus that the Pacific 'sooner or later
must be the world's great deciding ground for nations now reaching up
to maturity or waiting to test a developing youth of matchless might'.
Japan was now a 'Power in the first rank, and there she will remain'. For

the time being—until the completion of the Panama Canal—the Pacific was her lake. As the premier power in the region, she demanded respect the United States was unwilling to grant.[49]

The Anglo-Saxon nations of the Pacific basin all discriminated against Japanese immigration. Given British treaty obligations, the Japanese had little choice but to bear this affront from the dominions. With the United States it was different, and they reacted to proscriptive immigration legislation in California as example of the arrogant racism of an American 'albinocracy' which had to be 'exterminated not only for the sake of Japan, but of the world—yea, of humanity itself!'. If Japan was to teach these 'albinos' a lesson, she 'would have a far better chance of succeeding . . . while the Panama Canal is still unfinished'. It then took 'two months to steam from New York to San Francisco round Cape Horn,' while a Japanese squadron could cross the Pacific 'in less than three weeks'. The proposed California legislation was 'providing the pretext for urging the [Japanese] Government to early action'. And with relationships souring between the two powers, could the British Empire become involved? 'The issue between the United States and Japan' had already caused Canada 'to ask herself how she could defend British Columbia'. It 'is perilous to cherish the belief that Japan has no chance of victory should matters come to a decision of the sword'.

> In the event of war, the United States then will be the champion of the white man in the eyes of Australia, New Zealand and Canada, while Great Britain will be bound to Japan . . . If the Japanese assert their claim successfully the British Empire may be confronted with the same difficulty, for Australia will undoubtedly reject any claim by Japan to the Northern Territory.[50]

The crisis dissipated after the Panama Canal opened, permitting the *Sydney Morning Herald* to show a suavity it had not exhibited in the days of tension. Could 'any one in his senses suppose that Japan is seri-ously thinking of a life and death struggle with ninety millions of the wealthiest and most progressive people on earth?'. But the *Herald* took a less sanguine long-term view; so long as Japan was 'an ally of Great Britain', the dominions could 'shelter themselves behind British guns'. But the 'British-Japanese Alliance' was to end in 1915, and—'what then?'[51]

At the end of the year the *Sydney Mail* noted that it had been 'many years since such serious international complications have been threat-ened as were the case during 1913'.

True, no new war broke out during the year ... but the aftermath of the Balkan struggle created an international situation that demanded delicate handling during the whole time ... [and] the Balkan problem is still bristling with possibilities of trouble. The burden of armaments has grown well-nigh intolerable to the Great Powers.[52]

It came to a head nine months later.

CHAPTER THREE

1913: Nowadays we are most of us Nietzscheans

The thing at least is not inert and dead,
There's life and motion there, and rending force,
Colour-Niagara's thundering on their course,
Power that breaks like a great wave in spray—
And what it means we'll let To-morrow say.

'The Exhibition' (*Sydney Mail* 3 September 1913)

Two of the world's great cities

'By the late-nineteenth century', R. V. Jackson wrote, 'Melbourne and Sydney were already two of the great cities of the modern world'. By the turn of the century others had overtaken them, for the 1890s crash aborted schemes for accelerated development. By mid-Edwardian times, however, Australia was emerging from its slump. In 1908, with optimism once more in the ascendant, a Royal Commission was appointed to 'diligently examine and investigate all proposals that may come before us for the improvement of the City of Sydney and its suburbs, and to fully inquire into the whole subject of the remodelling of Sydney'. Its findings were meant to provide guidelines so that Sydney 'might be made nearly as perfect as she is naturally beautiful'. Sydney, during a decade-and-a-half of national stagnation, had fallen behind other cities. But now, in 1908, it looked 'as if we Australians'

> were going to do something big at last in the matter of civic Government. We have lagged behind every community in the world. Even China and some of the cities in Japan show admirable examples of city planning. Tokio and Kobe contain some most excellent examples of wide streets: and Shanghai is a fine city in many aspects.[1]

The 1909 Royal Commission's *Final Report* reads as a modernist *tour de force*. Sydney was meant to bristle with modernity. A bridge crossing the harbour would complement a 'system of underground electric railways for city and suburban passenger traffic'. Above ground:

> Improved methods of road-making have rendered it practicable to construct lighter vehicles, and this tends to an increased rate of speed. In a very few years hence, when we shall have done away with the lumbering omnibus, the lorry, and the dray, and when a horse in the busy streets will be as strange a sight as a motor car was some twelve or thirteen years ago, the speed will be higher still.[2]

This city of the future would borrow from other cities already showing the way; but not, it seems, from British cities. Well-travelled Australians probably knew them too well. Nor did American skyscrapers have many Australian admirers in 1908, and it was believed that the tenement-block lifestyle of New York or Chicago would inevitably 'produce a race of feeble physique that can never be the backbone of the nation'. What Sydney needed was a 'dispersion from the centre and [the] development of suburban areas'. It was to Germany 'where scientific principles have been applied to municipal methods as perhaps nowhere else in Europe' that Sydney must look; to Germany where 'the cities and towns have solved the housing problems'.[3]

Germany had been late to unify, to enter into the race for a colonial empire and to industrialise. Its rapid industrial expansion and unparalleled but apparently well-controlled urban growth now were perceived as providing Australians with worthy exemplars, the more so as the Reich's late arrival had left it with few outdated practices or technologies hanging over from the Industrial Revolution; Germany's modernity could be little else than State of the Art. This was particularly true of a city like Berlin; though a mere village in Jean-Jacques Rousseau's time, it was now the capital of what Eksteins calls 'the modernist nation par excellence of our century'.

> Berliners, unlike the natives of other German cities and other European capitals, seemed to be fascinated by the very idea of urbanism and technology and even developed . . . a romanticism from 'railway junctions, cables, steel and track . . . noisy elevated trains, climbing towers.' [The] Berliner enjoyed and consciously promoted his city's cosmopolitanism and sense of novelty.[4]

Admiration for Germany didn't end with town planning. 'Modern civilisation' it was noted in the *Technical Gazette of New South Wales* in 1912, was 'becoming every day more industrially efficient. It is leaving the battlefield and the forum, and wins its victories in the workshop.' No modern nation was having greater success than Germany, not only in training its working men for that workshop, but in inculcating in them 'the basic conception of true education', the ancient 'Greek ideal of human perfection in absolute mental and physical balance'. The German system of technical education had made of the Reich 'that great and puissant modern nation whose power and influence are practically ungaugeable'—an example Australia could well follow.

> Throughout Germany, the school, the polytechnic, the college, the univer-sity—each constitutes a unit, a rallying point, a focalising centre. Our Tech-nical College should likewise be our Alma Mater (Our Benign Mother), our Collegiate Commonwealth . . . [Every] member of our College can work to a standard worthy of the whole of us, as we expect our Australian cadets to do when the Compulsory Military Defence Scheme develops.[5]

But industrialisation came at a price, and Australian infatuation with German institutions and processes was counterweighted by the usual negative responses to both city life and industrialisation. Adelin Guyot and Patrick Restellini's description of the turn-of-the-century emergence in Germany of a 'neo-romantic and regional literature'—calling for 'unreal but sincere attempts for a return to the state of nature' as a response to the too-rapid industrialisation and urbanisation—could almost describe Australia in the previous decade. Australians, too, had long been encour-aged to believe that rural society was the 'sole healthy element of the nation. Rooted in the native soil, in permanent contact with the earth, living outside the city and its seductions', the rural population was the upholder 'of the purity of the race and its customs'. This shared attach-ment to agrarian truisms and distorted notions about Nietzsche would propel some Australian art of the interwar years in directions not dissim-ilar to those followed in the Third Reich under National Socialism.[6]

Despite often grudging acknowledgments from some of their right to exist, Australia's major cities in 1913 were conspicuously modernising and developing suitable technological and social infrastructures to launch cultural developments of complex possibilities. Looking overseas for examples of how best to organise the future showed a willingness to learn from the successes and mistakes of others, but it also ensured that the cultural cringe was never far from the surface. Every 'visitor from abroad' was said to notice 'how deficient Australians are in what may be described as the civic spirit'. Nonetheless, Sydney was still 'destined for civic greatness', and could expect 'within a few years' to have 'over a million people in the metropolitan area'. It was also 'following the cities of the world' in becoming 'almost wholly a motor-driven city'. Melbourne, meantime, was not lagging behind its northerly rival. In 1913 the 'first section of the electric light installation scheme for the city of

Brunswick' was activated, and a 'large number of applications received for premises to be connected up'.[7]

Larger Australian cities were not immune from evidence of less attractive aspects of city-life. 'In Sydney we sometimes boast that we have no slums', claimed the *Herald*, but there were 'nevertheless a number of places within the metropolitan area which are a disgrace to our reputation as a well-ordered town and a very serious menace to the health of those who are born and live amidst such surroundings'. Some thought this unavoidable, that there was a 'class of individuals' at whose hands 'any area would be a slum area inside 12 months'. But this under-class was not wholly to blame for its own plight. Professor Irvine was sure Sydney had made 'and is continuing to make many, if not all, of the mistakes of older countries', and would 'pay a heavy penalty'. He drew a picture of slums in which 'vice, among juveniles and adults' was 'allowed to go on unchecked', where fathers eschewed family responsibilities to 'seek the nearest hotel as the most cheerful place at night', and mothers sat 'on the kerbstones during the day gossiping and reading "penny dreadfuls"'. Babies were being 'brought up "literally in the gutters"'.[8]

As Austral-Britons, Australians were members of the race that made up the greatest empire the world had known, but even that didn't necessarily blind them to the shortcomings that made England the most 'emphatic example in the history of the world of national neglect of social laws'. Evidence was to be found 'in the condition of the immense volume of the "submerged" in England to-day, and the decadence of the race arising therefrom'. Attempting to help ensure such eventualities did not happen in Australia, J. F. Hennessy addressed the Institute of Architects on the subject of 'garden suburbs', endorsing 'the need for a well-planned healthy Sydney in order to prevent the social evils of the old world flourishing in this favoured land'.

> 'The basis for all reform,' he said, '(and few cities in the Empire require it more than Sydney) is to have a well-planned city, with adequate, wide, direct streets and traffic routes; to provide for the convenience of the people coming and going to their homes: for commercial purposes; and for the rapid transit of passenger and goods traffic by direct routes'.[9]

Hennessy saw the garden suburb's development as a State or municipal responsibility. Giving them power to erect 'healthy homes for the masses of the people' would ensure 'moral, sturdy, and happy children, and a stalwart race' better able 'to develop and if necessary fight for Australia'.[10]

If slums disadvantaged the Anglo-Saxons to the point of racial deterioration, then it was a further worry for the future that others seem to thrive in them. London's 'example' supposedly showed that while the 'Anglo Saxon perishes in the East End the Jew flourishes, and evolves to a higher social strata'.

> One or two generations takes the pure foreign Jew from . . . the slums to business premises in a decent quarter; another generation finds him comfortably or even expensively housed in one of the best suburbs, and a generation later he is in one of the best residential quarters . . . [It] is unquestionable that the virility of the alien Jew is more pronounced under slum conditions than that of the Anglo Saxon.[11]

Anti-Semitism in 1913 was one of the social ideologies of 'Anglo-Saxondom'. The Semitic origins of a prominent figure or criminal were rarely left unnoted. This was especially true in the *Bulletin*, as when it noted in 1913 that a 'Hebrew, Lieut.-Colonel Monash, of Melbourne' had been appointed 'to the important command of the new Thirteenth Brigade in the Australian National Army'. If the poor and the slums would always be a blight on the social landscape, then this was supposedly not true of the upwardly mobile Jew, who would become the victim of his desire for assimilation. 'The Jew has been killed by kindness', the *Bulletin* announced prematurely. The 'structure of Judaism' was 'crumbling away before our very eye'.[12]

Australian cities were not all slums inhabited by ne'er-do-wells, or grudgingly accepted cosmopolitans drifting towards the extinction of assimilation. Australians were often proud of their home towns. Sydney's alleged lack of 'civic spirit' was not typical of Melbourne, not according to the sometimes very parochial *Age*.

> Nobody can doubt the existence in Melbourne of a strong civic spirit. Most of us are conscious of a feeling of pride that we belong to Melbourne, and that Melbourne belongs to us; and that we are always prepared to champion the title of our city to be ranked first among Australian capitals in respect of each and all of the essential qualifications of metropolitan excellence.[13]

In the 1850s Australian cities were already large by world standards. Melbourne by the 1880s was nearing half a million, and 'was larger than Amsterdam, Milan, Birmingham or Munich'. When in 1913 the Sydney *Daily Telegraph* criticised Sir George Reid for his inability to recognise 'the increasing use of mind for doing what was in more primitive times done by muscle', it was recognising changes which had upset the rationale for a continual and unending flock to the land. Australians had to live with their cities whether they lived in them, liked them, or not. An

evacuation in favour of life on the land was as unlikely as it was economically absurd.

In Sydney and Melbourne minds, if not yet muscle, were being used
to visualise the form the cities of the future might take. Alderman
J. D. Fitzgerald, recently returned from a trip abroad, waxed lyrically
about New York. It was not only its 'huge buildings' of 'intrinsically
beautiful design' that inspired him. Taking that city's example, Sydney's
'harbour problem' could also be 'treated as negligible' by constructing
'tube ways' to provide 'immediate access . . . [to] sister cities on the
various shores of our convoluted harbour'. Berlin was the exemplar,
however, this time for Melbourne; it was Berlin's 'very modernity' that
was of 'special interest' to the Victorian premier, William Watt. The 'aims
which are being worked for in the great Australian cities are those that
have inspired the makers of Berlin'. City plans 'in ten or fifteen years'
time', claimed Sydney Jones, 'would show scarcely a single drawing of a
brick or stone building. The age of brick and stone was passing, and that
of concrete and steel taking its place.' Small buildings would be 'simply
passed out of a concrete mixing machine. Concrete and steel enabled
work to be carried out quickly, and durably, while they lent themselves
no less to beauty and good taste.'[14]

To Australians who shared Sir George Reid's aversion to the Australian
city, garden suburbs and technologies which facilitated rapid-transit
systems and the construction of multi-storied buildings merely added
creature comforts to a lifestyle that was already too soft, too parasitic
and too given to vice-ridden ways. C. E. W. Bean had been unenthusiastic
about Australian cities and those who lived in them since his return from
England. In 1907 he had complained that the 'decadence and vice of
twentieth century civilisation' was 'every bit as rampant' in cities in
Australia as it was 'in those of the old world'. In 1913 the leader of the
Social Purity Crusade took a similar tack, inveighing against 'orgies' in
Melbourne 'as low and vile as it is possible to find in Paris, the Bowery
of New York, in Berlin, or in the Paris suburb of Montmartre'. The
Reverend Spurr now despaired at finding such things among 'the men
and women of this country—a country which ought to be young and
clean-minded', and wondered 'what is the end of things to be?'.[15]

If orgies would always be with us, then times were changing and the
Bulletin was a good barometer to change; it had undergone transfor-
mations that would have made it unrecognisable to those who only knew
it in the 1890s. By now its audience was largely of the city, and its
contents still reflected a nationalistic and vaguely republican if sometimes
authoritarian position, compounded by a kind of belief in modernity for
its own sake. In line with this thinking, it saw Australia's future in a
British Empire whose history was 'very largely the story of muddling

through' as at best a short-term arrangement of convenience, and welcomed the news that the day was 'apparently close at hand' when the
'industrial toilers will outnumber the blessed "backbone"'. This bad
news for imperialists should be welcomed by true Australians, for it
meant Australia was 'slowly quitting the foolish practice of dragging
masses of raw material from the land and sending them away to be turned
into merchandise, and is beginning to do the work herself'. It envisaged
an industrially diversified and decentralised nation, so rich it could afford
to pick and choose to whom it might export, to the exclusion of 'people
who are likely one day to shoot at us'.[16]

Ignoring modern art

If Berlin was the model for future metropolitan excellence, London was
still Home to many expatriated Australian artists. To be 'hung' at the
Royal Academy was a mark of distinction for the ex-colonial but to have
really 'arrived' demanded Paris. Not that modernity's wake was crashing
against the embankments of the annual Salons, wherein could be found
the fashionable art of the western world. Audiences for cubism or futurism were limited to those prepared to risk the 'insanities' of the Salon
des Indépendants, so it was from the other accumulations of respectable
taste and values that most artists sought inspiration and verification. For
outsiders like Pablo Picasso or the Polish-born Guillaume Apollinaire,
Paris with its Haussmannian architectural legacy of 'barbarism and fri-
volity' was not so much a city of unbridled modernity, as an elegant,
grand and intellectually stimulating cultural centre, inhabited by some
supportive connoisseurs, in what was the capital of western art.[17]

Indeed, in the twenty-five year period leading up to the First World
War élite culture had lagged behind a technology which had only
recently begun to interest artists and composers. In 1913 the Italian
Filippo Tommaso Marinetti's Futurist Manifesto was four years old; the
Russian Igor Stravinsky's *Firebird* was three; Picasso's *Les Demoiselles
d'Avignon*, six. While Marinetti had once claimed part of the front page
of the *Figaro* for a day, Picasso and Georges Braque worked in comparative obscurity, for they had only recently received popular press attention. The year of the now notorious premiere of Stravinsky's *Rite of
Spring*, 1913, was also the year in which New York hosted the first major
New World exhibition of the latest art of the old one at the Armory
Show. The previous year, in London Roger Fry had staged the second of
his 'post-Impressionist' exhibitions, while elsewhere artists were actively
engaged in what then were often perceived as marginal, eccentric and

iconoclastic activities, in Vienna, Berlin, St Petersburg, London, Prague and Milan.[18]

Uniting them was not so much acquaintanceship or a common aesthetic thread—for most worked in relative isolation—as a reaction against the historical weight of the past and a desire to make responses appropriate to the age. 'I am nauseated by old walls and old palaces', the futurist Umberto Boccioni wrote in 1907. 'I want the new, the expressive, the formidable.' He would have found more to please him in the United States, where the modernity of the largest cities epitomised futurist enthusiasms. But the changes the world had seen were not confined to western Europe and the United States; there was also the industrialisation and subsequent rise of Japan (the 'Germany of the Far East'), as well as the emergence of burgeoning new societies beyond the frontiers of the older, more powerful nation states. In these new post-colonial nation states, the combination of rapid urban development, technological change and relative prosperity offered ingredients for, by 1913, potentially interesting creative cocktails.[19]

While Paris set artistic trends which finally filtered through to European-based societies, these were still mostly the Salon trends of annual subject fashionability. Much of the Salon art of that time now seems like soft-core kitsch: the impression upon a Salon viewer of acres of pinkish flesh can only be imagined from the monochrome reproductions of the catalogues. Kitsch does not apply to the demure painting the Trustees of the New South Wales Art Gallery bought off the wall in 1913, paying a figure beyond a cubist's wildest dreams—£1000—for 'one of the most important on the line at the Paris Salon this year'. Befitting an important work, Eugene Maxence's *Le Livre de Paix* was honoured by a full-page reproduction in *L'Illustration*'s Salon edition.[20]

L'Illustration did not ignore modernist art, but simply relegated it to the inside back cover among the *Annonces* in a crude comic strip asserting that the origins of cubism lay in primitive cave art. 'What struck me the most, is a painting without a number, the work probably of an idiot . . . of little squares of paint in red ochre . . . Can we not see here the origin of cubist painting?' Evidence of cubist and futurist works at the Salons can be found in Australian journals. A. J. Daplyn, in the *Sydney Morning Herald*, noted of the Salon des Artistes Français that 'newer styles are not greatly in evidence', but of another that there was 'far too much space occupied by the post impressionists, cubists, and symbolists. Their crude colouration and rough technique injures any serious work that may be in their neighbourhood.' The reviewer in the *Argus* ignored all modern art in Paris, as well as artists other than Australian, as if the Salons were at St Kilda or Toorak. Rupert Bunny was 'in' with a 'pair of striking compositions, and also a charming portrait. Mr. Bunny's recent trip to Australia has evidently filled his eyes with sunlight.' The Sydney *Daily Telegraph* used its Salon review to attack the new art forms. To an eye 'wearied by the insanities of Cubism and Post-Impressionism, the Old Salon' was 'refreshing in the solid merit of most of the work on its walls'.[21]

Whether in Paris, New York, London or Sydney, responses in 1913 to modern art took similar forms, ranging from outraged hostility to a kind of sullen indifference; as though to mention the enemy was to advertise the enemy's credibility. The pictorial and critical coverage in *L'Illustration* ignored modernist works, as did Raymond Bouyer in the *Revue Mensuelle d'Art Moderne*. For Bouyer the Salons were the appropriate events to find artistic developments. It was just that during 1912 and 1913 there had been few.

> 1913 . . . celebrates the centenary of the German Richard Wagner and . . . the tricentennial of the Frenchman André Le Nostre: but these two superb expressers of creative genius . . . would have been far from comfortable with the too-flat calm of two Salons where the most erudite savoir-faire has dethroned naive passion.[22]

Bouyer, Wagner and Le Nostre may have found 'naive passion' away from the Salons, but few Parisians could have told them where to look. Reviews in the *Figaro* in 1913 described the 'great' art of the day, as they continued to do throughout the war years, in terms that suggest it was not Picasso, Braque or Matisse who were esteemed as the masters, but Lucien Simon, Émile-René Ménard, Jacques Brissaud, Jules Adler, Eugene Maxence, Gustave Pierre and Georges Scott.

Wider cultural support for modernist art had to wait until after the war, which provided the often fragmented imagery of prewar modernism with a validation after the event that could be read as prophetic of the apocalypse. By the 1920s in Paris and Berlin the art of the modern movement was a more acceptable, understood and marketable commodity; Lionel Lindsay's belief that a 'confraternity of Jewish dealers' foisted it upon a gullible public was an anti-Semitic reaction by a man too old for the war, and who failed to recognise the chord it struck for the generation of Verdun and Passchendaele; a generation which now saw Salon art as hollow and pretentious.[23]

Accelerating change can either directly influence art, or bring about social change which affects the art being made, but this rarely translates into wide and immediate acceptance of innovation. To suggest that press awareness in Sydney in 1913 of modernist art was comparable to that in Paris runs counter to conventional wisdom, but it was already the age of instantaneous communication. The cliché of Australia's post-1889 isolation from the western cultural mainstream was only a factor for isolationism when Australians chose it to be. The year 1913 was not such a time: artists in Sydney and Melbourne had similar access to information and images to that which their contemporaries had in provincial cities like Boston, Milan or Prague; and some, at least, were interested. Australian institutions were also attempting to provide their public with examples of what were then considered to be significant examples of current practice. By drawing the distinction between what was fashionable and what was modernist, the purchase of Maxence's sugary *Le Livre de Paix* was at least an attempt by the New South Wales Art Gallery Trustees to fulfil the role of a picture gallery by showing an art that interpreted one aspect of 'the spirit of their time'—that spirit which guided the contemporary Salon exhibitors of the Belle Époque.[24]

In Sydney and Melbourne there was no shortage of artists who considered themselves contemporary: in respect of the world of art that they knew and believed in, they probably were. Nor compared with their overseas peers were they markedly inferior practitioners. There was little meaning to be attached to statements of the time to the effect that the Sydney Royal Art Society exhibition 'must be regarded as exceptionally weak', or that it was 'doubtful whether the general standard, in spite of a few good little works, averages above a students' exhibition in any other city as large as Sydney'. The implication was that somewhere else art was better. It was the critique rather than the art criticised that now seems redolent of a cultural cringe and provincial mentality; for the works of Sydney Long or Dattilo Rubbo hardly seem so inferior to overseas practitioners of similar styles that they could be compared to students elsewhere. Nor did such an observation apply to Norman Lindsay, then just beginning 'in the medium of oils':

> in which already he seems to have 'found himself,' [with] a fine collection of nudes—but nudes treated with a reticence and restraint that enhance their value as examples of consummate draughtsmanship and sound management of the problems of light and values that beset the artist in this field of work.[25]

In Salon catalogues there was no shortage of nymphets in fantasy landscapes similar to Long's, human interest pictures like Rubbo's, or allegorical paintings of nudes en masse like Lindsay's. Australians were not invariably inferior as exponents of styles they had adopted; expatriate artists like Hilda Rix Nicholas, Ethel Carrick Fox, Emmanuel Phillips Fox and John Peter Russell enjoyed international recognition at a level rarely equalled since by Australians.

This recognition was not based upon the Australian-ness of their subject material; rather, it was on their technical competency and ability to conform to the fashionable subjects of the day. Still, conservatism was not completely enshrined, for the idea that art was searching out new paths in which Australians were playing a role was an article of faith to returning expatriate Emmanuel Phillips Fox. 'One of the most noticeable features in the artistic world to-day', he stated, 'is the struggle for originality'. Phillips Fox did not mean cubist or futurist originality.

> 'Many Australian artists in England and the Continent, namely Lambert, Bunny, Longstaff, Streeton, Quinn, Coats [sic], and Burgess, are doing remarkably well,' he added, 'and they will I think, create a distinct impression on the English school.'[26]

With federation little more than a decade past, it seemed less important to this expatriate that an Australian school of art might be emerging than that Australians should make an impression upon the English one. London and Paris were unlikely places in which to evolve a 'school' which expressed Australia, and, although Phillips Fox and his expatriated contemporaries could hardly have expected it, 1913 was the last year in which the Salons and Academy would carry the prestige of being the events of the art world calendar for the upwardly mobile élite. Events were already overtaking them. Concerted moves were under way on two continents to impress the work and ideas of the modern movement upon a wider audience. None met with unqualified success. Progressives like American ex-president Theodore Roosevelt, who otherwise endorsed modernist technologies and social experimentation, were often content with the art they were used to. For art to be modern, it was enough to be up to date with trends and fashions based upon familiar values; it was not necessary to have the scene overturned and then wrecked completely. Art was too comfortable, too reassuring for such upheavals. Assuming it could find a purchaser, what place was there for a cubist painting above a fireplace in an aristocratic or *parvenu*, Belle Époque salon?[27]

An outbreak of modernism

Not all Australian artistic activity or interest centred upon the expatriates or would-be expatriates and their attempts to fit the European Establishment mould. If Australia increasingly came to resemble a provincial and backward cultural outpost in the 1920s, this was a recently contracted condition rather than one manifest in 1913. William Moore's later claim that 'Wakelin, Roi de Mestre, and Grace Cossington Smith, all students at the time, began to understand something about modern art from Nora Simpson, who brought out some reproductions in 1913' might reinforce the notion of modernism as a cargo-cult suitcase importation into a backward culture. Simpson's role seems to have been to provide awareness of the new uses of colour, as until the arrival of her books, catalogues and posters, knowledge of the new art was confined to monochrome reproduction. Wakelin later confirmed seeing such a reproduction of Duchamp's *Nude Descending a Staircase* in early 1913. By September it had been reproduced widely; enough to cause the *Sydney Mail* to show other cubist or futurist works rather than one already 'fairly well known' (see plate 5). The degree of tolerance evident in the *Mail*'s treatment of 'The Revolutionary Spirit in Art' was less observable in the *Age*'s music critic. 'New paths are ever fascinating to the young', he wrote, 'sometimes merely because they are new', but no less 'sometimes because ugliness is easier of achievement than the beautiful'.[28]

The term 'futurist' was used to described anything shocking, which included the (unheard) works of Arnold Schönberg. F. Mowat Carter now believed that, compared to Schönberg, Wagner was in his 'swaddling clothes, Richard Strauss not yet weaned, and Debussy an infant crying in the dark! So say his disciples!'.

> 'This Futurist is a man with enormous knowledge . . . who objects to melody in any shape or form' . . . [When] Sir Henry Wood [conducted] Schoenberg's 'Five Pieces for Orchestra' . . . every fresh explosion . . . caused roars of laughter. 'Even the players themselves were laughing. and there was a smile on the face of the tiger (Wood) as he left the desk at the finish.'[29]

Mowat Carter, if unsympathetic to this music, was not prepared to dismiss Schönberg's 'enormous knowledge'. Less equivocal in condemnation of the modern, a *Sydney Mail* reviewer lamented that a 'Women Painters' Exhibition' showed no departure 'from conventionalism, no tendency for leaving the well-beaten track', while simultaneously warning of the dangers to be found in sidetracks, for the latest phase 'in the evolution of art has reached the limit of absurdity'. He cited a Salon 'picture representing something like a multitude of microbes . . . entitled, "Ce Que l'on Voudra" (Whatever Pleases You). The artist's confidence in the public imagination is indeed touching.'[30]

The *Bulletin*, befitting a self-consciously radical journal, was prepared to give anything modern the benefit of the doubt, while retaining the right to poke fun at occasional excesses. Futurism was 'blatantly modern' and that was good. To futurists, 'a motor-car in motion has a higher aesthetic value than a Greek statue. He sees more beauty in a sky-scraper

"The Haunting Dancer."

By the Italian Futurist Artist, Severini.
"The futurist appeals to us only in a grotesque way."—See Article.

Post Impressionist Portrait.

This is a good example of the product of a school that probes into the most unlikely recesses of human nature for its inspirations, and that distorts in a wild attempt at originality. In other words, this is so-called Modern Art.

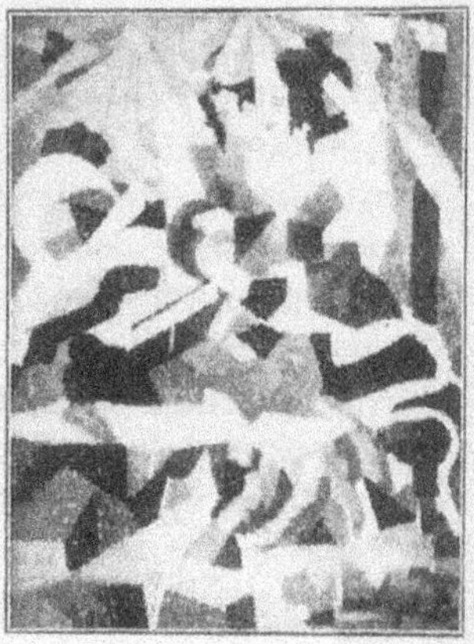

"The Milliner."

This is Futurist art. It is difficult to trace the milliner, but she is there. To the lay mind it suggests chaos at the ribbon counter.

THE REVOLUTIONARY SPIRIT IN ART.

THOSE who meet artists become accustomed to the remark, "It is personality that tells." It is quite true, but it is the idea of personality frenziedly developed to the borders of insanity that has given the world "futurism" in art. We have the Post-impressionists, the Futurists, and the Cubists, and they all riot in the effort after novelty. It is, of course, not all insanity. The Post-impressionists have a certain sincerity. Even when we turn to the Futurists and Cubists, a shred of truth remains in their work—just enough to base an argument upon. In their wildness and enthusiasm they affect to see in that shred the whole truth, and nothing but the truth. Duchamp's "Nude Going Downstairs" (which we do not illustrate, as it is fairly well known) is an example of this. Perhaps if a very drunken man were watching a nude running swiftly downstairs he might get some such impression as Duchamp affects to translate. It is only a hazard, but if a drunkard sees snakes there is no reason why he should not see Duchamp's nude, which is, of course, not a nude, but an impression of movement. The idea can be fathomed—that must be admitted—but the point is that the futurist appeals to us only in some strained or grotesque way. There is always something for an alert mind to grip, but one has to indulge in mental gymnastics to get there. This may be art for untamed artists, but it is not tempting to the refined or normal mind. It will be interesting and amusing while it lasts, and out of folly a liberalising influence may come, but that is the best that can be said of it. In Italy futurism asserted itself in 1911. By March, 1912, it had reached London, and an exhibition was held in the Sackville Gallery, Piccadilly. We are indebted to Miss Jacobs, whose art work is well known in Sydney, for a copy of the futurist manifesto. It has been quoted before, but is worth giving here in full.

Initial Manifesto of Futurism.

1. We shall sing the love of danger, the habit of energy and boldness.

2. The essential elements of our poetry shall be courage, daring, and rebellion.

3. Literature has hitherto glorified thoughtful immobility, ecstasy, and sleep; we shall extol aggressive movement, feverish insomnia, the double quick step, the somersault, the box on the ear, the fisticuff.

4. We declare that the world's splendour has been enriched by a new beauty: the beauty of speed. A racing motor car, its frame adorned with great pipes, like snakes with explosive breath . . . a roaring motor car, which looks as though running on shrapnel, is more beautiful than the "Victory of Samothrace."

5. We shall sing of the man at the steering-wheel, whose ideal stem transfixes the earth, rushing over the circuit of her orbit.

6. The poet must give himself with frenzy, with splendour, and with lavishness, in order to increase the enthusiastic fervour of the primordial elements.

7. There is no more beauty except in strife. No masterpiece without aggressiveness. Poetry must be a violent onslaught upon the unknown forces, to command them to bow before man.

8. We stand upon the extreme promontory of the centuries! . . . Why should we look behind us when we have to break in the mysterious portals of the Impossible? Time and Space died yesterday. Already we live in the absolute, since we have already created speed, eternal and ever-present.

9. We wish to glorify War—the only health-giver of the world—militarism, patriotism, the destructive arm of the anarchist, the beautiful ideas that kill, the contempt for woman.

10. We wish to destroy the museums, the libraries, to fight against moralism, feminism, and all opportunistic and utilitarian meannesses.

11. We shall sing of the great crowds in the excitement of labour, pleasure, or rebellion; of the multi-coloured and polyphonic surf of revolutions in modern capital cities; of the nocturnal vibration of arsenals and workshops beneath their violent electric moons; of the greedy stations swallowing smoking snakes; of factories suspended from the clouds by their strings of smoke; of bridges leaping like gymnasts over the diabolical cutlery of sunbathed rivers; of adventurous liners scenting the horizon; of broad-chested locomotives prancing on the rails, like huge steel horses bridled with long tubes, and of the gliding flight of aeroplanes, the sound of whose screw is like the flapping of flags and the applause of an enthusiastic crowd.

IT is in Italy that we launch this manifesto of violence, destructive and incendiary, by which we this day found Futurism, because we would deliver Italy from its canker of professors, archaeologists, cicerones, and antiquaries.

Italy has been too long the great market of the second-hand dealers. We would free her from the numberless museums which cover her with as many cemeteries.

Museums, cemeteries! . . . Truly identical with their sinister jostling of bodies that know one another not. Public dormitories where one sleeps for ever side by side with detested or unknown beings. Mutual ferocity of painters and sculptors slaying one another with blows of lines and colour in a single museum.

Let one pay a visit there each year as one visits one's dead once a year. . . . That we can allow! . . . Deposit flowers even once a year at the feet of the "Gioconda," if you will! . . . But to walk daily in the museums with our sorrows, our fragile courage, and our anxiety, that is inadmissible! . . . Would you, then, poison yourselves? Do you want to decay?

What can one find in an old picture unless it be the painful contortions of the artist striving to break the bars that stand in the way of his desire to express completely his dream?

TO admire an old picture is to pour our sensitiveness into a funereal urn, instead of casting it forward in violent gushes of creation and action. Would you, then, waste the best of your strength by a useless admiration of the past, from which you can but emerge exhausted, reduced, down-trodden?

In truth, the daily haunting of museums, of libraries, and of academies (those cemeteries of wasted effort, those Calvaries of crucified dreams, those ledgers of broken attempts!) is to artists what the prolonged tutelage of parents is to intelligent youths, intoxicated with their talent and their ambitious determination.

For men on their death-bed, for invalids, and for prisoners, very well! The admirable past may be balsam to their wounds, since the future is closed to them. . . . But we will have none of it, we, the young, the strong, and the living Futurists!

Come, then, the good incendiaries with their charred fingers! . . . Here they come! Here they come! . . . Set fire to the shelves of the libraries! Deviate the course of canals to flood the cellars of the museums! . . . Oh! may the glorious canvases drift helplessly! Seize pickaxes and hammers! Sap the foundations of the venerable cities!

The oldest amongst us are thirty; we have, therefore, ten years at least to accomplish our task. When we are forty, let others, younger and more valiant, throw us into the basket like useless manuscripts! . . . They will come against us from afar, from everywhere, bounding upon the lightsome measure of their first poems, scratching the air with their hooked fingers, and scenting at the academy doors the pleasant odour of our rotting minds, marked out already for the catacombs of the libraries.

(Continued on Page [illegible].)

The Exhibition.

I CANNOT shake away their wild control;
Their colours still go roaring through my soul,
Splurges of gold, and reds, and blues, and greens,
Huge malformed arms and legs, transalpine scenes,
Strange cubes evolving into half-guessed forms,
Cyclones of green, and purple rainbow-storms.
Thus artists on huge Jupiter might paint
(Or some mad star beyond the earth's constraint)
Maelstroms of limbs, great eyes that flame in gloom,
Moons red as blood, and sunsets hung with doom,
Malignant faces, pink sands, yellow flesh—
And every picture stabs the eye afresh!
Some madly launch in space, but, here and there,
A touch is seen that masters could not spare.
You go out with a whirlwind in your head.
The thing, at least, is not inert and dead;
There's life and motion there, and rending force,
Colour-Niagaras thundering on their course,
Power that breaks like a great wave in spray—
And what it means we'll let To-morrow say!

"N. Y. Independent."

"Dancers at the Spring."

This is serious Futurist art, title and all. The artist is Francis Picabia. As before, the lay mind sees a bargain sale. Suggested title of picture: "Chaos at the Cellar Counter."

than in the Grand Canal.' It poked half-hearted fun at cubism but admitted that as it 'continues modern methods,' we should 'see in it the only conception at present possible of the pictorial art. In other words, Cubism is at present painting itself.' The *Sydney Mail* outdid its weekly competitor in pictorial coverage and attempts at explanation (plate 5). As for the 'Post-impressionists, the Futurists, and the Cubists', it was 'not all insanity. The Post-Impressionists have a certain sincerity. Even when we turn to the Futurists and Cubists, a shred of truth remains in their work'. Talking of Duchamp's *Nude Descending a Staircase* the writer thought that 'if a very drunken man were watching a nude running swiftly downstairs he might get some such impression as Duchamp affects to translate'.

> [If] a drunkard sees snakes there is no reason why he should not see Duchamp's nude, which is, of course, not a nude, but an impression of movement. The idea can be fathomed . . . [if] only in some strained or grotesque way. There is always something for an alert mind to grasp, but one has to indulge in mental gymnastics to get there.[31]

While Australians were then limited to monochrome reproductions in newspapers or the occasional coloured illustrations brought back in magazines and reproductions by ex-students, their New Zealand cousins were not so hamstrung. In Sydney, on his way to install an exhibition of post-impressionist paintings in Auckland, Mr John Baillie, a 'well-known art connoisseur', wished the 'duty on pictures were removed throughout the Commonwealth. Nothing would please me better than to hold an exhibition here.' Although people 'used to come and roar with laughter at some of them', that had all changed, for 'their work is full of meaning'. It was necessary to 'study these things carefully', for modern art was no longer 'intended for the delectation of mere esthetic coteries. We live in an age of motor cars and aeroplanes. Artists today are interested in light, life, movement. We have no time for mere niggling drawings; art must express something.'[32]

Offering popular insights into the age of motor cars and aeroplanes was W. E. Rayner's 'Romance of Modern Life', which lay between biblical prophesy and the Futurist Manifesto. Rayner looked to the day when mankind would 'penetrate the great inarticulate mystery of Modernity',

Plate 5 Presenting 'The Revolutionary Spirit in Art' to its readership (*Sydney Mail* 3 September 1913, courtesy of State Library of NSW).
By late 1913 its readers evidently had some level of familiarity, not just with Duchamp's work, but also with recent European trends in contemporary art, showing that Australia was not necessarily the backwater isolated from the mainstream of modernity that some have supposed it to be.

which had 'cleft the air with noiseless wings' and 'bound the earth in a network of steel rails'.

> And the smoke of factories may be seen to envisage a captive genius, with strange and terrible powers, twisting iron bars like willow wands, and filling the land with machines that are well nigh sentient. And the poet of the future will sing not only of brooks and trees, of love and war; he will sing of industrialisation with its hundred hands, of science with its hundred eyes, of the delirium of speed, of the vision of a new world.[33]

In this hymn to modernity, as an example that afforded 'significant instances of . . . the entire obsession of a mass of people by an idea', the 'suffragist movement' was a manifestation 'of the wild and turbulent unrest of the times; the Zeit-geist of Romance that is the sign of a burgeoning epoch'.[34]

As for 'suffragism', Australian women had the vote and had little need for the middle-class militancy of their peers in the Motherland. As well, in Australia 'the superfluous woman does not exist; in Great Britain there are more than a million of her, and what to do with this excess of female over the male sex is a problem which is taxing the minds of reformers'. The *Argus* argued suffragism was due less to gender imbalance, than the mistake of educating women. 'A notable feature of the suffragette movement' was that it was 'supported, not by a rabble of ignorance, but by a rabble of the educated'; that 'the women who agitate most for votes only show themselves unfitted to receive them'. This 'campaign of crime by confessed anarchists' had finally 'become intolerable'.[35]

Australians could make themselves aware of more sophisticated views. In 'The Upholstered Cage' Miss Josephine Pitcairn Knowles's sympathy went out to the 'millions of young women of the middle classes whose lot is in many respects far less enviable than that of their humbler sisters'. She painted a 'sombre picture of their present and future' for middle-class women whose lives had become 'a drab round, where a tea party unpatronised by men is the height of giddy dissipation'. In the circumstances they became 'narrowed, their powers stunted, so that, even though they be willing, they are unable to engage in any serious employment'. The English journalist, novelist and social critic, Philip Gibbs— soon to become a major British Great War correspondent—already had a sizeable reputation in Australia, where he was read and reviewed as one of the prophets of modernity. Gibbs blamed many of the ills of the New Age on the 'feminisation' of society: the 'new man, indeed, has been created largely by the new woman'. But all the woes of the New Age could not be blamed on 'the conquests of the woman's spirit over the mind of man'. The 'new man' was the heir to 'intellectual, spiritual, and industrial' changes, which had 'broken down the old laws and creeds of his father and forefathers'.

> He has no authority to whom he can turn for guidance, because he has denied all authority. He has no absolute and unswerving faith, because he can find no evidence to convince him of a dogma of faith. He is afraid of all ideals, lest they should prove false, and of all laws lest they should prove tyrannical. He is the asker of questions to which he can find no answer.[36]

If God was dead, Nietzsche was already being deified in Australia. 'Nowadays we are most of us Nietzscheans', one local writer asserted in the *Sydney Morning Herald*. In 1913 Nietzsche and modernity were synonymous. For all his 'fierce individuality', he was 'as much a child of the age as Ibsen, or Spencer, or Wagner'. The same 'sort of time-spirit' was 'working in all these men'.

> When Nietzsche is ignorantly spoken off as mad, or immoral, all that is really meant is that he is a sane and not a superstitious critic of conduct . . . It is true that he proclaims a view of life that is frankly pagan . . . proclaims a society which is . . . aristocratic rather than democratic . . . goes further than the eugenist, and almost as far as Brahmanism, in the cult of a new sort of caste, founded on the national inter-selection of the 'few' from whom the 'superman' may be expected to develop; but stripped of their tantalising and aggressive presentment, most men who think at all . . . ultimately emerge not far from where he came out.[37]

Back to the bush

With the notable exception of the futurists, nationalism seemed largely irrelevant to a 'modern movement' deriving much of its impulses from immigrants to the big metropolises and other marginalised minority groups—citizens who often straddled two *patries* (or spiritual homelands). This could hardly be said of a homogenous national society like Australia, where the marginalised and culturally distinct immigrant was hardly present. Despite the homogeny, conceptions of what it meant to be an Australian were in a state of flux. A nation was hardly a nation at all without a representative national school of art, poetry, music or theatre; for every work of art was 'the expression of the human soul, either the soul of the artist himself, or collectively of the nation', with art thereby playing 'an invaluable part in the development of a young country'. That an Australian school had existed for a time around 1890 was accepted and some still thought that Australians could do worse than develop upon it by near imitation. Some, like C. E. W. Bean, thought a school already existed along these lines, although he had come upon it only in 1907 as a residue from the 1890s. Bean counted 'no critic worth listening to' who could not perceive 'that it is the bush which makes that poetry'. It was 'the same with painting. Every Australian does not paint, but those who do are obviously inspired by the bush and the bush alone. It is a genuine school of art, and peculiar to the country.' But by 1913, with the heady days of the 1890s long past, it was more common to lament the absence of a contemporary Australian school.[38]

'I have had a long experience in Australia as well as on the continent,' continued Mr. Fox, 'and I notice a distinct advance in Australia in the appreciation of art . . . At different times . . . I have heard people talk gloomily of the fact that there is no Australian school of art. That can only come after a lapse of time, when national characteristics have developed.'[39]

By 1913 urban sophisticates and acclaimed Salon exhibitors such as Phillips Fox, Bunny, and Lambert were unlikely to be interested in an art constrained to depict gum trees or heroic bush scenes. It was already recognised that a national school depending upon the representation of landscape had rapid potential for self-exhaustion; so the paintings of the Heidelberg School were usually considered only as pioneering beacons, rather than as exemplars, in the evolution of an Australian national art. The notion of what was acceptable subject matter was changing; one writer proposed it should be 'often the disagreeable thing, the ordinary and the commonplace in life, that to the painter hold the most significance'.[40]

Of drama dealing with the ordinary and commonplace 'Sydney knows practically nothing either of the aims, the tendencies, or the achievements of contemporary drama in England or Europe', lamented 'F.S.B.'. It was with 'the deep-seated conviction of this essential importance in the spiritual development of a young and vigorous people that one may plead the necessity of a national theatre'. While a national theatre would allow Australian access to the new plays from overseas, more desirable still would be Australian plays to stage in it. The drama of a country was, like its art, 'the expression of its national spirit'.

[Although] a drama indigenous to the soil . . . has not yet arisen here, evidences of a certain distinctive drama have been manifested . . . It has grown from the harsh crudities of melodrama. The outcome of a struggling civilisation has advanced past the rough farces and unskilled comedies of a vital, yet uncultured, community.[41]

'Indigenous to the soil' did not have to mean 'successful pieces dealing with the out-back pastoral life of this country'. There were possibilities beyond revivals of *On Our Selection*, or melodramas like Mr Jo Smith's *The Bush Girl*, with its 'brightly-written comedy scenes' set in 'the course of a story faithfully kept within a typical out-back atmosphere— so 'J.C.W.' believed (presumably this was J. C. Williamson, the famous theatrical entrepreneur). What marked the 'great modern dramatists' was their ability to use themes 'taken from contemporary life' in the 'epoch to which they belong', and still carry 'an indefinable, but none the less distinct, stamp of the race and country for which it is written'. Australia had 'melodramas of the coarse kind in plenty to point to, most of them drawn around the imaginary romance of the backblocks', but of plays 'throbbing and pulsating with the fire of real Australian life, holding up vividly a question or problem of our national conditions, there is not one'.

A play that is to have real national interest must have its theme centred around some distinct phase of national life. That may be found in the bush; but it is much more likely to be found in the bustling city. It is in the cities that the population of Australia lies, and it is the city and . . . in its circumference that a theme typically Australian in nature is most likely to be found.[42]

The year of J. C. Williamson's death was 1913: in March he had been on the record formally acknowledging that 'there is an Australian drama and it is improving. Like all young countries, it will have to grow and develop with the country'.[43]

The idea that the 'bustling' Australian city could provide world-class dramatic subject matter—and by implication material for literature and art—contradicted the belief that Australian cities were unremarkable if pleasant enough places. Nor, if the author were to actively seek out original themes, were the inhabitants of these cities accredited with traits that would mark them as distinct from cousins at Home. Foster Fraser had noticed little difference from the standard English type—responding in the affirmative when asked 'Do you think we talk cockney?'. Whatever distinguished the Australian was said to derive from the life in the bush. Like Bean and Francis Adams, Foster Fraser claimed he could 'differentiate' between the 'long, lean wiry' countryman and 'the average city man and city woman' who were 'rather slim in physique and not over the medium height'.[44]

If the national drama and the national art were to transcend clichés of backblocks and gum trees and station life, how was this to be done, given that the Australian city type not only claimed the vices of cousins abroad but had built cities which imitated theirs? Was there even such a thing as the 'national type'? Was it even desirable that one could or should exist? The *Sydney Morning Herald* thought not. It was 'out of the question' to wait for 'the early segregation of a purely Australian native type', even if this 'was a thing altogether to be desired—which in our opinion is not the case'. W. M. Fleming argued there was 'as yet no such thing as a fixed Australian thought or sentiment', let alone a physical 'type'. He saw therein an explanation as to why Australia had 'not yet much literature'.

> How could we expect more? The Australian is not yet a fixed type, or anything approaching it. Australians are not even a group of fixed types . . . We are a people of no settled ideas or sentiments, and appallingly few convictions. Even those which have been handed down through family records, the traditions of the Empire, or that great world of books which is open to us all, are in a state of flux. We accept nothing as permanent. The Commonwealth is a melting-pot.[45]

With neither fixed thought nor sentiments to call their own, Australians elucidated reassuring pearls of wisdom from returning expatriates and visiting British celebrities. The arrival of the popular novelist Sir Rider Haggard, a rural 'expert' with the Empire Trade Commission, whose main purpose was 'undoubtedly to develop and extend our trade and inter-course with the Mother-country', provided the opportunity for one Aus-tralian journalist to demonstrate the cultural cringe. Haggard explained that someone had been 'kind enough to send me a little parcel of Aus-tralian books, but they were of a rather scrappy nature', and he bemoaned the 'sort of cockney slang seems to have grown up in this country—the 'Arry and Arriet' business, only more so'. He understood that 'some good books have been written in Australia. I have read Marcus Clarke's fine story, but it is rather unpleasant reading.'[46]

Haggard's knowledge of Australian literature ended at some point prior to 1890, but interviewers dwelt on his every word. For as long as they liked, Australians could debate whether or not the national type had emerged, or what nationhood meant, and could speculate on the national theatre, art, music and drama; but, while there was still an urge to seek reassurance from outside that the efforts of the locals approached the mythical and arbitrary standards which were believed to exist at Home, what they aspired to was always likely to be second-rate. In the years after federation opinions about local standards were avidly sought on almost every subject from visitors, especially British visitors; they, like Foster Fraser, a self-confessed 'offensive British bounder who was insult-ing the Australian people', or Sir Rider Haggard, often responded in disdainful and absurdly patronising terms.[47]

In the four years since 1909 the absence of a 'national spirit' that Foster Fraser had detected could no longer be assumed. In the confused melting-pot of 1913, with questions of nationality, national arts, theatres and dramas and a thin but discernible layer of modernism, there is much that now seems exciting and admirable. But dreams of national theatre and drama, of garden suburbs linked by rapid-transit systems in a planned city, amounted to little. A national art of a kind emerged, though it was not based upon a fusion of the national spirit and modernism but upon a return to the imagined values of the 1890s, fused with hostility to anything hinting at twentieth century cosmopolitanism. For this, the Great War of 1914-18 bears vital responsibility; the war and the way the people of Australia were encouraged to interpret it.[48]

CHAPTER FOUR

1914–19: The gilding of battlefield lilies

The first victim of a war is the concept of reality.
Paul Virilio (*Guerre et cinéma I*, p. 44)

The last war, during the years of 1915, 1916, 1917 was the most colossal, murderous, mismanaged butchery that has ever taken place on earth. Any writer who said otherwise lied. So the writers either wrote propaganda, shut up, or fought.
Ernest Hemingway (cited by Phillip Knightley *The First Casualty*, p. 79)

An adorable, giant picnic

Something did appear to go desperately wrong in Australia between 1914 and 1919, but other societies suffered worse privations, lost more of their men and even, like Canada, survived internal conflict that put local conscription dramas into the shade. Pinpointing the conscription debates as the obvious point where disunity became apparent hardly solves the dilemma of what that something was, for anti-conscriptionists in Australia were not usually opposed to the war. Young Catholic men of predominantly Irish background continued to volunteer for the Australian Imperial Force (AIF) in proportion to their numbers in society throughout the conscription campaigns. What was at issue in the minds of many citizens, who otherwise believed in the crusade against Prussian militarism, was whether Australia, a small and underpopulated nation, could afford to commit all its young men to the charnel house and thus leave itself under-protected and apparently wide open to the by now traditional Asian menace to the north.

In Australia's case what was almost unique, and what can be pinpointed, was the sense of nationhood that had supposedly been achieved, which was reflected in a new national image, as though Australians had now won the right to be sole occupants of the vast continent they inhabited. Their national image had changed in four years from that of a rather self-deprecating people into one of a people who had been encouraged to believe they'd almost won the war single-handedly. It is not helpful for a small, new nation to have to deal with a press-inspired sense of national superiority; for its most logical consequence, apart from insularity, is almost certainly complacency. No more helpful, perhaps, is the formation of an image of nationhood based around military achievement, real or imaginary. National identity evokes complex subtleties: of language, customs, humour, landscape, art, literature, high and popular cultural objects and activities, cuisine, architecture, appearance, technological achievements, to name just some. The role of the soldier should be to protect the right of the people to develop their national life and their sense of oneness within a peaceful framework in a broader culture. Nationhood based upon the soldier puts the cart before the horse.

The Great War was the first Great Media War: what actually happened always mattered less for all but those violently engaged in it than what was reported to have happened; official censorship, moreover, ensured that Australians read news mostly indistinguishable from what their English cousins read. Most people—including even the soldiers at the front—relied on the newspapers for their understanding of the war. It was the interpretation placed upon this news—and the supplementary material provided by Australian correspondents—which suggested that Australians had won a place at the head of nations; that they were admired and extolled as had rarely happened in history. This overdone and, ultimately, self-defeating propaganda had little basis in fact and played no small part in the malaise of the 1920s.

By the early 1920s, too, C. E. W. Bean and General Sir James Edmonds, the official war historians of Australia and Great Britain respectively, were well under way with their respective projects and in fairly regular communication. As drafts appeared, each on behalf of the other sent copies to relevant Australian or British commanders, to ensure unreasonable offence was not given or to offer officers a chance, if necessary, to help revise the record in a more favourable light to themselves. With most Great War commanders still living, such an approach was perhaps unavoidable, but the tendency to whitewash history was no less a consequence. However, the Edmonds–Bean correspondence also details the near-breakdown of a professional relationship and, thus, goes some way to explaining why British and Australian versions of the same battles, or even the war, almost seem to be accounts of different events.[1]

Neither the English general nor the colonial journalist were professional historians. Both were 'gentlemen'; but Bean's origins and, according to Edmonds, lack of military understanding brought out in the Briton the kind of patronising airs that were most likely to rankle an Australian, even an Austral-Briton. This does not mean that Bean was invariably wronged in the exchange, which began with Edmonds's praise of Bean's

Gallipoli descriptions. By the time Bean's attention turned to Pozières, in January 1928, however, the Englishman was able to argue that Bean left 'the impression that there was nothing going on elsewhere and only the Australians were doing anything'. The next month he returned to the point.

> Your narrative time after time gives the impression that nothing was going on except at Pozières. If you will look at Sir D. Haig's Despatches . . . You will see that the most important fighting at the end of July was at Delville Wood and then at Guillemont. The Pozières fighting after the first attack falls among 'the operations of a minor character' . . . going on all along the British and French front. These operations get scanty mention in the war diaries, but those of the other divisions could be written up in the same way as you have done for the 1st and 2nd Australian Divisions.[2]

By 1932 the Bean–Edmonds liaison had soured. Of Bean's latest draft chapters Edmonds wrote that they 'do not seem to me to be up to the standard of your published volumes, and, as regards matters touching the higher command and really outside the scope of an ordinary corps history, they seem sometimes to be misleading'. He now claimed to speak for other Englishmen in his concern at the one-sidedness of Bean's depiction of the war.

> We all feel that the historian of the A.I.F. could afford to be a little more generous in his allusions to British units and formations. You are now aware perhaps that the home troops regarded the Australians and Canadians as the spoiled children of G.H.Q., who were given most rest, the pick of the fighting pitches and most of the praise.[3]

Yet, it would be wrong to assume the general and the journalist were always in a state of politely controlled contrariness. They shared too much common ground, having been partners between 1914 and 1918 in the process through which the war was relayed to the literate masses of the empire.

> The policy laid down was merely to say as little as possible, so as not to assist the enemy. You quote an instance in your account of Fromelles which would appear to support your contention. The question of how much a democracy should be told is a difficult one, but, from the purely military point of view, the less the better.[4]

For the 93 per cent or so of Australians who did not experience combat, knowledge of the war was gained through newspapers' reporting 'as little as possible'. So what filled the newspapers? On all sides wartime newspapers were packed with editorial comment, dispatches, communiqués and general items purporting to be about the war. But if the aim of the military establishment and its associated journalists was to leak nothing of value, then what is left is, by implication, either valueless or propaganda. In practice it was a mixture of both; flavoured with truthful material, when it suited. Recognising this was happening or distinguishing one type of content from another was clearly impossible at the time; it is not always easy even with the benefit of historical hindsight. What can be said is that the official military communiqué set the tone; a dispatch which disputed or by inference contradicted what was stated in a communiqué could not pass the censor. While journalists and correspondents were thoroughly under the thumb of the military, in one respect they were free. No restrictions applied to the glorification of one's own troops nor to the defamation of the enemy. With the war hardly a day old and nothing but rumours to go by, the editor-in-chief of *Figaro*, Alfred Capus, already had Germans 'cutting the throats of those they suspect of having guarded in their hearts the image of the old motherland' and 'shooting priests because they fear their prayers'. It was not a promising start, but in the propaganda war there was worse to come.[5]

Of those first days we are told that Australians 'had made up their minds and were ready and indeed terrifyingly willing to go to war'. But Lloyd Robson also points out that this enthusiasm was largely press-forced, that the 'daily metropolitan newspapers were enthusiastically imperialist; there were no serious party political divisions on the issue of the war; there was no organized opposition to Australia's entry into the conflict'. E. M. Andrews disputes mass enthusiasm. 'Historians who make much of the "rush to enlist"', he proposes, might 'do better to ask why *93.6 per cent of eligibles did not enlist*'. In Australia, 'voluntary recruiting was not to provide sufficient manpower, and, apart from the surge after Gallipoli, the numbers soon fell'.[6]

Andrews is supported from an unlikely quarter. In a war where lying was the norm and every battle could be presented as a victory, enemy 'lies' were often closer to the truth. The *Berliner Tageblatt* Australian correspondent, in late-August 1914 still under loose control but 'obliged under oath to report to the police that we wouldn't undertake anything hostile', had no obvious reason to lie and his report reached Berlin. The Australian was a man to whom all 'notion of "war" is unfamiliar: his land has never seen a military campaign, never corpses on the field, never smoking wreckage or crushed crops'. His depiction of the phlegmatic Australian character was not without affection and may still be recognisable.

Naturally the blood can also boil in him [the Australian], but there is no violent surge of the pulse. No impression is immediate; inspiration must first come in a round about way through reflection. He can do all kinds of things, but not with flushed cheeks. He collects for wounded soldiers, attempts in vain to catch the tune of the Marseillaise, fits out an expeditionary corps of voluntary troops ['freiwilliger Truppen']. The Federal Government has promised 22,000 men. Three weeks ago, although married men were accepted, London had to accept less than 4,000 enlistments.[7]

Recruitment was less than what was hoped for, as can be gleaned in the *Sydney Morning Herald*'s attempt to dispel the belief that only crack shots need apply for the Imperial Force, an idea which had been deterring potential recruits. If a man had 'never handled a rifle, and can not even claim to be anything approaching a good shot with the gun', he would still be acceptable, provided he was 'of good physique and willing to be placed where his services are considered to be most useful'.[8]

In societies without universal conscription, the need to attract bodies to the colours distinguished the way the war was reported: not only must newspapers provide 'news', but they must sell the idea of the war to waverers in the eligible male populations. This was unnecessary in Germany and France, whose general staffs could depend upon large standing armies and a mass of trained reserves, plus the fact that machinery was in place to ensure that recalcitrants had little chance of avoiding what had been made formal and inescapable. In the British Empire for most of the war a correspondent's duty was to provide copy to aid recruitment. 'Even the enormous, impregnable stupidity of our High Command on all matters of psychology', Philip Gibbs wrote, 'was penetrated by a vague notion that a few "writing fellows" might be sent out with permission to follow the armies in the field, under the strictest censorship'.

> Dimly and nervously they apprehended that in order to stimulate the recruiting of the New Army now being called to the colours by vulgar appeals to sentiment and passion, it might be well to 'write up' the glorious side of war . . . without, of course, any allusion to dead or dying men, to the ghastly failures of distinguished generals, or to the filth and horror of the battle-fields.[9]

War was, accordingly, presented as a dangerous but incomparably exciting team sport, too good to be missed, as this November 1914 letter to the *Times* from 'a cavalry subaltern at the front' illustrated.

> I adore war. It is like a big picnic without the objectlessness of a picnic. I've never been so well or so happy. Nobody grumbles at one for being dirty. I've only had my boots off once in the last 10 days, and only washed twice . . .
>
> The Indians had two men killed directly, and said 'All wars are good, but this is a bot'ucha war. Now we advance.'[10]

Plate 6 Grace Cossington Smith (Australia 1892–1984) *Soldiers Marching* ca. 1917 oil on paper on hardboard 23.7 × 21.5 cm. Purchased 1967 Art Gallery of New South Wales.
There is no sense here of the buoyant, imperial spirit of prewar military parades. Reflecting more modernist concerns, her foregrounding of the women and children—those left behind—acts as a counter to an imperial rhetoric of heroic warfare.

But it was also becoming clear that if the war was made too wonderful, with the Germans always losing, then there was little reason for waverers, who preferred a quieter life, to enlist. As some reality of what the war was like began to leak out, duty, obligation and even shame began to replace adventure as an inducement to recruiting. But it was still possible to be serious without being absolutely truthful, and from 1916 on British dispatches reflected this new earnestness. The French were relieved. War was war, and comparing it to sport trivialised its nobility. In early 1918 the *Figaro* was able to record that the day had already long passed 'since England had ceased to regard the war as a terrible and splendid sport'.[11]

Australia was odd-man-out in the white empire. The *Bulletin* as late as 1917 believed a correspondent's role was still to write aids to recruitment, complaining that the 'communications from the official correspondent have been colourless and no waverer's pulse has been quickened by them'. Bean, the correspondent in question, must have taken this to heart, for his succeeding dispatches abounded with fame, glory, and sporting metaphors. Enlistments for the whole of 1917, however, barely exceeded half those for the first six months of 1916. When it came to raising the number of battlefield effectives, there was nothing to compare with conscription.[12]

Still terrible, but fewer than we thought

Figure 4 reveals an unexpected sequence, one that even ex-prime ministers have not readily understood. But Malcolm Fraser no more than compounded a common truism when he claimed Australia's 'casualties in that war were, for our size, greater than that of other nations'. At worst, he is guilty of confusing the Anzac legend with history; as they are so intertwined, the legend and the history have become more or less indistinguishable.[13]

This legend began, as every Australian knows, on the morning of 25 April 1915 on the Gallipoli peninsula in Turkey. Australia's soldiers there showed to all that they were nonpareils; they made 'our people a famous people, so famous that every Australian is proud for the world to know that he is an Australian'. Bean wrote this almost four years after the assault at Gallipoli, elaborating in the process a legend he is sometimes credited with inventing. By then he was working in a recognised tradition already established some years before by others such as the leader writer who eulogised those 'brave Australian troops whose deeds have caused all eyes to be turned upon this Commonwealth' in May 1915 in the belief that Constantinople would fall at any moment.[14]

The idea that all eyes were fixed upon Australia grew in the war; by 1916 even the hard-headed *Technical Gazette of New South Wales* proposed that 'Australia's opportunity for realising upon her natural wealth was never so good as at the present time'. Nations who had 'scarcely heard the name of Australia before now know our geographical position and something of the characteristics of the Australian' because of the 'gallantry of our soldiers at Anzac'. This understanding of the way of the world's markets was sophisticated when compared with Cutlack's 1919 claim that the soldiers had 'made such a reputation for Australia that any

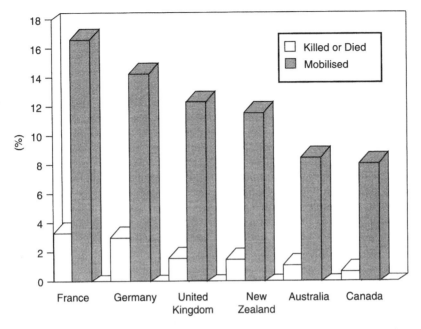

Figure 4 Mobilisations and losses as proportions of total populations: 1914–1918
SOURCE: From information in—Becker, *The Great War and the French People*, p. 6; *Census of the Commonwealth of Australia 1921*, p. 30; Bean, *Anzac to Amiens*, p. 532; Grey, *A Military History of Australia*, p. 119.

trade product sent into Britain or France or Belgium and branded "made in Australia" would be assured of a high place in the market'.[15]

It is hard to achieve undying fame in the twentieth century without media attention and this was in no way as universal and comprehensive in foreign reporting as Cutlack seemed to imply. Indeed, many diggers resented the way their work was credited to the British army. Among them, the VC winner W. D. Joynt believed that during the German offensive of 1918 'there was an official conspiracy of silence regarding the work of the Australian troops who largely retrieved the situation at this time', citing Monash's complaint that Australian 'press correspondents are forbidden even to mention that Australians are in this vicinity [in front of Amiens]'. Owing to its position in the British army and to the vagaries of censorship, the AIF did not always receive the recognition it deserved.[16]

The Australians who joined up in 1914 had joined a British imperial force. Australians were among the 'oversea' Britons to whom the King sent his 'message to the Government and peoples of his self-governing Dominions' on 10 September 1914. The *Sydney Morning Herald* leader that same day was devoted to 'The Expeditionary Forces'. It is only from

a sole reference to 'the soldiers of Australia' that it can be seen that the
march the leader described was not taking place in Manchester or
Glasgow, and that the expeditionary force referred to was in fact
Australian.

> The sight of trained men marching through the streets yesterday made each
> home-keeping citizen as he saw them feel that he, too, must do something to
> help the Empire. Everyone who noticed a friend in the ranks felt that he would
> be ashamed to meet that friend on his return if he had done nothing for his
> country in the interval . . . But after five weeks fighting the truth has been
> forcibly impressed upon every British citizen that the war will not be finished
> until after many months have elapsed, and grave dangers have been incurred.
> It would be quite in accordance with the British character if the news of the
> Belgian success at the outbreak of the war had delayed the influx of recruits.
> The better the volunteer the slower he is to come forward for a picnic
> expedition.[17]

By 1918 Australians were still 'British citizens' but it is unlikely a leader
writer would stress it, or that Australians would accept it as a term to
describe themselves. The Germans, not always for reasons of justness or
fairness, followed a similar course in their depiction of dominion troops.
Although the Germans believed at the start of the war that 'the military
assistance which her colonies can give to Britain is entirely negligible',
they had to admit anticipating that 'the whole British Empire would be
torn to pieces, but the Colonies appear to be closer than ever united
with the Mother Country'.[18]

Nonetheless, after the landing at Gallipoli, colonial troops were still
regarded by them in a poor light. The invasion force was written off as
'Canadian, Australian and New Zealand mercenaries' (*Söldner*); a 'mis-
erable collection of troops, got together anyhow' of 'coloured Englishmen and Frenchmen and colonial rowdies . . . Cairo Australians,
Canadians and so on'. They might be able to 'frighten old women . . .
and rob and plunder', but could 'do nothing against serious national
forces like . . . the Turks'. By July 1916 dominion troops were better
regarded, with the Australians at Fromelles now depicted in the German
press as 'sturdy lads', the sons of 'rich graziers and heirs to the land'.
What their 'fathers had brought to the wild colony, lay in their bearing
and eyes, and they were not to be taken lightly. Good shots, cruel fighters, steel-hard fellows.'[19]

It is difficult to find German references to non-French troops on the
western front, be they Scottish, Welsh or Canadian, which describe their
opponents as anything other than 'English'. This was not the case,
though, on Germany's 'blackest day'—8 August 1918, when the
Germans, unlike the British and French, stated the true order of battle.

'The enemy attack was mostly carried out with divisions from the dominions, Australian and Canadian. Seemingly only two French divisions were involved.' The *Berliner Tageblatt* paid almost as much attention to Monash—even though he went unmentioned in Bean's dispatches—as to Haig himself, in this 'greatest battle of the whole war'. Citing a copy of the 'Order of the Day by the Commander of the Australian Corps, General Monach [*sic*]', it claimed 'that the enemy's hopes were based on quite false premises, for German power is still unbroken' and 'the hoped for break-through has not succeeded'. But this apparent even-handedness, rather than being due to any sense of fair play, had more to do with convincing the German people that the Allies were so exhausted that they were now exploiting colonial troops in prime attacking roles. Throughout the war the Germans claimed England was using the rest of the British Isles and her colonies to fight her battles for her, which in its turn affected the way the British conducted their propaganda war, especially after Third Ypres in 1917.[20]

The French paid more attention to the presence of overseas British troops, and mostly reprinted British communiqués. The Canadians, however, enjoyed a special relationship based on the erroneous ideas that Canadians were half-French and that the 'C' in Anzac stood for Canada. That perhaps explains this dispatch, written about the artillery prelude to the battle of the Somme, when only Newfoundlanders among dominion troops were near the front line:

> When the local commander judges that projectiles and gas have accomplished their work of destruction, of stupefaction and of death, Anzac patrols,— Australians, New Zealanders and Canadians—solid and daring fellows, go out to verify the work.[21]

When Australians were singled out from the confusion of 'Anzac', it was in clichéd terms—nonetheless, terms which Australians would have recognised. Thus, no European should 'think of reproaching' them for their 'quite excusable provincialism', as no others had thrown themselves 'at the German with such a frenzy'. Described as 'broad-chested cowboys' who 'resembled the free horsemen of their country chasing cattle', or as 'slouch-hatted Australians, with their vigorous and supple stride', they were considered the 'most magnificent of Anglo Saxon specimens, thanks to their life in the wide open spaces and their passionate devotion to violent sports'.[22]

These descriptions date from later in the war; little was made of the Dardanelles campaign in the French press, and not until June 1915 were there attempts to describe the British troops involved. As the French Expeditionary Corps was made up of 'Senegalese riflemen, the colonial infantry and the Foreign Legion; all men accustomed to a hot climate', so:

> [The] English troops consist of volunteers from Australia and New Zealand, magnificent athletes, former shepherds or cattlemen, miners, farmers, etc. These chaps have a marked predilection for attacking with the bayonet, to cries of hip! hip! hooray! shouted with the same conviction as if it was a football game. The Turks didn't expect the arrival of these giants.[23]

After their arrival in France, French coverage of the AIF's exploits continued on a perfunctory basis, and it was not until the war was nearly over, on 2 September 1918, that the force earned a headline in the *Figaro*: 'Les Australiens à Péronne' (Australians at Péronne). Following 'the magnificent exploit of Mont Saint-Quentin', such was its proximity to Péronne that the *Figaro* felt entitled to prematurely claim the capture of Péronne itself (see plate 10).

> In fact, the ancient town fell twenty four hours later. Barely recovered from his surprise, on the morning of the 31st the enemy resolved to re-take Mont Saint-Quentin irrespective of the cost . . .
>   The 31st passed with continual counter-attacks . . . The Australians showed themselves as great in defence as they had been in attack, and even, while defending, they took more than five hundred prisoners on the 31st.[24]

It would be difficult to expect nations who had committed hundreds of divisions to the war to go out of their way to make note of a force of five divisions. Nevertheless, these same five divisions also made up about 10 per cent of the British army and—given also the ties of blood and language, together with the nature of the empire—it is not surprising that they were accorded a greater weighting in the British press than that accorded the continental powers. 'British press' also means the Australian press; a page from, say, the *Argus* at the time of the battle of Fromelles reads remarkably like an equivalent page from, say, the London *Times* of the same date—even to the inclusion of C. E. W. Bean's dispatch. Indeed, as during the landing at Gallipoli, Australians were sometimes less well-informed about the work of their own troops than Britons were; for, a notorious double censorship applied. The scissors of the Australian censor, according to one German report, often 'surpass their English colleagues in sharpness', sentiments with which Australian journalists might only have agreed. 'When matter has been censored here [London]', an Australian pressman told his London audience in 1918, and 'even official communiqués, we had them censored over again in Australia. We were supposed to be a fragile people who cannot read facts. (Laughter.)'[25]

For the Australian people it was no laughing matter to be less well-informed than the poorly informed British. The situation dated back to the first days of the war, when the 'colonial governments':

> handed over their men to the Empire in a spirit of blind trust. At the outset Australia and New Zealand exercised little more control over the disposition of their troops than the Lancashire County Council claimed for the Lancashire Division, which fought with the Anzacs at Gallipoli.[26]

'Blind trust' meant British official news control, and that meant keeping material flowing for the inhabitants of the British Isles. Except when it suited, colonials had to wait; consequently, the first notification Australians had that their troops had actually gone ashore at the Dardanelles came four days after the event in a message assuring Australians that 'their troops have landed on Turkish soil'. The next hint came in a message from the king to the governor-general praising their 'Splendid Gallantry', along with a claim by the Turks that they'd taken Australian prisoners. When these first reports came through, the *Sydney Morning Herald* seemed apologetic that the Australians were not in Flanders, reassuring its readers 'that in taking part in this enterprise' Australians were not 'merely releasing British regiments for more arduous work'. The next reports 'which at last the censorship is allowing to trickle through' did not deter the Sydney *Daily Telegraph* from claiming to have 'definitely' established 'the fact that the Australian troops have been landed in Turkey, and with the British and French are marching on Constantinople', whose capture was now 'imminent'. By 1 May there was still no hard news, but the *Herald* had ceased apologising and had suddenly discovered in these events in the Dardanelles a whole new meaning for Australia. These bore:

> witness to the beginning of a new era in our nationhood; and who shall say what influence they will have in shaping our national destiny? Australia is no longer isolated among the nations. New conditions have given birth to a new conception of our duties—our duties to our own people, to the Empire, and to the world at large. If proof were needed of it, the great war has furbished it.[27]

Fantastic tales

The foundations for what became the Anzac legend were thus laid about a week after the landing but, as it transpired, about a week before the appearance of a dispatch confirming the events of the day. In this news-free interregnum some fantastic tales were concocted, illustrating on the one hand how absence of material need not be a hindrance to an imaginative leader-writer and, on the other, the lack of censorship applying to extravagant claims of success. 'That Australian troops should now be approaching the gates of the old Byzantine citadel', the Sydney *Daily Telegraph* offered, 'with orders for the Turk to quit, and a sentence of eternal doom to Moslem power in Europe', was one of the 'most striking examples of the romance of destiny that ever the world has seen'. Australians were now 'writing in blood a new history of civilisation, in view of the site on which the walls of Troy stood', and this was a 'contingency that the boldest imagination would have hesitated to vision'.[28]

In view of these assertions, it seems odd that the *Telegraph* should criticise a lack of information so pressing that the 'greatest war of history, now staggering civilisation, is a war that will never have a history'. When the 'cataclysm' was over, 'all that the world will ever correctly understand is the effect that has been produced by it'. Angry questions were also beginning to be asked of the government.

> In the House of Representatives on Wednesday the Government was forced to confess that it knew nothing about the result of the action in which so many Australians have been sacrificed, and was totally ignorant as to whether the Light Horse participated in it or what brigades have been in touch with the enemy. As all this information has for some days past been in possession of the Turks, why it should be deemed necessary by the War Office in England to withhold it from the vitally interested public of Australia no one who is not in the confidence of the censors can imagine.[29]

On 3 May further sketchy information appeared in Australian papers, much of it lifted from London sources. The *Evening Standard* was quoted as relating that 'The fortune of war has at last given the Australians and New Zealanders their turn, and they are making the best use of it. The Dardanelles operations have special and peculiar dangers which are being met with special and peculiar skill and valour . . . '; while the *Observer* expressed 'confidence that the Australians and New Zealanders are not behind the Canadians in Flanders for resolute soldiership and contempt for death'. This may have been some comfort to Australians now facing their first wartime casualty lists, but it hardly compensated for the absence of a detailed dispatch.[30]

Making mockery of later claims that news of the 'new military wonder' was 'flashed all over the world after that first grim day', the first detailed dispatch on the landing appeared in the British press thirteen days after the event and in the Australian press the delay was exactly a fortnight.

Ellis Ashmead Bartlett's dispatch varies in content depending upon where it appeared; his image of a bayonet charge up a cliff which reached a seemingly grotesque climax when 'the first Ottoman Turk since the last Crusade received an Anglo-Saxon bayonet in him at 5 minutes after 5 a.m. on April 25' must have been considered too brutal for Australian sensibilities. In the *Anzac Book* of 1916 one Australian wrote that 'future historians will teach that Australia was discovered not by Captain Cook, explorer, but by Mr. Ashmead Bartlett, war correspondent'. Nowadays Ashmead Bartlett rather than C. E. W. Bean is credited as being the creator of the Anzac legend, but neither was responsible. Bartlett provided detailed confirmation and imperial benediction for an event already claimed as being the Australian national birth or rebirth. But the Birth of the Nation was notably lacking from Bartlett's imperial tract on the 'raw colonial troops', who in those 'desperate hours proved worthy to fight side by side with the heroes of Mons, the Aisne, Ypres, and Neuve Chapelle'. To a modern researcher, like D. A. Kent, this dispatch:

> can still produce an involuntary shudder in the reader. The men he described were heroic figures, 'a race of giants', whose courage and physical endurance were beyond measure. Bartlett's 'Anzacs' had about as much reality as Achilles and the besiegers of Troy just across the Hellespont; they were supermen.[31]

For the time, the heroics were not notably overblown; compared to what Frenchmen were used to reading, this almost seems understated. Of this 'race of athletes' it was said—'No finer feat of arms has been performed during the war than this sudden landing in the dark, this storming of the heights, and, above all, the holding on to the position thus won'. Above all perhaps, and in the rhetoric of the time to their undying credit, they were contemptuous of death.

> These Colonials are extraordinarily cool under fire, often exposing themselves rather than taking the trouble to keep in under the shelter of the cliff. One of the strangest sights of all was to see numbers of them bathing in the sea with the shrapnel bursting all around them.[32]

In Australian newspapers Bartlett's dispatch was reinforced by editorial leaders dwelling on the now familiar theme of the national birth. According to the *Sydney Morning Herald* the war had provided Australia with the 'promise of a national purification to come'.

> The statement so often repeated that a new country like Australia can have no real national life until it has passed through a great war means nothing unless it means that in the face of trials and sufferings the people shall realise

the imperative obligation of maxims they have previously treated as negligible.[33]

Bartlett himself only claimed that the Anzacs had added glory to the annals of Great Britain and her army. His 'Colonials' were proof that the British race was united and that the stock was breeding true at the extremes of the earth. The timing of his dispatch is significant, given the diminishing propaganda returns now available from Neuve Chapelle and given also that little, really, could be made out of the Canadians' hideous baptism of fire in a cloud of German gas at Ypres the day before the Gallipoli landing. If the Canadians' baptism of fire—on what was really the main battleground—had been more auspicious, it too might have brought forth an Ashmead Bartlett to ring Canada's praises throughout the empire. As it was, the *Toronto Mail and Empire* lamented how there had been no 'Canadian correspondents to witness and record the achievements of the Canadian regiments' at Ypres. From this point, as far as war publicity was concerned, Canada did something Australia never managed: she started to go her own way.[34]

For the time being Bartlett's praise discounted Australian fears that the imperial censorship was unfairly depriving the Australian people of vital knowledge about their troops, and ensured that Australia never went down the Canadian path. But Bartlett held no particular brief for the Anzacs. Above all he was an imperial correspondent, as is clear from his August dispatches covering 'Lonesome Pine' [*sic*] and the Suvla Bay landing.

> Thus closed for the time being, amidst these bloodstained hills, the most fero-cious and sustained soldiers' battle since Inkerman. But Inkerman was over in a few hours, whereas English, Australians, New Zealanders, Gurkhas, Sikhs and Maoris kept up this terrible combat with the Turks for four consecutive days and nights.[35]

He ended on a note of imperial bathos. Turks lay 'in masses, just as they have fallen,' and facing them were a 'Colonial, an Englishman, a Maori, and a Gurkha all lying dead, side by side, marking the highest point yet reached by the Imperial Forces in the Peninsula'.[36]

The Gallipoli campaign was Bartlett's great scoop. The dispatch from the Australian Official Correspondent, Bean, did not appear until a week later, on 15 May 1915, tucked away in editions now focused on 'Terrific Battles' and 'Furious Fighting' at 'La Bassee and Arras'. Bean claimed in defence for his tardiness that 'I would have reported earlier if I had been able to obtain leave from the admiralty', but his dispatch re-covers much ground already explored by Bartlett. Later attempts—by Bean himself and

Dudley McCarthy notably—to make the Australian out to be a different kind of correspondent, one with whom facts 'remained the cornerstone of his whole approach to his work' and therefore the writer of a different kind of Gallipoli dispatch, do not stand up to scrutiny: similarities in style, content and narrative-outline outweigh any differences. Neither man occupied the moral high ground in respect of devotion to facts or their embellishment, but this does not mean that propaganda distinctions between what these two men presented to their imperial audience were not profound.[37]

A reader of Barlett's account might easily have formed the estimate that this was dealing with a bunch of daredevil colonials attached to the British army; Bean left no such impression. There was no mention now of 'colonials'; in fact, Bean's dispatch is strikingly about Australians and Australia. The country around Gallipoli 'rather resembles that of the Hawkesbury River, in New South Wales', the cliff the Anzacs stormed is 'apparently as impregnable as Govett's Leap' [near Sydney], while the beach scene under shrapnel-fire 'looked more like Manly [a Sydney beach] on a public-holiday'. Nor were these men merely colonials under British command. Bean was at pains to stress the valour and resourcefulness of Australian officers. 'During the whole of this trying time, if one thing cheered the men more than another, it was the behaviour of their officers'. Of one, who went out to rescue a wounded man, he wrote:

> within a couple of seconds the Turks had a machine-gun on to him, and he fell riddled with bullets.
>
> Australia has lost many of her best officers this way. The toll has been really heavy, but the British theory is that you cannot lead men from the rear, at any rate, in an attack of this sort. It would be absurd to pretend that the life of an officer like that one was wasted. No one knows how long the example will live among the men.[38]

While one might be 'inclined to think this sort of leadership useless,' none who 'heard the men talking next day could doubt the value'.

The idea that officers were expendable and that it might be desirable that they sacrifice themselves in brave gestures was commonplace in French and British, but not German, reporting at the time. By showing that Australians were not just dashing troops, but dashingly led troops, Bean was dragging the Anzacs out from under the already stifling blanket of the British army. His future dispatches, when military action was their concern, scrupulously maintained this position often at the exclusion of material that could have provided a more generous and less one-sided impression. In so doing, he set the tone for much Australian military writing, from that in the press reactions of 1919 and 1920 to his own official histories.

Ashmead Bartlett's Gallipoli scoop was never imitated, nor was it necessary. After 1915 the loyalty of the dominions could be more or less taken for granted. Bean, except for a time in the Gallipoli campaign 'when the Age and the Argus had preferred the reports of their own correspondents' now had the most prestigious corner of the field to himself and provided most of the press coverage of Australians at war; his dispatches appearing in British papers as well as in Australian ones. Responsible not only for supplying Australians with information about their troops, but for providing a similar service to the British press, the impact of Bean's written words was unique. The words of praise which produced the 'fame' he claimed had been accorded Australia were often his own.[39]

Bean's dilemma

Bean's real problems as a correspondent began in France. Perhaps the worst prospect facing a conscience-driven war correspondent was to deal with a defeat—to turn it into something resembling a victory. His first battle contact in France, Fromelles, provided him with this situation; there, confronted by the magnitude of the disaster and incensed by the misrepresentations of the official communiqué, he had no choice but to put the best possible light on the situation. Apart from admitting that 'the losses among our troops were severe', no hint of disaster emerged in the dispatch.

> Yesterday evening, after a preliminary bombardment, an Australian force attacked the German trenches south of Armentières. The troops on the left seized the German front line and passed beyond it to further trenches of the first system. In the centre the Australians carried the whole of the first system and reached more or less open country.[40]

Facing 'shell fire heavier and more continuous than was ever known at Gallipoli', these men who were 'quite untried previously' nonetheless 'carried through' in a manner 'worthy of all the traditions of Anzac', and 'at least 200 prisoners' were taken. This was a figure he had no reason to inflate and which he knew to be untrue.[41]

Pozières presented him with the chance to describe a successful operation and his coverage reflected this, even if it did imply that the Australians had fought the Germans single-handedly. 'Shortly after midnight, by a splendid night attack, the Australians took the greater portion of Pozières'. These troops 'drove during a wild night through shrapnel, shell, and machine-gun fire', fighting:

> around difficult angles and through complicated stages with extraordinary coolness and success. They had a famous corps in front of them, but . . . showed discipline and capacity for being controlled intelligently amidst the awful surroundings of a night attack which only those who saw them in tight places in Gallipoli would have suspected. Australian officers sacrificed themselves with sheer carelessness of anything but duty.[42]

By now English reporters were protesting 'about Bean's name being published with his work', and GHQ was 'insisting that too much was being written about the Australians'. Bean, however, believed the Australians were doing most of the worthwhile fighting, and that the British press was deliberately down-playing their achievement.

> Reading the English paper you wd imagine that 10 Australians had been assisting the strong territorial divisions, between whom they squeezed, to move forward & steal a portion of German front. . . . They all spoke of this as the hardest nut to crack—Pozieres—before we got here. In three weeks we have already cracked that nut—it has been the sight of the battlefield . . . while movement elsewhere has been spasmodic . . . and we can't go much further until the English do something—we have fought the greatest battle in our history & one of the greatest in theirs—but not a suspicion of it would you get from the English papers.[43]

By the time of Bullecourt in 1917 Bean was confronting dilemmas that his peers could hardly have imagined. The failure of the conscription campaigns in Australia meant he was still obliged to churn out pro-recruitment material, with the result that not only did he have to deal with carping from the *Bulletin*, but now the *Australian Worker* accused him of cabling 'political news from the front with the idea of catching votes for the Fusion Party of Australia'. Bullecourt was a kind of personal watershed, that terrible battle where the Fourth Division would ultimately suffer what Bill Gammage called 'Australia's worst defeat', and Bean would see 'his Australia—past, present and future—destroyed'; but his dispatches suggest none of this and seem to offer justification for the *Worker*'s claim. Not that they were overtly political, just that they failed to present the desperate Australian actions of those days as other than a series of glorious adventures. In his dispatch of 18 April 1917 he recounted 'an attack by Australian troops which will live in history as long as history exists'.

In order to take the fullest advantage of the great successes near Arras, it was necessary that the Hindenburg Line should be attacked at the point where the Australian faced it. This line is defended by wire entanglements of whose strength the whole world has heard . . . By this time one of the 'Tanks' had got through the wire. Infantry followed it in accordance with plan, and entered the Valley of Hendecourt [north of Riencourt], 2,000 yards beyond the Hindenburg Line, within two hours of starting. The German infantry and transport were seen streaming towards the rear.[44]

This bears only superficial comparison with what Bean himself later wrote. From the onset he was aware of the complete failure of the tanks. 'Through his telescope', McCarthy noted, he 'could see some tanks blundering about and that "they never really got going" '.[45]

Two days later he described another German rout, likewise unnoted in the *Official History*. Now the Germans had 'attempted the biggest and one of the boldest raids yet known in this war against Australian troops opposite them'. Counter-attacking, the:

Australian infantry . . . advanced magnificently, sweeping the German guardsmen before them. By 8 o'clock the Germans were retreating by hundreds, utterly broken, with the Australians enjoying such shooting as they never before had against German soldiers. Our supporting troops were standing up watching as if at a football stadium. In the height of the retreat two Australians ran out from the rest and collected 70 prisoners. These two never thought to take rifles with them: their only weapon was the boot.[46]

Sporting allusions continued in a dispatch appearing on 11 May, which brought the first news of a second Australian assault on the Hindenburg line. In 1990 E. M. Andrews described this as 'perhaps the most serious rout of Australian troops in the war'. But Bean did not describe a rout. The Australians 'attacked the Hindenburg line between Bullecourt and Riencourt exactly at the point where, on April 11, they previously took it', but now the 'wire was wonderfully well-cut—better than in any attack the Australians have ever made'. At first only 'the heads of Germans were seen . . . and presently on they came'

. . . diving from shell-hole to shell-hole, two or three hundred of them together, for all the world like a school of seals. It is some new method of attack . . . irresistibly funny to watch. It was wiped out by our machine-guns and rifles. The men stood breast high over the parapet, with cigarettes in their mouths, and shot as they have seldom had the chance to shoot.[47]

Throughout that dreadful May of 1917, Bean continued to depict AIF successes. When the Germans counter-attacked and penetrated 'the Australian centre for about 30 yards', New South Wales troops countered so that by '11 o'clock no living German remained in the trench, but 200 dead were counted, and the trench was entirely recaptured'. In June he led off with another 'war as sport' analogy, about an 'old friend of Gallipoli', an 'Australian sniper' who was 'having good shooting': ' "My word," he said, "it's the best shooting I have ever had ... Sometimes they have the hide to try and cross the open—that's when we have some fun. ... " '[48]

Bean was not the only British correspondent to be still depicting war as fun or as great sporting spectacle, even as late as mid-1917. How much this owed to the pressures of providing stirring pro-recruitment material will never be known, but sometimes he drifted into Boys' Own Annual-style rhetoric, as in a dispatch from Third Ypres of 8 August 1917. This described an Australian artillery battery under attack by machine-guns, artillery and 'whirr! overhead a German aeroplane, flying under low cloud'. The men endured 'heavy shell-fire as the day went on', but 'carried out every order which reached them through a long day, exactly as if on a practice ground. "I had rather have lived those first six hours," said one to me, "than any other day of my life." '[49]

The year 1917 was a poor one for the white empire. New Zealand alone was apparently strife-free: the French Canadians were insisting on staying out of the war; the loyalty of Afrikaners was doubtful; Australia had rejected conscription twice and was in the grip of what was depicted as a sort of German-Irish inspired strike; unrest was continuing in Ireland. Perhaps in an attempt to raise the morale of empire, Third Ypres became a kind of imperial publicity-heyday, as troops from each dominion were praised in rote. This permitted the Germans to once more claim that the English were using others to fight their battles for them, and left the English wondering whether there were any English soldiers in Flanders. So, the last rays of this imperial heyday disappeared over the horizon with the publication in the *Times* on 6 October 1917 of 'some later figures as to the proportion of English troops participating in the war', which was 'desirable in view of continued German propaganda that troops from other parts of the Empire are being made to bear more than their share of the fighting'. News of the AIF's capture of Broodseinde was noted that same day in a leader, but in a diminishing context.

> The Australians fought in the centre of the battle, and had the signal honour of taking Broodseinde and the crest of the ridge: but the English troops had so great a share, both in the north and the south, that battalions from twenty-eight British counties joined in the advance.[50]

A month later the Canadians may have been another victim of this new objectivity, given the sober, almost glum response to their capture of

Passchendaele. While Canadian troops had won the village, its capture merely crowned 'the hard work of the British Armies in Flanders of the past two months'.[51]

The ground rules for changing the 1917 publicity climate had been spelled out in what seemed like the spirit of fair play: justice to the Englishmen who were doing most of the British Empire's fighting and dying.

> Since July 31 up to date the proportions of men engaged are as follows:—
> English 70 per cent.: Scottish 8 per cent.: Oversea 16 per cent.: Irish 6 per cent.
> The casualty proportions are:—
> English 76 per cent.: Scottish 10 per cent.: Oversea 8 per cent.: Irish 6 per cent. *Reuter.*[52]

This set in train the rationale for increased coverage of British at the expense of dominion troops. But, given that the Germans customarily described almost everything that wasn't French as 'English', and rarely bothered specifying which colonial troops were now being wasted in England's interest, the increasingly favourable coverage of British troops is difficult to justify. It is true that as the dominion divisions were generally crack, first-line ones, press publicity of their presence in a sector could give warning that an attack was imminent. This was not however, the argument used by the *Times*.

> The enemy have for some time been engaged in spreading the ridiculous fiction that the English have left the Scots and the Irish and the rest of the Empire to do the fighting . . . The fact is that the purely English contribution in man-power (and in money) in this war has been so greatly preponderant and all-pervasive that almost insensibly it became the complimentary custom to dwell chiefly upon the achievements of the other nations which make up the Empire. The share of the English was taken for granted.[53]

Plates 7 and 8 In 1917 Third Ypres (Passchendaele) produced some of the worst fighting conditions of the war (Australian Official Photographs, Australian War Memorial, Canberra).

(Above) Troops moving up to the Ypres front line, on Westhoek Ridge, near Broodseinde, November 1917. Owing to the mud, there was only one path, which left them exposed on top of the ridge. Hence, this location—called 'Idiot Corner'—came under constant shellfire, with guns and transports being wrecked or lost in the surrounding morass.

(Below) A fatigue party of Australians in the ruins of Ypres, 1 November 1917, collecting masonry for use as ballast in the construction of roads and rail-tracks.

AWM E1480

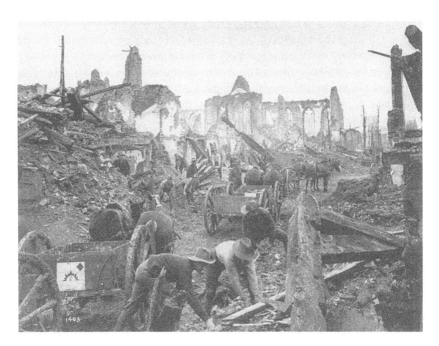

AWM E1403

Three weeks later Lloyd George stepped in. 'England had made 75 per cent. of the contribution in men, and 75 per cent. of the contribution in loss'. Paying formal tribute to the dominions, he ensured that the only feathers to be ruffled might be those of the loyal Kiwi.

> The Dominions had contributed between 700,000 and 800,000 men. 'And what a contribution!' Mr. Lloyd George exclaimed with enthusiasm. 'How well they had fought.' He passed in quick review their most glorious days, the Canadians at the second Battle of Ypres and Vimy Ridge, the Australians at Anzac and Pozières, the South Africans at Delville Wood.[54]

These political guidelines must have influenced battle coverage in 1918; but when the Germans broke through in March there were no dominion troops in the line, which was probably as well for them, for that offensive was of incomparable ferocity and brilliantly planned. The first to help stem the tide were the Canadians, followed quickly by the Anzacs. On 2 April Bean advised that Australians were now 'facing the head of the German advance', in place of 'outworn British infantry, who had been slowly retiring before the Germans'. Compared to the Tommies, the Australian infantry looked 'magnificently strong and bronzed', as they were seen 'marching downhill with a grand swing . . . eager and excited at the prospect of meeting the German attack'. The depiction of their arrival in a French village now seems almost like a shorthand notation for some of the narratives in his official histories; not only were they received 'with great joy by the villagers', but the 'hearts of our men, spoiling for fight, were uplifted at hearing cries of "Vive les Australiens" '.[55]

Bean had so far written about the Australians and nobody else with an almost single-minded devotion. On 18 April 1918 he radically broadened his brief, in one of his strangest dispatches of the war, devoted to the commander-in-chief. 'Exposing' a German 'lie', he endorsed the official line that English troops had borne, 'as usual', the brunt of battle. An Australian patriot could be a British sycophant if required.

> German war correspondents have been instructed to proclaim that Great Britain is, as usual, placing Colonial troops in the hardest and most difficult positions . . . So far from placing Dominion troops in the most dangerous parts of the line, Sir Douglas Haig, though he knew where the attacks were coming, had only English, Scottish and Irish troops there. One is inclined to believe this was done deliberately from a sort of pride, for the same reason which caused only troops from the British Isles to be employed in the opening stages of the battles of the Somme and at Ypres.[56]

Bean knew much of this to be untrue; one can only speculate on the pressures that caused him to write it—by now his aversion towards the word 'colonial', was on record. He believed that British Headquarters—

and therefore Sir Douglas Haig—'were expecting the main attack to be launched against the French in Alsace' and not on the Somme and in Flanders as was happening, and could hardly have forgotten that New-foundlanders, Canadians, Australians and New Zealanders had been in action of the first days of the Somme, Arras and Messines battles.[57]

Shortly after, as though to show that Australian officers were still as uncaring about death as they had been at Gallipoli, Bean highlighted the eccentric tale of a subaltern who at 'the height of the action before Strazeele' had 'mounted the parapet with a tin whistle and played "Australia will be there" '. Aiming to 'attract the Huns in greater numbers and thus provide a better target, he then played the "Watch on the Rhine," whereupon annoyed enemy machine-gunners concentrated their fire on him'. While this was of 'great joy to the men' and featured in Cutlack's *The Australians: Their Final Campaign* (1919), it fails to gain a mention in the *Official History*.[58]

At about this time the AIF received some of its best, albeit belated, imperial publicity of the war. Sir Douglas Haig was noted by a *Times* correspondent as having 'added special messages of thanks to General Birdwood and the whole Australian Corps for their "gallant conduct and magnificent achievements," with special mention of the "splendid service" of the Australian Division in the North'. Although only a couple of large paragraphs were devoted to the work of the troops, there could be no doubting the sentiments. Australian behaviour had 'been superb'. They had not only 'shattered the German attacks . . . about Dernancourt [and] Morlancourt', but 'when the line north of the Somme fell back to Sailly-Méricourt l'Abbé', the Australians 'held the chord between the streams, and have beaten off every attack since'.

> To the share of the Australians in the recapture of Villers Bretonneux on April 24 and 25 full justice was done at the time. It was an admirably planned coup, and most vigorously executed . . . .
>
> In the North . . . Australians took over the line east of the Forest of Nieppe to Merris . . . There was never a moment in this fighting when . . . the Australians were not 'all over' the enemy . . . earning the heartiest admiration of the French troops fighting in their vicinity.
>
> Altogether, theirs has been a splendid record.[59]

In August, following the German break-out on the 8th, the Australians were in the news again, largely thanks to W. M. Hughes, who was in London and functioning as an unquenchable publicist for 'his' troops. On 19 August he claimed that 'the past fortnight would be remembered as one of the greatest periods in the history of Australia'. In the 'great battles of the past few days no Army of the Allies had achieved greater success than the Australians', who shared with 'the Canadians the honour of having reached the farthest point attained by any Allied troops'. Three weeks after the 8 August break-out, the British at last admitted that men 'from the British Isles had only a small part of the attack north of the Somme', their role being 'to protect the Australians south of the river.' The honour of the 'first advance was shared by the Australians and Canadians'.

> In structure it was chiefly a Canadian battle . . . The Canadians are, I think, right in claiming that the fighting of those first two days was the biggest thing that Canada has done in the war not excepting the capture of Vimy Ridge . . . [The] battle in the latter phases was an Australians' battle . . . [One] finds it hard to get words to do justice to their fighting qualities, whether of dash or of tenacity. Pozières itself was not more glorious.[60]

The triumphant progress of the Australian Corps across Picardy in 1918 meant Bean no longer had to disguise disasters like Fromelles or Bullecourt, nor write sycophantic praise for imperial masters, nor fill in bleak periods with human-interest trivia. With so much happening, all he had to do was keep up and report facts. After Mont St Quentin, he cited a 'message of warm congratulations' sent to the (by him) unnamed Australian commander (Monash) from Rawlinson, who was 'filled with admiration for the greatly surpassing daring' of the troops who took Mont St Quentin. The *Times* leader claimed 'the dashing capture of Mont St Quentin by the Australians' had now rendered Péronne untenable. On 5 September Bean wrote of Mont St Quentin that the country at that angle is more like Gallipoli than any the Australians have seen in France. The capture of Mont St Quentin reminded him of that 'first swift rush up the hills by Ari Burnu which brought the Australian soldier into fame'. Where once he had likened Gallipoli to the Hawkesbury, now Péronne-Mont St Quentin was likened to Gallipoli. This was to be the AIF's crowning achievement. They fought on for another month but failed to receive

Plates 9 and 10 In 1918 their assault on Anvil Wood, followed by the capture of Mont St Quentin and the neighbouring town of Péronne, provided the AIF with a major publicity coup in the Entente press. But the cost was heavy (Australian Official Photographs, Australian War Memorial, Canberra).
   (Above) Anvil Wood, 2 September 1918, showing the gap in the barbed wire through which some of the Fifty-third battalion advanced on the previous day in the face of heavy machine-gun fire.
   (Below) Péronne after its capture, 2 September 1918. This machine-gun position was established by the Fifty-fourth battalion on the previous day when the attack through Péronne was in progress.

AWM E3149

AWM E3183

more than communiqué mentions. In this final comparison Bean climaxed the AIF's publicity on a formally cyclical note, suggesting that all future Australian endeavour could be judged by comparison with the example set on 25 April 1915.[61]

CHAPTER FIVE

1919–20: Blowing the national trumpet

Propaganda is to democracy what violence is to a dictatorship.
attributed to Noam Chomsky
(in Achbar and Wintoneck *Manufacturing Consent*)

'The First Great Day of Pain'

In January 1919 the idea that the war had seen modernity run mad on the western front had yet to take hold in Australian society. Little in the sanitised reporting in the British Empire had emphasised technology's role in the nightmare of modern battle experience: 1914–1918 had often been portrayed in a manner which might not have been out of place describing Waterloo. Nor in Australia would the slackening of the reins of censorship aid in the development of popular understanding of its hideousness. Instead, in 1919 and 1920, Australians were fed a diet of militaristic propaganda designed to reinforce an image of the digger as the incomparable inheritor of a tradition dating back, through Drake and Hawkins, to those heroes of antiquity who had also fought near Troy. Australians now knew that their new nation had been born in war, specifically on 25 April 1915, which endowed that April date with a spiritual meaning equivalent to that of 4 or 14 July in the republican United States or France. But the sense of nationhood held in those republics differed from the one Australians believed they had won, in that it existed at a mystical, rather than constitutional or political level. Australia had 'secured a sort of recognition as a self-governing nation, and not a mere colony', but the dominions were still 'not independent communities'.[1]

So the world, when it noticed at all, was content to accept Australia just as it had before 1914. Japanese criticism of Hughes at the Peace

Conference, that he had 'no better status than the representative of a British colony' whose 'voice in the discussion' was because 'he had Britain at his back', matched American fears that 'the new status of the dominions is part of a British design to "stack the cards" in the League of Nations'. While mayors in French villages promised: 'France Will Remember', French statesmen looked on 'with mixed feelings at the diplomatic honor conferred on the British Dominions'. Should not France's colonies 'have special representation on a par with Britain's self-governing Dominions'? Why should the world 'recognise the Australian flag', when Australia was 'politically incorporated in the British Empire'?[2]

When W. M. Hughes in January 1919 boasted that Australia's 'fighting record surpasses that of any of the nations', he was not only stating the unprovable but indulging in the inflated rhetoric of a victorious war-leader facing an exhausted, and potentially disenchanted, peacetime electorate. Australian identity, so elusive and uncertain in 1913, was now suddenly wholly formed and its image was that of a soldier. In this simplistic mood, patriotic orthodoxy during the first full year of the peace became the truncheon with which to bludgeon a host of supposedly related alien influences: internationalism; pan-German militarism; the One Big Union; the IWW (Industrial Workers of the World, or 'Wobblies'); Sinn Fein; and the most evil of all, bolshevism.[3]

Coexisting with the image of the digger was that of the classless Australian Imperial Force (AIF); a 'happy band of brothers', which had immortalised Australia's 'name on a hundred battle fields'. But the constructed image of the digger often seemed more bearable than the returning daily reality Australians now faced. 'The digger is back', noted the *Bulletin* after Armistice Day 1919. While he wandered 'about the streets seeking to be "repatriated"', the only people who took 'a genuine interest' were 'the publicans'. It was 'so much "safer" to take under your patronage the dead who can ask for nothing, and who never make you feel uncomfortable by getting drunk and riotous'. But the shadow between ideal and reality was probably no less dense in respect of the classless AIF. The bishop of Bathurst, and ex-brigadier-general, the Right Reverend George Merrick Long, had long preached against so-called class warfare. In 1913 he characterised 'the man who talked about class consciousness as the greatest traitor'. Australians had to 'learn to distrust and repudiate people who tried to erect a mountain between class and class'. In 1919 Long, now popularly known as the 'digger Bishop', was once more preaching the 'futility, nay, the obstruction of old prejudices, and especially those of caste and class'. Former socialist W. M. Hughes also stressed his repugnance for what he had once striven. The road to salvation lay 'not by class warfare, but by co-operation'. This was also a view endorsed by General Brudenall White, as a *Sydney Morning Herald* leader explained.

When the soldier comes home to learn that a class war is being preached in Australia, that the 'Labour' officer must regard his best private (who may happen to be a capitalist) as an enemy of society, and that the 'capitalist' officer must hate his most trusted Labour 'non-com.,' that in any case all those who served their country in the hour of need are 'legalised murderers,' one may well despair of the future. But happily these sentiments are not universal even in the official Labour party, and there are many who will be inspired by General White's appeal to a greater appreciation of the fact that if we are to be worthy of our fighting men we must live and work for Australia rather than for our sectional interest.[4]

To work for one's 'sectional'—that is, class—interest was now, by implication, unpatriotic. But what was Australia? And whose were the sectional interests? Attempts to achieve social justice could now be smothered under the pillow of patriotism; the 'classlessness' of the trenches rendered political aspirations for a fairer society socially undesirable and replaced them with mystical concepts of the national good and the national being. In face of this press-imposed consensus, Irish Catholics and those that F. M. Cutlack dismissed as the 'crowd that didn't go away' (those who didn't enlist) could but duck for cover, take an inconspicuous if sometimes fruitful part in the national life, and leave uncritical ceremony and pomp to those whose experiences and beliefs best fitted what was becoming the pervasive orthodoxy.[5]

To most citizens the context for the war had been provided by verbal tableaux in the pages of the mass-circulation dailies: in the peace the elaboration of the Anzac legend and its hold on Australian culture became the prerogative of respectable patriotic journals with—although few then noticed it—somewhat discredited reputations. What they printed in the first eighteen months of the peace now seems repetitious and banal, even mind-numbingly boring—for it is in the nature of propaganda to become boring—but little of it was then readily disputable. Most diggers, similarly to soldiers in other armies, had no better understanding of how the war had been conducted than civilians who had stayed home. Thus, the Anzac legend took off in the press during the first full years of peace in an uncritical climate marked by an ignorance of recent historical events—for which it was the press itself, although often no less ignorant than other sections of the community, that had been the sole source of enlightenment.

It would be false to depict a mainstream press devoted to a single position, for there was no absolute consensus yet to its ideological trappings. Between Sydney and Melbourne, between free-traders and protectionists, agrarian conservatives and industrialisers—between all of these there existed differences of interpretation. As for the legend in its emerging purist form—of a physically magnificent 'race of giants' symbolising the vigour and virtues of an agrarian and uncorrupted society that had gained the awe-struck admiration of the world—its main sources in Sydney were Bean's former employers, the *Sydney Morning Herald* and the *Sydney Mail*. Even in Sydney, however, the city where the patriotic trumpets blew loudest, the *Bulletin* was hostile to the image of the digger as a reincarnated pioneer; in Melbourne the protectionist *Age* sometimes took a similar view. Indeed, the legend's loudest support came, not from liberal, urban, middle-class sources articulating an increasingly independent Australian nationalism—the *Age*'s apparent constituency—but from agrarian conservatives who stressed the maintenance of the imperial status quo.

In January 1919 the armistice was holding, but a return to the relative normality of prewar relations was far from the minds of editors crying in support of claims for reparations. Few seemed to believe that they had experienced the war to end wars; there was little reason to presume that the world of 1919 was much less dangerous than that of 1913. The innocence of a youth that had supposedly welcomed August 1914 was gone forever. Though the full awfulness of early-modernist trench and mechanised warfare was yet to be popularly recognised, casualties suggested it had been of unprecedented ferocity and that technical advances would guarantee that future wars were even more barbarous. What the Allies had fought for—the defeat of German militarism—even seemed a Pyrrhic victory. There was a feeling of inevitability that the 'Hun will come back', even if there was 'no fixed date for the event'.[6]

The threat of a German-inspired bolshevisation of civilisation and the pneumonic influenza were not the only dangers ready to sweep down upon Australia from the north. The war had brought the Yellow Peril closer. Japan would now have mandates over former German colonies in the Pacific; deep concern, 'even alarm, will be caused throughout the Empire by the threatened internationalisation of the Pacific islands and the possibility of the islands some day going back to Germany'. With the British Empire now 'at best the second Power' and 'degeneration' forced upon European peoples whose 'fighting quality has diminished', there was little consolation to be drawn from the knowledge that 'Our Uncle' (the United States) had achieved 'first place among the Powers, a mortgage on the planet and the war habit', since Japan had gained 'money, experience and the removal of its great rival [Russia?] in Asia'. For an emerging nation, there were few reassurances.[7]

In January 1919 most of those who'd taken part in Monash's offensive in August 1918 were in Europe. Many of the troops were still enrolled in the educational schemes organised in Belgium and England by 'digger Bishop' Long. The grounds for the AIF's triumphant return were seeded by reports now freed from censorial control. Just how important the Australian part had been in the last months of the war was unclear, though the praise of French village mayors suggested it was substantial.

> It is to you, soldiers of the British army, above all Australian soldiers, that we extend at this moment our most grateful and warmest thanks. You have saved for us our beautiful city of Amiens, with its superb cathedral, one of the joys of the world . . . We know of your powers, Australian soldiers. We had here for twelve days one of your most brilliant conquests, the Bertha that bombarded Amiens. It told afterwards to Paris your glorious exploits.[8]

Already the first postwar books on the war were appearing, with H. W. Nevinson's cited for its claim that no 'finer set of men than the Anzacs' could 'be found in any country'. Sydney's Lord Mayor noted how a 'day hardly passes without the daily press publishing a warm tribute to their worth as fighters'. He was sure 'that the glowing reports which have been circulated on the other side of the world by these heroes of ours in regard to Australia's future as a wealth producer will result in a constant stream of immigration'. In reviewing Sir Douglas Haig's now published dispatches, the *Daily Telegraph* had eyes only for the 'numerous references to the Australian soldiers at the front'.[9]

The idea that the war may have had a positive cultural impact was also abroad. In early March Bertram Stevens reviewed 'Australian War Literature' for the *Sydney Mail*, tying together the strands of the Anzac legend. Described as culturally 'conservative but open-minded', Stevens was one of Henry Lawson's old drinking mates, a former editor of the *Bulletin* Red Page and the compiler of anthologies of Australian verse. Now co-editing *Art in Australia*, he had excellent credentials to provide the Anzac story with high cultural credibility. A common 'aim and a common sacrifice' had 'given the scattered inhabitants of the Commonwealth a spiritual unity they could not have had otherwise'. Australia had 'found her soul and became a nation'.

> The framework . . . had been made by politicians, but no paper Constitution could bring the people of the States together in reality . . . When Germany challenged . . . all Australians felt as one; and over three hundred thousand of her sons went forth . . . Their heroic deeds have placed Australia's name high on the scroll of Fame.[10]

Spiritual unity or soul was the theme of the literature under review. Stevens believed the 'Gallipoli campaign found its one true poet in Leon Gellert', but the ideologue of the legend's more short-lived nihilistic—

even modernistic—side was not a digger. Adrian Consett Stephen had 'enlisted in England with the Royal Field Artillery', and subsequently won 'the Military Cross and the Croix de Guerre avec Palme'. Nonetheless, he 'thought often of his country and his fellow-soldiers from Australia, especially after Gallipoli'. Upon reading 'Masefield's prose epic' and then learning about the conscription vote he wrote:

> Australians do not seem to realise their own significance, that each one of them is guardian of a name and a nationhood that has suddenly been revealed to the world. More than that, Australia has at last found a 'soul'—there was no denying that . . . before the war we were the most soul-less people alive, as a nation.[11]

By voting 'no' to conscription, Australians lost a chance that did 'not come often in the life of a nation—of realising and cementing their nationhood, of showing their reverence for the new-born soul of their own nation'. To Stephen, war was a test and what was important was not that Australians passed or won, rather that they showed 'their determination at all costs to sacrifice everything to keep that soul unsullied and place their nation at the forefront of all the nations'. The life of a man was 'as nothing compared to the continuity of a nation, to the greatness of its soul'. Stephen's understanding seems uncannily close to Ernst Jünger's discovery of Fatherland.

> And almost without any thought of mine, the idea of the Fatherland had been distilled from all these afflictions in a clearer and brighter essence. And so . . . life has no depth of meaning except when it is pledged for an ideal, and . . . there are ideals in comparison with which the life of an individual and even of a people has no weight.[12]

Bertram Stevens also noted 'Charles E. W. Bean has yet to publish his history of the Australians in action'. Although bound to 'be a big book' it would 'be a good book, for he is a trained observer and an admirably lucid descriptive writer'.[13]

For its 'anniversary of the First Great Day of Pain' the *Sydney Mail* featured Gallipoli's 'one true poet'. Leon Gellert had collaborated with Norman Lindsay—at the instigation of Bertram Stevens, with whom he now co-edited *Art in Australia*—in the production of *Songs of a Campaign*. In Gellert's view 'Torment, both physical and mental' was 'a necessity in the individual life of man'. But hating pain 'as Man does, it seldom strikes him what an unbearable existence this world would offer without that perpetual menace'.

Without Vice there would be no appreciation of Virtue, and none of that strength that arises from restraint and resistance. Without the eternal threat of the physical Sore, there would live no just pride in the vigour of limbs. Pain is the obstacle from whose defeat and ashes is born the independent right to live.[14]

Gellert's sado-masochistic brew of torment, suffering and pain applied as a 'law' to all 'Nations, as it does to the Individual.' The 'health' acquired in war ensured the 'power' to fight more wars. Social Darwinism was still alive and well. War was still racial hygiene.

The health that follows after the triumph over affliction is not a restoration, but a new-born state, with the additional and inseparable ingredients of gratitude and the realisation of the power of Self. After the destruction of despair, the victorious mind holds an almighty reinforcement in the knowledge of its Power to fight again.[15]

As well as an 'almighty reinforcement', Australians had now gained the right to a legendary–historical past, one dating to antiquity. The 'latest Spartans' had been 'found worthy of the latest Troy, Hectors . . . killed a thousand times, and Mount Gargarus of the hills of Ida is a little thing in fame beside the Anafarta Ridge'.

The influenza epidemic of 1919 caused restrictions on public gatherings, and so the first peacetime Anzac Day was anti-climactic. The *Bulletin* on 24 April was low-key as was the *Argus* on the day itself, when it ran a strange leader about the benefits of war on art and literature. 'Great though the sacrifices at Gallipoli were, Australia has reaped advantages that will be permanent.'

The influence of the campaign upon literature and art are already marked . . . [The] books and the verse of writers that comes to us in fragmentary forms show how great was the stimulating effect of these tragic experiences. On art, too, the great adventure has given a new direction in creative efforts.[16]

The *Age* vowed that pride of 'race and country' would never 'blot out the heroism of the Anzacs'. Anzac was to Australia 'what Grenville and the Revenge are to the British Navy, or Badajoz and Balaclava to the British Army. It showed that the Commonwealth is peopled by a manhood ready to fight to the death for its national and racial ideals.' Otherwise, it was in parochial mode. Victorians had 'the honor of landing the first gun on Gallipoli' and the '8th Victorian Battalion' had 'greatly distinguished itself by its magnificent fighting, when attack after attack launched by the Turks was sent reeling back at the point of the bayonet'.

Previously, 'despite very heavy losses sustained in the boats before they reached Anzac Beach', the

> Victorian troops never faltered, and once ashore they pushed straight ahead, penetrating in that first wild charge far beyond the ridges where the front line trenches were eventually established. 'B' Company of the 7th Battalion, which was composed almost entirely of Essendon men, suffered very heavily at the landing.[17]

'A race of Avatars'

Responses north of the Murray were even more energetic and enthusiastic. The *Daily Telegraph* really let its hair down.

> *They came a race of Avatars;*
> *And in old Europe's sight amazed*
> *A new and unknown flag they raised,*
> *A standard strange with southern stars!*
> *That banner, blood-bedewed and torn,*
> *Flew out, upheld by dying hands,*
> *When on the oldest of all lands*
> *The newest nationhood was born!*

> It was not in vain. Gallipoli is ours; Anzac is ours. The same unconquerable and imperturbable spirit that led the Anzacs up those bullet-swept cliffs carried them triumphantly against the common foe in the fields of France and on the plains of Palestine. The Anzac spirit saved Amiens and the Channel ports, smashed the Hindenburg line, conquered Jerusalem. It was all part of one vast battlefield, of which one famous corner was Gallipoli.[18]

In 'the first revelation of those military virtues which were the foundation of all our successes', Australians had 'proved themselves worthy to fight beside the bravest troops of their Mother-country'.

The *Argus* followed up on 26 April with a cautionary sermon which suggested that a mood of nationalistic militarism might not be conducive to a thriving national culture. 'If the flame of nationality burns too fiercely it will lead to nothing but disunion, and then to competition, jealousy, and hostility'.

> There are certain extra-national interests . . . which touch all civilised nations, and by which all civilised men may be held. There are such things as science and art. For science and art . . . are not inter-national but extra-national. If we could only educate the peoples . . . to take an interest in these extra-national things, instead of their being immersed in histories which are filled with

nothing but wars and nationalism, then the result might be a tendency towards a peaceful competition instead of towards a warlike struggle.[19]

The *Daily Telegraph*'s follow-up bore none of this introspection or doubt. 'No one needed to be told that yesterday was Anzac Day', despite the fact 'that its ceremonies lacked the customary parade and official ceremonial'. Australia's 'most sacred anniversary was yesterday honored in our remembering hearts'. The appearance of 'a new custom' was also noted. Many women were now 'wearing a sprig of rosemary "for remembrance"'.[20]

Meanwhile, in London, W. M. Hughes was making it clear that 'Australia's future' would be 'built up upon the foundations laid on Anzac Day, when Australia was born'.

> The shores of Gallipoli had made the 'digger' what he is. Australians in Gallipoli, France, and Palestine earned the right to be called the bravest of the brave, because they fought for liberty and freedom . . . Australia also fought for the right to keep Australia for the Australians and to govern their own land in their own way.[21]

Hughes's was not the last word on Anzac Day. Journalists continued, in New South Wales especially, to dig up from foreign journals and publications anything that could add to the litany of praise devoted to the 'extraordinary military qualities' possessed by all 'ranks of the Australian and New Zealand troops'. If the *Sydney Mail* could find nothing new, it simply repeated itself. The '25th of April has a significance far transcending that of any other unit of the great British Commonwealth, for until then we were recognised by the world as a mere outpost of Empire'. With more books arriving for their review, writers celebrating the Anzac as creator of the nation and saviour of the world were getting a second wind.[22]

Empire Day was given over to Greater Britain. The saturation coverage of the digger abated while citizens were asked to ponder on how the war was 'likely to operate as the strongest of all consolidating forces'— for the Empire. Out-of-context utterances by Rawlinson and Foch were highlighted to mean something other than patronising words of praise thrown by generals at any massed parade of victorious troops that happened to fall within ear-shot. With native-son senior commanders returning, these too were interrogated regarding the international worthiness of the Australian soldier. General White confined himself to noting 'the extraordinary increase in patriotism and the development of a national character', and to praising the future war-historian: there was 'no finer man in this Commonwealth than Mr. Bean'. General Glasgow was unsurpassable. The Australian was the 'finest man in the world', and the country had little to 'fear if the troops only displayed in civilian life those qualities that had made them such a power in the field'. Not only were there returning generals on-board ship, space had also been found for some of C. E. W. Bean's sacred relics.[23]

> Within the last few weeks guns captured by the Australian forces in France, mostly of the great offensive of 8th August last year at Villers-Bretonneux, have reached Melbourne, and have been placed in the Domain camp . . . From to-day the public will be allowed to inspect the guns . . . Mr. C.E.W. Bean, official Australian war correspondent, has prepared a description of the guns, which represent almost every variety used in the field against the Allies.[24]

At this point the *Age* was content to mention the 'report prepared for the Commonwealth War Museum Committee by Mr. C.E.W. Bean', outlining the role of the future War Memorial. It noted that in 'addition to war material, the war museum would also contain pictures by A.I.F. and official artists, and models of battlefields'.[25]

On 24 June it fired a broadside at the whole concept. While the people of 'Australia naturally desire to have a collection of war trophies which will have a historical, educational and sentimental value', what was planned went too far. 'If Australia is to house a collection of all the junk that has any connection with the war, the population, sparse as it is, will be crowded off the continent.'

> A Commonwealth War Museum Committee has been appointed, with apparently unlimited power to spend public money. It proposes to have a 'central war museum' at Canberra, and . . . that means another palace added on to the row of palaces that are to adorn that lonely piece of Bushland . . . The Government . . . has apparently lost all sense of discrimination. It apparently argues that if the public is interested in seeing one machine gun it will be 3000 times more interested in seeing 3000 machine guns.[26]

'Not until we have . . . cleaned-up Europe for every relic of nearly five years fighting will we really have a War Museum worthy of the ideals of the Federal Government.' The *Age* was not finished yet. Within the week it turned to an associated theme, citing the 'war books, records, opinions, truths, half-truths and genuine romances' that were 'issuing from the Press by thousands of tons', it despaired for a future historian 'studying all the original documents, in order that he might keep up the status of his profession by giving the world the precise facts and the unassailable philosophy'. A pile of records in 'crowded shelves that extended for miles' would be 'higher than the Himalayas'.

Australia is only beginning. Its soldiers and writers have already produced a whole library, covering all the battle fields. In order that the history which Captain Bean is writing of Australia's part in the Great War may be strengthened by illustrative exhibits, there is to be a great War Museum in the Federal Capital.[27]

The day of 19 July was a holiday set aside to celebrate the signing of the peace treaty. With most of the diggers back from Europe, Peace Day also offered Australians a surrogate Anzac Day to make up for the real one, which had been spoiled by the influenza epidemic. That same day, 19 July, was also the anniversary of Fromelles—or as it was then called, Fleurbaix—and Senior-Chaplain James Green's exposé of the Fifth Division's terrible baptism of fire brought a sobering touch to the otherwise elated columns of the *Sydney Morning Herald*, together with an uncustomary hint that the war may not have been a succession of triumphs for the AIF.

More befitting the mood, and released two weeks before Peace Day—therefore timed to catch a patriotic market inspired by rousing speeches, blaring bands and the crash of hobnail-booted marching feet—was C. E. W. Bean's *In Your Hands, Australians*, which received full endorsement from his former employer, the Fairfax Press. In exhorting 'his fellow countrymen to prove themselves worthy of the great traditions established by their army, Mr. Bean's argument is briefly that Australia pulled together magnificently in war; her army, a happy band of brothers, immortalised her name on a hundred battle fields'. While Bean 'would be the last to blow the trumpet of the Australians undeservedly', he was nonetheless 'sincerely convinced that for certain qualities of initiative, determination and self reliance they are unsurpassed'. Two days after these favourable comments, on 7 July, Bean himself spoke of the 'marvellous mass of material' to be taken into account for his future history; 'if it is written properly, it should make one of the most magnificent stories in the world'.[28]

Bean was destined to play a major role in the celebrations, and the *Herald*'s stablemate chimed in with testimonials to his achievements. General White averred that 'That man (Mr. Bean) faced death more times than any other man in the A.I.F., and had no glory to look for either.' As with Anzac Day, Peace Day was treated more boisterously in Sydney than Melbourne. The *Argus* quoted from acting-Prime Minister Watt's message, which stayed within the familiar line of the war having reasserted 'the links of the Imperial tie between her [Britain] and the Dominions overseas'. In Sydney the *Herald* asked that Peace Day be greeted 'not with boasting or vainglory, but with sober gratitude and praise for those who have fought and those who have fallen for us'. This was easier said than done. The minister for Education—speaking from a Sydney school (Neutral Bay) that 'had the honour of sending probably the youngest English [*sic!*] soldier to the war', a child of 13 years 11 months—led the way in ignoring the call. The Australians 'had covered themselves and their country with glory'.

> They had heard from the reports of the most distinguished generals that the Australian forces were the best for an emergency, or to throw into a breach when disaster threatened. On all such occasions they showed themselves the equals, and more than the equals, of the seasoned shock troops of Germany. (Applause.)[29]

C. E. W. Bean's 'inspiring address on the war' was 'read in all the schools on the occasion of the presentation of peace souvenir medals'.

> During four long years, in good fortune and ill, they so bore themselves that when the tide changed the great and free nations beside whom they fought and with whom they emerged counted Australia amongst them. She has been given a place in the conference of nations; the great world has recognised her right to mould her future as she pleases.[30]

Senior-Chaplain Green's disquieting disclosures on Fromelles appeared in a newspaper which during that period did not otherwise deviate from a fixedly predictable path of comment. A middle-class Sydneysider who took the *Herald*, *Telegraph* or *Mail* must by now have known the Anzac story by heart. The Peace Day leader in the *Herald* was typical: 'our men's gallantry and tenacious purpose won the war'.

> The Australian battalions which took the key-position of Mont St. Quentin . . . surprised the whole military world, achieved what was regarded as impossible at that moment . . . These are the qualities which are wanted to make Australia the peaceful and prosperous land she ought to be; yet . . . Australia is suffering from industrial turmoil and social unrest, and there are in our public life a querulousness and a lack of confidence in one another which are disturbing and distressing.[31]

F. M. Cutlack's book *The Australians: Their Final Campaign, 1918* was announced in late July. 'It is singularly appropriate that the first consecutive account of the work of the A.I.F. on the Western front in the last year of war should reach Australia coincidently with the Peace celebrations.' In a book that didn't 'purport to be "history" ', aiming rather to 'follow the five divisions through their almost superhuman fighting of 1918', this non-history was made up of anecdotes and testimonials. The 'sight of the Australian infantry going into battle' was capable of lifting 'a man above all thought of death and wounds and physical difficulties'. They possessed 'a fire and a bearing for the battle which awakes in the breast as you watch them, the drum beat of Macauley's tribute to the Ironsides of Cromwell, fighting in the same distracted Flanders'.[32]

The *Victory Celebration Number* of the *Sydney Mail* followed a few days after Peace Day and featured, as had its Naval Number in 1913, C. E. W. Bean. It reprinted in full his special 'address which was read out at each school prior to the presentation of the children's peace medals on Friday'.

> Australia rides safely in harbour to-day, a new nation . . . To-day, the men who went to fight for her have placed her high in the world's regard . . . She has been given a place in the conference of nations; the great world has recognised her right to mould her future as she pleases. That is what the Australian force . . . has done for Australia . . . They who raised Australia to the very height of the world's regard.[33]

Bean enjoyed a status and credibility that can rarely have been accorded an Australian historian; not least one yet to write history. As guest at the Millions Club on 8 August he warned of the dangers facing Australia, how 'city life in older countries had been ruinous to the people of those countries', and how Australia 'had now to face the problem of removing . . . the causes of national decay (Hear, hear.)'. His ideas featured again in the third of a series of essays in the *Sydney Morning Herald* by H. N. P. Sloman entitled 'Some Lessons of the War'.

> 'Australia lies in your hands now . . . You have a much bigger task facing you than the force in France and at Anzac had. It is the same great task really, but the A.I.F. only began it.' So writes Captain C.E.W. Bean in the opening paragraph of his inspiring book, 'In Your Hands, Australians,' a book which must be read by every citizen of the Commonwealth.[34]

Sloman claimed an 'amazing fertility of resource, a versatility greater than that of the ancient Athenian, were especially characteristic of the Australian soldier in war'. Like Bean, Cutlack and Long, he deplored 'the idea of a class war and over-emphasis of class-consciousness' as 'sadly narrow conceptions, which can never delude those who formed part of an army on national service. National not class solidarity is what we need in peace as in war.'

In September the Prince of Wales's forthcoming empire tour resurrected tales of imperial glory, but the future king added only to the mass of repetitive banalities. With Armistice Day looming, journalist and editors had the chance to dust off the texts of the earlier months and

re-word some. The *Bulletin* saw it more as an Anzac event than an imperial one. If 'Australian valor just turned the scale at a time when either
the Allies or the enemy had to begin that downhill slide which could
only stop at the bottom of perdition, then this country saved itself by
the narrowest of margins', and if Australia and New Zealand had done
'more than others it was because they had more at stake'. The *Sydney
Morning Herald* embraced imperialism. On this day tribute was paid 'not
merely to our own Australians, but to all the brave men, from whatever
clime, that fell under the Union Jack', but especially to those Australians
who had 'filled the gap' before Amiens, 'and in the heroic actions of
Villers Bretonneux and Dernancourt, where a few brigades of Australians
beat off as many divisions of Germans'. These triumphs would 'live
forever among the feats of British arms'.[35]

F. M. Cutlack, in his essays for the *Herald*, seemed to believe Australia's future was best left to the 'Little Digger'. Looking 'at Australia to-day
and at the khaki about the streets of the returned soldiers, and listening
to the various unhappy and despairing cries', Cutlack found a land racked
by class-hatred. Was 'there nothing . . . to resurrect any of the old ideal
of the war? The Nationalist leader, "the Little Digger" of the Peace Conference, had at any rate his heart in the A.I.F. over there, and he fought
in Europe and in Australia the same war as the A.I.F. did.' Working against
both Hughes and the diggers now was the Australian Labor Party.

> In June 1918, after the Australians had just saved Amiens at Villers Bretonneux
> while the British army was fighting 'with its back to the wall,' while the
> brilliant Australian attacks at Merris and Morlancourt were inspiring the whole
> army with new hope, the men who are now against Hughes were sitting in
> conference in Perth and passing resolutions for a crawl-out in France on any
> terms they could get from the Huns. Had these men then, or have they now,
> the diggers' vision of the future of this great country?[36]

As Cutlack's digger consensus about Australia did not extend to incor-
porating ideas hostile to those of the 'Little Digger', patriotism was
painted with a party political hue. To be a patriot implied accepting a
politically correct stance.

Later in November Sir Arthur Conan Doyle's latest volume in his war
history provided the *Sydney Morning Herald* with the chance to warn
Britons never to 'forget the debt which they owed to Australia at the
supreme hour of destiny. The very sight of these lithe, rakish dare-devils,
with their reckless, aggressive bearing, or of their staider fresh-faced
brethren with the red facings of New Zealand, was good for tired eyes.'
Another book was reviewed, *Diggerettes*, containing 'some capital
cartoons by Mr. Cecil Hartt'. Hartt's diggers hardly differed from the

Herald's version of Conan Doyle's—'hard-featured, weather-beaten individuals, inveterate "leg-pullers," with a sardonic brand of humour peculiarly their own'.[37]

On 27 November the return of Australia's military leaders was noted, although how Birdwood could be considered to be returning 'home' is unclear.

> General Birdwood has ever since Gallipoli been G.O.C. A.I.F., and from the landing of the Australians in France in 1916 till June, 1918, he was commander of the Australian Corps . . . as well. In June, 1918, General Monash took over the command of the corps, while General Birdwood . . . was promoted to command the British Fifth Army. Australia, *whose name abroad is greater for the reputation of her fighting men than it has been for anything else she ever produced*, owes a deep debt of gratitude to both of them.[38]

Having great commanders was one thing, having outstanding troops to follow their orders was another. Australia was doubly fortunate in both respects. It was the 'selected' British blood which had made the troops and, thus, the nation great. 'We did not breed the original strain here; that came from our forefathers of the British peoples at home.'

> Great Britain rose on individual self-help, independence, enterprise . . . it was this spirit rather than militarism which spread the Empire. Drake, Frobisher, Raleigh, Cook, were, in the best sense, adventurers, not men of war. The Australian spirit and stamina . . . came to us in the blood of our British ancestry. What we may congratulate ourselves upon is that we have kept the qualities of the stock good and pure.[39]

In another *Herald* leader citing 'Mr. John Galsworthy' and 'Mr. John Masefield', Bean's 'lessons' were rammed home; Australians were again told how physically outstanding they were. But they still needed to be on guard, for the 'falling-off of the Englishman's athletic prowess is only one aspect of a general physical decline for which the crowding into cities has been responsible', and of which the war provided 'striking evidence'. While 'Mr. John Masefield has written how profoundly he was impressed at Gallipoli by the stature and bearing of this army of athletes', Australia still had to had to take note of Bean's warning. 'A nation which herds into the cities must suffer in the long run; the process may be delayed, but ultimate deterioration is inevitable.'[40]

With Christmas approaching the *Sydney Mail* advised readers how thankful they should be for the war. Now Australians knew first-hand 'those countries that had been extolled so long by their forefathers, and whose charms had been droned into their ears from infancy'.

Hitherto, with few exceptions, they had never been out of Australia and their life-long teachings had been such as to lead them regard their homeland as the Cinderella among nations—a very poor sort of country compared with the old worlds. It could produce nothing worth while, even the men themselves, as the amusing Foster Fraser iterated, were deemed inferior of the old stock and the wonders they still bred oversea.[41]

The war had changed all that. Australia was 'The Best Land After All'. And as if to find external verification, the Christmas number of the *Mail* included a 'fine tribute to the Australians who served in Egypt'. Dr William T. Ellis, 'the special correspondent of the "New York Herald"', believed that the:

> most important of all the discoveries of the last five years in Egypt and the entire Near East has been—Australia! Out here . . . amidst the ruins of successions of ancient civilisations, this new nation has fixed its place in modern history, and established, for all mankind's admiration, the character of its people.[42]

Nor was the year allowed to escape without a home-grown contribution.

> With dreams of high endeavour
> They faced the distant sea
> To hear the grim Death calling
> In far Gallipoli.
>
> Alone in distant Flanders
> They lie, and where they bled
> Slow foreign feet pass over
> Our sixty thousand dead.[43]

On 7 January 1920 the *Sydney Mail* announced it had the rights to 'General Monash's book on the war' and in February it reviewed the first serious history of the war by an Australian. Although there was 'an elaborate official history of Australia's part in the war under way', one was 'glad to have so concise and well-prepared a history of our military and naval doings in the great years 1914-18'. The Hon. Staniforth Smith's *Australian Campaigns in the Great War* was a sober and fairly dependable overview. He introduced, though, statistics of Australia's incomparable loss, which were taken at face value by successive historians.

> He has not attempted any fine writing . . . The record itself in its barest form is sufficiently eloquent. A country of only five millions of people . . . raised over 400,000 men and sent 330,000 into action. Of these we lost 59,038 killed, and 166,817 were wounded . . . The percentage of Australian casualties to

the total strength is 68 which is higher than that of any other part of the Empire.[44]

A total of 225,855 casualties from a force of 'over 400,000 men' represented at most 56.5 per cent and not 68 per cent; a figure now directly comparable to Britain and New Zealand.

The Fifth Division's history was reviewed in March. 'Captain A.D. Ellis, M.C., is to be congratulated upon the completeness and apparent accuracy of his "Story of the Fifth Australian Division". It also offered a *Sydney Mail* reviewer the chance to dust off old hyperbole. 'The brilliant deeds of the Fifth Australian Division in France and Flanders are not likely to be forgotten by Australians, and will be counted in history as some of the greatest achievements of the Allies in the recent war.' This may give the wrong impression about another sober Australian history. Ellis was probably as critical of the events at Fromelles as was then feasible: 'few incidents of the war deserve a closer attention from the Australian public'.[45]

An outburst of sycophancy

If Australians had ever doubted the imperial nature of their 'national birth', Edith Reddall's Anzac Day poem for 1920 may have cleared up the misconception. She avoided mentioning Australia or Australians altogether.

> On far Gallipoli the noble dead lie still,
> And once again this April morn are hearts athrill
> With love and homage fresh to wreath their mem'ry dear,
> Which Britons for all time shall honour and revere . . .
> Blow gently, breezes, o'er the sacred soil where lie
> Those gallant sons of Britain, bred 'neath southern sky.
> Bloom sweetly, flowers of spring, upon each lonely grave;
> Speak in your beauty of the glory of the brave.[46]

General Birdwood was now in Australia to preside at the Anzac Day celebrations. His pending arrival had been the occasion for a veritable outburst of sycophancy, which was all the stranger given the comparatively muted response accorded to the native son, Monash. It was at Gallipoli that "Birdie" and the Australians first got to know each other' and from then on 'the General enjoyed the whole-hearted esteem and affection of officers and men of the A.I.F.'. In his honour, the *Sydney Mail* conducted a readers' competition for 'Birdie Yarns' while the man himself in one of his first outings told Lithgow ex-diggers they 'were all the better for having been at the front'. That same day the *Sydney Morning Herald* replayed the sentiments of Anzac Day 1919.[47]

> . . . to-morrow we honour the day on which our men proved themselves in the eyes of the world, and won immortality at a single bound. Never has an army received such generous and universal tributes, as that which five years ago stormed the blood-stained slopes of Gaba Tepe. Untried though they were, our men had convinced all who saw them that here was a 'corps d'elite.' All observers were impressed by their bearing and physical grace.[48]

In Sydney it rained on Anzac Day 1920, which meant a second successive peacetime disappointment, despite Birdwood's presence. There could be no new rhetoric, but if the Anzac cult was to be a secular one, the leaders of more orthodox faiths were not faint-hearted in adding to the mountains of words. The dean of Sydney claimed that in 'the commemoration of Anzac Day we are making a memorial to time itself, and which will last as long as history'. The Anzac spirit had 'ensured for Australia her place amongst the nations of the world', and it now remained 'for Australia as a nation to keep the principles for which these men fought and died bright and burning'. In 'a special Anzac Day address in All Saints' Cathedral', Bishop Long returned to his idée fixe, reiterating opposition to those who gave vent to 'the cry to divide and stir one section against the other'. Australians would not find in such people 'the great note of patriotism and unifying influence', discovered 'in the sands of Anzac Cove and in France'. They could never 'be great Australians through differences and divisions'.[49]

The *Sydney Mail* almost outdid itself. Not only were the eyes of the world on Australia, but the 'stories of the heroes that have for hundreds of years supplied the world with material for picturesque romance' were 'now displaced'. Historians now agreed that 'the deeds performed on that memorable date have no parallel in military history'. It failed to mention which historians, but may have had in mind the history in the raw of Philip Gibbs's *Realities of War*. But the most the *Mail* could really claim was that, of 'Australians generally he [Gibbs] expresses admiration more than once'. In fact, Gibbs's concern had been for the English soldier, who had not 'been given his share of the honours that belonged to him—the Lion's share'.[50]

By early May 1920 most of the diggers were back, and the 'staffs of the "Sydney Morning Herald" and "Sydney Mail"' met 'to welcome home their comrades who had served in the war'. James Fairfax officiated and appeared to be trying to make a claim that Villers Bretonneux 1918 was deserving of equal status to Gallipoli as the event which 'brought the nation to birth'. The idea hardly survived that function.

'It is appropriate,' continued Mr. Fairfax, 'that this gathering should have held so close to Anzac Day, and so close to that double anniversary of Villers Bretonneux. That was a glorious day. It brought the nation to birth . . . it was the finest bit of soldiering and the cleverest piece of fighting that the Australians had carried out up to that day . . . [That] fighting achieved something, not only for Australia, but for the Empire. (Applause.)'[51]

The propaganda levels of 1919 and early 1920 were never again sought or attained. Australians, particularly in Sydney, were subjected to a sustained and intense barrage of propaganda which promoted a vision of the nation that was limiting, old-fashioned and biased against urban life and culture. During the war the idea that the soul of the AIF was agrarian, and the digger was the bushman reincarnate had become generally accepted. The unrelenting propaganda bombardment of 1919–20 had a predictable result: the city bushmen re-emerged from their dugouts and reoccupied territory lost after the 1890s. They owed their come-back to the war.

CHAPTER SIX

The return of the city bushmen

It was pleasant up the country, City Bushman, where you went,
For you sought the greener patches and you travelled like a gent,
And you curse the trams and buses and the turmoil and the push,
Though you know the squalid city needn't keep you from the bush.

Henry Lawson 'The City Bushman'
(in Cantrell (ed.), *Portable Australian Authors*, p. 156)

On 9 September 1914 the *Sydney Morning Herald*, acknowledging that there had been a shortage of 'those who came before the enrolling officers yesterday', also noted that this was 'more than counterbalanced by the quality of the applicants'.

> There was a good mustering at the barracks of men from the country. They quite outclassed the material offering from the metropolitan area. Not one man who came by rail was rejected. All had a full knowledge of the responsibility attaching to their service, and were prepared to serve in whatever regiment they could be of best use to the Empire.[1]

This less than overwhelming response to the call of empire soon brought forth attempts to shame recalcitrants: 'There are two classes of Australians in this war, those who go to it and those who stay behind', and admissions that Australians were doing 'something a little under our share up to the present'. But the image presented of Australia's Expeditionary Force offered no great incentive to city menfolk, who were already encouraged to see themselves as inferior.

> The men coming forward from the country are particularly of the class desired. They do not want to pick their positions. They go cheerfully to the ranks, believing that the officers know best where their service will assist the Empire. None of them have, so far, suggested the formation of a Bushmen's Contingent, such as has been mooted by correspondents.[2]

126

'As in South Africa, so in Europe, the Australian horseman will be able to do a service to the allied armies which they can expect from no other of their reinforcements.' It was not as though city applicants were completely useless. They might never ride with the Australian cavalry across the European plains or sight down their rifles at a Hun, but they were still needed 'to do the work of craftsmen' as 'sail-makers, bootmakers, farriers, electricians, engineers, saddlers and harness makers'. Before a shot had been fired or an enemy even sighted, the legend had already surfaced that the élite of the still-to-be-named Australian Imperial Force (AIF) came from the bush. This, despite what was already clear: that the war being fought in Europe was a different kind of war, demanding different skills or qualities perhaps than those exhibited by mounted bushmen in the Boer War.[3]

Bushmen, cowboys and gauchos

It is likely that in those first drafts the men from the bush did stand out physically. Robson notes that 'scarcely 2 per cent of those men who came from the country districts failed to pass the medical examination' but also pays due credit 'to the work done by [country] police in pre-sorting the men offering their services'. Deducing from this any kind of proof as to the physical superiority of the countryman is problematic; for, the disproportionate number of British-born joining in those early days—Andrews claims 27 per cent of the first contingent, almost double that of the population at large—might no less suggest that the native-born was lacking in vital respects when compared with 'new blood' from Home. But little of this prejudice in favour of the country was actually new: the idea that the Australian country-man not only looked different but was fundamentally superior to his city cousin, had, by 1914, been current for generations. Many of the traits ascribed to the bushman were admirable in a military context, which is not to say that the city man may not have possessed other desirable traits, just that for much of the war these were not what propagandists were looking for. The farm labourer ideal of 1913—who, either as immigrant or locally born, could by hard work acquire his own patch, marry, and help spread population across Australia—was now the soldierly ideal of 1914. In the process a vision of a 'post-modern' non-industrialised Australia received a hefty boost.[4]

French historian Raoul Girardet described nationalism as an eighteenth century and nineteenth century product of the 'new intellectual elites and the proletarianised masses'. While it was therefore 'a principally urban phenomenon', it could also take another form, developing 'in a rural milieu from the moment where the old communities commence to disperse, where the old solidarities become untied, where the structures maintained by the past, familial, village or tribal, commence to collapse'. This might have been written to describe Australia after about 1880, when the traditional ways of Manning Clark's 'Old Australia' began to disappear. Well before the 1890s 'the curse of the town with the railroad had come':

> And the goldfields were dead. And the girl and the chum
> And the old home were gone, yet the oaks seemed to speak
> Of the hazy old days on Eurunderee Creek.[5]

The depression of the 1890s cushioned change for about a decade. During that respite, poets could find comfort in the belief that the life they idealised was not really on a path to extinction. Much of the work of that first golden epoch celebrates disappearing Australia, as might be expected from city bushmen burdened with idealised and hazy views of bush life, and no less simplified generalisations about city poverty and vice. City living, even before federation, was associated with a deficiency of patriotism, as when Henry Lawson complained about 'Australians who are not Australians, but who loaf in the towns by the seas', people with:

> No glimmering sense of duty
> To the great land that made her so . . . [6]

To Lawson and most of his 1890s peers, it was the people of the bush that made Australia great, not the sub-citizens of the 'great, ant-swarming, useless city'. After federation he softened and by late-Edwardian times Lawson made his peace with the city as he 'turned his back on the bush and all that it stood for', an act which may not have been accompanied by great heartache.[7]

Eurunderee Creek had not been all rosy days. From childhood and adolescent experience Lawson well knew how harsh bush life could be, impressions which adult re-acquaintanceship did little to mollify. 'Banjo' Paterson—the model for Lawson's 'city bushman', although the term also befitted Lawson himself—had only good memories: his bush childhood had been rosy, idyllic even. So too, assuredly, was C. E. W. Bean's childhood. On his return in 1904, after a decade and a half in England, Bean gained early journalistic opportunities from Paterson, the man who 'had been a boy at Sydney Grammar when Edwin [Bean's father] was teaching there', the man to whom Bean owed more than just an introduction to the world of journalism. The 'Banjo' then edited the Sydney *Evening News* and was near the height of his popularity as a poet. His poems delighted Bean, who 'embarked on what was to be a life-long love affair with the country of which they were an expression; a powerful influence in shaping many of the views that were manifest when he came to write of the people of this country in war'.[8]

It was now well over a century since Rousseau had pronounced his fear of the *moderniste* and since the appearance of the bundle of truisms and idealisations that Richard Hofstadter called the 'agrarian myth'. Originating in the northern hemisphere as a literary idea, 'a preoccupation of the upper classes, of those who enjoyed a classical education, read pastoral poetry, experimented with breeding stock, and owned plantations or country estates', this agrarian myth made its first ideological conquests in the United States. Central to it was the conception that the yeoman farmer was 'the ideal man and the ideal citizen', and as this type acquired relevance in Australia through the opening up of vast tracts of land in the mid-nineteenth century for settlement, so the myth took hold, not only among Australian aspirants to this yeoman class, but also among city folk. But unlike in America, where it lingered mainly in Hollywood movies and cowboy art as 'a kind of homage' to the 'fancied innocence of their [American] origins', in Australia the agrarian myth survived not only as a half-believed romantic image but as a functioning ideology, too.[9]

In the United States the centrepiece of this agrarian myth—ironically, considering the real role of Mexicans, Indians, and even black Americans in cowboy culture—was what E. J. Hobsbawm calls the 'white Anglo-Saxon (and fortunately non-unionised) cowboy of the wide open spaces'. Elsewhere the type went by other names—vaquero, bushman or even gaucho—someone who, when domesticated, could be posed in front of small homestead on a plot of land accompanied by wife, children and horse. If this was ideal man in the ideal circumstances, then the antithesis was the lower-class inhabitant of the 'dangerous antheaps of the swelling great cities': the Australian version of this antithetical type Bean recognised, in 1907, as possessing 'a sort of hectic cleverness, an almost unnatural sharpening of the wits', but who otherwise would be better off if he turned his back on modernity, threw in his city job, and 'went on the land and stayed there'.[10]

When Bean's views on the subject first came to public attention in 1907, the notion of a future checkerboard, Australian settlement-pattern of farms and farmlets, where only the most hopelessly barren and remote desert land might be immune from the 'scientific' technologies of modern farming, had been a patriotic article of faith for decades. But first it would be necessary to break up the existing pattern of large holdings. 'Do you think we shall ever make a nation with sheep-walks?' the New South Wales Secretary for Lands asked in 1883. These 'ought to give way to population, and those who occupy them must recede and give way when the land is required for bona fide occupation'. Of such attitudes,

J. M. Powell wrote how 'ridiculously, the old vision of yeoman farms in little Englands beckoned, consigning the threatening realities to the cob-webbed vaults of a collective subconscious'. What was ridiculous in the last decades in the nineteenth century, was ludicrous by the end of the First World War. Nonetheless, it retained immense credibility, supported by a formidable advocate whose own credibility had been greatly enhanced since learning bush lore from the 'Banjo' in 1904.

> Every schoolboy in Australia knows that, where the back country is good enough for farms and agriculture, it is better for Australia to have it covered with farms than held in huge sheep—or cattle—stations . . . To put it simply, in an extreme case, Australia, which would hold only five million people if it were all sheep runs, would hold fifty million if it were all farms. And we want fifty million for safety's sake.[11]

What schoolboys know as provable fact and what they are encouraged to believe may not be the same. Bean's article of faith in 1919 was no mere logic so clear that even children could recognise its justness: it was merely agrarian propaganda. In 1907 he had derided the 'pessimism' of graziers 'and even farmers, [who] shake their heads at the prospects of closer settlement'; they should look to the 'example' of what had been done 'in the drought-stricken deserts of Western America', where 'again and again and again' it had been shown that there was 'no reason what-ever why energetic men should not combine to irrigate the land, farm it in five and ten and twenty acre plots, and live in real comfort'. Emphatic reiteration—'again and again and again'—as surrogate proof without sup-porting validation, is a rhetorical trick often used by Bean. It could hardly have been otherwise, for he had 'seen nothing of the outback', nor had he lived or worked on a farm. Neither had he been to the western United States.[12]

By 1919 Australians were at last attempting to put into practice some of the wishful thinking of 1883. So pervasive and persuasive had this thinking become among articulate, influential and sincere patriots, that by 1919 even the protectionist *Age*, at the same time as it espoused the need for urban industrial development was arguing that the 'problem that our legislators have to face is how to keep country people in the country and how to attract a fair percentage of city people to take up rural pursuits'. Among middle-class journals, the *Bulletin* remained a voice in the wilderness, disputing all claims that it was 'in the national interest that as many returning soldiers as possible shall engage in the primary industries'. Nor did it accept parallel claims that it was 'equally desirable, and for the same reasons, that a considerable proportion of the people in our grossly overcrowded cities should go back on the land.'

It observed that: 'Countries that are almost wholly agricultural . . . are all poor'.[13]

In the years before the war, when imperialists like Foster Fraser and Sir Rider Haggard had admonished Australians about their ever-swelling cities, it was not the size of Australian cities per se that so much dismayed imperialists, as the fact that increasing numbers of Australians were gravitating to industrial pursuits. Neither was a change to this imperial status quo in the interest of established colonial agriculturalists. 'Free trade allowed primary producers overseas to exchange their products for British manufactures.' It also reinforced:

> the symbiosis between the United Kingdom and the underdeveloped world on which British economic power essentially rested. Argentine and Uruguayan estancieros, Australian wool-growers and Danish farmers had no interest in encouraging national manufactures, for they did very well out of being economic planets in the British solar system.[14]

Britain's dependence upon the empire and Argentina for foodstuffs had become critical. She had 'let her own food production decline during the Depression' (of the late-nineteenth century) and by 1905–09 'imported not only 56 per cent of all the cereals she consumed but 76 per cent of all her cheese and 68 per cent of her eggs'.[15]

By 1919 to be a confirmed Australian patriot meant also supporting the tenets of the ambiguous sense of nationality contained in the precepts of an imperial destiny. An Australia, Canada, or New Zealand 'covered with farms' that would sop-up the surplus unwanted of industrial cities and 'surely drain the great pool of social discontent in Britain' was sought by all good imperialist Britons—at Home or abroad—as was an empire in which the colonies and dominions supplied raw materials while the Motherland processed them. For the English aristocracy and *nouveaux riches* this tidy arrangement abetted visions of a 'restored English countryside with such pleasurable associations—"hunting, shooting, farming and so on" ', the proviso being that the colonies and dominions refrain from major industrialisation. The white empire was meant to be a kind of exclusive Anglo-Saxon trading club, which could only function if the members abjured competitive industrial activities among themselves. Encouraging the mother-country's agricultural production to decline would not only serve the interests of Tory and would-be Tory squires, but would assure guaranteed markets for the dominions and colonies at Home.[16]

A motivating concern for Rider Haggard and the other members of the Trade Commission of 1913 had been Germany's increasingly successful competition in the dominions, where it was making deep inroads into traditional British markets. Between 1883 and 1913, German exports had grown 'from less than half the British figure to a figure larger than the British'. Worse, excepting what Hobsbawm calls the 'semi-industrialized countries . . . the actual or virtual "dominions" of the British Empire', German manufacturing exports 'had beaten the English all along the line'. With 'the Hun' due to 'come back' some time after 1919, postwar relief from this competition would be short-term. Tired-out and debt-ridden Australia, having fought for its place in the empire, was in no shape to counter the preconceptions of Whitehall even had it wanted to: in fact, dominion statesmen were often more aggressive in espousing their imperial patriotism than British ones were.[17]

As though confirming the wisdom underlying existing imperial understandings, Australian cities were already showing signs of the after-effects of industrialisation: it could be read as being in Australia's interest that the Motherland should continue to do the dirty work and Australia be quarantined from any further unhappy side-effects. Industrialisation went hand-in-hand with the growth of the city—and, by implication, its slums and their mobs—and that, the Australian middle-classes were told, was about the last thing Australia ought to want. 'As soon as a nation begins to shut itself up in cities', Bean wrote in 1907, 'it begins to decay'. Bodily strength 'and along with that its moral strength, declines. The new generations that have to bear the responsibilities of the old are smaller in body and weaker in courage and resolve than their forbears.' The worst aspects of city life were already to be seen in Australia; they were not new, but part of 'an old, hoary-headed, decrepit European civilisation, which appears half the world over, to be tottering to its grave'. The Australian city was 'already decadent. Its amusements show it; its literature shows it.' But Australians had the chance to create something new; a 'civilisation up country [which] is more or less a new thing in this world', in which 'you can see that the people are vigorous and healthy and strong—a young nation as it ought to be'. Those who remained in the city, however, were doomed to 'the fate of every city-bred people of any consequence that the world has known' which had 'been invariably the same'.[18]

Prognoses of this kind were losing much of their potency in Australia's late-Edwardian economic recovery; by 1913 they may have had little popular meaning. But in 1919, with a 'back-to-the-land' movement in full swing, the events of the First World War were read as validation of what may have been a flagging cause. To intellectuals like Bean—who had been to France and had seen first-hand how the railways that crisscrossed northern France had acted as conduits along which were funnelled millions of boys and an assortment of monstrous technologies, which finally faced each other across the battlefields of a modernity gone mad—the war had indicted faith in the machine's ability to provide a better future. But if the diggers were meant to react against these technologies with revulsion and, on their return, join the vanguard of a 'back-to-the-land' retreat into the past, there were disturbing indicators that many men had been captivated by what could also have been an Ali Baba's Cave of mechanical wonders on the Western front. 'The first and the largest group' undertaking courses in the AIF's educational scheme, directed by Bishop and Brigadier-General Long, 'consisted of those men seeking training in all varieties of trades, crafts, and industries'; only a 'comparatively small number seemed to favor a future spell on the land'. Not everyone considered this was necessarily a bad thing: on learning that many of the troops 'expressed a desire to go in for mechanics, particularly motor mechanics,' General Glasgow agreed that this 'was an occupation which he thought would suit many of them very well'.[19]

The coming agrarian man

Enrolling to become motor mechanics was not a response to be expected of men disenchanted with modernity; so disenchanted as to—hopefully?—prefer the isolation of a plot of land, a few primitive tools, and a mystical oneness with the earth. But, while the war had been an eye-opener to many young Australians and introduced them to skills, techniques and knowledge which otherwise might never have come their way, few could ever have questioned that it had been other than an incomparable disaster. It was not yet completely understood that the war had been made infinitely worse by Luddite-like commanders whose thinking often barely went beyond that required to re-fight Waterloo: in their maladroit hands, it was as though the machine had been granted, through war, a life of its own. In the immediate wake of war, 'degenerates' in Berlin and Paris in the 'madness' of their Dada might still believe in a cultural future where the machine could be benign, the past scrapped and art dead; but the urban-sourced decadence of cosmopolitanism was inappropriate to a young and vigorous nation whose boys had proven themselves against the world's best and validated the heritage of the pioneers.

In respect of the ongoing pioneer era that seemed so desirable, by 1913 it was no secret that the 'strenuous struggle of the pioneer days is past'. Farming columns in the newspapers confirmed that the 'bygone age' of 'the genuine pioneer, the man who ventured out and opened up country where there was no other settlement', was something 'still well remembered by men who are not yet old'. If fifty was the age of such a man, the actual end of the pioneer era dated from about the mid-1880s, suggesting that the 1890s literary and artistic heyday coincided with the end of an era; the soon-to-become 'extinct bushman of Lawson and Furphy' was already an endangered species as the bush poets were beginning to write about him. It is, therefore, little wonder that, in Judith Wright's words, the life 'traceable in old memoirs ... set against the unsubtle generalizations of Paterson, O'Dowd, McKee Wright and even Lawson, seems strangely unfamiliar'.[20]

The agrarian myth provided a *Weltanschauung* which saw industrialisation as a scourge, city life as a downhill ride to racial deterioration, and the soul of the nation tied up with images of character, landscape and race. In respect of race, as recently as the 1870s and 1880s there had been a flurry of interest in the subject of the 'Coming Man in Australia'. What if Australia had to look forward, not to 'a "Coming Man" who is to lead us into a land flowing with milk and honey, to a heaven on earth, but to a number of coming men who are to lead us, or rather our descendants, to a Hell on earth'? As for the qualities of the future Australian stock, this same writer considered 'the prospect is one rather for the Pessimist than the Optimist'; he was 'not quite thankful' to be living 'in a colony which is, in the figurative sense, "going to the dogs"'.[21]

Not all agreed that a colonial type had to be inferior to stock at Home. By the centenary (of white settlement) in 1888—that is, about the time of the Eiffel Tower, of the *Exhibition of 9 by 5 Impressions*, and of some of the 'Banjo's' early triumphs—the belief in an '"improved type" evolving under the Australian skies' was current. To Francis Adams this was a fait accompli. The bushman was already the 'fons et origo, of the New Race'.

> Nothing but the intense, the overwhelmingly and horribly intense character of the climactic conditions of the Interior could account for a differentiation absolutely defined after two generations ... The bush is the heart of the country, the real Australian Australia, and it is with the Bushman that the final fate of the nation and the race will be.[22]

In 1888, also, it was held that by '1988 Australia will be a Federal Republic, peopled by fifty millions of English-speaking men [*sic*]', and that by then 'a separate and recognisable type' would have developed. As the old world became increasingly congested, the 'stream of emigration' would 'turn to Australia' with 'the overspill of Germany and the United Kingdom ... pouring to the South'. There, 'room for all and land for all' would be found. This 'Australian Republic' would be 'mistress not only of her own continent, but of the Eastern Archipelago,—that is, of the lands which in all the world are richest in minerals, forests, and the means of yielding all that the tropics can produce'.[23]

By this time the myth of a vast inland sea—at least one above ground— had been exploded, and the trials of the inland explorers had shown how hostile much of the continent was to the agriculture of European civilisation. But for editors sitting at desks in Sydney or in London, for politicians passing laws in plush European-style chambers, and even for the artists and poets depending upon a clientele of urban sophisticates, the bush was a state of mind; their prospects of ever seeing, let alone experiencing, the inland was remote. It was simple to compare Australia's area with the area of Europe and the United States and make European-based judgements. The population growth of the United States was, thus, surely the benchmark for Australia. To cater for the millions due to pour in from the overcrowded Anglo-Teutonic nations meant pushing the frontiers of settlement, and dividing the sheep runs into family farms.

At the end of the second decade of the twentieth century few seemed to dispute this credo. Among those who did, T. Griffith Taylor argued that the 'contemporary margins of settlement already closely approximated the limits which had been "set" by the very nature of the physical environment'. The real challenge to a 'young community seeking some national goals and collective identity did not reside in romantic nineteenth-century frontiering, but in the clarification of more rational objectives'. With uncanny accuracy, Taylor predicted 'a total population of 19 or 20 million by the end of the century'. Not unnaturally, he was reviled by British and Australian imperialists as a 'croaking pessimist'. In those immediate postwar years Taylor's was a voice in the wilderness, as bona fide occupations of the idealised kind came ever closer to fruition in closer settlement and soldier settlement schemes.[24]

Hofstadter's agrarian myth takes on an air of deeper unreality in this Australian context. Yet it was this myth on which the Edwardians, who became the cultural guardians of the 1920s, cut their teeth. The bundles of truisms about future population, national destiny, rugged individualism as exemplified by the pioneer-yeoman and racial superiority had already taken wing by the golden nineties, when these men were youths. Yet by Edwardian times many Australians were thinking in more complex terms: there was little, aside from the preoccupation with finding immigrant agricultural labourers, appearing in the metropolitan press to suggest Australia was much other than an urbanised and industrialised society, with a prosperous and comparatively well-educated populace, coming to terms with modernity.

By 1919 broadsheets that had been notable in 1913 for their coverage of foreign news were now parochial. Who needed foreign heroes when we had so many of our own—homo sapiens and equine? Pages in the

Sydney Mail that once had been devoted to art or literature were now filled with photographs of race-horses or of diggers 'pioneering' in near-suburban Bankstown. Now it was said that nothing was 'more important to mankind than the production of food'. The world had 'been awakened brutally and decisively to a keen realisation of this truth by the events of the war. The solution of the problem of feeding the people mainly decided the war.' Australia could not fail to be the great beneficiary of this new understanding for 'without augmenting her area under wheat by a single acre, [she] can increase her yield enormously'. In the 'grand time coming for Australia', Australians would be able to 'work for ourselves, knowing we are working for others whom the war has dispossessed'.[25]

The *Argus* at that time saw the national future in agrarian terms, too, expressing amazement that 'there should still be persons holding the view that there is something inferior in the work performed by country people'.

> Without that work Australia and the whole of her factories and her imposing cities would not last a month. Yet the shallow notion is still expressed by men of small minds that the more the Commonwealth can be 'developed' and 'diversified' and 'encouraged' into avenues other than rural pursuits the greater will be its prosperity and the higher will be its intelligence. There is no reason to be ashamed of advancing the opposite theory.[26]

The *Age*, typically, was having it both ways. Australians had 'a continent to work upon; land and climate that can produce in any quantity practically everything that grows'. It was 'the country that builds the city; the city only handles what the country produces'. If, therefore, the city was 'drawing people away from the country so that the number of primary producers is decreasing, the city is creating the conditions of its own decay'. On the other hand, if Australia was to develop 'a race of vigorous, intelligent people' capable of 'enjoying the happiness that comes from a just distribution of its earnings', then it was necessary that we do our own manufacturing'. There were too many 'scores of millions of goods brought from abroad', often 'made from Australian raw materials' which ought 'to be made in Australia'.[27]

To the Sydney-based Fairfax press, large-scale manufacturing had long been more trouble than it was worth, something best left to the Motherland. Bean's *In Your Hands, Australians*, described by Michael Roe as one of the 'two most important manifestos of post-War idealism', with its vision of an Australia covered with farms, decentralised into many country towns and almost devoid of industry, provided perfect material for its 'back-to-the-land' movement. On 11 July the *Herald* devoted a

leader to the theme of 'The Toll of the City', endorsing the ex-corres-
pondent's views on the consequences of city existence. Bean had just
spoken 'of the damage to the physique and the moral of a nation which
is the inevitable result of the world-wide tendency during the last century
to gravitate to the cities'; this he had been able to see for himself 'in the
armies of the various belligerents'. Throughout his life Bean insisted the
Australian country-man was 'more valuable as a soldier', but the *Herald*
in July 1919 was more cautious about ascribing soldierly qualities to one
group at the expense of another than it had been in September 1914.
Now it was careful to point out that these 'natural laws' did not apply—
yet—to Australia.[28]

> City and country contributed equally to the A.I.F. and the recruits were of
> uniform quality. Our townsmen have not as yet had time to be affected by
> the natural law . . . But we should not flatter ourselves too easily. Already in
> Australia more than a fifth of the whole population is gathered in two centres.
> The proportion of urban to country dwellers is being constantly reduced, and
> this is the worst possible augury for the future of Australia.[29]

It took up an associated theme the following day. 'Where else in the
world is there a continent capable of supporting a population of scores
of millions, yet held by a handful of white people, who insist that only
their kith and kin shall help them to fill this empty space?' How were
the kith and kin best absorbed? How else but by more farms. All this
presented an opportunity 'for teaching the children' the valuable 'elements of social science' and encouragement for a leader writer to create
a panegyric to the 'young soldier who carried our six-starred flag into
the world's battlefields' and displayed 'under the severest test known to
humanity, the qualities of virile manhood and true nobility of character'.[30]
    The *Bulletin* was avoiding inflated rhetoric of this kind and remained
trenchantly hostile to the idea Australia was an imperial farm-lot. Indeed,
it argued that the nation already had 'an absurdly large proportion of its
people on the land, considering how few are this country's agricultural
products at present'. Germany and the United States, it said, the countries
that had 'jumped to the first and second positions for wealth and importance', hadn't taken the 'S.M. HERALD'S advice'; for, it was a 'slave's
game' to go '"back-to-the-land" and grow surplus grain for exports to
markets where prices are regulated by Hindu and Chinese and African
competition'. In most countries 'the agricultural section of the people is
generally, as a matter of course, the worst paid section'. As an example
of what should be done, it pointed to the 'Anzac tweed industry' as 'a
kind of test case.' Since being founded as an 'occupation for partially
crippled soldiers by the War Council', 'hard figures' now showed 'that

it could be run—was being run, in fact—at a profit, and there was a great demand for hand-woven tweed'.

> Orders for years ahead were forthcoming, and any number more could have been had if there was a chance of supplying the goods . . . This proved industry only asks for . . . less than MILLEN'S Department can spend in an hour in putting a dozen impossibly-mortgaged ex-troops with no agricultural experience on a 'farm.'[31]

Manufacturers, or those assisting manufacture, were taking similar lines. Alexander Pentleton Stewart pleaded that it was not enough 'to produce wheat and other commodities from the ground, shear the wool from the sheep, or raise stock, dig metals, and other raw materials'.

> To settle people on the land in the belief that production alone would solve labour problems would be absurd. [If] every acre of Australia capable of bearing crops were under cultivation we would still be a long way from solving the economic problem . . . The coming struggle will be one in which the Allies, the late enemies, and the neutrals will marshal all their forces. Australia . . . should export the manufactured article . . . Develop our own resources ourselves![32]

With a nascent agrarian political grouping now at the point of coalition with the postwar Nationalist party, and as though to console British imperialists disturbed by such colonial rumblings, W. M. Hughes maintained a 'definite policy' that would 'give British manufacturers preference in their home markets', and simultaneously ensure that the dominions' raw materials obtained 'a larger market within the Empire'. If such an arrangement was not maintained, not only would 'Imperial trade suffer, but the Empire will tend to disintegrate'. Hughes's faith in the empire was not as limitless as that of L. S. Amery, who, despite wayward prewar prophecies, was still gazing into the crystal ball. Amery believed that 'as the nineteenth century was the century of the United States, so the twentieth would be the century of the British Empire'. The century would close 'with the British Empire having 200,000,000 white citizens, enjoying a far higher level of prosperity than the United States to-day'.[33]

Labor leader Frank Anstey was not as sympathetic to this federalist imperial vision, or to the way imperialism had operated to Australia's disadvantage in the past. He drew 'attention to Australia's war debt of £300,000,000', and asked why America had 'got greatly higher prices for her wheat and meat from England than Australia' and Canada had obtained 'better prices for products than Australia'. His questions fell on stony soil. On his return from Europe W. M. Hughes claimed to have the answers, but all he could offer was a burst of unspecific demagoguery.

Five million people have to carry a war debt of £400,000,000 and the economic loss involved in the death of 60,000 young men and the disablement of 40,000 more. We are living on capital—it is as if a man was drinking his own blood. There is one plain and obvious course—the production of more wealth . . . There is only one way out. It is work. Let every Australian get his shoulder into the collar.[34]

'Work—Yes, but What Work?' asked the *Bulletin*. Erecting 'pyramids and statues of JUPITER'? Building 'a cathedral or fighting a bigger man than yourself about nothing in particular'? The construction 'with money borrowed at 6 per cent. of the railway from Dryvale in the county of nowhere to Bone Mountain in the county of Gordelpus'? It derided soldier settlement schemes as examples of misdirected energy and wasted money.

And genuine work is done at some of the places where [Hughes's] colleague MILLEN is putting returned soldiers on the land—to plough and sow and harrow three acres for six bushels of wheat, and cart water six miles and watch the horse drink half of it on the road, and listen to the mortgage gibbering by night.[35]

Soldier and closer settlement

The superficial gloss of soldier settlement was well-tarnished even by this early stage. Eight weeks after the Armistice, the New South Wales minister for Lands had already been forced on the defensive against charges 'criticising the Government relative to the settlement of returned soldiers on the land'. It was, nonetheless, conceded that among the soldier settlers caught up in the 'back-to-the-land rush' there might be 'a number of city youths, unfitted by experience, and often by temperament' to become 'tillers of the soil'. But there were still 'possibilities in most of these types'; for, if they showed 'any capacity for work,' they were 'offered every assistance to fit them to become good agriculturalists.' It was not as though anybody could come off the street and succeed on the land, as Sir Rider Haggard had suggested might have been the case. At the Macquarie Vale Soldiers' Settlement, a 'few miles from Bathurst':

Most of the settlers have had no experience in the growing of vegetables, and they have to be taught . . . Each settler receives a sustenance allowance, varying according to whether he is a single or a married man. For the married men cottage homes are provided, which are substantially in advance of anything of the kind that has ever been attempted in the district.[36]

The results from soldier settlements in mid-1919 were still 'described as remarkable'; however, individual States ran their own schemes, which remained uncoordinated federally. New South Wales claimed it was 'doing more in the direction of settling her returned soldiers on the land than any other State'. But a 'good deal of criticism' was emerging by June 'regarding the quality of certain areas of land selected and the prices paid for them, also concerning the difficulties that have had to be faced by some of the new settlers'. The back-to-the-land *Sydney Mail* remained sanguine: 'no matter what mistakes or miscalculations have been made, there can be no doubt about the success of the scheme as a whole'.[37]

Nonetheless, even in late April 1919 the ministerial equivalent of extreme caution had been expressed about the 'difficulties connected with settling a great number of men on the land'. It was admitted that possibilities for 'settlement in grazing, wheat-growing, and dairying industries were all limited owing to the present conditions'.

> For instance, dairying was limited on account of the impossibility of getting sufficient cows to provide so many new men with herds. With wheat growing they had to consider the market possibilities. When the market opened again there might be room for considerable improvements here, but at present there must be some limitation.[38]

What the 'present conditions' were, and what these 'limitations' might have been were prescribed by the ferocious drought that ravaged the continent in 1919–20. To the city bushmen and their metropolitan journals it was as though drought was as predictable as snow in Alice Springs. For soldier settlers it was desperately different. One pastoralist estimated that 'during the present drought over one million sheep have died in the Far West of New South Wales', and the 'small man out there, the settler,' was 'having a frightful time'. He believed that to put 'soldiers on such country as settlers is sending them to certain ruin'. It was 'no place for a man who does not know the country, and he must have the big area'.[39]

In the lush and fertile Hunter Valley of New South Wales, by November 1919 it was 'an uphill fight'. Many soldier settlers were 'right "up against it"', even the secretary of the returned soldiers' Baerami settlement, a man who had 'worked on the land before going to the war', had packed for the city to 'get a job'. Of the twenty-five blocks in this settlement, settlers 'on eight were about to leave, as they could manage no longer'. Those who had taken up 'farming for the first time' were 'unable to do anything, and are throwing up their blocks'. With the drought intensifying into 1920, the *Sydney Mail* offered desperate settlers a cheer-up letter.

'Two years ago I was a journalist, with twenty years experience behind me. To-day I am a sheep and dairy farmer, crammed full of hope, no loose cash, but happy in the free and independent existence of the man on the land. I am happier in my work than I have ever been in any other vocation, and I can see in the future success to the degree of my energy.' By Ex-Sergeant-Major, A.I.F.[40]

It was all a matter of the 'energy' of the settler. In the view of city bushmen, failure on the land could always be read as a lack of character making the individual less likely 'to stick it out'.

The vulnerability of an Australian back-to-the-land movement, carried out by under-capitalised would-be yeomen in a continent where the best of the land was long gone, now seems obvious. However, the rise of pastoral, political groupings and the absorption of the values of a pioneer ethos by influential members of the cultural élite meant that societal and cultural recovery from the damage of over-simplistic agrarian romanticisation would not be rapid or simple. The reality of closer, soldier or other yeoman settlement was irrelevant to the crusade to establish a new kind of civilisation. With drought already looming ominously, the *Sydney Morning Herald* continued citing Bean's ill-informed truisms and ignored the obvious. Science and technology could not 'defeat' nature. The idea that Australia could accommodate tens of millions of yeomen was, therefore, no more than a dangerous fantasy—one for which many young ex-diggers were giving up their future and that of their families.

CHAPTER SEVEN

Aliens among us

Those who are not for us are against us. (Cheers.)
W. M. Hughes (*Times* 27 August 1918)

There are Bolsheviks everywhere. Our own soil is not free from them.
Sydney *Daily Telegraph* 8 January 1919

Bolsheviks, bolsheviks, everywhere

A numerically small and essentially homogenous society, spread lumpily around a vast continent, must almost inevitably have felt threatened by nations of greater numbers, of differing culture and race, who were said to regard the habitat of this society as a 'wide, rich, undeveloped squattage'. The Victorian forts still to be found in the harbour and around the coastal foreshores of Sydney and Port Phillip Bay testify to the fear that isolation can induce; but neither the Russians nor the French were more able or likely to invade in the 1850s, 1860s or 1870s than the Japanese could land in 1913 in the north, march across the desert and invest Canberra. It is difficult to overestimate the deep-seated sense of vulnerability that caused Australians to put so much at stake in the idea of empire and the belief, still espoused by W. M. Hughes in 1919, 'that the full protection by the British Fleet was necessary for Australia's defence'.[1]

Underestimations of the geographical nature and immensity of the continent encouraged those agrarian fantasies of a vastly increased population, which, if spread evenly over the continent, would act as a deterrent to the potential invader; the continent's potential ease of conquest being exaggerated in apparent inverse proportion to its geographic dimensions. The Russo-Japanese war of 1905 intimated that Australians might be dealing in the not-distant future with an expansively minded and technologically advancing nation, making C. E. W. Bean's 1907 warning of a race war 'so ghastly and gruesome that if you want any sleep to-night you had much better not try to imagine it' seem plain commonsense. Many Australians also agreed with Social Darwinist dicta that a place in the sun was only justifiable through a process of eternal conflict: that there could be no cessation of the age-old struggle between white and non-white. Bean proclaimed in 1907 that Australia was *already* 'fighting the coloured nations of the East to-day in the same cause in which Themistocles fought with Xerxes, Pompey with Mithradates, Richard of the Lion Heart with the Saracens, or Charles Martel with the Moors'.[2]

In Great Britain, too, imperialists were warning of 'Interminable Conflict' between 'East and West' and forecasting a 'Yellow Invasion' in which 'Australia and Western America will be the scene of the next phase of the conflict with Asia'. For this Armageddon to come, Australia was poorly placed; at the current rate of population increase it would 'not be able to stem the yellow invasion for a century'. These Jeremiahs who anticipated such pessimistic scenarios were not only providing a disincentive for potential emigrants to the danger zone but—more than a generation before Singapore's fall—they were despairing at the British Empire's capacity to fight, if not on two fronts, then in two oceans. The only 'chance of salvation' for the white race in the Pacific would be if mastery passed 'into the hands of the United States'.[3]

To imperialists at Home or abroad, the prospect hardly bore thinking about. But, as well as a sense of vulnerability that was part and parcel of existing at the end of the earth, in those first decades of the century other factors abetted the development of siege mentalities and insularity in Australia: not least of these was the near-monolingual ethnicity of a white Australian society in which peoples from the Mediterranean and Asia—outside their inner-city or isolated rural cantonments—were rare enough to be regarded as exotics. The waves of multicultural immigration that had transformed the United States had no Australian counterpart until the 1950s; in 1911 Australia was probably more 'British' than Britain (figure 5).

By 1919 the threat of the Yellow Peril seemed to have moved closer through the Japanese takeover of former German possessions in the Pacific. While an Armistice applied in Europe, peace seemed far from being under guarantee. As late as March 1919, the Germans were reputedly 'discussing the Russian overtures for the formation of a German-Russian-Hungarian alliance against the Allies'; not until the ratification of the peace treaty after July 1919 would threats of the recommencement of the war abate. Australia and Britain were both by now deeply indebted and had had to endure the loss of many promising young men. Nor was there compensation for Australia in the news that between 1914 and 1918 a neutral trading competitor, Argentina, had made a commercial killing.[4]

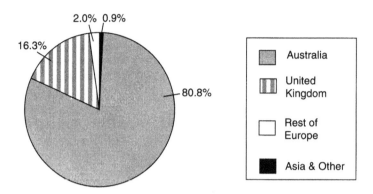

Figure 5 Australians, by birthplace: 1911
SOURCE: *Census of the Commonwealth of Australia 1911*, vol. I, Statistician's Report, pp. 145–47.

Economic matters were not all that was causing anxiety to patriotic middle-class Australians in the first year of peace. There were also the political developments that had occurred during the war and in its aftermath—even if the First World War itself had not been fought for political ideologies. Absolutist and reactionary monarchies allied with democratic republics to fight other absolutist monarchies, or allied themselves with societies that had hardly advanced politically since the Dark Ages. Socialists and internationalists, encouraged by kaisers, kings, presidents—or even social democratic prime ministers—had turned into ardent nationalists. A war often spoken of as a crusade above politics was now spawning unpalatable political offspring. Fascism was not yet known, though its precursors were present; the chief threat to civilisation, however, was said to be the ideas espoused on behalf of the proletarian masses by their agents and leaders.

If the Prussian military menace by late-1918 was in eclipse, the fight was only beginning against its alleged political successors. By transporting Lenin across the Reich and then signing a separate peace with the bolsheviks, the Germans had 'proven' their complicity with, even their control over, the bolshevik regime. Inside the Reich itself fear of 'Asiatic' bolshevism and the need for a strong German army to repel it was the theme of the day, even in liberal journals of record like the *Berliner Tageblatt*; but outside Germany, revolutionary developments and civil unrest were seen as a grand German design to bolshevise the world. Russia was to be the first pawn and Germany meant to 'disorganise its enemies by setting one against the other, by promoting internal disorder over Irish or other questions, and by financing bolsheviks and One Big

Unions'. In time an equally exaggerated connection between Judaism and bolshevism would be 'established'.[5]

For insecure wartime political leaders fighting to hold on in an unstable peace, bolshevism was a political godsend which could be used to smear any left-seeming opposition. The *Sydney Morning Herald* endorsed, even praised, such opportunism on the part of W. M. Hughes, who it hoped would 'seek at once to rid himself of certain elements of the old Liberal party' and 'convince the country that a vote for Labour to-day is really a vote for bolshevism'. The *Argus* took a similar view. With its journalists apparently fossicking through world sources to rake up stories of bolshevik atrocities, anti-bolshevism was an editorial crusade. And so the Red Scare dominated Australian conservative journals from the Armistice until the formalisation of the peace treaty.[6]

The February 1917 Russian revolution had first been interpreted as anti-German: loathing for the Czar's German-born wife—allegedly under the spell of the pacifist Rasputin—was interpreted as the motivating force behind the rising of the masses. 'The Russian Revolution is pure and simply anti-German', claimed the *Figaro* in March 1917. But while it was 'necessary that Russia remained true to the cause of the Entente and accomplishes her great destiny', the real 'lesson of Petrograd' was 'a crushing blow for Germany'. Casual optimism quickly eroded. By September the question was would the Allies be 'content to be present with arms crossed at this collapse of Russia'? or would they 'try to save the Russians who appear more and more incapable of saving themselves'? After the October revolution, no longer was it pretended that the Allies might gain from developments in Russia, which now represented a threat to established orders in nations whose working classes had bled in a cause that for many was increasingly obscure.[7]

That year, 1917, was a bad year for the Entente. Despite calls for 'no more Sommes', the British army had been wasted in inconclusive slogging matches at Arras and Ypres, while the French, fighting en masse since August 1914, were brought to mutiny by the Nivelle offensive. By year's end the events in Russia, although disguised at the time, constituted another disaster on a disheartening list.

For the first time in the world, a purely socialist minister proclaimed himself the master of a country and so realised the golden dream cherished by Engels and Marx: social revolution by the monopolisation of power . . . Already, at the Soviet, visionaries and traitors were announcing the fall of thrones and of governments under the irresistible wave of the proletariat of the world. And, in this collective madness, the like of which only the middle ages had known examples, could be distinguished above all the funeral knell of an immense country.[8]

By January 1918 the Russian people were ruled by the 'caricature' of a government, in which 'visions of slavery and of tyranny, successions of abuse and of violence, pretence of social progress and a real return to Barbary', represented the true 'spectacle of Petrograd under the Bolshevik regime of terror'. But the Treaty of Brest-Litovsk ended any illusions the Allies might have held of affecting political developments. Russia was now almost a German colony; Petrograd on the first May Day of the New Era was filled with 'German ex-prisoners of war freely promenading' in 'prewar uniforms'. The Germans were 'now the masters there'. Amidst this turmoil was another development of, as yet, hardly more than marginal interest—the apparent appropriation by a totalitarian regime of a modernist art form.

> The mayoral palace is decorated with three immense futurist paintings. Opposite, the Hotel Astoria also has one. Futurism has become the official art, I would say almost the academic Bolshevik art . . . immense paintings covering sometimes the whole complete facade of a house offer witness to the joy of artists celebrating the 1st of May and the arrival of the new era of universal happiness.[9]

The Entente now faced a contagious political virus, which was capable of spreading revolution among war-weary working-class masses and infecting them through its radicalising art. Germany's part in Lenin's rise enabled them to infer German machinations behind the scenes. 'The Kaiser organised the bolshevik Revolution' the *Figaro* cried, offering as proof 'seven publications reproducing a series of official documents that American agents seized in Russia'. Germany had been preparing 'its plans for world conquest before the assassination at Sarajevo'. It was now clear that Lenin, Trotsky, 'and their principle associates' were 'German agents in the pay of Germany'. The German High Command had organised the bolshevik revolution 'down to the finest detail', plunging Russia 'into an orgy of crimes unsurpassed in history'. It alone was responsible for the 'Russian Plague', when it transported in 'deluxe carriages' the 'Bolshevik rats who spread the plague in Russia'.[10]

The wild man from Australia

It was into this hysterical ambience, in the northern summer of 1918, that W. M. Hughes made his re-entry onto the European stage. By now, crushing the Reds was as important to him as defeating the Hun: they may have been indistinguishable. During his first wartime European visit in 1916, his determination to crush Germany and his espousal of an imperial destiny had been widely welcomed, in London and in Paris, too, where he was described as one of 'the most striking figures' at the Allied Economic Conference. The English it was said, 'rightly' considered him 'already as one of the most remarkable men of the Empire. This impression is today shared by all those who've been able to approach him.' By 1918 the empire was taking the major role on the western front and the Australian prime minister's agenda reflected his increased importance.[11]

By 1918, too, the Germans were taking the 'Wild Man from Australia' seriously; it is testament to the irritation he was causing that the *Berliner Tageblatt* should devote an editorial to him during the critical period following 'Germany's Black Day'. In the war Australia, a 'country of the most glaringly contradictory political, also particularly military-political, contrasts', was permitting its sons to be sacrificed on the altars of English imperialism and Hughes's personal ambition. Hughes had become a menace to 'the point where not long ago in the House of Lords he was given unambiguous advice to abide by the basic rules of etiquette, which apply even to an Australian'. This he disregarded, by 'meddling in things which were none of his business. Hopefully Hughes won't take this advice too much to heart, and make up his mind to go home too early'.[12]

Hinting at divisions in enemy alliances was a frequently used editorial device on all sides, which does not mean there was never any fire behind the smoke. The man stalking the corridors of imperial power in 1918 was not quite the calm consensus-seeking statesmanlike W. M. Hughes who had gazed out earnestly from his official portrait in 1916. Nor had he merely come to Europe to pay 'tribute to the splendid work of the Australian troops in the last big offensive on the Western front'. As had occurred in 1916, he was once more adopted by the French right, but now for his 'anti-pacifist and anti-bolshevik crusade'. This 'ferociously anti-bolshevik' ex-trade-unionist was also 'the most ardent of imperialists, in the good sense of the word'.

> From the first minute he was the implacable enemy of the Germans . . . [taking] all necessary measures to eradicate from Australia the tentacles of the German octopus. He made the Australians vote on conscription. He failed through the manoeuvres of the Irish Catholic clergy and Irish Catholic trade-unionists . . . But at the general elections which followed, Hughes and his colleagues defeated their adversaries and Australia is today unanimous in its approval of the extremist anti-German politics [la politique anti-germanique à outrance] of its Prime Minister.[13]

Hughes had 'converted Australia to his ideas', using 'good sense with a clarity and logic that could be envied by the clearest thinkers of the Latin race'. But if the French saw him as a fellow Celt, the Germans had reason

to see the last of him with his denunciations of their appeal for peace
by negotiation and warnings against 'the danger of Germany's insidious
attempt to divide the Allies and deceive the workers'.

> We dare not be meal-mouthed, lulled into false security while this poison does
> its deadly work ... The pacifist is at best the unwitting agent of our
> enemy ... doing the enemy's dirty work. We must fight the 'peace by nego-
> tiation' cry as our soldiers and sailors are fighting in the field. (Cheers.)[14]

Hughes was also making enemies among the prewar British politicians,
many still in power, who he claimed had 'left our citadels open to the
enemy'. Had he not 'advocated compulsory service in England in 1907
as I did in Australia'? If Britain had been 'a quarter as well prepared on
land as she was on sea Germany would never have dared to make war.
(Cheers.)'[15]

Hughes had been in international-statesman mode since his arrival in
Europe, and was not confined to hectoring the politicians of the Motherland. Italians, too, were counselled to turn away 'from the siren voice of
the Bolshevist and the pacifist'. The 'disaster of Caporetto' provided a
'warning which I am sure Italy will not need to have twice repeated'. Italian
troops had been undermined by 'the insidious and treacherous propaganda
of the Bolshevist, the Internationalist, and the German agent', and Italy
should 'profit by this lesson', and close 'her ears to all this chanting humbug
about internationalism'. Pacifism, internationalisation, the Sinn Fein and
bolshevism: all were, in Hughes's view, aspects of an evil against which
only nationalism and patriotism could prevail. By now, French anti-bolsh-
eviks were already forging connections between pan-Germanism and Prussian militarism and, latterly, Judaism, though an 'immortal' of the French
Academy, and editor-in-chief of the *Figaro*, Alfred Capus, as late as September 1918 had still not inculpated the Jews.

> Bolshevik atrocities, German atrocities, the two terrors are controlled and
> issue from the same abyss ... It is therefore logical that the Bolsheviks have
> become the auxiliaries of Germany and have recourse to this system of terror
> that we have seen functioning for four years in the invaded countries ...
> When they unite, as in the current connections between imperialist Germany
> and bolshevism, we watch the entire universe upset by this monstrous
> association.[16]

Jews, capitalists and bolsheviks

After October 1917 the Jewish connection became an issue: if Trotsky
was a Jew, were Lenin and other prominent bolsheviks also perhaps

Jews? On 14 September *L'Illustration*'s correspondent offered what seemed to be proof of a more intimate and fundamental Jewish involvement in Russian bolshevism. The 'more one studies this second revolution, the more one is convinced that bolshevism is a Jewish movement'.

> [Everywhere] in Petrograd, in Moscow, in the provinces, in all the police stations, in the suburban offices, in Smolny, in the old ministries, in the Soviets, I've only met Jews and still more Jews.
>
> A Jew, this suburban commissar, a former broker, with a bourgeois double-chin. A Jew, this bank superintendent, very elegant in the latest thing in neckties and his fancy waistcoat. A Jew again, this tax inspector with the hooked nose: he understands wonderfully how to pressure the bourgeoisie to make good the deficit of the Bolshevik budget which rises, for the half-year of 1918, to 14 billion roubles![17]

By mistreating their Jews, the Russians had brought calamity upon themselves. Jews were now returning as 'internationalists, because they've not felt the gentleness of the motherland'. Sour at heart, 'full of hate and bitterness, indifferent to suffering, grasping', they wanted 'to make others suffer as they had suffered'. Their 'vengeance was terrible and bloody'.[18]

Australia was remote from the tumult and shouting of revolution but it was not insulated against the shock waves. Industrial tensions in the aftermath of the conscription battles were high, and a sizeable Irish Australian element was now tainted with 'disloyalty' along with the anti-conscription rump of the Australian Labor Party. If nationalism was to be the defence against the 'siren voice of the Bolshevist and the pacifist', then Australia's newly gained nationhood was yet to be tested politically: it was unknown whether Australians would take their lead from the 'classlessness' of the Australian Imperial Force (AIF), or whether it would be business as usual on a turbulent industrial front. Industrial action could be made to seem as unpatriotic as it had been in the war, with anything threatening to the established cultural or economic fabric blamed upon importations extrinsic to British ways. In 1919 the Red Scare was as alive as it would ever be in the 1950s; through the fear and reaction it created, it would help anaesthetise the cultural life of a generation.[19]

For journals like the Sydney *Daily Telegraph*, two months after the Armistice bolshevism was already a 'very real foe' that was 'threatening this country, and every other country'. It could 'wreak a havoc worse than that which the plague now being beaten back from North Head has caused in others of the countries it has devastated'.

> Bolshevikism [*sic*] reduces the countries over which it gets mastery to a worse form of slavery than militarism, and until it is rooted out of Europe civilisation will remain under a menace more deadly than that from which the overthrow

of Germany has set it free . . . [Civilisation] can afford to take no chances, either here or elsewhere.[20]

Nor did it require imagination to implicate an Australian Labor Party carrying motions 'expressing sympathy with the Bolsheviks'. Had not the Trades and Labor Council tarred 'itself with Bolshevism's brush' by supporting a movement now steeping 'Russia in blood and debauchery', and about to bring 'about a similar state of things in Germany'?[21]

The federal government was 'carefully watching in Australia events which savor of Bolshevik tendencies'. Claiming to be 'in possession of several reports bearing on happenings not above suspicion', it sought to prevent the entry of bolshevik propaganda 'which may endanger the Commonwealth'. In late-January 1919 Australians received further warnings about 'that hideous thing born of the agony of once mighty Russia'. Bolshevism, or any of the malaises associated with it, was un-British.

> The madness which had sundered the Russian Empire and caused unimaginable woe and injury to the workers themselves was a false growth, which . . . like the threatened visitation of the dreaded pneumonic influenza, should be promptly met and finally destroyed, ere it tainted the atmosphere of any of the wide lands peopled by men of our common British stock.[22]

The *Sydney Mail* announced a 'scheme of the Bolsheviks (or Spartacusians) for revolutionary conquest'. The bolshevik government had 'plans for a revolutionary conquest, and was raising an immense army to carry out its plans'.

> We have a million men to-day, and will double our strength in six months. The Hungarians will soon join us . . . Then the Red Flag will be carried into Austria. As soon as we cross the German frontier the greater part of Germany . . . will rally to Bolshevism in order to escape crushing peace terms. We shall then have millions of trained German soldiers at our disposal. There will be no difficulty in organising an army of 5,000,000 men with which to overwhelm Western Europe.[23]

The bolshevik crisis raised another insidious problem. The 'great want of the Commonwealth' was still population, but what if Australia took in immigrants infected by bolshevism? The possibility of a political and class-based quarantine was canvassed as early as January 1919.

> Bolshevism, acting on the disturbed mentality of the European masses caused by war conditions, has greatly increased . . . It is for self-protection against Bolsheviks and their like that America is about to prohibit general immigration.

We, therefore, should also adopt some selective method for the same purpose.[24]

Considering that the likely infectious class was 'sufficiently represented' in Australian society, why risk an influx that might 'turn the whole course of our destiny wry'?

In April 1919 the reaction against bolshevism in Australia became tangible. In Brisbane 'nine men were proceeded against for having carried the red flag in a procession through the streets'. One, Hermann Bykoff, claimed he 'had been stabbed and beaten with sticks by some ignorant and probably drunken soldiers'. This self-confessed Industrial Workers of the World (IWW) sympathiser and Russian 'Maximalist' received six months in gaol. Bykoff was described by the magistrate as a 'boisterous person' who was apparently 'under the impression that if any laws in Australia were regarded unfavourably by him he could defy them with impunity'. The Queensland Returned Soldiers League responded with a 'vigilance committee' that was 'assured of a big financial backing'. To the League, people of German or Russian origin were likely bolsheviks. It 'had the names of 64 Russians and Germans working in the Ipswich railway workshops while 300 or 400 returned men were walking the streets of Brisbane looking for work'. By 7 April the vigilante idea was taking on proto-fascistic overtones.

> At a meeting in the Exhibition grounds this afternoon under the auspices of the Returned Sailors and Soldiers Imperial League of Australia about 2,000 volunteers were enrolled as an army to fight disloyalty . . . The commanding officers addressed the various sections, and in every case impressed the fact that they had been banded together with one object—the upholding of law and order.[25]

This was not great news for Australian democracy, but the action of the ex-soldiers was read as a display of worthy patriotism. W. M. Hughes also took the formation of a White Army in his stride, telling reporters in London that he 'was delighted with the way Australian soldiers had dealt with the Brisbane Bolsheviks'.[26]

In April 1919 Hughes announced that while the signing of peace would 'bring to an end the special circumstances which brought about the formation of the National party on its present basis', the danger posed by undesirable elements necessitated its continuing existence.

> Though the war is over . . . it is inconceivable that the strong party which has grown up to combat all undesirable elements in the community, such as the Bolsheviks, the I.W.W., and the Sinn Fein, should completely disintegrate. These forces have still to be reckoned with, and, in the coming fight, all who

desire the conservation of law and order, and the maintenance of the integrity of the Empire, must combine to defeat them.[27]

Outside signs were not promising, adding an apparent sense of urgency to Hughes's appeal. Although Germany was 'dethroned as a world power', there was still evidence of 'serious coquetting on the part of the German governing classes—particularly the militarists, with the Bolsheviks'. So the Germans were now contemplating the 'alternative of "going Bolshevik" and dragging the world down with them', in the belief that Germany would 'recover more rapidly than other nations'.[28]

When it came to promoting the Red Scare, the *Argus* was an incomparably prolific scaremonger. But its editorial comment was often thoughtful, as when it attempted an analysis of the phenomenon. Discounting the idea that bolshevism was 'a kind of epidemic or plague which is both infectious and contagious', that may have an "explosive" outbreak in any community', the *Argus* saw it instead as 'a door opened into the primeval savagery of human nature'.

> Bolshevism is an open door into the meaning of history and the strangeness of human nature; not an external disease, not an alien germ foreign to humanity which has had an exuberant culture within humanity, but just the opening of a door into the mind and character of humanity, showing its possibilities and its mystery, and giving a key to its growth.[29]

It was, thus, a symptom of a general human decline caused by the loss of the best in war. Just as 'during the long ages the human race, by natural selection, built up certain strong, useful, powerful stocks [so] during the short historic period these stocks are being destroyed, the human race is consuming but not renewing its capital, the species is deteriorating'.

> In 1789, as in 1871, men broke away from the gains and restraints of the past, led by the glory of a vision of the triumph of mankind over all their ills. Their programme was as beautiful as a dream. But the reality was butchery ... When they broke away from the restraints which mankind had built up, then human nature fell back on Nature, and it was revealed in all its possibilities of animalism.[30]

Such critical introspection was rare, not only in Australia. The German ex-kaiser was not one equipped to add much to the sum of understanding on the topic. Evidently concerned at his place in history now that he was credited with making Lenin's success possible, he explained to an interviewer in Holland that bolshevism was 'a criminal alias for Freemasonry, and Freemasonry for him is "Satanism"'. And with pejoratives like

'Bolshevik', 'I.W.W.', 'Sinn Fein' and now 'Satanism' available to put into disrepute any idea that was disliked, not even the aspirations of Australia's original inhabitants were immune. 'I.W.W. doctrines', it was claimed, had 'penetrated to the aborigines in the Northern Territory'. Jimmy Nundal, described as 'an aboriginal I.W.W., only more so', had 'induced five other boys from the dormitory to leave and "make corroboree"'. In this same report mention was made of 'rumours of massacres of blacks' but 'it had not yet been possible to investigate them'.[31]

With his party constantly being tarred with the bolshevik brush, Labor leader J. H. Scullin counter-attacked. Despite 'the "new war-hoop" of Bolshevism', the war had not been the work of labour agitators. 'The bloodshed, the destruction, and the colossal lawlessness were planned by mighty rulers, and their aristocratic secret service, with its devilish diplomacy, urged on by the Tory press, the mouthpiece of capitalism.' These 'minions of the capitalists, guilty of the blood of millions, dare to charge the workers with the unholy desire of plunging the country into the throes of red revolution'. Although Scullin's disavowal of bolshevism was 'welcomed by all', the *Argus*, speaking on behalf of 'the public', asked whether this was 'not inconsistent with the eager acceptance by the party of the support of sympathisers with Bolshevism'. It would be 'better satisfied with the character of the official party if it would expel from its ranks the Bolsheviks who infest the movement'. If this was not done, 'the public will rightly conclude that zeal in the defence of the Empire is more abominable in the eyes of Labour than is Bolshevism'. The Labor Party was not helping itself with motions for 'the speedy triumph of Bolshevism in every country', even if the phrase 'bloodless Bolshevism' was inserted as an afterthought—considering 'the welter of bloodshed in which Bolshevism moves', the idea of 'bloodless Bolshevism' represented 'a contradiction in terms'. And the Victorian Labor Conference was still 'full of war approval'.

'The forcible seizures of banks and bank funds, of factories and warehouses, as tending to bring about the common ownership and workers' management of the means of production, have the same objects as the international Labour movement in general and the Australian Labour party in particular,' says the resolution, and therefore the Labour conference wishes speedy success to the cause.[32]

By June, with the formal ratification of the peace treaty now seen as inevitable and Germany's real weakness all too apparent, the heyday of the Red Scare had passed. The *Age* now attempted objectivity. 'The suggestion that Germany will patch up an alliance with Russia', so as 'to defeat the peace terms, emanates from the type of mind which matches a fearful joy from dire forebodings'.

> While, temporarily, Germany may be very weak, she can gain no strength from alliance with a national paralytic . . . [The] present regime in Russia is nearing its end, and . . . Bolshevism, the rule of Lenin and Trotsky, will give place to another authority . . . More significant still is the desperate anxiety of the once arrogant Lenin to negotiate with any and every country for recognition and support.[33]

This did not mean Australians should not remain on guard at home against the 'Labor extremist, or "industrialist" ' who knew 'neither country nor countrymen'. The *Age* marshalled considerable invective against the internationalist who insulted 'the Australian by introducing the foreign language of servitude'. These 'grovelling foreign doctrines, the product of tyranny and serfdom' were 'grossly repugnant to this free country, yet the Labor conferences are foul with them'.[34]

In Sydney the *Sydney Morning Herald* was not letting down its guard. It was 'well to remember', it warned on the day before Peace Day, 'that we are still at war. The enemy in our midst is active, and he is aiming at the destruction of all we hold dear.' Labor leaders were asserting the 'inevitableness and righteousness of a class war of extermination', through the:

> overthrow of all authority except that of the Big Union boss; an endorsement of the horrors of Bolshevism, on the score that the end justifies the means . . . the repudiation of war loans, and by parity of reasoning all other loans and Government obligations to the 'capitalists;' the abolition of 'wage slavery,' and the dethronement of the 'present capitalist system'.[35]

'A.D.', writing for the same paper, described bolshevism as a 'practical exposition of the doctrines of the Germans Nietzsche and Haeckel', which 'glorified the might of force'. It represented a 'serious menace to the peace of Europe, and to a successful League of Nations'. H. N. P. Sloman, in an article which might have been written for the likes of 'A.D.', attempted to put the Red Scare into a more realistic perspective.

> We have only to instance the loose use of a term like Bolshevism by people who could give no clear account of its main principles. Our intellectual dishonesty is the amazement of the French, who are a fearlessly logical people, and who, consequently, will . . . solve the many problems of reconstruction far more easily than we shall.[36]

As year's end approached it was clear that the Red horde would not race across Europe within the foreseeable future. The unholy alliance of Prussian Junker and Soviet Commissar had come to nothing. With political leaders in Russia making tentative overtures to the West, Lloyd George accepted that 'Bolshevism could not be suppressed by the sword, and that other methods must finally be employed'. In Australia this new note was endorsed. The *Sydney Morning Herald* acknowledged that 'even to treat with Russia' would be 'tantamount to an admission that our previous policy . . . had been a blunder', but accepted there was no choice.

> Only the other day we heard of the systematic 'colonisation' of certain western provinces of Russia by discharged German soldiers. Lenin has frankly said that if Britain refuses to listen he will woo Germany. Any policy which would have the effect of driving Russia into Germany's arms may well prove disastrous in the future; any settlement by which such a consummation can be avoided deserves serious consideration.[37]

Its weekly stablemate continued to beat up the Red Scare. In its Christmas 1919 issue, the *Sydney Mail* warned of a 'fresh European conflagration' inspired by overwhelming bolshevik successes in Russia. Civilisation may 'soon be faced by something even more fiendish than the war out of which we have just emerged'. While bolshevik propagandists were 'trying to convince the people that they represent nothing less than a new form of democracy', Australians should 'keep prominently before us the awful picture of the track they have laid waste through Russia by murder, rapine, torture, and every kind of hellish crime'.

> No matter what ideals, if any, may have been held originally, by the leaders of this terrible creed, it is apparent to-day that it represents . . . a homicidal madness born of the desire for easily-gotten wealth, fanned by the excitement of blood and carried on by a current of the most shameless debauchery in fine fettle.[38]

So far the French had led the way the way in depicting bolshevism as a Jewish-led movement. The Jewish–bolshevik conspiracy theory as accepted fact appeared in Australia by, at the latest, March 1920. 'If there were any doubts about the Lenin–Trotsky regime, they would be dissipated by the circumstantial account of the experiences of Mr. John Pollock, a Fellow of Trinity College, Cambridge, as related in "The Bolshevik Adventure" '.

> The Bolshevik leaders, he said, are nearly all Jews . . . [who] fled or were exiled to Germany and America; they have no sympathy with Russian nationality . . . [They] desire to root out all sense of patriotism. To do that

they have tried to crush or destroy the educated classes in Russia who were pro-Ally and generally pro-British.[39]

In April 1920 this new perspective on bolshevism's origins had filtered through to a *Sydney Morning Herald* leader writer, to whom Lenin was the creature of a 'motley gang of clever Jews' that by implication now controlled the Soviet state.[40]

With central Europe in crisis and the prewar textile region of France and Belgium devastated, Australia now seemed temporarily cut off from traditional centres of cultural input as well as major sources of national income. So far as Germany, at least, was concerned, W. M. Hughes was determined to make this temporary isolation permanent. The courage and combativeness that helped make him an effective war-leader were not necessarily virtues in peacetime. Though prepared to squeeze Germany for the last drop of reparations, he would not permit the open trade policies that would provide the Germans with access to markets and, therefore, the means to earn money and pay them off. The unbolted door of free trade, which had 'left our citadels open to the enemy' now had to be bolted and locked. Australia 'could not afford and would not allow goods of all nationalities to flood the country'. In promoting his 'Closed Door Policy', he elaborated upon what 'all nationalities' might mean. With prewar markets in disarray or rejected, the empire could hardly fail to take on crucial significance.

> Mr. Hughes . . . said he was glad to know that Australia had proved herself worthy of being part of the Empire. Peace was at last practicable. We would invite disaster if we opened our gates to Germany. He would never be a party thereto, but he would do all he could to develop Empire trade with the Allies.[41]

The argument in favour of tariffs is that they can allow infant industries the chance to develop through relatively unimpeded access to local markets, until they might compete in their own right against the products of the world. What Hughes was proposing was that tariffs and restrictive practices be used to cripple Germany. If the Germans were 'helped or permitted to resume trade with Great Britain, as they did before the war', then Germany would gradually 'creep back to her old position, and the war will have been fought in vain'. While he 'hoped that the terms of peace would compel Germany to repair the ravages and cost of the war', how could they if cut off from their traditional markets? And would Germany be the only loser?[42]

Not only had Australia been one of Germany's major trading partners, but the balance of trade had been one-sidedly in Australia's favour

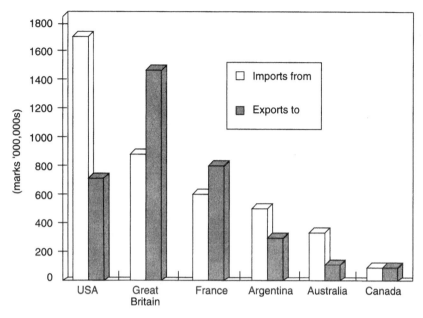

Figure 6 Germany—Imports from and Exports to: 1913 (in marks '000,000)
SOURCE: *'La "carte de guerre" economique par André Fribourg', L'Illustration,* 20 July

(figure 6). By quarantining itself from German products and denying Germans access to the market which had formerly existed for them, the Commonwealth was not only cutting itself off from a major source of prewar wealth and the supplier of some of the best machine tools in the world, it was steering itself further away from a position of real national independence and consolidating its position as an imperial dependency.

As for the former Allies that Hughes might deign to do business with, the United States was near self-sufficiency in respect of what Australia produced and Hughes's attitude was hostile to the wartime Asian ally to the north. As early as January 1919, it was noted of the 'interviews which Mr. Hughes gave to the American Press' that they had already 'offended the Japanese'. At the Versailles Peace Conference Japan had asked for racial equality in its dealings with the occidental powers and confirmation of the right of its citizens to enter their domains, but Hughes was adamantly opposed. Baron Makino for the Japanese insisted that Japan, while 'not too proud to fight', was 'too proud to accept a position of racial inferiority in her dealings with the associated nations'. Japan sought 'nothing but justice'. But while Hughes denied that 'the rejection of the Japanese amendment of the Covenant of the League of Nations' was due to him, Australia had been 'the only country objecting to the amendment'—an objection based ingenuously, not on racial grounds, but on the excuse that 'Japan does not enjoy the same industrial conditions'.[43]

His stand was greeted enthusiastically in Australia. To the *Bulletin* he might have been the same old 'lamentable Foreign-trader and importer's hack', with an 'out-of-date schoolbook idea of political economy', but Australia had 'every right to be grateful to HUGHES', for 'the stand he took over Japan's demand for the free admission of its people to all Allied countries'. But the racial slight simmered in Japan. When Japan had 'signified her willingness to participate in a League of Nations', it was because 'the League was based upon justice and humanity'. Now the Japanese were having second thoughts, as they saw how the notion of 'racial equality based upon justice and equality has been rejected by advocates of the League'. They seemed amazed that this 'representative of a British colony' who had so 'bitterly opposed' Japan's 'racial equality amendment', could have finally gained such international support.[44]

Anti-Alien Law

On 24 April 1920 Australia responded to the international climate by introducing anti-alien laws, which defined as aliens anyone who was not British, and potentially included the British-born, even Australian-born wife of an 'alien'. The relatives of Australian Irish in the Free State were now aliens too. Anyone 'who communicates with an alien . . . before registration will be liable to a penalty. An aliens' registration officer may require from any alien his signature and finger prints . . . The penalty for breach of the provisions will be a fine of £100 or six months imprisonment.'

> The bill defines an alien as any person over the age of 16 years who is not of British nationality, and includes the wife of an alien . . . Children of aliens must be registered on reaching the age of 16 years, the parent or parents being liable for any breach of this provision . . . No alien may change his abode without giving notice . . . An alien may not change his name without notification . . . and persons believed to be aliens must give the information sought from them.[45]

Two days later, in a post-Anzac Day address, the 'digger Bishop', George Merrick Long, asked for an 'an expurgation from Australian ideas of all those things that are alien to real Australians'. He 'feared for Australia, because there was not enough of a note of real Australian patriotism to be found'. The true patriot could only look to the classless example of the AIF.

On the hills of Gallipoli and the sands of Anzac Cove and in France they were one. We must learn to think things out as Australians engaged in our own special problems . . . If I wanted to be a real Australian Protectionist I would be against the madness of bringing in holus bolus strange ideals in an effort to plank them down as suitable for Australia itself.[46]

Anti-Red hysteria was now beginning to impinge on high culture. During the war it had been simple for anti-modernist critics to deride modernism as unpatriotic, and showing symptoms more readily associated with the enemy. The fact that, by 1920, futurism could now officially be tied to bolshevism offered a new field of possibilities to criticisms of this kind. This appreciation was not long in coming to Australia. At about the time the 'digger Bishop' was pronouncing on the need to be a 'real Australian Protectionist', in the foreword to his scholarly monograph on the colonial painter Conrad Martens, Lionel Lindsay used the occasion to vent his outrage against 'strange ideals' in the contemporary world of art. Martens was an early example for Australians of a dedicated artist, working in the long-established tradition that Lindsay admired. It was to artists of this type, rooted firmly in the national soil that Australians should look now. The tolerance of 1913 was light years away. Modernity had become the enemy. The futurist was now the 'Bolshevist in Art'; and his dealer almost certainly had to be, what else but, a Jew?[47]

CHAPTER EIGHT

Blues in the Jazz Age

The old world is dead. Let it die.

'Foreword', *Vision II* August 1923

One great trouble in this young country is that there is a certain diffidence in the Australian mind as to whether, owing to its extreme youth and distance from Grandpa G. Britain, it is possible to produce anything as good as is done by those important people.

Margaret Preston, 'Australian Artists Versus Art' (*Art in Australia: The Art of the Year* (3rd series) No. 26, December 1928)

The new futurist menace

In March 1919, with the formal ratification of peace months away and editors in Paris and Berlin behaving as though the war had never ended, space was found in pages in the *Figaro* for an essay by Eugène Montfort on the subject of 'New Art'. Although it had once hosted Marinetti's manifestos, the *Figaro* was the epitome of patriotic and bourgeois respectability. Its art reviews prior to and during the war were written as though there was no such thing as cubism, except when it could be derided and spelt with a 'k'. The treatment now showed no improvement. Cubism was a symptom of the 'malaise that the introduction into our universe of so many elements showing new aspects has caused in architecture, in street art, exterior art', a malaise which had 'produced, in intimate art, in house art, in painting, the phenomenon so curious that it has been called cubism'.

When you walk across Paris you only see now squares, rectangles, cubes and circles: our taxis, our auto buses and our tramways. These *mécaniques*, as Laurent Tailhade called them with disgust, are of an extraordinary ugliness . . . It can not be surprising therefore that our recent painters, having deserted the countryside and being completely city dwellers, have been affected by all these inhuman forms? And what's so surprising about cubism coming from this?[1]

160

This ugly art, it continued, with its references to 'the drawings of infants, and to the sculptures of Negroes' would surely by now have been on its last legs were it not for 'gallery dealers' still marketing cubism as the latest thing, promoting it on the art market 'as one would sell a gold mine or an oil field at the stock exchange'.[2]

If there was a commercial killing to be made from modern art in Paris in 1919 or 1920, D. H. Kahnweiler, the man whose 'head for business' made Picasso—as well as one or two others—millionaires, would have been surprised. A German citizen who felt no sympathy for his Father-land's cause, Kahnweiler spent the war in Switzerland. Now, back in Paris, he was forced to bid at auction for Braques, Picassos and Légers that had been confiscated as reparations by the French state from his pre-war collection. He was able to buy most of them back at modest prices. There were few other bidders; the idea that modern art was a fad that would soon go away was already in vogue. Even Picasso 'the father of cubism, a fellow with a fine sense of humour' was supposed to be 'abandoning cubism. Between two cubes he's now making academic paintings.'[3]

With an alliance through futurism to Judaic bolshevism well 'estab-lished', the standard interwar critiques of modernist art were already evident in March 1919: it was a fad that would soon go away; it was made by rootless, urban cosmopolitans with foreign-sounding names, people who set themselves apart from the world of true beauty that lay in the countryside; its value was inflated out of all proportion by a few dealers, who often, like Kahnweiler, were of Jewish origin. The idea of the Jewish dealer with shady links to a world of conspiratorial high finance had yet to surface on the Australian art scene in 1920, but Lionel Lindsay's likening of futurists to bolshevists and anarchist bomb-throwers suggests that most of the rhetoric of anti-modernism was formed before the appearance in Australia of the first modern-looking European paint-ings. These arrived in 1923, ten years after John Baillie's exhibition of English post-impressionism was shown in New Zealand; and though 'Modern art was minimally represented', Mary Eagle notes, 'it received most attention'—but not, it seems, positive attention. The exhibition's function seems to have been therapeutically but clinically pedagogic: the New South Wales governor, opening it, ventured the opinion that he 'was glad to see that Australian artists had not succumbed to the temp-tation of "advanced art"'.[4]

It was the last exhibition of its kind for fifteen years. If an 'exchange of artistic ideas' was necessary 'for any art to survive', this apparently did not mean ideas contaminated by modern attitudes. A cultural quarantine is never meant to be all-inclusive, merely to obstruct or if possible bar entry to that which the quarantiners feel should be excluded in the interest of those who identify with their values: such a quarantine was now being massaged into place. The enthusiasm with which, in 1913, Roland Wakelin and his associates were able to receive the 'first glimmerings of what is now called "modern art"' was no longer regarded as mere youthful innocence, but as hinting at decadent preoccupations. By the early 1920s these artists were running foul of an Establishment that looked askance at their use of 'vibrating colour' and the 'new ideas in composition' that they picked up from reproduction of work making headway in the old world. Word of this experimentation had leaked out and, in a move that almost typifies 1920s-style reaction, a special meeting of the Council of the Royal Art Society was called 'to stop the rot'. Fortunately, their teacher Dattilo Rubbo 'bravely defended us and finally won the day'. It was a Pyrrhic victory for Wakelin, and one that Rubbo years later felt bitter about. Wakelin's work was now 'extremely unpopular with critics and public'.[5]

De Mestre and Wakelin did have a brief moment of glory in 1919, in a joint exhibition which may have left them with a degree of hopeful anticipation. Despite 'its oddity and militant avant-gardism, the critics liked their colour music; only Howard Ashton dismissed it as "elaborate and pretentious bosh"'. But the following years became plagued with uncertainty. 'We were repeatedly told that we were "on the wrong track" and really wondered if we were, and I think, unconsciously drifted in some degree back towards the academic.' Still, on the votes of George Lambert and Thea Proctor, de Mestre won the New South Wales Society of Artists' Travelling Scholarship in 1923, and in 1924 travelled with Wakelin to London and Paris, where 'the sight of the original works by the Masters we respected stirred again our old enthusiasm. We decided that on our return to Australia we would pursue our former course without compromise.' In 1928 Wakelin noted a 'more general interest awakening in our work'; but, at the onset of the Depression, de Mestre, 'finding little understanding and encouragement at that time', exiled himself in London.[6]

What must even now be asked of the members of the Royal Art Society who tried to censure the activities of three relatively youthful art students is: who or what was on trial? Why was such action necessary? These same self-appointed judges and jurors accepted in the name of art the supposedly shocking anti-wowser pictures of Norman Lindsay; the point being that, while Lindsay's art was degrading to women, it set few formal or aesthetic challenges either to the elders of the Royal Art Society or to the petit bourgeois 'wowsers' it was meant to disturb. It still looked like art, especially the Salon art of the late Belle Époque, deriving from a tradition of depicting nudes whose precursors could be found on the walls of Pompeii. Lindsay's art could be understood and valued for its technical, formal and auto-erotic qualities without going too deeply into its alleged meaning. But art that did not show clear evidence of the traditional skills or the usual methods of applying paint, even at the uncomplicated levels demanded by three young Sydney art school graduates, was too much.

Absurd 'intellectual' pressures were applied in the early 1920s to these artists, so they compromised, and wondered whether they mightn't be on a false path; their creativity withered for lack of meaningful criticism or even want of a sympathetic dealer who might have tided them over or provided moral support. In these devitalising years Australian culture lost much, not only from these members of what until recently was dismissed as 'a weak minority movement among Australian painters of the 1920s and early 1930s', but from others who might have entered with them into the challenges they had only begun to meet. These early post-impressionists became the victims of time and place; a situation which de Mestre recognised in 1930, when he like Streeton before him flew the coop and became 'in his art an Englishman'.[7]

In this reactionary climate, culture was already so marginalised that there was no need for an authoritarian-minded politician to threaten to cock his pistol at the sound of the word. Apathy ruled except when it came to sport, which had succeeded war as the peacetime expression of the national character. With art, literature and theatre at base level on the scale of priorities, Sydney Ure Smith was like a voice in the wilderness when he complained that 'the arts of painting and drawing were only mentioned on the occasion of exhibitions'. In fact fine art, or at least painting, was the best served of those named, as it at least received some press coverage. But Ure Smith had a point. Where in 1913 newspaper columns had included essays 'Concerning Modernism' and about 'The Philosophy of Nietzsche', or 'Art Study in London', this now seemed esoteric for readers fed a diet of bolshevik atrocities, war heroics and a great mass of horse-racing and other sporting trivia. The society had already moved some distance down a path deplored by C. E. W. Bean in 1943.[8]

> When nations or classes have to find their amusements in gambling—whether in expensive, elaborate entertainments (in horse-and-dog racing, huge public spectacles, prize fights, commercialized sport) or in simple gambling such as 'Two Up'—it is a sure sign of under-education.[9]

Ironically, the direct beneficiaries of the climate of the early interwar years post-1919 were conservative upholders of the art Establishment. With few young men showing interest in art and the younger women marginalised or patronised, it was no challenge to preserve the Australian art world as an Edwardian gentleman's club, contentedly encouraging the practices of the late-nineteenth century. Few outside the art world were likely to care what happened: it was a climate made-to-order for the special interest groupings of which, aside from the nationalists—who gravitated naturally to landscape and found sustenance in the Anzac legend and the traditional bush myths of the 1890s—the most influential were centred around *Vision* magazine. These self-styled Dionysians held themselves above conventional nationalism, and certainly above the modern world, in their attempt the create an 'Hellenic world of strong and free spirits'. While it may have seemed 'futile to try to answer that voice from Australia where so little of the mechanism of culture exists', those who heard 'Nietzsche's voice calling desperately for a return to courage, laughter and beauty' could rest assured that, given 'the sterility of Europe, a response here would mean that Australia alone maintains stability and vitality'.[10]

Grocers' lads a-plenty

While this Dionysian ideology was 'under any possible examination of it, precisely the opposite of national or Australian in outlook', the seeds of P. R. Stephensen's Australia First Movement were already planted. Australia could and should go it alone, dragging the rest of the world or inspiring it to follow. The imperial traditions and ambiguous nature of Australian nationality forbade such extreme positions among the landscapists, who probably preferred their isolationism inside the empire. The landscapists and the Dionysians did, however, interact and the distinctions between them were always clearly defined. Both of these groupings gained from what was believed to have been the experience of the war: the heirs of the city bushmen could find in the Anzac legend validations of a pioneering tradition that provided their art with its 'racial' justification; drawing on the nonpareil quality and fame of Australian soldiers, the Dionysians took the chance to present themselves as the élite of what was already a racial élite, one that really was capable of taking up the mantle of Hellenic and Roman civilisation.[11]

There was nothing egalitarian about this. The Australian working-class might have proven itself in war the finest of its class in the world—but 'of its class' was the operative term. In Norman Lindsay's opinion the role of the lower orders was to help feed the artist and then, if necessary, die for him so that he might continue to create 'beauty'. In response to Elioth Gruner's enlistment in the Australian Imperial Force (AIF), Lindsay was 'forced to recall Nature's forgotten formula of forgotten values'. The lives of men were 'not of equal value, though all may rise to an equal greatness in the moment of sacrifice'.

> War brings out reverence for man to a common level, but our hearts must recoil from this democracy of Death. Grocers' lads may be had in plenty, but there is no choice of Gruners so that we may pick one for war and let the other remain to develop his creed of beauty.[12]

To be an artist was to belong to a class and caste. That a grocer's lad might be educated to become a fine artist did not enter Norman's calculations, nor those of his brother Lionel, nor those of J. S. MacDonald, who fully endorsed Lionel's belief that 'enforced education has more to answer for than the cheap press and over industrialisation'.[13]

Indeed, the Anzac legend's egalitarian facade was probably distasteful to them. Lionel Lindsay claimed that Australian 'racial consciousness' had been 'emphasised', not by Gallipoli, but by the 'federation of the States'. Otherwise, his essay for the catalogue of the London Royal Academy Australian exhibition of 1923 followed well-traced lines.

> The Englishman, transmuted by climate and different conditions, had changed a little his skin and modified not a little his ideas. He had become the Australian, that more casual Englishman, whose character had been formed by drought and flood, vast distances and the sovereignty of the sun.[14]

In his ability to express uniquely Australian qualities, Lindsay believed Streeton to be peerless. 'I never stand before a good Australian "Streeton" but my mind lightens, and the love of my native land stirs my blood.' But in taking us 'back to the bush townships of our childhood', Streeton also made use of a sense of 'that "limpedezza" dear to Nietzsche, which is also the characteristic of our own atmosphere'.[15]

Nietzsche was back. A prophet who had been reviled in the Anglo-Saxon world between 1914 and 1918 was now an apostle of reaction to artists with whom he may have had little sympathy. Others in Europe were endorsing Nietzsche in ways that would have shocked those seeking to remake Western civilisation through art and 'creative effort'. Ernst Jünger's ideas on beauty were as antipodal to Australian Nietzscheans as was his concept of the *Übermensch*.

> Today we are writing poetry out of steel and struggle for power in battles in which events mesh together with the precision of machines. In these battles on land, on water, and in the air there lay a beauty that we are able to anticipate. There the hot will of the blood restrains and then expresses itself through the dominance of technical wonder works of power.[16]

Instead of the machine that 'destroys all culture', here the machine dictated for the better modern cultural evolution. Nor would Jünger have felt other than distaste for the idea of sending grocers' boys to war as proxies while artists toyed with beauty. War was an indispensable personal process, part of 'becoming modern'—a state Jünger aspired to with as much will as the Australian Nietzscheans sought to avoid it. And no one can doubt Jünger's claim to a Nietzschean heritage.

> Yes, the machine is beautiful. It must be beautiful for him who loves life in all life's fullness and power. The machine must be incorporated into what Nietzsche . . . meant when he . . . insisted that life is not only a merciless struggle for survival but also possesses a will to higher and deeper goals . . . The artistic individual, who suddenly sees in technics the totality [*Ganzheit*] instead of a functional assembly of iron parts . . . is finding the deeper and more elevated satisfactions of the machine, as the engineer or socialist is.[17]

The critics were not impressed

The 1923 London exhibition that occasioned Lionel Lindsay's praise of Streeton's talent for 'limpedezza' had actually been opposed by Streeton and other Victorians, who considered it dominated by members of the Sydney Society of Artists. It was. Not that those Victorians were likely to have objected at the central thrust, which was, according to Mary Eagle, encouraged by the 'tremendous hope that old-fashioned Australian art might prove its excellence world-wide'. But it was also an opportunity to attempt to export Norman Lindsay's 'personal dream of an Australian Renaissance' to London; for it was to landscape and to the 'imaginative work of Norman Lindsay' that Lionel Lindsay expected the 'English people to look for whatever is fresh and original in Australian art'. London critics were unimpressed. To Norman Lindsay, a man who in his own land had been told that his etchings were 'strangely original' and 'absolutely unlike anybody else's work, save, perhaps, that of Goya and Rembrandt', and even that his name 'will, no doubt, in time be classed with them', it must have been depressing. The response of P. G. Konody, the 'celebrated critic', was typical. Admitting that Norman Lindsay's drawings might 'astonish the observer by their amazing dexterity', he felt nonetheless that the work did not really 'bear looking into'.

> [For] while there is the greatest power of draughtsmanship displayed in rendering the textures of velvet, lace, flesh and sky, there is also any amount of bad drawing. His types too, are debased, and the same frenzy . . . with blatant

nudity and excessive finery incongruously thrown together, stands him in
even less stead in the water-colours. In many of these there is much positively
bad drawing, the faults of draughtsmanship being all the more accentuated by
bad colour.[18]

There was little for the artist to salvage from this, and even less from Sir
William Orpen's opinion: 'Norman Lindsay's figures are extremely badly
drawn, certainly vulgar, and show no sense of design'. In Lindsay's
defence it was said that 'his best work has not come across the water',
though why an artist would not send his best for this important exhibition is unclear.[19]

The previous Australian painting exhibition in London had been in
1898, and Konody later recalled how Streeton's art had come 'upon us
as a delightful revelation of personal vision and sound technical accomplishment'. Just as many survey exhibitions of its kind did, the 1923
exhibition claimed a hypothetical objectivity that was hard to justify in
practice. When one considers the numbers of women artists and the part
they were beginning to play, they were woefully under-represented;
while de Mestre, of the more or less acceptable modernists, was represented by one tame work, selector and organiser Ure Smith was able to
show six. No one questioned Hans Heysen's Australian prestige, but
twelve works displayed and reproduced was a lot, given that Thea
Proctor and Margaret Preston were restricted to two each. It further hints
at dubious selection politics that J. S. MacDonald—then *Art in Australia*'s Melbourne correspondent and soon to be appointed director of the
New South Wales National Gallery—was represented while Cossington
Smith and Wakelin were not. In 1913 MacDonald had been attempting
to make his career, not as a critic or curator, but as an artist; the *Bulletin*
then noted that 'Jimmy Macdonald [*sic*]' had been seen 'chasing sunshine
for the last few weeks ... at Ringwood'—Jimmy, the 'son of lawyer
Macdonald, is out after the Wynne Prize'. While serving in France in
1918, MacDonald came second in an official AIF painting competition
judged by Will Dyson, Fred Leist and John Longstaff and was promptly
appointed to be a kind of artist-in-residence accompanying the Fifth Division. He didn't last long. Bean, who had control over war artists, wrote
in August that he had 'examined the A.I.F. Artists work and consider that
in the case of Scott, McCubbin, Benson and Longstaff they should be
confirmed in their appointments'. MacDonald however, was 'unfitted for
the work by reason of his shaky health'.[20]

MacDonald's inclusion in an exhibition of art in 1923 was a political
gesture that could only have added to the overwhelming conservatism
of the show. A more progressive-looking feel may well have been possible using the work available in Australia, but it could not have been

selected by a committee representing the Royal Art Society and *Art in Australia*. Founded in 1916, *Art in Australia* had its clique of contributors, editors and favoured artists that in 1923 formed an Establishment centred around Ure Smith, Leon Gellert, Bertram Stevens, the Lindsay brothers and MacDonald. In the early-1920s these men published each other's poems and reviewed each other's art, in a generally uncritical manner. No work hinting at change was welcome at the expense of art which reinforced their values. When *Vision* cursed the Edwardians of the 'generation which produced the war' as 'damned utterly', it did not mean those Edwardians.[21]

If the organisers had intended an open and fair survey, Lionel Lindsay's introductory catalogue essay did not reflect it. He revelled in Somerset Maugham's charge that Australian art was 'old fashioned', as though the alternative to old-fashioned art was cultural bolshevism.

> It would seem that a certain stigma attaches itself to the epithet 'old fashioned,' as to one not quite alive. But if to be alive is to be one of the Red Army of art that has trampled upon the great tradition we inherit from the Greeks, then I am thankful for the appellation, and find in Mr. Maugham's implication of provincialism a delicate compliment.[22]

His validation for backwardness was found among the greats of the past. Australians were 'in good company, with old-fashioned folk like Constable and Corot; like Vermeer and Rembrandt and all the great ones who founded their art upon sincerity of mind and skill of hand'. Sincerity was thus equated with old-fashioned virtue, while insincerity marked the modern. As to provincialism, this too was not 'so bad a thing', for it offered 'escape from all the revolutionary manias of a rotted world' and left Australia 'unaffected by the "stunt" art that has ravaged the older civilizations'. Lindsay allowed his anti-modernism free fall, attacking 'all the patent art theories' which were now 'exposed, stark and coverless, the degeneration of the creative instinct in art; all that base egotism, brother of the Revolution, which strikes in envious hate, upwards, at everything most noble in man's past achievement'.[23]

As though to suggest a certain tolerance, Lindsay also pointed to the presence in the exhibition of works by 'Miss Proctor, Mrs. Preston and Mr. John Moore', who were 'with the modern movement. Their work has its roots in Europe; its inspiration owes nothing to this country. These are cosmopolitans.' With so little of value to be found in the art of the modern world and his marginalisation of those who tried to find value in it, he could claim with justice and perhaps a sense of relief that Australia had 'nothing to teach the Motherland'. English critics agreed that their artists had nothing to learn from it, and Konody felt it a pity there was 'such a sameness, a kind of monotony, lack of experiment, about the whole exhibition'.

> In a country having no tradition of its own, one would have expected new, virile modes of expression to have been adopted, so that the vigorous strength of a young nation might be expressed. Instead of which all its artists are employing the technique and using the spectacles of painters in these islands of fifteen or twenty years ago.[24]

Australians exalted their landscape tradition but Konody was less sure: it was 'impossible to say' there was 'such a thing as an Australian School in the sense that one may speak of the Canadian School of landscape painting'. Otherwise, only two 'paintings of flowers by Miss Margaret Preston' provided a 'new note in the show'. The London *Daily Telegraph* swam against the critical tide, reading as 'a sign of health' the absence 'of impressionism or post-impressionism, or any artistic mannerism', but the *Times* critic shared Konody's disappointment. He expected that 'in a new country like Australia new movements would find a rich soil for development', but the:

> converse seems to have been the case. Perhaps the very distance of Australia from the old-world centres of art, and incidentally from their occasional fads and fancies, has prevented the successive waves of the various modern movements from reaching its shores.[25]

While this response must have been disappointing to artists and organisers alike, its consequences were not all bad. The young, vigorous nation had been rebuffed, not for adolescent high jinks, but for being pedestrian and boring. What should have been of concern to Australians was that they were considered, not as inheritors of the great traditions of the past, but as provincials caught up in the dated fashions of academic and Salon art of the *fin de siècle*.

Lionel Lindsay's catalogue essay made him appear the natural spokesman to Australians now aware of English criticisms. In 'regard to the criticism levelled', he now claimed that with 'few exceptions the press had been very fair', and that the 'dissatisfaction which had been expressed with the work was notably that of a small coterie'. For this he blamed 'Sir William Orpen, who was a fellow member of the Chelsea Arts Club with Mr. Arthur Streeton and Mr. George Lambert'. Though Orpen had not 'been alone in his display of bad taste', he had broken one of the golden rules.

> It had been laid down as an axiom that as regarded the work of contemporaries an artist might write an appreciation of good work, but it was not within

his province to attack their failings. It was pre-eminently a case in which silence was more eloquent than words.[26]

Lindsay was now distancing himself from involvement in the exhibition. He would have 'preferred to send the 1922 Exhibition [Society of Artists] to England' but the selection committee 'took care of that'. He noted, too, that Arthur Streeton 'was bitterly opposed to the exhibition, but Mr. Ure-Smith wished to show how much our art has progressed during the quarter of a century which has elapsed since the last purely Australian exhibition was held in London'.[27]

Vision fails

By 1924 Norman Lindsay might have been wondering whether the gods were against him: not only had he been singled out by English critics for rough handling, but *Vision* had just failed after less than twelve months in existence. In hindsight it is not difficult to see why *Vision* failed, for it was as much an organ of virulent anti-modernist propaganda as a literary magazine. Norman Lindsay had originally toyed with the idea of such a publication in 1920, at the time when he fell out with Bertram Stevens, a generous and tolerant friend to artists and writers who was then editing *Art in Australia*. What led to the falling out was that Stevens had reprinted in *Home* Somerset Maugham's criticisms of Australian art. As a result, Lindsay attacked his former friend, who had edited his pen drawings in 1918 and first 'encouraged him to write fiction', as 'an epitome of the whole human race, muddled, helpless, moribund and stupid'. Not content with such verbal abuse, he sought to have *Art in Australia* 'renamed "Vision" and to have his son Jack replace Stevens as editor'.[28]

In this he failed, but it did not deter him from using *Art in Australia* as a forum for his ideas: in an editorial section in 1922, entitled 'The Quick and the Dead', he assaulted the modern world.

I hate to think Shakespeare has lasted 300 years.

—Bernard Shaw

Of course, but then, Shaw is dead. Naturally he is annoyed with Shakespeare for being alive.

* * * *

Shakespeare (to Shaw); 'I had a momentary terror that you were going to praise me.' . . .

* * * *

Rubens (to Velasquez): 'I commiserate with you, my poor friend: the twentieth century admires you.' . . .

* * * *

Any Modern: 'I'm alive, but Shakespeare, he is dead, poor fellow.'[29]

In those years anything modern drew the ire of Norman Lindsay and like-minded commentators. Bernard Hall, the long-serving director of the Victorian National Gallery and consultant to the War Memorial Art Committee wondered, in view of the 'far-reaching changes and significant tendencies' whether it was possible that one was 'witnessing the gradual passing of the period of Art and the coming of the Mechanical age'. Could this be 'a distinctive as well as penultimate phase of every old and declining civilisation? Man, plus machinery, spells super-man, but dependence upon machinery must in the end overmaster and destroy him—first spiritually, then intellectually, and last, physically.' Hall's description of man's decline mirror-imaged what C. E. W. Bean been saying, for Bean had always placed physical decline first.[30]

With the advent of *Vision* in 1923, a vehicle of expression existed for a full-blooded assault on modernity; on its art, its literature, its machines, its cities, its mobs and its fascination with primitive or tribal art. 'It is the sense of Vision that is lacking in all Modernism which sets its criterion in a morass of primitive sensibility.' 'Primitivism in the Arts' was the product of 'a deliberate intellectual choice'; unless 'consciousness' took an 'upward turn, vitality will sink too low to ever recover'. The war was only the latest 'surface expression of a devitalisation that went far deeper than political causes or all the laws of the belly stated by Marx'.

> In England such people as Macaulay, Ruskin and Matthew Arnold hardened all moral values to their limit in smugness and self-satisfaction. In France the rationalist, the intellect that petrifies all to stone, cried triumphantly: 'We have dissected a corpse and learnt all about life.'[31]

The 'bludgeon of English morality' and the 'dissecting-knife of French rationality' had brought on the European 'paralysis of spirit'. There had 'never been a single profundity uttered in the French tongue', James Cunninghame cried. It was the 'French mind' rather than Prussian militarism that had 'devastated Europe'.

> Wherever we find a dead or disintegrated condition of mind, or wherever mind becomes diseased and poisonous, we can almost always trace to France the cause of the decline . . . The French are primarily shallow; their frantic response to the emotion of the moment is a mark of febrility, and their intellectual perception goes no deeper.[32]

France, 'more than any other country', was in 'the hands of the sick in spirit'. It was a 'morass of depression and ugliness' in which the primitives and 'the depressed ones' had conquered, and 'struck at the mental stability of the world'. Without Paris, 'Modernism could never have got the hold it has'. Disgust and horror were 'the only emotions' the French had 'to transmit; these are the basic elements of their reaction to life, and they are the absolute antithesis of the Dionysiac acceptance of earth'.[33]

With English life 'swaddled in shame' and France damned as 'The Abyss', where could the younger generation—'those who had experience in the war and yet had sufficient courage to survive its horror' and on whose shoulders lay 'the burden of the world to-day'—turn for inspiration and ideas? To Nietzsche, inwards and to the distant past seemed to be the answer, at least for *Vision*'s 'legionnaires of the Roman spirit to reconstruct earth'. The idea of a renaissance of world civilisation led by Australian supporters of the Lindsay aesthetic was in vindication of their 'possession of Youth' and rejection of 'all that is hieroglyphic, or weary and depressed'. If Australia, 'alone in the world', was doing this, then 'both the onslaught of expression and the analytic attack must begin from here also'. The ideas or art of a small or medium-sized nation can make disproportionate impressions on the world stage—as demonstrated by the overseas impact of Australian film in the 1970s and 1980s and by Aboriginal painting in more recent years, though this was probably less a possibility in the more parochially spirited 1920s. But the idea that the local branch of the Dionysians might have led the world into another Renaissance appears a monumental conceit.[34]

A reader tackling *Vision* today would quickly glean what it hated, but not much else. To counter the evils of modernity, it offered nostalgia for an idealised Greco-Roman civilisation, together with racism, and Nietzschean one-liners. As such, its ideology was in the mainstream with other anti-modernist reactionary movements elsewhere, which is a clue as to why it could only remain parochial and derivative. What *Vision* may now explain about Australian culture in the early 1920s could be related as much to the magazine's formal layout as to its predictability of content: Norman Lindsay's archaic-looking pen-drawings of fauns, mythical beasts and adolescent nymphets were offset by slick new-objectivity advertisements extolling modernist consumer products—whatever caused *Vision* to fail, it could hardly have been lack of advertising.

The final edition of *Vision* was followed, the month after, by an issue of *Art in Australia* carrying English reviews of the Australian exhibition in London. In the unsympathetic responses to Norman Lindsay's work existed evidence that the visual manifestations of the Lindsay aesthetic were not exportable. English comments were taken to heart by some local artists, among them Elioth Gruner, who benefited from 'constructive comments' made by Sir William Orpen 'that were to change Gruner's style dramatically'. In that case the exercise of sending art for the approval of Mother was not all wasted. A chastening of local conceits made a few locals better for it; it sent Norman Lindsay huffing back to Springwood and helped keep brother Lionel off the scene while he spent 'unnumbered hours' looking at 'exhibitions of contemporary art' in European galleries, none of which, as far as the short-term acceptance of contemporary art was concerned, could be considered as unsatisfactory.[35]

Lionel Lindsay's salad days came after the London Exhibition and its tame Wembley follow-up in 1924. Where the 1923 exhibition tried to assert that something had changed in the antipodes since 1898, the Australian Pavilion at Wembley—by hanging a few modern de Mestres alongside Lamberts and Streetons from the turn of the century—stated that hardly anything had. Lionel Lindsay's arrival in London would have seen him considered, if at all, as just another colonial artist—and a very middle-aged one at that—trying to make a mark for himself in an already very crowded London art world. Australian artists after the near-debacle of 1923 were hardly sought after. But insofar as any colonial could 'make it' in those days, Lionel Lindsay did. What brother Norman could never achieve, Lionel managed.[36]

For the Australian artist who seeks 'an important place within the development of a truly international and cross-cultural arts practice' the road to success is clearly no easy one. It was easier in 1927, when 'international' to an Australian meant London primarily and then perhaps Paris; but to be taken seriously and to rate headlines in the British journals of that day was no mean feat either. The acclaim attending Lindsay's work had nothing to do with any radical conceptual or formal realisations; rather it was owing to technical redevelopments in the medium of print-making that Lindsay had resurrected from near disuse. Naturally, the local press dropped its general disinterest in art matters to find praise for the local boy made good. 'Dame Margaret Greville's taunt that Australia has no art', the Sydney *Daily Guardian* gloated, 'has been strikingly refuted by the success of Lionel Lindsay's exhibition'. Not only were the London critics hailing him 'as a master', but even 'before the show opened £200 worth of etchings and dry-points were sold'.[37]

The London *Morning Post* recognised his skill, but saw nothing particularly Australian in it. 'Mr. Lionel Lindsay (of Sydney, New South Wales) might be of Amsterdam, Madrid, London, or Philadelphia so far as his art is concerned'.

> It may be that we expect too much from young Australia in the way of new
> vision and original ideas in art . . .
>   Australia, like other countries of the Empire, is working in an age of prep-
> aration, and there are signs, especially in Canada, that art is slowly but surely
> passing its cosmopolitan stage to one of experiment, which will lead to self-
> determination and national independence.[38]

It took the Melbourne *Herald* six weeks to find out, but when it did, on
25 June 1927, it greeted the news with banner headlines: 'Lionel Lindsay's Triumph—Big London Show—64 Pictures Sold in First 48 Hours—
London, May 3'.

> Australian Art may now wear a new and brilliant feather in its best cap. The
> exhibition of etchings and drypoints by Lionel Lindsay, which is being held
> this week in the Colnaghi Galleries in New Bond Street, according to London
> art critics, has caused more interest and speedier sales than any exhibition in
> London during the past few years.[39]

A generous man to those whose work he understood, Lindsay shared his
moment of glory with compatriots. There was 'no artist over here who
is doing better pencil portraits than those of George Lambert; no one is
painting landscape better than Will Ashton; Hans Heysen and Streeton
are doing work that compares with anything I have seen in any of the
big art centres.' Which wasn't necessarily saying much; of '"modern" art
in London, Paris, Rome, Vienna and Berlin', he thought 'much would
"die an early death"', noting encouragingly that Australia 'fortunately'
was 'too far away to be influenced to any extent by these rapidly-changing fashions in art'.[40]

'I am no Anti-Semite . . . but . . . '

As a celebrity-etcher, Lindsay was 'honoured to propose the toast on
etching' at the Royal Academy, and asked the gentlemen of the Academy
whether he might attack ' "the modernist movement when I've spoken
to the toast!" "Splendid," was their acclamation'. Modernism, behind
which lurked the spectre of the Jew, was responsible for the ills of British
society.

> What is wrong with your public and the times? You all know the reason—
> this malady of modern art. And who is to blame for the continental infec-
> tion?—the press and a people that England has so long welcomed, the Jews.
> I am no Anti-Semite . . . but I am decidedly hostile to the dealers who bribe
> a corrupt press.[41]

He later reckoned this his finest hour: he 'certainly never held an audience better'. As he left the banquet 'Sir Edwin Lutyens, the great architect, embraced me, and kissed me on both cheeks, a courtesy I returned, as he said, "At last an honest man"'. The following morning, the 'consequences' of his 'courageous' denunciation were made plain to him by the dealer Harold Wright. '"I hear you made a great speech at the banquet and attacked the Jewish dealers. Your work won't get further notices in any of the papers that have modernist tendencies."' But Lindsay, after sell-out shows, was now going home. How English critics might have treated him was not, for the moment, a primary consideration.[42]

He was now an imperial celebrity and, as was the custom in those days of sea voyages, returning celebrities were greeted by journalists at each Australian landfall. For the Perth *Daily News*, Lindsay announced 'that English art at present stands considerably the highest in the world'. The standard in France had 'gone down, and art in Germany is practically dead'. For the Melbourne *Sun News Pictorial* he launched into a favourite topic.

> 'This modern movement is loaded with the leprosy of the ages,' he said vigorously. 'It is disgusting to any man with a sane eye. Only a few cranks are buying it. They lay on paint worse than house-painters.'
>
> It is easy to call the modern movement 'jazz in art,' he says, but thinks it is not so easily explained. 'It is an expression of the profound unrest of a world that has been lacerated and wounded, and seeks to find an anodyne and a new stimulus.'[43]

Under the headline 'Modern Art is Dangerous', he followed up with much of the same in Sydney, claiming that a 'lot of people abroad are afraid to say anything against modern art, because they may be regarded as old fogies'. But as far as modernism was concerned Lindsay conceded that all was not necessarily lost, but that 'some good has to come out of it, where artists have been capable of using it'.[44]

Indeed, following the 1923 London exhibition there had been change that warranted a certain degree of circumspection before launching into anti-modernist tirades. Margaret Preston's comparatively enthusiastic English press reception in 1923 seems to have earned the regard of Sydney Ure Smith, who was becoming 'a great admirer of her work'. Perhaps under Preston's influence, *Art in Australia* in the latter part of the 1920s came increasingly to appear as a peacemaker between warring factions, placing itself above the petty squabble. This 'continuous spectacle of rancorous hostilities' between 'equally bitter and inflexible' camps would 'bring about a destructive state of bewilderment and misgiving'.

> So strong is the prejudice against the introduction of Modernism—a prejudice that extends to our Gallery Trustees, to our critics and to our Press, which prefers to condemn before even examining, that it is left to a few enterprising art dealers and a few itinerant picture-buyers to introduce the work of the modern world to Australia.[45]

Where once *Art in Australia* had been content to let the rest of the world—excluding the Motherland—go by, it now criticised the 'international silence' of Australia, 'which fear and a mistaken form of self-protection have forbidden us to break', and backed this with articles by Roland Wakelin and Preston, and by reproducing modernistic works by Preston, de Mestre and Kenneth MacQueen.[46]

The following year, in 1929, in an issue devoted to 'A Contemporary Group of Australian Artists', *Art in Australia* could claim 'with all modesty' to be an upholder of the Modern Movement. It found local 'prejudice against the more modern art ... difficult to understand.' Despite the acceptance of modern designs in 'clothing, curtains, furniture, rugs, glass, china and lighting fixtures', much of which was 'designed by modern artists':

> [We] are confronted with the inconsistency of a woman in a gown designed by a modern French artist and completely surrounded by the products of a modern decorative artist's brain, condemning 'modern' work, by an Australian artist, which would fit so well with her modern home. To quite a number of people, anything modern can be appreciated in anything except pictures.[47]

Basil Burdett, who had established the Macquarie Galleries with John Young in 1925 and stood against MacDonald for the directorship of the New South Wales Gallery in 1927, wrote deploring the prejudices that generated 'luke-warm, sometimes ill-mannered and vindictive—and frequently ignorant—press responses to modern work. He warned that the 'history of art should teach us caution'; for we have seen 'how the Whistlers, the Constables, the Manets, live on their work to confound the parochialism of their day'. Australians knew that these masters had 'come to take their place naturally in the body of an art which is infinite in the variety of its expression. Similarly, we have among us artists who are concerned not to destroy what we know, but to amplify it.' Despite this, Australian modernists were still faced with a parochial hostility in which an 'unfamiliar turn of style can give rise to vague but sinister suspicions in this country. The words "modern," "cubist," "futurist," are murmured with all the sinister import with which a total misunderstanding of their real meaning can invest them.'[48]

Burdett then attempted to lay to rest some of the sacred cows of Australian cultural isolationism. Accepting that 'we must strive for expression in our own way' did not mean 'ignoring the gifts and influences brought back to us by our returning students and painters'. While a great deal had been 'talked about the value, and conversely, the disadvantages of our distance from the old world', no people could 'legislate for a country's artistic development, nor can we produce it artificially; it must happen within its own conditions'. This, he hoped, would be 'great in its own particular way, and so of peculiar significance to the world'. But in the view of the economic crisis now beginning to beset the country, even inspirational words about art and culture must have seemed almost irrelevant. The effects of the depression reached deep into society. With artists now wondering where the next meal might come from, there were more vital issues at stake than provincialism and internationalism.[49]

CHAPTER NINE

Fissures in the imperial landscape

The idea of empire as a solar system with England as the sun and the colonies as satellites was out of date. Alongside the development of transport should go the development of oversea settlement. Emigration was an evil word. A man could not emigrate to Australia. The word should be reserved for foreign countries.
Leo Amery (cited in *Morning Post* [London] 14 November 1919)

We have a sort of loose, changeable machinery for the standing together of the English-speaking sea States which we call the British Empire.
C. E. W. Bean (*In Your Hands, Australians*, 1918 p. 45)

A wider patriotism

The federated and equal imperial partnership that Leo Amery envisaged in 1919 was to be the final phase of a project, based on compromise, which grew out of unease in Victorian times with the rising tide of colonial nationalism. To imperialists at Home and abroad not only was the example of ancient Rome salutary but more recently there was the great Hispanic empire of Latin America. It had fragmented into a checkerboard of independent republics whose *hispanidad* remained as a vestigial attachment of linguistic and minor cultural ties: Argentina, the most prosperous of the secession states, had even attempted to align itself economically with the British Empire. The lesson seemed clear. Even great empires could succumb to peripheral nationalism. If the British Empire was not to disperse in a medley of weak post-colonial republics then a compromise version of self-government was a necessity, for the long-term interests of Great Britain as much as that of the colonies.

Dominion status diffused breakaway sentiments, not to mention republican ones, and made it possible for the ex-colonials to indulge beliefs or even fantasies in an exclusive domestic nationality, while offering them another shared nationality secure in a uniquely powerful and well-protected trading and cultural bloc. To English imperialists, in theory at least, 'importing' foodstuffs from Canada or New Zealand was no different to bringing them from Wales. This didn't quite work in practice, as the increasing British trade and investment in the 'Sixth Dominion', Argentina, might suggest. Nor was blood always thicker than water to hardheaded dominion businessmen. If the Germans or Americans could supply as good or better-quality goods on time, at an agreeable price and provide efficient after-sales service, then business would go their way.

To imperialists in the dominions 'The Spirit of Patriotism' by Edwardian times was expressed by the 'Imperial sentiment, this wider patriotism', which meant 'the sure growth of a sane local patriotism, based on a full knowledge of our past history'. This ideal was bound to be more reassuring and attractive to English-, Scottish- or Welsh-born leaders in the former colonies—or those that still insisted on calling most of the British Isles 'Home'—than to the sizeable Irish Australian, French Canadian or Afrikaner minority populations. Doubts about the benefits and eternal viability of the empire were not restricted to ethnic minorities, either. Political groups on the left at Home and overseas wondered whether the interests of the British industrial worker were really best served by policies that protected the interests of Australian fruit and sugar farmers, or whether the implied disincentive to dominion manufacturing was really in the interests of ambitious Australian manual workers seeking more challenging or better-paid employment. Some even doubted whether the empire was anything more than a temporary arrangement of convenience that would serve until something better came along. 'The history of the British Empire', the *Bulletin* argued in 1913, declaring its hostility to the creation of a chair of Imperial History at Sydney University, 'is very largely the story of muddling through'.

> There has scarcely been a trace of design or indication of national purpose in the whole business. India was a great field of plunder; Canada a chance possession taken from the French with the idea of hurting France . . . Australia was a convenient dumping ground for convicts which happened to attract a little settlement . . . South Africa, after being taken from the Dutch, was turned down as useless, and at last taken over again because it lay on the road to India . . . In connection with none of these had England any settled policy or national plan.[1]

At that time neither the *Bulletin* nor those upholders of an 'Australian socialist tradition' who dreamt 'of founding in our remote seas an ideal republic from which the evils of the old world would be shut out' were ready to cut the painter. The world was dangerous and the empire remained the imperfect means to the end implied in a powerful, self-contained and heavily populated Australia: if any proof were needed, the Great War was it. Although it is difficult to tell what Germany's attitude to the dominions might have been in the event of a German victory, the major units of the British Empire were as one in rallying against a threat perceived to be as great to them as to the Mother-country herself.[2]

The dominions' baptisms of fire were initially portrayed in the main-stream press of the empire as proof of imperial and racial solidarity: but not for long. By 1919 it had long been recognised in Australia that the Birth of the Nation was what the war was about: the nation had fought, according to Bishop Long, the 'digger Bishop', not 'for Empire or to defeat the enemy so much as to make the name of Australia honoured'. Long was no anglophile any more than was C. E. W. Bean, who saw the value of the British race as a stock for future generations of Australians, and was fond of something like a federated empire of equal parts that might even incorporate the United States of America. At Gallipoli Bean had been appalled enough by the weaknesses of a British Empire to confide to his diary: 'We don't deserve to win wars'. By 1917 he was hoping Lloyd George would 'act like either a radical or a socialist & clear out the English class system—& I wouldn't hesitate—abolish the mon-archy because it perpetuates the snobbery which paralyses England'.[3]

Even on the public record, Bean was often patronising about the Mother-country, as when in his book *In Your Hands, Australians* (1918) he described it as 'steadfast, old-fashioned, slow-going England'. But he was no upholder of the *Bulletin*'s isolated military and economic 'fortress Australia'. A heavily populated Australia, with perhaps 80 per cent of its population involved in farming and a minimal industrial infrastructure needed 'for defence—certain industries', would need great and powerful friends with their complementary industries as never before. The land 'covered with farms' was to become an integrated component in an Anglo-Saxon-dominated world order based on the apparent pre-destiny of this race at the head of the races.

> The existence of the great Anglo-Saxon Republic on the other side of the ocean is an all important fact for us; just as the existence of the great Australian State just overseas will be about the biggest fact in the world for America when we are an Anglo-Saxon State of sixty or seventy million inhabitants.[4]

What had seemed conceivable in 1919 or 1920—a future based on the eternal production of food—was less certain by 1927. Few heavily com-mitted combatant nations survived the war without economic damage. Australia was no exception. It had expanded rapidly after 1904 when rising worldwide foodstuff prices 'encouraged the Australian rural sector to diversify', and that 'greatly increased the supply of rural produce, resulting in a boom in manufacturing activity that continued until World War One'. But, as N. G. Butlin notes, 'expansion slowed between the two world wars'.

This heralded reduced growth prospects: Australia had lost the special advantage that natural resources had provided in the nineteenth century; there were severe constraints on improvements in rural productivity; and the traditional British market for Australian goods was in the doldrums. Efforts to encourage the growth of domestic population depended on relatively low productivity manufacturing. In addition, investment in infrastructure was no longer the prime mover it had been in the nineteenth century, but rather added to external indebtedness.[5]

Australia's prime minister for most of the 1920s was Stanley Melbourne Bruce. He had fought at Gallipoli but not with the Anzacs. When war came he received his commission as a Guards' officer and duly appeared on Gallipoli with the British Twenty-ninth Division. This only confirmed the impression held by many Australians, that he seemed more English than an Englishman. But while Bruce's lack of the common touch was widely deprecated in a society that liked to see itself as egalitarian, a majority of Australians continued to vote for the agrarian–conservative coalition he headed throughout the 1920s. At the beginning of 1927 he seemed at the apex of his power and prestige, having just come back from an imperial conference in London with what were portrayed as far-reaching and important achievements to his credit. He played a significant role in the conference's promotion of unity in an empire that had 'amongst its constituent parts a broader spirit of co-operation than has existed in the past'. Now, in theory at least, Australia had 'absolute autonomy without weakening the ties of Empire', which were its assurance that it 'was safe from attack.' For Bruce, in 1927 Australia was at last 'assuming the obligations of nationhood'; for many others, however, the events of 25 April 1915 signified that Australia had already been meeting these obligations.[6]

To Manning Clark, at that conference Bruce 'sanctioned the throttling of Australia, financially and economically, by the Shylocks of Great Britain'. In view of the ethnic origins wrongly attributed to Niemeyer, the man finally sent out to Australia to act in the British banks' interest, 'Shylocks' may not have been the happiest choice of words. But Australia had gone deeply, though not necessarily wisely, into debt—and for government spending to boot. Not all the fault lay with Bruce and his government. The residual debt of 1913 had blown out during the war, but successive governments thereafter had not seemed prepared to rein it in, only to compound it. Despite the rhetoric of 'obligations of nationhood', nothing of political substance had altered since 1915, while economic dependency was as high as ever: instead indebtedness to London had soared and nationhood was still defined in diffuse national–imperial terms.[7]

Ghosts in the imperial landscape

It is not perhaps coincidental that the two national–imperial artistic *tours de force* of the interwar years should both date from about the time of a rare royal visit—the pomp and circumstance of the opening of Parliament House in Canberra in 1927. Of the first of them, Streeton's *The land of the golden fleece*, Ian Burn suggests that it conveys 'a "national emotion" and "the spirit of a new order" in the postwar world'. If it does, this must mean that the 'new order' had hardly changed from the old; for, to all but the initiated, the painting could have slotted into an exhibition of the artist's early-1890s output with only slight jarring, and that a technical one. Indeed, it was now clear to all but his most fervent admirers that over the decades of English castle painting Streeton had lost a certain legerdemain. But if this 'new order' was really the old one— with the timeless and under-populated land of the golden fleece ever present and reassuring irrespective of the tumult and disorder in the international background—Australia was a kind of last refuge in empire. The empire—or rather Britain alone—underwrote Australia's role as the eternal primary producer and thus encouraged such a perception, sourced in the agrarian myth, of a privileged lifestyle in an antipodean Arcadia.[8]

In common with most works of art *The land of the golden fleece* can be read in different ways, but what is unambiguous about this painting is that it is, unmistakably, an Australian landscape. Will Longstaff's *Menin Gate at midnight*—which is supposed to share 'many similar values' with Streeton's painting—was painted by an Australian expatriate living and working in London and finally bought for the Australian government. That apart, there is nothing in the painting that specifically suggests Australia at all. The Menin Gate memorial in the old ramparts at Ieper (Ypres) in Belgian Flanders is dedicated to soldiers of the empire who fell in the Ypres salient between 1914 and 1918; it was designed by the British architect Sir Reginald Blomfield and inaugurated by Field-Marshall Plumer in 1927. In Longstaff's midnight painting, the 'overall modulated blue field is interrupted only by the eerie pale moonlit gateway and fields'. In those fields 'the spirits of dead soldiers rise up . . . their steel helmets creating the illusion of a field of poppies' (plate 11).[9]

When *Menin Gate at midnight* was seen by George V at his private viewing or the citizens of Manchester and Glasgow, it is unlikely they could have thought of Australians in other than a grander imperial grouping: they must, first of all, have thought of Englishmen or Scots. Had this painting toured the other dominions, Canadians, New Zealanders and South Africans would have been reminded of their own dead, and

Plate 11 Will Longstaff (Australia 1879–1953) *Menin Gate at midnight* 1927 oil on canvas 137 × 270 cm Australian War Memorial (9807).

These imperial ghosts struck a chord with people, which was evident from the enormous crowds the painting attracted whenever it was exhibited, and the large numbers of reproductions that were sold.

endowed the work with a specific Canadian, New Zealand or South African meaning. The spirits of the dead soldiers that rise up wearing their British helmets are the spirits of *British* soldiers; *Menin Gate at midnight* is an imperial painting, therefore, acquiring national meaning only through the context of the place in which it is displayed. In this sense, it is an appropriate painting to depict the sense of ambiguous imperial nationality prevailing in 1927. Whatever else may be said of it, it was imperial propaganda par excellence.

The big Gallipoli scandal of 1927

The sense of postwar imperial solidarity conveyed by works like *Menin Gate at midnight*—in stone or as depicted in oil-paint—or by royal official visits, or empire film quotas can be misleading. In 1927 there were rumours afoot—far from encouraging rumours to loyalists at Home or in Australia—that at one point overspilled to leave a residue of bitterness. At the centre of what for a brief time became a storm were perceptions of that most sacred of national virtues—the attitude shown by the nation's youth when first subjected to enemy fire. Antagonisms between colonial troops and Tommies had manifested themselves in the Boer War and were fairly well-known of in Edwardian times. As late as 1913 the *Bulletin* noted the superior 'self-reliance of the Australasian troops sent to the Boer War' over the 'ignorant mechanical obedience of the Tommy'.[10]

After 1914 not only were such observations unpatriotic but unless couched as the most careful hints, the censor ensured they were also impossible. After the war a gentlemanly aversion to holding up to critical gaze the inadequacies—real or imagined—of kith and kin who had fought in the same British Army became a kind of ingrained habit. Whatever tacit gentleman's agreement existed, it came publicly unstuck in 1927, however, and the very unwilling catalyst for the unsticking was the Australian official war historian. By 1927 Bean's first volumes had already appeared, and represented a mine of incalculable value to the British historian of the invasion of Turkey, Brigadier-General C. F. Aspinall-Oglander. At about that time the reciprocal custom of exchanging draft material for comment between British and Australian war historians had been instituted; so, draft copies of Aspinall-Oglander's history of the Dardanelles campaign had been sent to Bean, with the understanding that copies of this material were to be forwarded to former Australian Imperial Force (AIF) senior commanders at Gallipoli, of which there were six still living. This was duly carried out, and in early September 1927 Bean told Aspinall-Oglander that he was unimpressed with the Englishman's version of events at 'the Landing'.

I do not think the true facts of the Landing can be correctly depicted by saying (1) that the G.H.Q. plan was practicable, and (2) that the troops were brave, but did not come up to the standard that would be expected of trained soldiers, and, in particular, included an extraordinarily high percentage who would not face their duty; and that is the impression which your story, as it stands, has given me and other readers out here.[11]

Aspinall-Oglander claimed Australians at Gallipoli had exhibited cowardice, citing an officer who'd been forced to draw his pistol and threaten stragglers. While Bean now admitted that a 'small part were shirkers', he insisted that 'a great number were troops who had bona-fidely lost themselves and come back for orders'. As for the officer in question: 'The mention of M'Cay [McCay] threatening with his pistol some men whom he found behind the lines is, to anyone who knew that general, only another confirmation of his excitability and of the foolish extravagance which robbed him of the respect of the men he led'. Bean thus implied that this was an isolated action by an unstable commander, into which too much might be read. But Bean had actually been with McCay on another similar occasion and then seemed to approve of his action.[12]

> He said: 'How are the others coming on?' I looked back and said: 'I expect they'll need support pretty quickly, won't they, Sir?' We were talking about it in this spirit when M'Cay said: 'Well, Bean, this is where I suppose I have to do the damned heroic act', and up he jumped on the parapet and waved his periscope. 'Now then, which of you are Australians? Come on Australians . . . !' I saw him with a revolver in his hand—he had been talking to some chap in the trench 10 yards to my left. I heard afterwards it was a sergeant, and M'Cay threatened to shoot him if he didn't get out of the trench damned quick.[13]

Lieutenant-General Sir J. W. McCay was hardly the diggers' favourite commander: they held against him not only the infamous II Anzac Corps desert march of March 1916 but also, to some extent, the debacle at Fromelles. He had supposedly objected to the desert march; as to Fromelles, according to what Bean later wrote, McCay was no 'more responsible than the humblest private in his force'. Indeed, Lieutenant-General Sir C. B. B. White—the man 'often referred to as "the brains of the A.I.F."'— claimed in 1937 that McCay, when compared to Monash, 'was the abler soldier' despite Monash's advantage of a 'brain like that of so many of his race [that] was quick to grasp and quick to learn'. Neither White's opinion nor McCay's promotions support the suggestion of an unstable character prepared to draw a pistol on troops without reason—what Bean was now, in private, accusing him of doing.[14]

What had been a private affair between generals and historians exploded publicly on 7 October; it was the same day the *Sydney*

Morning Herald announced that Mr Lionel Lindsay, who had 'left Australia about 18 months ago', was returning to Sydney. 'English artists to-day, said Mr. Lindsay, were the best in Europe. Modern art was at a standstill, and had made no progress in the past 15 years.' The big item that day, however, was not carried by the journals of record: a former AIF general had leaked confidential information to the London *Daily Express* and the Sydney *Daily Guardian*, and from there it had spread like wildfire. 'Flung Back—Slur on Gallant Anzacs—What of Tommies!—Monash's Counter-Attack; Incomparable Diggers', were headlines greeting readers of the Sydney *Sun*.

> Now two British officers have written 'The History of the Dardanelles,' in which they state that the Australian troops who landed at Anzac were herded together on the beach, and allowed other men to storm the heights.
> This slur on 'the flower of Australian manhood' has been flung back in the teeth of those officers by Australian generals, including General Monash, who says that Dominion generals were compelled to form a very poor opinion of most of the British troops at the Landing . . .
> 'Just another of those depreciations of the Australian soldier, which appears every two or three months in England,' said Sir John Monash.[15]

Bean immediately fired off a telegram to the man who seems to have been the source of the leak, Major-General Sir John Gellibrand, then the federal member for Denison in Tasmania. 'Guardian's article today most unfairly fails recognise that Aspinall's typescript was sent us spontaneously asking for comment or suggestion and exaggerates statement by purporting quote.' But by now it was out of Gellibrand's control. It was too good a story and the press was running with it. 'Digger Officers Slate War Historians' was the Sydney *Daily Guardian* headline on 8 October. The 'Little Digger' had joined Monash in buying into the affair and now condemned as a 'Vile Slander' this 'libellous and dangerous stigma cast upon the behaviour of the Anzazc [*sic*] Division at the landing'.[16]

On 8 October the serious press tried to hose the whole thing down. Citing the opinion of 'a distinguished officer who was closely associated with the preparation of the History of Gallipoli', the Sydney *Daily Telegraph* argued that it was 'absurd and mischievous to suggest that there is ill-feeling between Australian and Home authorities'. Stories that Bean

Plate 12 Cracks in the imperial facade (*Daily Guardian* 7 October 1927, courtesy of State Library of NSW).
Impugning the Anzac legend was seen as a gross act of betrayal on 'Mother's' part, but the carefully fostered illusion of imperial solidarity was coming under pressure in other areas, too.

ANZACS "RABBLE" SAYS HISTORIAN

HIGH AUSTRALIAN OFFICERS ENRAGED AT LIE

VILEST LIBEL OF WAR

PROTEST WILL BE MADE BY OUR GREAT GENERALS

"Nothing more or less than a disorganised rabble."—How English war history proofs insult the Anzacs. Who wrote it?

Canberra, Thursday.

The immortal first Australian Division that made the name of Anzac has been grossly libelled in the yet unpublished volume of the British official history dealing with the Gallipoli landing.

Proof sheets of the contents of the volume have reached Australia, and have been the subject of indignant comment by the few whose privilege or misfortune it has been to peruse them.

Anzac "Wild Cats" Lauded by Hamilton Only Two Days Ago

GENERAL SIR IAN HAMILTON, who was C.-in-C. of the Empire troops at the Dardanelles, at a dinner in London on Wednesday, in connection with the War Office film of Gallipoli, said of the men who made The Landing:

"I always will remember the Australians and New Zealanders with rifles and bayonets, and very little else beside, fighting themselves like wild cats unto the rocks of Gallipoli.

"I have never seen anything more splendid."

SO serious, so scandalous are the allegations that the proofs were submitted in turn to Sir Harry Chauvel, Sir John Monash, Sir William Glasgow, Sir John Jellibrand, General Blamey, and Capt. C. E. W. Bean (Commonwealth Historian) in order to present a united protest against the statements made. Among the other things it is re-

corded that the Australians on the Sunday night of the landing were

"nothing more or less than a disorganised rabble." It is asserted that a vast proportion of their number were herded on the beach, while a scattered few held the heights.

The whole tenor of the book is regarded as a challenge to the authenticity of Capt. Bean's careful and painstaking record of events.

The "proof" was despatched to Australia for perusal prior to publication. The matter it contains will certainly meet with the full-throated protest of every living person in the Commonwealth.

One who is acquainted with the contents of the "History" told "The Guardian" to-day:

"It is the vilest libel of the Australian dead that has ever been put to paper."

Another Australian officer says:

"The English history was compiled by members of General Sir Ian Hamilton's staff, who lived on the Aragon. The whole army knew the headquarters ship Aragon, which rested behind the destroyer-proof booms of Mudros, many hours steam from the guns of Anzac. It was the common jibe of men who knew the ship that after the evacuation it was found almost impossible to shift her for the empty champagne bottles that clung like barnacles to her bottom."

was convening 'a conference in Sydney to refute the allegations contained in the proof copy' were simply untrue. All he had done was to suggest 'that the draft of the history of the Dardanelles campaign be sent to the generals who took part in the Gallipoli landing'. By now the Sydney *Sun*, too, was apparently beginning to entertain second thoughts: '"Example to All"—Their Everlasting Fame—Official History's Tribute', these were its follow-up headlines. In England the British official historian Sir James Edmonds was now quoted as telling the *Sun* that the draft forwarded by Aspinall 'did not contain the phrases alleging that the Anzacs were "an ill-led rabble," or anything equivalent thereto'. The British account of Gallipoli, he claimed, was 'more laudatory of the Australians than Captain Bean's own story of Anzac'. On 9 October the illustrious *Observer* entered the fray.

> Any Australian who can imagine the Anzac's part in the great war being subject to depreciation here must be extraordinarily out of touch with British opinion. The statements of Sir John Monash and Sir John Gellibrand, M.P., make readers here rub their eyes . . . It is astonishing that some responsible person did not immediately detect the absurdity of the story, and most regrettable that inflamed comment should have passed without investigation.[17]

On 11 October Bean sent a report to the minister for Defence—the ex-Fifth Division Commander Sir Thomas Glasgow—on the 'grossly inaccurate notices' that had appeared in the press. As for the 'Source of Leakage', he appeared to cover up for Gellibrand: the 'press articles were so widely inaccurate' that no real blame could be attached. 'On the whole, it at first seemed to me that someone to whom General Gellibrand had spoken had very inaccurately repeated his remarks, which thus at third or possibly fourth hand had reached both the correspondents of "The Daily Express" and "The Daily Guardian".' He knew who was responsible and, without naming him, said so in a letter dated that same day, to Sir James Edmonds.

> I have not had time to write to you fully about the deplorable publication of false reports concerning the draft of General Aspinall's history. Unofficially I may say that it is almost certain that the disclosures originated through a high military officer, who had read the draft, making inquiries of certain comrades who were present at the Landing as to facts of the 'straggling' upon that occasion.[18]

The leak had come about because a former AIF general and politician passed highly sensitive and controversial material to representatives of the popular press. The eagerness with which others who had also read Aspinall's draft, most notably Monash, jumped in indicates their depth of concern at what they considered a slur. Edmonds, having said his piece for the press, now kept his counsel. The Australian representative at the British Historical Section noted that Edmonds was 'amused at the whole affair', but handled it with 'moderation and fairness'. He was, however, disquieted that Edmonds made no mention of Bean's 'several reservations' about Aspinall's history. Nor had Edmonds been 'accurate in declaring that the British Official History treated the Australians much more generously than their own Official History'.[19]

At this point the embarrassing affair should have been over. That a less than amicable imperial relationship existed in the last war, not only between enlisted soldiers but between officers, had been confirmed at the highest level. While Monash, Gellibrand and W. M. Hughes would later recant to some extent, the only way they could really retract what they'd said was by appearing to endorse the idea that Anzacs might have shown cowardice at Gallipoli. By mid-October most participants probably wished the whole affair would just go away. *Smith's Weekly* beat it up again, inferring a conspiracy of silence that was not wholly inappropriate, at the centre of which were Bean and the Australian prime minister.

> How annoyed the A.I.F. official historian (Mr. Bean) was that the public should get to hear of it is already known, but it will be news to most people that the Prime Minister was all for keeping the manuscript secret, too.
>
> The psychology of both Mr. Bean and Mr. Bruce was to keep the 'beastly thing' a matter between Mr. Bean and General Aspinall as officers and gentlemen—an attitude that can be understood and forgiven in the light of the early training of Mr. Bruce and Mr. Bean among the best gentlemen of Oxford and Cambridge, with Mr. Bruce's additional experience as a captain of the guards.[20]

For both sides the 'beastly thing' was too embarrassing not to be put to sleep as quickly as possible. But the shared doubts and recriminations now covered up again had not been properly addressed, and probably never would be. Nonetheless, with imperial-spirited governments in power in London and the new capital of Canberra, a rosy imperial future began to seem reassured again: the depression of 1929, however, meant it would not be that simple.

Imperial preference comes unstuck

Unemployment in Australia never dropped below 5 per cent in the 1920s. In 1928 it topped 10.8 per cent while the public debt, which had soared during the years of the Bruce-Page government, reached £1,043,531,642 (about A$400 billion in today's terms). Behind the protection afforded by a wall of tariffs, attempts at diversification, by government and private enterprise alike, had been only been half-hearted. The nation was still dangerously dependent on non-value-added exports. Canada, admittedly much closer to the western world's economic dynamos, had entered earlier into large-scale competitive industrialisation, and had been more aggressive and successful in its attempts to diversify the national economy. While primary products accounted for 95.5 per cent of Australia's export earnings, it made up only 46.2 per cent of Canada's; manufactured goods, which represented a mere 4.5 per cent of Australia's exports, formed 50.9 per cent of Canada's. By July 1929 the Canadian minister for Finance could contrast Canada's 'record of national progress and prosperity' with Australia's 'sorry tale of increased debts, deficits, and industrial and trade depression'. The free-trade *Argus*, which in 1919 had endorsed the idea that Australia's future might lie solely on the land, now blamed the 'high and exclusive tariff' for having failed to provide the 'royal road to what is the desideratum of every country, a well-balanced diversity of production within its own borders'.[21]

The imperial preference was a form of tariff directed against those outside the imperial trading club. It had been initiated by Canada in the 1890s 'as a friendly expression of sentiment, with no suggestion of reciprocity', but Joseph Chamberlain followed it up with proposals 'as an overture for reciprocal arrangements'. Little support was forthcoming since, for the products of dominion farmers to be given preferential treatment, tariffs would have to be imposed against all food items from outside the empire and successive British governments were firmly 'against the taxation of food or raw materials'. Thus, when the newly elected British Labour government announced in July 1929 its intention to 'repeal all preferential duties, including those to the Dominions', this was a proposal not so much to change long-standing and wide-ranging arrangements as to put on notice that those few existing arrangements would be wound down and that there would be no attempts to create others. Great Britain was no longer under 'obligation to display paternal solicitude for the Dominions', which the *Argus* now considered only right and fair. Even if this move were to 'affect prejudicially, say, Australian interests there can be no good ground for protest', for the British government had 'determined upon a course which the majority of the British electorate so clearly approves'.[22]

It was not over yet. Leo Amery led the Conservative opposition's rally to the cause of empire. The Labour chancellor (Phillip Snowden), according to Amery, did not know 'what Empire trade meant'. Great Britain:

> could better afford to cut herself off from the whole of outside world than the Empire. The conditions to-day were infinitely more favourable to a closer

Empire union than ever before. Mr. Amery continued:—'We may not be able to get complete free trade within the Empire, but let us take steps to bring us nearer to free trade when the disposition to meet us half-way is stronger than ever.'[23]

Snowden retaliated, quoting the imperialist's oracle, Joseph Chamberlain himself. There 'could not be Imperial Preference without a tax on food and raw materials', and that was a policy to which the Labour ministry 'would never subscribe'. Taxes and duties all put food prices up, and duties still applied in Britain in favour of the dominions.

> Britain could not give preference to the Dominions if she did not take their food and raw materials. He [Snowden] . . . hoped that when he left office he would have swept away all the food duties, including those on sugar and dried fruits. The preferences on these duties would naturally go too. He meant to enquire into the difficulties of producing sugar in the colonies, but he would not assist them by tariffs.[24]

Prime Minister Bruce was concerned that the British proposal would damage the sugar and dried fruits industries particularly. His minister for Market and Transport was already darkly hinting at reprisals—which, however, were unlikely to be carried out. Australia 'could not be expected to make this sacrifice without some reciprocity'. Surely the British parliament would never 'support a proposal to abolish the limited list of preferences granted to kith and kin overseas'. While the Australian Labor leader, James Scullin, 'could understand' the position of the British Labour government, he could also recognise that 'the removal of the preferences on sugar and dried fruits would be a serious blow to these industries'.[25]

The *Argus*, while supporting the principle behind Britain's decisions was not unaware of its short-term consequences. It would be 'a serious matter for Australia' if the proposals came into effect, as all 'tariff provisions made by any of the countries comprising the British Empire must affect all the others, more or less'. However, not only could there be no argument with a decision 'accepted by the great majority of the electors of Great Britain', but Australians were getting by far the better deal in the arrangements as they stood at present.

> Over the whole range of industry, including wool, wheat and foodstuffs generally, Britain offers an absolutely free market to Australia. As a supplier of foodstuffs Australia has an open door where the demand for foodstuffs is practically unlimited. There is no open door of that kind in Australia. Britain exports metals and machinery, woollens, and many articles of luxury and

necessity. Against them, with few unimportant exceptions, there is a substantial duty determined entirely in the interests of Australia.[26]

Britain now had a government less interested in imperial grandeur than in shoring up the living standards of its constituency: the British working-class. The British people were 'determined that the cost of their food shall not be added to, and in their opinion that is the effect of Imperial preference'. And what was the point of British workers paying more for traditional staples to aid the well-being of Australian farmers if heavy dominion tariffs discriminated against British goods? Where did this leave the empire?[27]

In Britain, the MacDonald Labour government's proposals had broad cross-party support, Conservative imperialists excepted; it also had the support of some British industrialists, who for some time had complained of the less than fair deal they received from kith and kin. Lord Austin, the motor magnate, warned of a possible 'dumping of American cars on

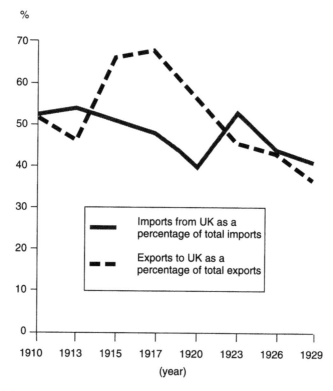

Figure 7 Australian trade with the United Kingdom: 1910–1929
SOURCE: Based on figures in Vamplew (ed.), *Australians Historical Statistics*, pp. 193 & 196.

foreign and dominion markets' which would make it 'ridiculous for us to try and compete there', especially as British manufacturers faced a 'real difficulty' in trying to 'persuade the Empire to buy British cars. I sometimes feel annoyed with the Dominions—for example, Australia—where there are eight foreign cars to one British car.' But tariff reductions alone could not overcome the design and construction defects that the pounding of Australian roads, long distances and a hot climate had revealed in these products. Australians were no more likely, despite the ties of blood, to buy unsuitable cars than Cockney labourers would choose to help Australian farmers by paying more for their food. The fallacy underlying imperial preferences had been clouded over by empire-first rhetoric which had long had a hollow ring. While the economic bonds of empire had been tied more firmly by war, they had loosened in the peace. On the eve of the Great War the United Kingdom took about half of Australia's exports and provided half its imports. By 1929 imports and exports had both dropped to about 40 per cent and the trend was downward (figure 7).[28]

The imperial preference row caused odd but predictable alignments. The majority imperial wing of the Conservative Party and its supporters in the press now found themselves on the side of the dominions, whose most publicised spokesman was Stanley Melbourne Bruce. The London *Daily Telegraph*, lacking an economically cohesive argument that could support both free trade and imperial preferences, dropped economics altogether by portraying Bruce as the occupant of the moral high ground. Snowden's announcement had 'seriously disturbed the public mood of each of the Dominions'.

> Even a slight knowledge of the public feeling in the Empire overseas would have warned Mr. Snowden that preference is not regarded solely as a matter of business . . . [but] a manifestation of sympathy and a desire for a more intimate inter-Imperial relationship. Mr. Bruce says what is true of all loyal sentiment in the Dominions when he declares that bad as are the economic consequences of the disappearance of the British preferential duties, much more disastrous is the impression created in the minds of the people of Australia. Mr. Bruce . . . is apprehensive, as every statesman in the Dominion must be, of the moral consequences not merely in reducing the range but in ending the whole system.[29]

With almost every edition of Australian newspapers telling of the plight facing Australian farmers and hinting at the near collapse of the soldier settlement schemes, Snowden's timing could hardly have been worse. In apparent response to dominion agitation, he appeared to soften his line by announcing that he did not mean 'to convey the impression that the preferential duties would end within a year or two'. Beaverbrook now entered the fray at the head of a 'crusade on behalf of free trade within the Empire', his papers advocating an 'Empire merger' which would ensure 'that neither capital nor employment suffer. By this arrangement of quotas and compensations practical men can work out a practical scheme.' The Labour-supporting *Daily Herald* opposed not only Beaverbrook's line, but French Foreign Minister Briand's advocacy of a united states of Europe. The British Labour movement would 'not support plans which aim at carving the world into separate competing units'.[30]

Australian farmers and their political representatives in the Country Party were opposed to tariffs that increased the prices of the machinery or equipment they needed. But in their view imperial preference, which applied a duty at the importing end on foreign competitors, was good and fair and in the best interests of the empire. On 16 July 1929 the rationale behind any tariff or preference argument was disputed in a report to the Australian government by 'an informal committee of economists appointed by the Prime Minister'. Its conclusions resembled those accepted by the British Labour government. The academics responsible argued that Australians' calculations of the net benefits:

> of Australian preference to British manufacturers overestimates the amount of real benefit accruing to Great Britain . . . Imperial preference imposes greater costs upon both countries than the benefits to be desired, and the further extension of preference is rendered difficult by the tariff policies of Great Britain and Australia.[31]

Bruce's own advisers were disputing his government's policy-making assumptions. With the economic props cut away, Australian support for the retention and expansion of preferences now had to be marshalled on emotional lines. Almost the only rural industries to show a growth in male employment since 1913 had been those 'protected by the tariff'—like dairying, dried fruits and sugar, where large numbers of soldier and closer settlers and their families were engaged in yeoman-style farms. That these small farmers, now facing ruin, had been enticed into rural industries based on the unstable illusion of Britain's giving preference to their products into eternity, was something no Australian politician wanted to own up to, or acknowledge. The British decision was now said to be set to 'break down a system which is doing more good than can be estimated in cementing and bringing together the various trading interests of the Empire'; concerned at the fate of soldier settlers, the Returned Soldiers' League took a similar line, implying the 'inevitable ruin of thousands of former soldiers engaged in the dried fruits industry, among them soldier migrants'. It feared for 'the development and even maintenance of the present spirit and policy of Empire trade'.[32]

To Professor Giblin, advising the prime minister, the present row reminded him of 'an old lady, rather worried, and harassed, trying to feed her children; and a number of well-fed, lusty nephews tugging at her skirts and blubbering loudly because the customary distribution of chocolate creams was not taking place'. Clever metaphors were small consolation to soldier settlers, though not all settlers sought to blame the British Labour government for their woes. A settler's conference motion to the effect 'that the fundamental basis of the troubles of primary producers was not in Britain, but here in this country', received a show of support. Preferences 'which depended upon the varying fortunes of British political parties, would never be a permanent remedy for the wrongs suffered by settlers, and they should seek to remove the basic cause of their unsatisfactory position, which was the high cost of production (Applause.)'.[33]

The news that there would be an imperial conference to debate the preference issue defused it for the time being. Bruce played it down further on 23 July, disputing the opinion of those who 'believed that any action by Britain on the lines suggested by Mr. Snowden would cause the foundering of the Empire. It would not do anything of the sort.' In any case, Bruce was now in election mode. Australians faced a new 'Era of Prosperity Ahead' if only they would show 'a real optimism, and a little courage (Applause.)'; the 'outlook in Australia was better to-day than ever before in the country's history'. The *Argus* agreed 'that optimism is preferable to pessimism, especially if the terms are not defined', but otherwise was sceptical.

> A false optimism did more to bring about the present state of affairs than anything else. That spirit has permeated legislation in its many forms and to some extent it has communicated itself to general enterprises. It has found expression in excess of borrowing and in a trust that the future will repay that which is borrowed in the present. The growing load of unproductive debt is sufficient answer to that spirit.[34]

This might not be an unfitting epitaph for the 1920s. True, not until Britain's entry into the European Economic Community (EEC) would dreams of an exclusive imperial trading bloc become defunct, while as an emotional union based on the proposition that blood is thicker than water the spirit of empire still hovers. But by 1929 only the most optimistic of imperialists doubted the heyday had passed. Lulled by the apparent promises of a guaranteed imperial market and an optimism founded in 1919–20 when the world was short of food, Australia in the 1930s paid dearly for the belief that much of a continent lay ready for the plough, and that prosperity could be assured by borrowed money and

high tariffs. By mid-1929 with the Wall Street crash still months away
there was already talk of an Australian 'trade depression which was
evident early in the year'.[35]

The 'world's Pastoral'

No one can tell how much the deepening economic crisis, by the grim
year of 1931, might have impinged upon the life of J. S. MacDonald, the
director of the National Gallery of New South Wales (as it was then
called). Being well-trained in the observational skills of the draftsman, it
seems unlikely that he could have failed to notice the increasing numbers
of shabbily dressed men, occasionally encamped or decamping in Sydney's grassy Domain, opposite the National Gallery, although there is no
hint from MacDonald's writing or notes that he did. But, if he did notice
them, he could only have taken their presence as proof of the failure of
industrialisation to secure a better life for all; for MacDonald was no
advocate of any national aim to achieve 'a well-balanced diversity of production'. Diversity meant industrialisation and his ideal was a land
covered with farms.

In 1931 he asked Australians to look at Streeton's paintings and see
why they didn't have 'to be like the rest of the world'. If others were
'bent upon it to mass produce themselves into robotry; thinking and
looking like mechanical monkeys chained to organs whose tunes are
furnished by riveting machines', that was their affair.

> We do not need to do these things. We have the pastoral land, and if we do
> not realise it sufficiently well, we have Streeton's pictures to stress the mirac-
> ulousness of it. That is ours; ours is the world's Pastoral and all it implies of
> herds and flocks and vines and hives, orchards olives and grain. Are smoke-
> stacks prettier or healthier than groves or do they give rise to finer emotions?
> Hardly.[36]

If Australians learnt from Streeton, they could become 'the elect of the
world, the last of the pastoralists, the thoroughbred Aryans in all their
nobility'.

> we are not only a nation but a race, and both occupy a particular territory
> and spring from a particular soil. The racial expression of others will not be
> ours nor the methods of interpreting their own country and folk. We will be
> mainly contented only with our own imagery expressed in our own indepen-
> dently minded sons, and of these, in landscape, Streeton is the protagonist.[37]

Plate 13 Arthur Streeton (Australia 1867–1943) *The Gloucester Buckets* 1894 oil on canvas 80 × 152.5 cm Purchased 1918 Art Gallery of New South Wales.

Streeton, with his Arcadian view of the Australian landscape, represents the key reference point for the quarantine masters of the interwar period, such as J. S. MacDonald and Lionel Lindsay.

Few passages can so adequately or eloquently define a 1930s position adopted by many Australians. If Australians were not to have the factories and smoke that went with manufacturing or the processing of wool and meat that created added value to primary products, who then was? It was simple. Australia could have Arcadia and somebody else could have the value-added profit. It was a line imperialists had peddled for decades and one R. G. Menzies met as late as 1935. He found Australian politicians less well thought of in London than their New Zealand counterparts, but the 'reason was clear. New Zealand had no secondary industry and was "therefore the good boy"'.[38]

Throughout the 1930s MacDonald would remain a persuasive advocate for followers of a landscape tradition he saw quantifiable with the expression of a national culture and soul. These artists he upheld against the rootless cosmopolitans who flirted with modernism and represented no culture at all; for were not culture and race tied intimately to the concept of nationhood? In arguing in these terms, MacDonald muddied the waters of nation, race and culture, which years later would be filtered by Claude Lévi-Strauss: 'There are many more human cultures than human races,' he wrote, 'because the ones can be counted by the thousands and the other in single figures: two cultures developed by men belonging to the same race can differ as much, or more, as two cultures rising from groups racially distant'.[39]

It is not difficult to endorse Humphrey McQueen's judgement that MacDonald 'wrote splendidly', or even that he possessed a 'ferocious intellect'. What Bernard Smith called MacDonald's 'ecstatic survey' of Streeton's work was a formidable piece of agrarian propaganda and an inducement, given his curatorial position in one of the nation's greatest gallery-museums, to Australian artists to go forth, follow his dogma and Streeton's exemplar, and then prosper. But it was also an impressive piece of art writing, eschewing the usual banalities of brush-stroke, light, paint, technical skill, composition and divine inspiration, for a real attempt to treat Streeton's work from the standpoint of a socio-political ideology. And while it does represent propaganda for a particular vision of nationhood locked firmly into the past, that is not, in itself, remarkable. Most art and what has been written about it has been propaganda for one ideal or another for centuries.[40]

Postmodern overviews of interwar art, centred upon the national landscape tradition, give MacDonald a rather better press than an outright reactionary probably merits. In contrast, C. E. W. Bean—a far more influential figure in the cultural landscape—receives less than he deserves, with what discussion and controversy there is being largely restricted to military history. For men who seemed to inhabit opposite polarities on the progressive–conservative spectrum they shared much in common.

Both saw Australia's futures almost exclusively in farming terms; both were intensely nationalistic and saw the landscape tradition as the appropriate national school; and both owed a kind of unstated and possibly reluctant allegiance to the empire as the structure that rendered possible their particular Arcadian visions.

An art writer's prescription for an ideal aesthetic and economic state is unlikely to carry weight beyond the art world. Quite another matter is a prescription written by a nationally famous journalist, correspondent and historian, which is reviewed enthusiastically in the leaders of the major national newspapers and recommended to the attention of school teachers—even if the opinions expressed seem much the same. Neither Bean nor MacDonald, even in the context of the 1920s, could be credited with offering viable contributions to the debate of what Australia was to be. A land covered with farms and with only some defence industries where manufacturing took place, in an Australian continent of forty million or so souls, would be hopelessly at the mercy of seasonal forces and changes. Indeed, it would be destined to remain at a kind of permanent third-world level, dependent on a guaranteed market for veritable mountains of foodstuffs in the eternally benevolent and larger outside powers, who were at the same time prepared to do the dirty work disdained by Arcadia. And battered old slow-going Great Britain was the only such power Australia had. But by 1929 the lesson was clear. The imperial safety-net was simply not there for protected rural industries and any future imperial arrangements were subject to repeal every time a Labour government was elected to office. The 1930s would see a revival of the imperial dreams and dreams is what they seem to have been. Mother England and her young offspring could never truly go it alone as a trading bloc, and the fear in the dominions that they could not go without Mother says something about the substance of the nationality they claimed to have won for themselves.

CHAPTER TEN

Crash and aftermath

> *Alfred Noyes says:—'Contemporary art has been blamed on the Allies
> but the fact is that: Hitler thrust it out of Germany in the belief and
> hope that it would corrupt the morals of the Allies.'—It did to a great
> extent.*
>
> J. S. MacDonald, ca. 1934 (ANL MS 430 Box 1 Notebook p. 30)

> *A contributory cause in the decline of France—the writing was on the
> wall when the Jew Stavisky was discovered to have bribed more than
> half the members of the Chamber of Deputies—modern art was the
> outward visible symptom of a spiritual malady.*
>
> Lionel Lindsay (*Addled Art*, Preface, 1942)

A sound-money banker

The Scullin Labor government achieved its 'glorious triumph' in the
month of the Wall Street crash, October 1929. Scullin told the Australian
people not to expect the new government to immediately 'usher in the
millennium' and he sent a half-veiled warning to English bondholders not
to engage in 'stupid meddlesomeness'. He was soon in electoral trouble,
as many potential voters forgot the profligate Bruce-Page years and began
to blame his government for the economic calamity facing the nation.

> The numbers of the unemployed grew each month. the amount of money
> paid in unemployed sustenance increased each month. The Commonwealth
> and State Governments complained of lack of funds. The churches protested
> they could not meet the demand for free meals.[1]

By mid-1930 Scullin was acknowledging that 'Australia's financial position
required the use of the best brains the nation could bring to its solution',
and asked the High Commissioner in London to make inquiries. He was
referred to the Bank of England, which proposed an economic mission
of banking and economic experts be sent out under Sir Otto Niemeyer.
Niemeyer had 'strong views, particularly about sound money, and was
not easily shaken'. This he had shown when, as principal adviser on all
financial matters to the chancellor of the Exchequer, he had insisted on
the 'return of sterling in 1925 to the gold standard, at the pre-war parity'.
The chancellor, Winston Churchill, 'reluctantly acquiesced in the

decision and defended it brilliantly in Parliament', but it was a controversial decision, although hardly more so than an Australian Labor government's acceptance of this sound-money conservative as a consultant to help the nation sort out its indebtedness.[2]

Niemeyer was a banker, not an economist, and his reputation for strict financial orthodoxy was not unknown to the Australian government. So, on meeting Niemeyer in July 1930, Scullin was in no doubt as to the advice likely to be forthcoming, especially as Australian governments had fallen into the habit of raising 'loan money in London to meet their interest payments on previous loans'. In August 1930 Niemeyer addressed a meeting of Australian political leaders, at which he came out with a predictable recipe. Australia would have to balance budgets and cut wages 'at all costs'. According to Manning Clark, the assembled premiers, treasurers and prime minister 'were penitent. They had sinned against the laws of political economy through their "own most grievous fault".'[3]

The labour movement was in no doubt what wage cuts meant and who would bear the brunt of them. Lang's *Labor Daily* denounced the Scullin government as 'bluffed, well and truly, into handing over our present and our future into the clutch of foreign Jews'. The *Australian Worker* no less angrily claimed that workers who had 'spilt their blood to save England's war lords' were now being asked 'to go hungry to fatten England's money lords'. Lang, then leader of the Opposition, fought the 1930 New South Wales election on a mixture of demagoguery, paranoia and occasional anti-Semitism. In announcing his opposition to the banker's proposals, Lang warned that the English financial interests Niemeyer represented were conspiring to 'degrade, by economic pressure, the Australian standard of living'. On 25 October he won in a landslide, with fifty-two seats going to Labor and twenty to the National Party.[4]

With the largest state in Australia now controlled by a Labor Cabinet opposed to the policies of a federal Labor government, a split seemed imminent. In April 1931 the New South Wales Labor Conference exacerbated existing class and loyalty tensions by passing motions committing the party 'to a Soviet-style five-year plan of socialization', recommending 'that Empire Day be no longer observed in the schools', and that 'Imperial bias' be 'removed from the textbooks'. On 7 May J. A. Lyons became leader of the United Australia Party, made up of former National Party and Labor men who transferred allegiance with Lyons. Niemeyer's recommendations were now put aside in favour of the 'Premiers' Plan', further isolating Lang and those depicted as the New South Wales extremists, and this plan was duly adopted by federal Caucus. But in the federal election of 19 December 1931 the bleeding Scullin government suffered a landslide defeat. With the first Labor foe disposed of, anti-Labor forces turned their attention to New South Wales and Jack Lang. They didn't have long to wait. On 13 May 1932 the governor, Sir Philip Game, told Lang 'I cannot retain my present Ministers in office'. He was seeking 'other advisers'.[5]

Throughout the developed world, the depression led to extreme reactions on the right no less than on the left. In comparatively placid and supposedly apathetic Australia, fears of a socialist revolution were played up in the conservative press throughout 1931 and 1932, which utilised the work of cartoonists given to portraying the class enemy in a vicious and bloodthirsty manner that was almost devoid of any leavening of humour. At the height of these troubled years the *Sydney Sun and Guardian* gave over its front page to a 'vivid article' by Howard Ashton: 'If Revolution Came to Sydney: Death, Fire, Plunder . . . Gunswept Streets and Mob Rule . . . What Communism Really Means'. It described 'some of the horror and misery and slaughter that Red Revolution would mean to Sydney'.[6]

Ashton didn't directly implicate the Jews, nor did he have to. The idea was already entrenched that there was a 'motley gang of clever Jews' orchestrating bolshevism—now communism. And as Lang and other demagogues had made clear, the Jews were implicated at the other extreme also. In international high finance, in the London loan market, wherever one looked, in whatever shady financial deal—was there not a Jew, lurking in the background and pulling the strings? Into this ambience the arrival of Sir Otto Niemeyer was a godsend to Lang; but for the federal Labor government, and to the British themselves, Niemeyer was a public relations disaster. It was hardly what he did or recommended that mattered in the end; any important, if none too imaginative, banker at the time would have probably recommended the same. Niemeyer suffered from an image problem: that he was of Anglo-German descent but had a Jewish-seeming name; that he had something of a Semitic-looking physiognomy and, in an age when news photography was being featured in the pages of even journals of record, a distinctly un-photogenic air. Gangling, bespectacled and so habitually untidy that even his friend and admirer Montagu Norman considered he ought to 'smarten himself up', Niemeyer was easily made to resemble less an important figure of the world of high finance than a caricature of a Shylock. If Mother England were sending out the Jews to tell Australians how to get their house in order, then what did that say about Mother England?[7]

Sport—the great distracter

Even in the midst of an economic crisis, perhaps particularly so at such times, life goes on and people seek diversions—although 'diversion' is hardly the word to use in connection with Australian attitudes to sport, particular in the early 1930s. Since the First World War this national obsession had been fed by a national press increasingly catering to the perception of a community need: Australian newspapers were noticeably less parochial and had less coverage of sport in the Edwardian and early Georgian times than became normal in the 1920s. Henry Mayer's comparison of the Melbourne *Herald* in 1900 and 1925 is not, as he admits, conclusive but it does represent a tendency observable across a range of journals: in 1900 the *Herald* devoted 4.8 per cent of its contents to sport and 29.0 per cent to foreign news; by 1925 sport represented 19.2 per cent and foreign news 8.2 per cent.[8]

The evolution of modern team sports, most of them Anglo-Saxon in origin, and the colonisation of Australia were largely synchronous. Much of populated Australia enjoys a temperate climate that encourages outdoor activities. Add to that the kind of background likely in emigrants seeking new lives and the type of physically active life likely to greet them, and it is hardly remarkable that Australians should become sport devotees, or list sport high among desirable national traits. Indeed, sport played no small role in unifying colonies which, despite having set up customs barriers against each other and built railways of different gauges, agreed to select an Australian cricket team to play in test matches against England a quarter of a century before federation.

As Niemeyer was making his way around Australia in 1930, Australians could rejoice in the fact that Don Bradman was in the process of ripping off a record 974 runs for a series in England, and that it might have been more except that two of the Tests 'were badly interfered with by the weather'. Bradman seemed unstoppable; if an attack including bowlers of the quality of Larwood and Tate was unable to make a dint in his armour, then what hope was there for the future? Bradman was only twenty-one years old. But a ray of hope shone for England, when in the last test at the Oval on a rain-damaged pitch, the English fast bowler Harold Larwood noticed Bradman flinching at balls rising into his body. This might just be the Achilles heel. Larwood's observation passed from his County captain to the man who would captain England on the 1932–33 Tour in Australia, Douglas Jardine.[9]

For many Australians 1932 would be the worst year of the depression. On the sporting field the world seemed filled with mean-spirited and downright dangerous enemies, made worse perhaps because they were kith and kin. In early April it was announced that the mighty Phar Lap had 'Gone the Way of Les Darcy', falling 'Victim to Dire Risks He Was Asked to Run in Foreign Land'.

EVERY sportsman and non-sportsman was staggered when the cableman broadcast the fatal news. It cast a gloom over the whole continent and in the Dominion across the Tasman, the birthplace of this racing phenomenon. Every man who had wagered on the champion, whether it was five shillings or £100, felt pangs of remorse steal chokingly into his throat.

AMERICA has a hoodoo on Australian champions. Les Darcy died there. Funny rumors got out about that. It now turns out that Phar Lap has been poisoned—Well, America can say good-bye to a lot of her goodwill in Australia.[10]

Before twelve months was up, in other sporting interludes, England would have said good-bye to a lot of her goodwill in Australia, too, beginning with a savage, brawling Rugby League Test in Brisbane, where players set out to maim and which has gone down in sporting annals as 'The Battle of Brisbane'. But a Rugby League Test was really a working-class battle between players from New South Wales and Queensland against others from Lancashire, Yorkshire and Cumberland; few in Melbourne, Adelaide or London were likely to have known anything about this Test other than, perhaps, that England won. The real Tests were cricket Tests, which in those days were played before crowds in Sydney or Melbourne of up to 50,000, almost exclusively male as photos of the soberly hat-bedecked crowds attest.

The announcement of Jardine's team raised eyebrows in Australia. It went against the conventional wisdom of the day by its inclusion of four fast bowlers, three of whom had spent the previous English season bowling versions of what was called 'Leg-theory'. This had long been practised, but what Bowes and Voce now exploited was a modified version: it confronted a batsman with short-pitched balls rising into the body, for which his natural defence, strokes to the leg side of the wicket, was now inhibited by a packed leg field. Against bowling of this kind batsmen faced the dilemma of prodding away balls into the packed-leg field and running the risk of being caught, or of not playing a stroke at all, and taking the full force of the ball on the body. A cricket ball travelling at over ninety miles an hour is no mean missile. Cricket was shaping up as a dangerous, even potentially lethal sport.

Jardine was Niemeyer's logical successor as an imperial public-relations disaster. Tall, angular and aloof, newsreels of the time reveal that he also spoke with the kind of upper-class English accent that Australians love to hate. On the field he wore a Harlequin cap that made him seem the personification of the arrogant born-to-rule upper-class toff that legend now said had callously sacrificed brave Australians in assaults on German positions at Pozières, Fromelles and Bullecourt (see plate 14). For his part Jardine reciprocated; indeed, he regarded Australians and Australian crowds in particular with barely disguised loathing. Niemeyer might have been concerned about public image, but not Jardine—he had come to Australia to win back the Ashes. To achieve this, he would first have to clip Bradman's wings. He had the fastest bowler in the world and the plan to do just that.

What became known as bodyline bowling was first unleashed in the Australian XI versus MCC match in Melbourne. Larwood in his first serious work-out of the tour built up impressive speed and seemed to have Bradman rattled. 'That he lasted three quarters of an hour and made as many as 36,' Ronald Mason wrote, was 'solely attributable to the fact that he was a great opportunist batsman and that even in these circumstances opportunities occurred, which he took'. Bradman missed the first Test in Sydney but the tactics of the English team meant the match was played 'in an atmosphere of screeching, mindless pandemonium'. Australian batsmen now had to come to terms with the fact that 'the Larwood of 1932 in Australia was yards faster than the Larwood of 1930 in England'; all of them were 'finding it hard to come to terms with his new method of attack'. In the process many were being hit. England won the match and to describe the new bowling methods an old Australian Test player used the phrase 'half-pitched slingers on the body-line'. Larwood and Jardine both hated it, which probably ensured that 'bodyline' would stick. It did.[11]

Bradman played in the second Test in Melbourne, scoring 0 and 103 not out, suggesting that he was mastering the English attack. Australia won, setting the scene for a dramatic third Test in Adelaide; a match that at least one commentator has called the Battle of Adelaide. At the English practice sessions before the match, crowds turned out 'booing and yelling and demonstrating to the English players'.

> With internal and external susceptibilities so quiveringly at stretch, it is not surprising that when the match itself began, as it did under a high hot sun and before a tremendous crowd, the situation was standing ready for some kind of eruption, small or great.[12]

As England batted first, this eruption took place in the Australian innings, when the Australian captain Woodfull was struck over the heart by a rising ball from Larwood. Jardine reputedly called 'Well bowled, Harold,' loud enough for the non-striker Bradman to hear, and while Woodfull struggled in pain to regain his composure Jardine packed the leg field. In the crowd pandemonium reigned.

Plate 14 (following) Some interesting action from the Poms (*Sydney Mail* 26 October 1932, courtesy of State Library of NSW).
 The infamous 'Body-line' team of 1932, with the soon to be execrated Jardine, the captain, wearing his celebrated Harlequin cap (*top left*).

The English Cricket Team : S

D. R. JARDINE (SURREY).
Wearing his famous "Harlequin" cap.

G. O. ALLEN
(Middlesex).

W. R. HAMMOND
(Gloucester).

L. AMES
(Kent).

Additional interest is added to the inclusion of Allen in the visiting team by the fact that he is an Australian by birth. Allen is included as a fast right-hand bowler, but he is also a bat to be reckoned with, as he showed by scoring 57 in the second innings of the second Test match played during the last tour of the Australians in England.

H. SUTCLIFFE
(Yorkshire).

F. R. BROWN AS BOWLER AND BATSMAN
(Surrey).

THE

ne Interesting Action Studies

D. R. JARDINE, CAPTAIN,
Making a late cut.

G. DUCKWORTH
(Lancashire).

R. E. S. WYATT
(Warwickshire).

W. VOCE
(Notts).

Voce is a fast left-hander, who during the season just closed in England obtained 136 wickets at an average of 16.87. He played for his county against the Australians during the last tour, and captured 4 for 86 and 1 for 112. Unfortunately Voce has injured his ankle, and it is possible that the injury may prevent him bowling for some time.

H. VERITY
(Yorkshire).

E. PAYNTER
(Lancashire).

H. LARWOOD
(Notts).

Even old men of conservative habits, and normally most moderate tempers, seated in the Members' Enclosure, rose to their feet blood-red in the face as they first hooted and later, joined in chorus to count Larwood and Jardine 'out'. And for a time it was touch and go whether the less conservative barrackers on the opposite side of the ground would jump the fence and mob the English players.[13]

Worse was to come when the Australian wicket-keeper Oldfield was struck in the face by another ball from Larwood, though Oldfield sportingly admitted that this accident was partly his own fault. Woodfull complained to the English manager but it didn't stop there. The Australian Cricket Board of Control was formally 'preparing to crystallise national feeling into official utterance', and on 18 January 1933, the last day of the Test, despatched a telegram to the MCC at Lords Cricket Ground, London, which stated that 'Body-line bowling' was making 'protection of the body by the batsman the main consideration'. The final sentence ominously implied that unless stopped, it was 'likely to upset the friendly relations existing between Australia and England'.[14]

Twelve days later Adolf Hitler became chancellor of Germany. Jardine continued for the rest of the tour to use bodyline tactics, winning at Adelaide and in the remaining two Tests. From the Australian point of view, relations with England had probably hardly been lower since the days of transportation. The 1932–33 series gave vent to an anti-English sentiment that may always have been there in some form, but had been obscured by the rhetoric of empire and race. That depression-summer may have also been the nadir of Australian isolationism. After such a dreadful year the only way to go was up. For a society in which sport had come so close to symbolising the national psyche, the assault by kith and kin was like a declaration of civil war. England had betrayed Australia by sending out the 'Shylock' Niemeyer to lecture Australian leaders on how the interests of English capital must be preserved; now she rubbed salt in the wound with the even less attractive Douglas Jardine. Apart from the dominion across the Tasman, it must have seemed that Australia in 1932 and early 1933 had not a genuine friend in a treacherous world.

A mild recovery in the art world

A depression is no time to seek out richness in cultural developments. Publishing outlets and the publicising of Australian artistic activity was at a twentieth-century low. Will Dyson in a 1929 lecture entitled 'Australian Art; a Plea and an Indictment', chaired by R. G. Menzies, proposed that Australian 'neglect of the creative literary artists was stunting the growth of the other arts and depriving itself of the full benefit of science'. He worried that 'the culture that grew in universities was being stultified for lack of a medium of public expression'. Even the 'second coming' of the Heidelberg School in the 1920s, promoted by Lionel Lindsay and J. S. MacDonald, was not sufficient compensation, least of all according to W. K. Hancock, who wrote, in 1930:

> For the artist, every habit is bad. Streeton left Australia in 1897 and did not return until after the war; but the habit of imitating Streeton's work of forty years ago still persists, so that one frequently feels, after attending an exhibition of Australian paintings, that one has seen them all before.[15]

In the early years of the depression de Mestre left for good and Lionel Lindsay toyed with the idea of leaving; Basil Burdett, 'frustrated by parochial attitudes towards the arts in Australia', went to Europe in 1931 with few fixed plans for the future. Art school attendances were down and exhibitions were few. But there were signs that the old guard was now being forced onto the defensive: articles in defence of modernism were once more appearing in the press after almost two decades. One brought this rejoinder from Lionel Lindsay, who now argued as far as modernism was concerned, that 'to-day the game is up'.

> Nothing new has been forthcoming since 'Expressionismus' and the art dealers of New York are lamenting the four million dollars expended on international 'masterpieces,' which they are unable to unload on a depressed market . . .
> Mr. Wilkinson seems to have forgotten that a very complete selection of modernist art was made by its champion, Mr. Konody, and brought to Australia in 1923. In the five years I spent recently in Europe I saw very little except the abominations of German Expressionismus that was not included in that exhibition.[16]

As the depression lifted, even in conservative journals a shift in attitude towards the encouragement of the ideas and ideals of modernity was clear. Perhaps some of the old illusions of time, place and imperial identity had been bruised too much between 1927 and 1932; but it is also likely that the image of what Russel Ward called the 'old digger', as a 'conservative and an Austral-British imperialist', was no longer of relevance to a generation who had been children in the war and were bored by the tales of their fathers or, more likely, elder brothers. Even the shrines now appearing in capital cities to mark the Anzacs' sacrifice reflected less the pompous imperial values of a Thiepval Memorial or a Menin Gate than the new image of sleekly acceptable internationalised

Australian artists who were open to modernist influences during the interwar years,
Dupain and Cossington Smith (plates 15 and 16) among them, were interested in
images drawn from the contemporary world—from the modern city rather than from
the idealised nineteenth century bush.
Plate 15 Max Dupain (Australia 1911–92) *Pyrmont Silos* 1933 gelatin silver
photograph 26.2 × 19.6 cm Purchased 1976 Art Gallery of New South Wales.

Plate 16 Grace Cossington Smith (Australia 1892–1984) *Circular Quay From Milson's Point* ca. 1928 coloured pencils, chalks, 45.7 × 34.5 cm Purchased 1967 Art Gallery of New South Wales.

modernity—art deco. In 1935, a year in which there was a mild Australian cultural renaissance, another 'swing' to modernism was underway.[17]

With the exception of photography, where the quarantine seemed hardly to apply and young men like Max Dupain and Athol Shmith produced images which would not be out of place in any international history of photography of the time, women effectively dominated Australian interwar art practice but picked up few of the glittering prizes. While there were many more women doing it—and usually doing it better—the structure of Australian painting practice was loaded against them. If art was not a suitable career for most talented young Australian males at that time, nor was it a profession readily accessible to women. Yet, looking back now, while Mary Eagle's claim that Grace Cossington Smith was 'the most brilliant artist of her generation' may be disputed if only in terms of personal taste, it is difficult to think of many male painters at that time who possessed either her talent, wit or willingness to explore. A conservative and somewhat genteel person she may have been, but like many of her female contemporaries she was not weighted down at a critical stage with the kind of nationalistic ideological baggage that even de Mestre—who flirted with slightly modernised versions of the national art, landscape, in the mid-1920s—seemed to be obliged to carry and which a new generation of Australian male painters only really began to discard at the time of the depression.[18]

In the 1920s the members of the Edwardian generation that dominated positions of critical power in gallery/museums, newspapers or magazines were in step with the conservative societal attitudes that were fed to the population at large through the media of the day. If the *Argus* and the *Sydney Morning Herald* mainly delegated art and cultural matters in general to their down-market weekly stablemates the *Sydney Mail* and the *Australasian*, then at least their imperial-national ideologies worked to reinforce the rationale for the kind of national art which was encouraged. But from 1927 there had been a change in media attitudes towards a grudging acceptance of modernism, and too much had happened to the imperial relationship for anyone to be able to push with quite the same fervour after the depression the solidly imperial 'farmer as the nation's backbone' line that dominated in the 1920s.

In view of the misery of the previous years, comparisons like Bishop Long's of 1925 between 'the play boys of the beaches and the work boys of the bush', after the depression seemed unfounded, even vindictive. Equally, in the reality of crashing soldier settlement schemes and the mounting evidence of the impracticality of a land covered with farms, Long's opinion that it was 'those nearest to the soil' who alone gave Australians 'the moral right to hold this continent for our own race' was no longer universally acceptable. With the truisms that held together the mystique of 'Old Australia' now rather tattered, an old-fashioned landscape art that had been their high cultural propaganda arm was exposed as being as obsolete as the ideologies it implicitly endorsed. At the height of the depression Norman Lindsay, returning from a voyage to England and the United States to 'Liberate People', announced that for his new Australian publishing venture stories 'of bushrangers and bushwhackers were not wanted. What was wanted was a description of life in Australian cities.'[19]

With Hitler in the Chancellery and the bodyline series as yet unfinished, Daryl Lindsay, Norman's brother, told Australians they inhabited a cultural desert. 'Australian artists and critics were about 20 years behind the times and did not realise that through these moderns art was reverting to the good old days of solid painting and drawing.' It was not a perception of modernist art that Lionel could endorse, any more than he could welcome Daryl's opinion that 'the best of the so-called moderns are doing nothing but going back to the beginnings of art—the primitives—and Australian artists could learn a lot studying them and practising some of their theories'. The times were changing, and though MacDonald extolled the national and racial virtues of landscape and Lionel Lindsay fired press salvoes at anyone poking a helmet that bore a modernist insignia above the trench lines, it is also clear that theirs was a losing cause. Australia was moving under and away from them.[20]

By 1935, for better or for worse, modernist art was fashionable. In both Melbourne and Sydney, art was beginning to be taught in art schools as though it might include Cézanne. The *Australian Woman's Weekly*, hardly a bastion of radical thought and attitudes, endorsed just such a school—or rather the work of two teachers in a school—in describing an exhibition by 'youngsters on view at Julian Ashton's'. As is so often the case with art students the work was not as radical as they might have believed, but it was made to appear that the post-depression generation was at last shrugging off the deadweight inherited from an Edwardian Establishment.

You will be amused at first, but you will be vastly impressed in fine. There is a new school among these youngsters in art, whose members are as modern as the 'maddest' of the Continental schools. This is the Crowley-Fizelle school. Fizelle will be remembered not so long since as a painter of high talent who was developing along conventional lines. Of a sudden he said good-bye to all that and set about a new technique, a new viewpoint, a new colouring, and a new everything. This is not by way of experiment, but as the genuine outcome of a new revelation leading to an immediate conversion.[21]

The press baron takes interest

Lord Beaverbrook, as far back as 1917, had played an important if not always deliberate role in the wider acceptance of modern art in Canada.

The role of another press baron, Sir Keith Murdoch, as a modernist ben-
efactor in Australia was not so dramatic or perhaps crucial, but it would
nonetheless be significant. Murdoch had tried to become Australia's official war correspondent in 1914, standing against Bean, but was not
embittered by his defeat. He went on to publicly expose the mismanagement and poor generalship dogging the Gallipoli campaign and, less
attractively, to conspire with Bean to have Brudenal White made commander of the Australian Corps instead of Monash. In 1935 he was the
proprietor of the *Herald and Weekly Times* group in Melbourne and
determinedly interventionist. Not only was he taking his flagstaff journal
consistently up-market, but he was blessed with a streak of patrician
benevolence: the National Gallery of Victoria and Melbourne University
Fine Arts would both have reason to be grateful to him.

He was by now associated with the National Gallery through the trustees and, concerned at poor attendances and a general disinterest, determined to use his main newspaper to encourage interest. In January 1935
he wrote to Lionel Lindsay.

> What chance is there of you settling near Melbourne for a year or two and
> trying with us to stir the dulled brain of this State into a wider appreciation
> of the beauties of life? ... What would you say to ten guineas a week for
> doing all the art shows and Gallery work, and an extra article each week after
> consultation with the Editor or myself?[22]

Ten guineas was reasonable money in 1935, particularly as Murdoch was
prepared to add in with the deal 'a pleasant cottage in the hills ...
Montrose, where Blamire Young lived'. No artist's career actually blos-
somed in the depression and Lindsay was no exception. Making the offer
even more appealing, Lindsay's wife was not well and Sydney's humid
summer climate was not helping her. Lindsay demurred. The Melbourne
Herald already had a critic, Basil Burdett, who represented a quite
opposed artistic ideology. Murdoch consoled him. Basil was abroad and
showed 'no signs yet of coming back, and I think he will stay away a
good while'.

> When he does come back he will want to go in for practical journalism, which
> is going to be his life's work ... In any case you would not be interfering
> with his development. He is going to be a distinguished journalist, and with
> that end in view must cover a wider field.
>
> You are the man for this position. You will ornament it and do most useful
> work. I think Melbourne will be very lucky if you can make up your mind to
> come.[23]

Lindsay accepted, but instead of a cottage in the hills, settled for a flat in St Kilda. The art world Establishment was pleased. Streeton wrote to the editor congratulating the *Herald* on its choice of 'Lionel Lindsay as your writer upon Art. Victoria has suffered the loss of J. S. MacDonald (now in Sydney); Blaimore [Blamire] Young, and Bernard Hall:—I feel sure that Lindsay will be a tremendous help to us in every way.'[24]

Up to a point Murdoch got what he wanted. Lindsay's occasional art appreciation essays on works from the collection of the National Gallery were prominently highlighted and illustrated, well-written and totally appropriate to a collection which as yet had few modern works. His exhibition reviews, given the changing climate, were another matter. Lindsay's Melbourne *Herald* sojourn seems to have ended abruptly but, given a correspondence with Murdoch that continued for many years, amicably enough. In December 1935 Murdoch wrote a memo instructing editors to 'cease calling Lionel Lindsay The Herald art Critic, because Burdett will be taking up this work'. While the *Herald* might still publish 'a few more articles from Lindsay on the Melbourne Gallery', he wanted to 'encourage Burdett fully as art Critic'.[25]

Burdett's long-term enemy, J. S. MacDonald, was meanwhile having troubles in Sydney with the trustees of that city's National Gallery. He seems to have made few friends and fewer allies, particularly among artists; even the kindly Douglas Dundas remembered him as 'a rather aggressive person, a journalist almost by profession; a painter too, but not a very distinguished one, and somehow a rather unpredictable character'. In October 1936 MacDonald wrote to the New South Wales Under Secretary and director of Education, then responsible for the gallery, announcing that he had had enough. 'For seven years and ten months I have had to suffer and endure talk and opinions which would make a gathering of painters either dumb with astonishment, helpless from laughter or purple with indignation; jackdaws strutting in peacocks' feathers.'

> Will Ashton would be a good man, but already plans are made for gagging him . . . Mr. Ure Smith does not know enough and Mr. [Lionel] Lindsay does whatever Mr. Smith asks him to do. With the exception of Mr. B. J. Waterhouse, none of the rest knows anything worth writing about. They would be better employed assessing the relative merits of Diesel engines and Parsons turbines.[26]

When MacDonald had applied for the position, Basil Burdett had been an opposing candidate. In 1937, when MacDonald applied for the directorship of the sister gallery in Melbourne, 'Mr. Burdett, with both Sir Keith Murdoch's and Mr. Ure Smith's blessings, again presented himself'.

MacDonald was once more successful. But his tenure would be cut short and he would leave under a cloud.[27]

MacDonald's arrival at the National Gallery of Victoria coincided more or less with the foundation of the Academy of Art in Sydney. This establishment and the reaction against it, the Contemporary Art Society, seem demarcated as much by the attitudes of their respective figureheads and cultural spokesmen as by the work produced by the artists they ostensibly represented. Norman Lindsay, who seems to have adopted a policy of a pox on both their houses, summed up the problem as well as anyone. 'It is possible to centralise art in London. In Australia, both Melbourne and Sydney have an equal claim in art qualifications, and are more or less always at war with each other culturally.' He was right, for 'the liberals in Melbourne sided with the C.A.S. and in Sydney with the Academy'. Nonetheless, while Dobell showed with both and Sydney painters Cossington Smith, de Mestre, Preston, Proctor, Rees and Wakelin favoured the academy, the young Turks Drysdale, Nolan and Tucker, as well as the social realists de Hartog, Bergner and Counihan, were all with the Contemporary Art Society. Although the Academy soon ceased to exist, it may not have been so much a matter of the Contemporary Art Society winning the day, as that a younger, predominantly male and largely Melbourne-based generation was taking over.[28]

True, the conservative and even reactionary attitudes espoused by R. G. Menzies were unlikely to go down well with those of a post-Spanish Civil War generation who no longer considered art to be above politics, but it remains one of the curious ironies of that time that Menzies, a Victorian, supported the Academy, whose members were mostly in Sydney, while Sydney's own H. V. Evatt opened the Contemporary Art Society's first exhibition at the National Gallery of Victoria in 1939. Mary Alice, Evatt's wife, featured among the 'youngsters in art' of the Crowley-Fizelle school in 1935, was quoted at length in the *Woman's Weekly* earlier that year. Returning with Evatt after his overseas sabbatical, she and her husband had been 'privileged to see the works of the modern masters. In essence they stand for what is best in the masterpieces of the past.'

> In color and design, much of their inspiration comes from the Primitives and also the superb sculptures of ancient Egypt. Moreover, in spite of ill informed criticism, their draftsmanship is impeccable . . .
>
> My husband was lucky enough to see much of Picasso's new work. In the last two years he has painted more than a hundred pictures. He is one of the greatest personalities in Paris.[29]

Mary Alice Evatt was 'less impressed with contemporary art in England. "Much of it is dull," she said, "and I agree with the general feeling that the Royal Academy Exhibition was unusually feeble. Such is the inevitable tendency of official art in every country." ' As for Australian art, she felt it 'a great pity' that so much of what was sanctioned seemed 'devoted to gum trees, sheep, koalas, misty impressionistic seascapes, and supposedly academic color photography of a kind that is well known'.[30]

The differences between artists who chose the Academy or the Contemporary Art Society, or both, might be less important than that these organisations provided an early platform for those long-term antagonists Menzies and Evatt to choose opposing sides. This time Evatt was a winner; Sir Keith Murdoch, no admirer of either Menzies or his friend MacDonald, put his weight behind the Contemporary Art Society and sent Burdett away to organise the first exhibition of contemporary European art to be held in Australia since 1923. This was staged at the Melbourne Town Hall shortly after the outbreak of the Second World War and nine works, including paintings by van Gogh, Braque, Utrillo, Picasso and Vlaminck, were selected from it for submission to the National Gallery Trustees and Felton Bequest Committee. MacDonald attacked them as 'exceedingly wretched paintings'.

> There is no doubt that the great majority of the work called 'modern' is the product of degenerates and perverts and that by the press the public has been forcibly fed with it. As owners of a great Van Eyck, if we take a part by refusing to pollute our gallery with this filth we shall render a service to art.[31]

Given that the president of his Board of Trustees was the patron of the exhibition concerned and was also the most notable pressman in the country, MacDonald might be admired for courage if not for either tolerance or political acumen. Murdoch had already shown he was prepared to be as interventionist a president as he was a newspaper proprietor, countermanding MacDonald's recommendation for the purchase of two Norman Lindsay watercolours in terms that resembled P. G. Konody's of 1923.

> They are in bad taste, in the main badly constructed, and their subject matter ill-chosen. They will have no interest to succeeding generations. The two chosen for our decision have been selected because they contain no repulsive Lindsay nudes, but they are none the better for this. To my mind they are ill-constructed, lack substance, and are unworthy of our Gallery.[32]

MacDonald's days were numbered, and Daryl Lindsay replaced him as director in March 1941. This other Lindsay brother sided with the progressives but kept a door ajar for the old guard as well. How far he endorsed his brother Lionel's opinions and judgements on a 1940 Contemporary Art Society exhibition will never be known.

> I saw no single work that, from its own pronounced manifesto, was original. Everything I had seen before dozens of times in Venice . . . in Paris . . . and in London, to which I returned between the years 1926-1935 on five separate occasions. During those years I gradually learned how a few dealers of Paris had—exactly like the Nazi propagandists—established the market . . . In England belief in Sargent and Corot, Puvis, Millet, was undermined by Wilenski (Duveen's dog) and Konody (two Jews). In France, a German Jew, Uhde, was the big noise . . .
>
> I would like to stress the internationalism of it all. Modernistic art really started in Middle Europe, and it was the entry of the Jew (always a corruption), into the market he already controlled, as a practitioner; Kissling [*sic*], Soutine, Gris, Chagall, Modigliani, Grünewald, Menkès, Pascin are all Jews. Picasso, a Malaga tough, who, so I believe—and he looks like it—enjoys knocking women about. Not that this has anything to do with his quick-change cafe-circus acts. Max Ernst, Kokoschia [*sic*], Kandinsky, Feininger and Klee are mostly German Jews.[33]

Lionel Lindsay was no longer the Anglophile of yore. 'I can't forgive England [for] forcing these Jews [refugees from Nazi Germany] on Australia, it's the dirtiest return for our war effort that could be imagined. They fairly stink in Sydney.' A very much enlarged but, of necessity, pasteurised version of the above, called *Addled Art*, was offered to the general public at about the time the first train rumbled into Auschwitz. But well before then there were signs that Lindsay's implacable hostility to internationalism and modernism was out of step with what more tolerant Australians were thinking. One wrote thus to the *Sydney Morning Herald*.

> I find, for example, that gum trees of Hans Heysen are a pleasant rendering of something that anyone can see with their own eyes, and quite unoriginal. If we must talk of 'degenerates' versus 'academic,' I find that the work of Max Ernst gives me infinitely greater stimulus.
>
> I do not know if Mr. Lindsay visited the Exhibition of Degenerate Art in Munich in 1937, and compared it with the orthodox exhibition nearby . . . There were admittedly some works among the 'degenerates' which one would not wish to have in one's home . . . although the orthodox exhibition was a dull and stifling collection of 'second-hand symbols and formulae.'[34]

CHAPTER ELEVEN

Whatever happened to the 'lost generation'?

> *[War] embraces much more than politics . . . it is always an*
> *expression of culture, often a determinant of cultural forms, in some*
> *societies the culture itself.*
> John Keegan (*A History of Warfare* 1993 p. 12)

'Something appears to have gone desperately wrong in Australia during the war years', Gregory Melleuish recently wrote, 'but no-one seems able to pinpoint exactly what it was'. He thus joins the ranks of writers who have identified a fundamental problem for which the cause remains frustratingly elusive. But while there remains a considerable degree of consensus that the consequence of apparently losing the plot sometime between 1914 and 1918 was the cultural and economic malaise of the 1920s and 1930s, there are still some who look back on the interwar years less with criticism than with nostalgia. In a sense these years can also be seen as the last hoorah of an Anglo-Celtic Australia, which the Second World War and waves of non-British immigration would change forever. In the hazy light of nostalgia, the interwar years have become a golden time of California bungalows, Ginger Meggs, Smith, Phar Lap, Vegemite and Aeroplane Jelly; seminal-seeming images of the stuff of a postmodern creative director's advertising dreamtime; reassuring, soft-focus and comfortingly bland.[1]

Bean takes aim

There are other relics of the age which seem less reassuring than the nostalgia-provoking hazy colourised images now used to sell true-blue Australian products and values: for example, the 'Hawkers and Canvassers Need Not Call' notices that still sit rusting on the occasional rheumy inner-city gate, sullenly bespeaking a time when men were forced to beg, or do 'work' which did little more than attempt to dignify the image of the beggar. Indeed, for the working and lower-middle classes, even for those still in employment, they could be and frequently were terrible times. By the time the worst had passed in the mid-1930s, the illusionary froth and bubble of the Jazz Age—symbolic of the recklessness, witless planning and get-rich-quick mentality that marked a decade which had culminated in the depression—was but a memory, now tainted, it seemed, by emerging and unforgiving criticisms of its isolationism, conformity and complacency. In those years the cliché that Australia was somehow a decade, or even a generation, 'behind' some unspecified other place apparently took hold based on the sensationalist headlining of newspaper interviews with returning celebrities like Daryl Lindsay or Mary Alice Evatt. Australians had to wait until the Second World War before a notable Australian would bluntly admit that in the interwar years 'we failed, failed wretchedly'. From 'twenty-one years of opportunity to mould the future of this young nation', C. E. W. Bean wrote in 1943, 'there came, in a great part of Australia, barely a single change of any value'.[2]

In 1943 when he wrote *War Aims of a Plain Australian* Bean was in the public spotlight to an extent unmatched since 1919 and 1920. His dream, the Australia War Memorial in Canberra, had recently been completed, to time perfectly with the publication of the final volumes of the 'principal literary monument' of the epoch, his own *Official History*. For its time *War Aims* was unusually brusque. The First World War had provided Australians with a 'chance' which they fumbled. And he seemed in little doubt who was to blame for this 'deadness that fell on Australia between the two wars':

> in political, social and religious effort; when our labour parties forsook their fine ideals to busy themselves with lotteries, dog races and similar trash, and our 'National' parties forgot the development of this great land in the hurry to liquidate the public industries their predecessors had established; for the departmental narrowness and lack of vision that bound our educational system at a time of vigorous experiment and progress elsewhere; for the public lack of interest that gave openings to corruption in every political party and encouraged young Australians to meet every project with the question: 'What do I get out of it?' . . . —for this deadness we are all of us responsible.[3]

Bean's indictment of Australia between the wars remains one of the most damning. How could a people aspire to 'the greatest achievements in science, invention, art, music, literature', when its 'classes have to find their amusements in gambling'? But obsessions with 'Two-Up' or dog racing remain symptomatic of an underlying malaise rather than being a cause. Bean in no way inculpated events or attitudes formed in the First World War, which for him had a wholly positive potential, as now did the Second: 'We do not often have two such chances in a lifetime; but the same devotion of the co-operative peoples that brought us that chance in 1918 will bring it to us a second time in the near future'.[4]

War Aims reveals Bean softening his formerly trenchant racist thinking. Though, like most Australians, he was concerned that the 'intermixture of peoples' was 'so often the cause of perpetual strife', no longer was the Briton the sole desirable potential immigrant. A 'degree of intermixture, increasing in the long run, seems to be certain here and probably in all countries'. Bean's increasing liberalism on this and other matters did not extend to any revision of the Anzac story—it was still the great moment in national history that had given birth to the nation. Even if he had doubts, which seems unlikely, Bean was not the man to speculate on a possible down-side to a legend in whose creation he had been a major shareholder. The wartime 1940s was not, in any case, an appropriate moment to bring it into closer scrutiny; nor was the Cold War 1950s necessarily more so. The 1950s had some conformist-style similarities with the 1920s, critical analysis then being too-easily dismissed as left-wing-inspired; the first full decade of the Menzies government, thus, was not an easy time for academic historians wishing to raise new or potentially controversial criticisms of early-twentieth century political and cultural attitudes, in whose consolidation many still-influential political leaders had played roles.[5]

Views from the 1950s

Social histories were not exactly thick on the ground in the 1950s, and Gordon Greenwood's pioneer work *Australia: A Social and Political History* (1955) probably deserves more attention than it has actually received. A collaborative work, it was the first postwar 'broad yet comparatively detailed survey' written 'not exclusively for historians' and was, for its time, as critical of the recent past as circumstances permitted. Yet, just as other academic histories from the post-Second World War period did, it seemed to play down the political, social and cultural consequences of the First World War. Greenwood's sketchy twenty-nine-page chapter on the First World War is little more than a condensed paraphrase of Bean's official histories; the war is presented as an unwelcome, almost unconnected interlude between the sixty-two pages devoted to the period of 1901–14, and the fifty-seven pages on the 1920s. Greenwood viewed the post-federation prewar years as something of a golden age in which 'the range and rapidity of national development was remarkable'; a time when liberal and labour leaders alike had:

> a belief in experimentation, a sense of Australianism, a recognition of the necessity for remedying social injustice by State action, and, in the larger view, an optimistic acceptance of the social democratic doctrine of progress, all [of which] sprang from genuine conviction.[6]

Cautioning that the 'achievement prior to 1919 should not be exaggerated', he nonetheless made the appropriate connection between art and dominant socio-political ideologies; indeed, the 'national mood' of the time was 'best expressed by the painters and writers. Art and literature in those years show in their development not only remarkable resemblances to one another, but together reflect the ascendant national and social tendencies.'[7]

The 1920s, in Greenwood's view, 'began a new phase of Australian development'. Although he made no blanket critique comparable to Bean's, the pervading mood he evokes is no less one of disappointment at the lost opportunities and mismanagement of the decade. An admirer of prime minister 'Bruce's intellectual quality and in particular his capacity for the most telling analysis of highly complex situations', Greenwood held no similar brief for Bruce's coalition partners. The Country Party's influence was 'plain to discern in the legislative policy of the Bruce-Page government', and 'showed again and again that it was sectional in interest and materialist in outlook, and too often in its thinking on such matters as censorship or the basic wage or arbitration paid scant respect to the importance of the individual'. Surprisingly, considering a profligate 'expenditure of loan money' which had led to 'losses because too frequently there had been either inadequate inquiry or an over-optimistic assessment of the financial prospects of settlement and public works schemes', Greenwood felt that 'it would be difficult not to be impressed by the closely integrated programme of the Bruce-Page government'. Between conception and realisation however, a shadow must have fallen, for he also noted that 'it must be admitted that the plans were often more impressive than the results achieved'. But it was the cultural repercussions of the dominant socio-political ideologies of the 1920s that brought forth Greenwood's most consistently negative critique.

> Even as social experimentation and creative political experiment declined in the twenties, so in education, art and literature, there was often aridity, a lack of works of first-class imagination and a seeming lack of passionate purpose on the part of those who wrote or painted ... The culture of the times mirrors an uncertainty about values apart from an emphasis upon utilitarian goals ... Music, art and literature broadly reflect the same social inertia.[8]

Russel Ward's *The Australian Legend* (1958) aspired to, and assuredly achieved, the same non-specialist but educated market Greenwood and his collaborators were aiming for. Where Greenwood sought to explain cultural development as the product of political and economic forces, Ward was not concerned to write 'a balanced or complete view of Australian history'. Ward's intention was, as he was later obliged to explain, rather to 'try to trace and explain the development of the Australian self-image—of the often romanticized and exaggerated stereotype in men's minds of what the *typical*, not the *average* Australian likes (or in some cases dislikes) to believe he is like.' Women only rated mention in 9 pages out of 283—of which 2 deal with prostitutes and 6 are devoted to the lack of women in the bush—and there is no attempt to see the evolving legend as other than a male-centred organic process, a view that minimises the role of 'poets, publicists and other feckless dreamers'.[9]

Ward was not wholly uncritical. In admitting the Anzac legend exaggerated what were supposed to be Australian qualities, he found compensation in the observation that 'not even the *Bulletin* exaggerated more fondly the "independence" of the Australian character than did some cartoons in the London *Punch* of the war and post-war years'; this, perhaps inadvertently, implies a far greater British acknowledgment of Australian soldiers than was in fact the case after 1916. He was, however, concerned at some of the exaggerations and bush-inspired oversimplifications of C. E. W. Bean—notably Bean's belief that the bush and the bush alone made the Australian soldier—wondering, for example, 'whether, even in 1914, most city slum-dwellers were wont to spend camping holidays in bush'. But this mildly critical mood did not endure, for he also claimed that 'no one knew better than Bean that up-country values were not acquired in such direct and material ways'. Indeed, in Ward's view this male-centred Australian legend and its Anzac sub-section seem to come value- and judgement-free. All that remains is to adapt and modify it to current needs.

> But nothing could be more thoroughly within the tradition than to 'give it a go'—to venture boldly on new courses of action, and so modify, and even create traditions as the anonymous bushmen, and later, the men of the nineties did. Today's task might well be to develop those features of the Australian legend which still seem valid in modern conditions.[10]

A down-side to the Anzac legend?

Women have always stood outside the Anzac legend; indeed, there is little place for them in it. It should not be surprising, therefore, that they could dare to tread where few males dared to go. Women became early

critics of a legend so sentimentalised now and enshrined into Australian
life and the monolithic perception of Australian nationality that to criticise it was, even as late as the 1960s, to court the automatic accusation
of unpatriotic behaviour in the eyes of the inordinately powerful RSL—
and not just that organisation. Judith Wright's *Preoccupations In Australian Poetry*, written as Australia began conscripting twenty-year olds for
service in Vietnam, covered much of the territory explored by Ward. It
too dealt with the Australian legend, but differed from Ward's interpretation inasmuch as now the legend was no longer the result of some kind
of osmosis; rather, it was a product in which poets, publicists and even
a few 'feckless dreamers' had played a prominent creative role. As Ward
had done, Wright incorporated the Anzac legend—or at least its most
overtly prominent manifestation—into a more generalised construct of
Australian self-identity but she drew some substantially more negative
conclusions.

> O'Dowdian rhetoric, Lawsonian and Patersonian colloquial heroics, while we
> may overtly reject them, seem to have built themselves slyly into our char-
> acters; they are traceable in Hansard reports, at public dinners, in newspaper
> leaders and letters, at Anzac Day services. The nationalist and reformist
> writers, by so drastically simplifying the issues for us, left us a dubious legacy
> that it seems we may take another century to outgrow.[11]

The Vietnam War helped change Australia into a more doubting but
rather more liberal society. No longer was a war fought at the behest of
large and powerful friends or even brothers necessarily a just or a good
war: it was possible at last to be a pacifist and, in the eyes of all but the
trenchantly reactionary, still be a decent Australian patriot. F. J. Crowley,
who had contributed towards Greenwood's study in the 1950s, almost
twenty years later replayed Greenwood's editorial role in his similar, and
similarly targeted, but much updated *A New History of Australia*. By
now the kind of hedging and cautiousness that had marked earlier
attempts to explain away the 1920s was in the past. To Heather Radi,
the 1920s was marked by its 'dead level culture', in which the image of
the Anzac was made to flourish and bridge 'the gap between pioneering
and the present, by giving to the people of the city the right to the
qualities of the outback'.[12]

Manning Clark's magnum opus, finally published in the late 1980s, was
no less intended for the non-specialist market. Though admiring of the
valour the war allowed young Australians to reveal, Clark had a mostly
negative view of the war and its repercussions on Australian society and
culture, which he saw as dictated by imperial considerations. The
'Empire was at war, Australia was at war. All the resources of Australia

were in the Empire, for the preservation and security of the Empire.' As
far as the emerging legend was concerned, this too he saw in only bleak
terms. 'Australians were abandoning their hopes of creating a society free
of the evils of the old world.' Australians now had a faith, but 'what that
faith was no one could say'. The poets now 'were using the language of
religion to describe a secular experience. Anzac Day was becoming a
secular religion.'

> [The] void left by loss of belief in God and the life of the world to come had
> been filled by worship of a site and heroic deeds which held out no hope for
> the future. Australians had acquired a sacred site. Gallipoli was the 'most
> sacred corner of Australian soil'. The Anzacs were transfigured into folk
> heroes.[13]

From such a base he could hardly find much that was positive in the
1920s, particularly given his distaste for W. M. Hughes and Earl Page, the
men who along with S. M. Bruce ruled Australia for almost the whole
decade. For Bruce—despite soldier settlement, the misplaced devotion
to empire and poorly thought-out development schemes—Clark retained
some kind words. After his 1929 defeat 'he came to see that his faith in
the harmony of British and American economic interests and in the intention and capacity of the British to provide for the defence of Australia
was misplaced. Bruce had the wisdom to turn a public defeat into a
personal victory.'[14]

As far as Clark was concerned, Streeton, Roberts and Lawson represented and symbolised the quality and vigour of 1890s and later-prewar
culture: the problem facing them was either to 'observe the rules of the
bourgeois game, or be reduced to wrecks'. In the depressed cultural
milieu of the interwar years Norman Lindsay—a man who saw 'revolu-
tionaries as the men with brutish faces' and who during the war had
'portrayed the Germans as the monsters inside himself, and then painted
naked women to tickle to madness the puritans in Australia'—negatively
fulfilled a similar role. Otherwise, Clark paid little attention to art: Cossington Smith, de Mestre and Heysen are simply not present: Margaret
Preston is—for her efforts to change the way Australians thought about
Aborigines and her comments on the Sydney Harbour Bridge.[15]

Clark's indifference to the cultural life of the 1920s and 1930s is
perhaps its own critique: it hardly matters because, in his view, there
was little in those decades to matter. Australian interwar culture was
merely the logical outcome of the kind of conformist, dull and reactionary anti-modern thinking that first saw light in the war, with a mean-
spirited Norman Lindsay as its perfect symbol. There is a fair degree of
overlap between Clark's melancholy interwar culture and the one in

which Bernard Smith became active towards the end of the 1930s. In his 1988 compilation of essays, *The Death of the Artist as Hero*, Smith also drew a line between the Anzac legend and the deflated culture of the interwar years. He claims to have been:

> impelled by the angry conviction that an Australian cultural history of a totally evil kind was being written from the perspective of a nationalism that had soured gradually from the first Anzac Day and had gone rotten. By the late 1930s it was stinking to high heaven, and no where more so than in our high art circles.[16]

He went on to accuse J. S. MacDonald and Lionel Lindsay—both were 'racists and both were anti-semitic'—of attempting to manufacture 'an account of Australian culture that seemed to me, and to many of my generation, not only an evil in itself but possessed of a great potential for the corruption of culture in Australia'.[17]

A lost generation—and a generation lost

It is not claimed that the authors surveyed above represent the definitive academic position on the status of the Anzac legend or attitudes to the 1920s. What they do represent is a body of respected and widely read opinion, taking in five decades and ranging from Ward's mellow acceptance of legend or myth as being fundamentally benign through to the indictments of interwar Australia by Clark and Smith—and by Bean insofar as it went. Indeed, whether they implicate the Anzac legend or not, few commentators find much to praise in the interwar years, aside from sentimentalised comments about the last decades of 'true-blue' Australia. But, as Melleuish has found, it is far easier to discern the symptoms than to discover what might have caused them. Australia was not alone in suffering from something akin to a cultural malaise in the 1920s. The relatively buoyant cultural life enjoyed in the 1920s in societies such as France, Germany or Russia was finally thwarted by the emergence of countervailing reactionary tendencies which became dominant in the 1930s. France, Germany and Russia nonetheless managed to have moments, even years, of vitalised cultural life of a kind virtually unknown in other European societies or their cultural satellites and they also happen to be the ones that had the greatest losses proportionately of men in the war—a warning flag, surely, to those wishing to speed down a 'lost generation' path to simplified conclusions.

The idea of the lost generation of the Great War is rooted in Social Darwinism: only the best volunteer for war, and the best of the best die first, offering themselves up selflessly as an example to those who might follow. In this way, it is said, societies lose only the very best of the young menfolk, and thereby create for women a chance they would not have otherwise had. The idea of the lost, or 'gutted' (Robert Hughes's term) generation, by which the cream of a generation's talent always lies on an old battlefield, is one of the most powerful Anglo-Austral myths to emerge from the Great War, despite the fact that Australian and empire war losses pale beside those of Germany and France. It is too easy, however, to blame the rise of fascist dictators in the 1920s and 1930s on the loss of 'a generation of leaders', or to attribute the pre-eminence of women among progressive Australian interwar artists to the absence of men. Hughes's claim in front of television cameras on an old Somme battle-site that it is 'probable' a Picasso of England lies in a battlefield is, while powerful television myth-making, hardly justified by what is known.[18]

Bernard Smith, too, has become a proponent of something akin to the 'lost generation' idea. While his assessment of the consequence of isolationism in the 1920s is difficult to dispute, his claim that war loss is more important invites disputation.

> [The] isolationist attitude of the 1920's is not, in itself, a sufficient reason for our lack of contact with the contemporary movement. The First World War is probably more important. Sixty thousand dead and 226 000 casualties was not a small proportion of the young men of a nation of less than 5 million people.[19]

It is not suggested here that a national population loss of about 1 per cent in the space of some three years is of no consequence. But even in societies where this loss approached 4 per cent there was no wounding so grievous that the culture took another generation to recover. National societies, unless they are politically dismembered, show great resilience in adapting to war losses. In Germany, which has been twice disassembled, the outright loss of 1.8 million soldiers in the First World War, plus another 3.2 million soldiers and a similar number of civilians in the Second World War—amounting to about 8 million war dead in just over thirty years—did not result in either an enfeebled economy or a depressed cultural life.[20]

Of course, war demands uneven sacrifices: total population losses only tell part of the story. Ducasse, Meyer and Perreux in *Vie et mort des Français 1914-1918* cited France's loss of the 'young of eighteen to twenty-seven—the hope for the future'. The 1921 Census suggests a similar, but less drastic situation in Australia. Almost 55 per cent of the men in Australian Imperial Force (AIF) embarkations were under twenty-four years old and single. The unmarried youth of Australia did flock to the colours, but only conscription could have forced older and married men into the ranks. These older men, who by age and career-continuity were poised to succeed the Edwardians in influence in the postwar years, were not in short supply by 1919; for the majority of eligible Australian males did not, or could not enlist in the AIF (figure 8).[21] The continental system of universal conscription ensured that those who did not enlist in Germany and France almost exclusively comprised men whose work was essential to the war effort, or men so unfit or handicapped as to be useless for military purposes. After 1916 conscription made inroads into the ranks of non-volunteers in the United Kingdom, New Zealand and British (but not French) Canada. Australia's experience was thus unique, and this carried unique postwar consequences.

A lost generation implies more than just a dead generation: Gertrude Stein's *'génération perdue'* is made up of the living, of men so damaged, disturbed or brutalised by the experience of war as to be virtually incapable of peacetime civilian readjustment—a generation lost. The war also meant a break—all too often permanent and irretrievable—in many a young man's education or career advancement. It is this aspect of the lost generation that Bernard Smith also used to provide a possible explanation for Australia's lack of modernist 'leaders able to challenge the ideals and authority of the Edwardian generation'. He meant male leaders; for, because of the comparative absence of males, 'women artists played a greater part in forming contemporary taste in Australia than they have before or since'. Women, thus, succeeded because men were either dead or had suffered a break in their education; an observation that has rightly brought on the wrath of more than one subsequent critic.[22]

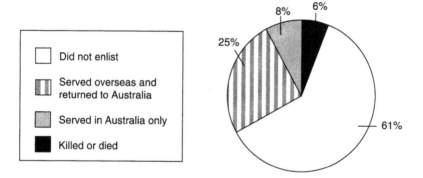

Figure 8 War service of eligible Australian males, 18–44 years old: 1914–1918
SOURCE: Based on information in—*Census of the Commonwealth of Australia 1911*; Scott, *The Official History of Australia in the War of 1914–18*, vol. XI, p. 874; Bean, *Anzac to Amiens*, p. 532.

Plate 17 Max Dupain (Australia 1911–92) *Doom of Youth* 1937 gelatin silver photograph 92.1 × 35.8 cm National Gallery of Australia, Canberra.
By the 1930s urban and industrial motifs, now well-established in the lexicon of Australian modernity, could seem emblematic at times of a generation sacrificed on the flywheel of history or of a new kind of modernistic future, perhaps (*plate 18*).

Caroline Ambrus has convincingly demonstrated just how active women artists were in those years and how effectively they have subsequently been marginalised or even written out of subsequent art histories. But what had happened to the men? They were not all dead, but the younger, up-and-coming ones seem to have been hardly present nonetheless. 'Had there been no war', Smith speculated, 'a student body who had made direct contact with fauvism, cubism, and abstract art, would have come back from their art studies in Paris and London', and the Australian art scene would have witnessed a vastly different outcome. Perhaps. But what of those who couldn't afford what was then, in peacetime at least, a virtual king's ransom to make such a trip?—'those who survived the war and wished to turn to art'. According to Smith, they also suffered insomuch as 'art training was not so easy to come by as after the Second World War' but perhaps it would be closer to the truth to say that there were more opportunities available and taken up after the Second World War. Availability has a nexus with demand; given the mood of the 1920s, what existed then, as far as potential male artists were concerned, was adequate. The romantic idea that the war caused young Australian males to be deprived of a kind of modernist art education in Paris is highly debatable, too.[23]

Art in popular disfavour

Between 1916 and 1919 nearly 300,000 young Australian males went to Paris and London in what was the greatest population movement over the longest distance in the shortest time ever known. Those interested in something other than the sights, spectacles and fleshpots would have found considerably less art on display than had been shown before the war—and, as in 1913, hardly any of it was fauvist or cubist. Not that many seem to have been interested in art. Calls for war artists in 1917 and 1918 unearthed a number of middle-aged men who had established prewar practices, but few young talents; equally there is no record of young men clamouring for art training when Bishop Long's AIF Education Scheme was set up. The message seems clear. For whatever reason or reasons, art fell out of favour with young Australian males during the war. Perhaps nothing shows this more clearly than the drop in male enrolments in Sydney's National Art School between 1912 and the 1930s.

Attesting to the kind of prejudice they have traditionally faced in carving out subsequent careers, female student have always been in the majority at art schools. At the National Art School in 1912 the male-female break-down was normal for the time: 101 women and 62 men 'successfully passed art examinations'. After the war, when the same

institution introduced diplomas in art, between 1926 and 1945, it grad-
uated 109 students, of whom only 5 were men. Perhaps Sydney's situation was unique, but to presume so seems as logical as accepting that in
the 1920s the largely male staff of National Art School suddenly developed a phenomenal prejudice against male applicants. It is true,
however, as Bernard Smith claims, that the war interrupted the studies
of the likes of Rah Fizelle and Daryl Lindsay, just as it interrupted the
studies of Otto Dix, Fernand Léger, Ernest Hemingway, Robert Graves,
John Heartfield and Lázsló Moholy-Nagy. But what cannot be justly
claimed is that potential male artists after the war were deprived of
educational opportunities. What existed was more than enough; young
Australian men, whether returned soldiers or civilians, were just not
interested in using resources that existed.[24]

The figures for the 1920s reflect a situation common in the nation as
a whole concerning mainly young people who were children during the
war. The massive drop of male enrolments in the interwar years shows,
not that young men had disappeared in battle, but that art had lost appeal
to young men. Something changed in cultural attitudes between 1913
and 1919. Women in a sense between 1919 and 1940 carried the mantle
for men and against odds, for not only was their practice frequently
belittled by the established male critics of the day, but for the most part
they had grown used to this. At art school they had learnt from men,
been assessed by them and seen examples of the great works of the past
that had been made by men. They had perhaps even accepted the notion
that men had something special that made them superior, a kind of divine
inspiration that passed women by. Women artists were well-conditioned
to be marginalised by an entrenched and largely unchallenged Edwardian
Establishment that only occasionally took them seriously.

War can create internal divisions which, as Gammage suggests, may
linger on to affect or even poison relationships in the peace. 'Had there
been no war'—rather like supposing, had there been no Industrial
Revolution or Renaissance—the privileged Australians who could have
undertaken study in Paris would have done so under teachers who had
about as much sympathy for the modern movement as the elders of
the Royal Art Society in Sydney. Had there been no war, European
modernism would have run a different course, or may not have run a
course at all. What such speculations ignore is the relationship of this
phase of modernity with the Great War, and the difficulty of imagining
Europe manoeuvring through the 1910s without a war. Whether in
1914, 1916 or 1919, a political assassination or a diplomatic slight was
bound to set the train of alliances into clumsy motion towards the
apocalypse. Over four decades Europe had structured itself for war.
Europeans were spoiling for it. A major continental war was the

safety-valve that had to blow, with late-prewar modernist art a periph-eral expression of tensions becoming unbearable.

The Great War was not an international optional extra that inter-rupted the expected course of modernism or the studies of colonial art students, it was a component part of the modernist experience. Not until the early postwar years did modernist art begin to become under-stood and established in Europe and start to become academic. In the 1920s when overseas study again became possible, some Australian artists, from their different positions and prejudices—Cossington Smith, de Mestre, Wakelin and Lionel Lindsay among them—availed themselves of the opportunity. What they and others brought back to Australia added to the residue left over from 1913 and the information gleaned from publications comprised local understanding of the so-called modern movement by the late-1920s. But if they passed on their new-found knowledge, understanding or insights or hostilities to others, then it was mostly to young women or ageing men.

Between 1913 and 1919 art had become a devalued cultural activity in the medium from which people took their cultural leads, the press of the day. The lack of interest males now showed in art was a reflec-tion of this media devaluation and also of the kind of image of manhood they had been encouraged to identify with in the war. Late-prewar coverage had taken in the noteworthy events and exhibitions and included lengthy serialised features on 'Art Study in London by Arthur Mason', or even lengthier treatises on the paintings of Velazquez. But in 1919 Sydney Ure Smith could be found urging 'that the daily news-papers should be leaders of public taste as well as opinion. They ought to devote more space to art matters than they do.' At that time Nettie Palmer also was despairing of the nation becoming a cultural desert, lamenting the absence of 'some medium of expression for all that the *Argus* and *Age* omit and smother'.[25]

Genius in a far-off grave

It is possible that the Picasso-to-be of England, or for that matter of Australia, lies at Gallipoli or in a Somme battlefield. But, even accepting the remote possibility that he may have existed, the question is left begging: had he lived, would the societies in which he was destined to make his postwar art have provided the kind of support mechanisms that even the restricted audience for cubism gave to Picasso prior to 1914? As it transpired, some of the great works of earlier-twentieth century culture were the products of those in a *génération perdue* who—excited, stimulated, inspired, disgusted or appalled by the war—refused to simply become war's living victims and instead incorporated the experience into their life and art.

Indeed, the problem with the idea of a lost generation is that it takes a remote possibility, turns it into a probability, and then uses that as an excuse for whatever kind of malaise—political or cultural—that seems to require explanation. In the end it solves or explains nothing; in fact, it obscures, for to refute the idea of a lost generation goes against all the notions of incomparable losses and self-sacrifice that intertwine in the history and myth of war. Because we find a myth compelling, that does not make it a realistic explanation. The consequences of the war were complex; the lost generation serves, as do most myths, to make the near-inexplicable simple. Perhaps the final word on the subject might be best left to Roland Barthes. 'Myth deprives the object of which it speaks of all history', he wrote. 'In it, history evaporates.'[26]

Conclusion

The culture of the warrior

Between 1914 and 1919 many attitudes changed in Australia; to judge from the press of the time, foremost among them was what being an Australian meant. Until the first dispatches from Gallipoli, the *Sydney Morning Herald* had written of Australia's part in the conflict as though the nation were part of the British Isles: imperialism was the 'sanest' form of nationalism; Australians were really off-shore Englanders. After Gallipoli the *Herald* wrote as though there might be something like an Australian identity, if not exactly the sought-after Australian 'type'. Nor was it alone in this respect. Where once the words 'Australia' and 'Australians' were rarely headlined in those imperial-centred papers for which ties to Britain or England outweighed any formal loyalty to a federated Australia, now Australian valour was extolled. The nation had arrived on the world stage and Australians would not be allowed to forget. At the height of the early-postwar Anzac publicity deluge, in 1919, the *Bulletin* offered this interpretation of what new, or reborn, nationhood meant.

> The war has made Australians nation-conscious to a remarkable extent. Its young men, after measuring themselves against the world, have come home confident that they are as good as the best. They feel that they can make steel goods with Sheffield, cotton with Manchester, small-arms with Birmingham, beer with Munich, wine with France. The great gamble of the war has given their country a start as a manufacturing nation; and the young men know it.[1]

Those who disputed the *Bulletin*'s advocacy of a mixed industrial economy and for whom its hostility to 'back-to-the-land' was anathema could at least agree that there had been a rise in Australian self-assurance after that successful military measuring-off. The belief that the Commonwealth was no longer a motley federation of old colonies but had, at last, become a nation, was almost universal in the land.

Nationhood, however, was one thing. Big-noting about how that was achieved was another. The Landing and Lone Pine were now presented as among the great military feats of all history, while Pozières was represented as being effectively the battle of the Somme and Bullecourt, the battle of Arras. When the time came in 1919 to praise unqualified military successes at Villers Bretonneux and in Monash's subsequent drive across Picardy, the supply of superlatives was already near exhaustion. From now on the language of success could only be that of repetition, as it was until beyond Anzac Day 1920. The Anzac was now the greatest thing Australia had ever produced. The image of the man-at-arms, merged with the long-standing if near-defunct bushman-yeoman type, was a reinvigorated national ideal. A soldier cult was now ascendant in the land.

The 'culture of the warrior', John Keegan recently wrote, 'can never be that of civilisation itself'. Qualities used to describe military virtue, like courage, physical strength, mechanical adroitness, dash, hardness, love of a stoush, loyalty, obedience and—sometimes blind—faith, had long been synonymous with the Australian ideal. 'The Australian is always fighting something', Bean wrote in 1907. 'In the bush it is drought, fires, unbroken horses, wild cattle; and not unfrequently strong men.' All this fighting, 'with men and nature, fierce as any warfare, has made of the Australian as fine a fighting man as exists'. With the postwar national image narrowly associated with physical and violent virtues, the incentive for men to find or encourage what was contemplative or sensitive in their hearts and minds was not high. It is in retrospect predictable that challenging works and new modes of expression should be difficult, if not impossible, to find among Australian menfolk of the war generation in the interwar years.[2]

A brand new taste-maker

Indeed, during those interwar years the institution most directly dedicated to the task of ensuring the 'lost generation' would never go unremembered and that their 'sacred relics' would be preserved into eternity, took over by default much of the cultural power which was meant to belong to now-moribund State galleries. Although Bernard Hall, the Victorian Gallery's director, was on the War Memorial Art Committee, he sometimes felt 'embarrassed because he finds that we are very keen on pictures of which he does not form a favorable opinion', and tried to ensure that 'any decisions to reject would be announced as the decisions of the Art Committee and not as his personal opinion only'. His aesthetic opinions were often ignored even though the 'Committee wanted his expert advice', but only 'with a view to ensuring that it gets good value for money spent on pictures'. When it came to the final decision, the War Memorial usually deferred to Bean. Phrases like: 'It now remains for you to express your opinion', or 'subject to your approval', conclude much of the correspondence on art from the Memorial's director, J. T. Treloar, to the man who, busy writing his official histories, still found time to act as consultant for the institution.[3]

Hall did a good job of ensuring artists were well-paid: the £200–400 most of them received for single commissions represented good money in those days. And Bean worked hard chasing up artists, encouraging and cajoling, visiting their studios where necessary and seeking out new talent. He knew what he wanted and that was not modern art. But his taste was at least as advanced as Hall's; when the Victorian wrote off Arthur Murch's work as 'weak' and that of an 'immature artist', Bean thought that, while his works were 'clever and in the modern style', he was 'quite one of the coming men, but possibly a little young'. Bean went out on a limb for his friend George Lambert. H. S. Gullett, who detested 'controversial works of art', countermanded Hall's half-hearted approval of Lambert's 'Port Said Memorial Group' (now called 'The Anzacs' and on display in the Australian War Memorial's foyer), feeling this was 'all Lambert and precious little Light Horse'. But Bean lobbied for an 'exceptionally fine work of art', which he considered to be 'almost certainly one of the finest pieces of sculpture produced by an Australian', and finally won the day.[4]

By now, so unimpressive were the National Galleries that the War Memorial was a preferred space even to the great Streeton, who was 'sorry that the "Mt. St. Quentin" picture was given to the Melb. National Gallery when *it is hardly seen* instead of to the war Museum'—quite an indictment of the state of the galleries. Through Bean's energy and commitment, the Anzac tradition now had a vital, institutional, cultural force, but at the cost of a militarisation of the culture. And, unlike in Weimar Germany, Britain, or surely Canada, this cultural militarisation was never formally opposed by a solidly based pacifist grouping, nor by an outspoken counter-group pleading that society had had enough of war and military ceremony. The religiosity attaching to Anzac Day not only made it seem unpatriotic to criticise but almost blasphemous. But then neither the British, French or Germans could claim their nation's birth in a war now presented as a sacred cause. 'Battle-weary Europeans', as Robin Gerster wrote, could 'afford to be cynical'.[5]

Conscription dilemmas

Australia was not the only nation in the British Empire to see its national birth or rebirth as deriving from the war. But unlike Australians, New Zealanders held no visions of a future as a world power and were content enough to be little Englanders in a far-off place. In Canada the war, instead of unifying, had exacerbated a grave ethnic split: the immediate postwar future of that bilingual and bicultural white dominion seemed to depend on hosing down the inflamed memories of internal ethnic conflicts of the recent past and, if possible, suppressing the divisive memories of the war as quickly as possible.

Certainly, the war also created divisions in Australia, and on the same conscription issue that bedevilled Canada. But French Canadians, feeling little loyalty to an English empire which they saw as holding them in bondage and less to a France which they believed had deserted them two centuries before, were at best reluctantly patriotic Canadians and at worst violently rebellious and unpatriotic ones. No such accusation after 1916 could realistically be levelled, despite the efforts of some Protestant leaders, against Australian Irish Catholics. Conscription divided Australia but not on the issue of fighting the war, just on who should go. Compared with Canada, divisions were mild; Australian troops, for example, were never called upon to fire on crowds in their own country in response to a declaration of martial law. True, the introduction of conscription for Australian men may well have changed that.[6]

It is, in fact, this absence of conscription which marks Australia out from the other major belligerent societies on the Western front, where Australians, in numbers, ranked equal fourth among those fighting. As a unique all-volunteer force, the Australian Imperial Force (AIF) was not only a uniformly dedicated one; it was made up for the most part of men at the high tide of masculine vigour, strength and audacity. The trawling nets of conscription, which elsewhere picked up most of the more cautious middle-aged and married men with family obligations, were never cast in Australia. As a consequence, the AIF was disproportionately filled with *single* men, of twenty-five years of age or under (about 55 per cent of all embarkations); it was inevitable that this group should do most of the dying, and its drop in numbers in the Commonwealth censuses between 1911 and 1921 shows that it did. In view of its youth and general homogeneity, there is a compelling argument for considering the AIF by 1918 as a *corps d'élite*, dedicated to a cause, and with few of the radical, bolshevik or pacifist elements that constituted morale-lowering presences in other forces.[7]

It would be simplistic, however, to suggest that the all-volunteer AIF was made up solely of those who believed ardently. There were young men who joined because of peer pressure, fear of a white feather in the post-box, or because six bob a day, clothes, board and tucker represented a better prospect than none of this at all in a society where unemployment hovered between 5 and 10 per cent and the welfare state was still vestigial. Some, too, doubtless joined for adventure or to see the world—the two are interrelated. For them the war seemed a once-in-a-lifetime chance that transcended abstract notions like nationality or empire. But what all these volunteers had in common was that they had willingly offered themselves to the empire to have done to them the empire's bidding. Among them, it is unlikely that there were any Irish Catholics outwardly hostile to Britain or the empire, or any pacifists, anti-imperialists, anti-militarists, Quakers, cowards, or men who did not want to kill or be killed.

The postwar 'rift between those who had fought' and 'those who had not' that Bill Gammage noted, was unlikely to have been brought about by men who had not volunteered and were now trying to find acceptance in a society encouraged to perceive them as second-class men. Those of Cutlack's 'crowd that didn't go away' now had no choice but to accept marginalisation: so long as the image of the ex-digger represented all that was great in Australia, they, along with women, were forced into non-participatory subsidiary positions—passive spectators only to the ceremonies of the Anzac heritage. But they were still Australians and it was their duty, as they were repeatedly told, to glory in the solemnity and sacrifice of it. For these spiritually marginalised souls, the war was something perhaps best not spoken about. Neither they nor returned soldiers were now likely to be sources of postwar anti-war sentiment or pacifism.[8]

In the case of the ex-serviceman now settling into a peacetime routine, he may have loathed the war but it had been his choice to pledge his life to fight in it. While European ex-conscripts and some of their volunteer ex-officers now emerging to prominence in European cultural life gave voice to a more general sense of disgust and disillusionment, the ranks of the all-volunteer Australian Imperial Force held firm. As the 1920s rolled on, a kind of chauvinistic disaffection was manifested by old diggers and their leaders, aimed not at the insanity of the war per se, but at British officers and even the poor, 'physically inferior' and hard-done by British Tommy. These were cheap shots, but otherwise no one seemed willing to break ranks. Unlike so many continental Europeans and Britons, they had volunteered to offer up their lives for the state and if their lives were to retain meaning, they were hardly likely to disown the idea of the war as just, sane and worthwhile after all. All this brings to light a curious dilemma: the possibility if conscription had been brought in, by offering every eligible male a similarly uncertain destiny and by throwing the AIF open to the radical, socialist or pacifist elements, it may actually have worked as a democratising, radicalising, or liberalising on all the soldiers in that army.

Had the first conscription referendum succeeded, W. M. Hughes would have been able to quickly draft somewhere between 100,000 and 150,000 additional men into the AIF. Some of these first conscripts might well then have found themselves in action at Bullecourt; or certainly at Third Ypres, arguably the worst battle of the war. Speculative though the possibility be, is it unreasonable to imagine that surviving conscripts, after having lived through such an initiation, would reject notions about being part of a 'happy band of brothers'? Would they not react with the kind of sullen disaffection that British, French and German conscripts were by now demonstrating? In the event that one conscription referendum had succeeded, would those 'silent accommodations reached by post-war Australian society' that John Rickard noted, and which gave 'the impression of a greater unity than in fact existed', have been so accommodating and silent? Together with a less conformist sense of monolithic patriotism, a more positive and open response to the process of coming to grips with modernity may well have been a by-product.[9]

Retreating from modernity?

Australia faced 1919 with a kind of almost naive optimism. The comparison with continental Europe is striking, and not only because Australians seemed to be celebrating what Europeans—if the press of Berlin and Paris is a guide—were desperate to put behind them. In Europe, surrounded by the ruins of their desperately crippled societies, many young ex-conscripts and ex-volunteers alike now felt, despite the prevailing political oratory, that it might all have been in vain: a period of peace might be little more than an interregnum before an even bloodier conflict. They were disillusioned, nursing scars and psychological wounds, and harbouring the resentment that their generation had been wantonly and callously used up by an incompetent military-political ruling caste.

Among this *génération perdue*, some ex-conscripts like the Dadaist and Surrealist artist Max Ernst now believed it was a duty to help, as he would describe it much later, 'overthrow by force all foundations of western civilisation, beginning with the cult of reason, logic, conventional language, religions, philosophies, conventional beauty, conventional poetry; in short, conventional stupidity'. His use of 'overthrow by force' was of course rhetorical and he soon simmered down, his desire for violent change sublimated into art that assaulted the conventional bourgeois society of a civilisation so stupid and hidebound by archaic conventions as to allow itself to blunder into the cataclysm. But while Ernst disavowed a personal share of responsibility for the calamity, as a European he had little choice but to deal with what was left to him. There was no possibility of his retreating to a happier, sunnier, more permanently tranquil clime, and evidence of his personal stand lies in his art; a vital element in the tough and politically motivated modernism that began to assert itself in European culture at that time.[10]

Ernst was a German in the act of becoming a Frenchman, revolted but energised by his recent European heritage. For Anglo-Saxons it was different. Only Anglo-Saxons, after the Armistice, could leave Europe behind them, generally with a mixture of relief and disgust. The point where withdrawal becomes a retreat is moot, and with Europe racked by Spanish flu but also beginning to produce some of the wildest, most thought-provoking and radical manifestations of this latest, disillusioned, cultural phase of modernity, the act of leaving Europe could easily turn into a retreat from the latest 'shock of the new'. Not that this retreat could ever be full-scale. Western continental Europe was not the sole or natural 'home' of modernism. Two of the world's most advanced industrial powers were 'Anglo-Saxon', though in cultural terms the larger of these was still making attempts to come to terms with the ideas, art, literature, and even politics that had begun to emerge from Europe in the first decades of the century. Indeed, well after the war the United States was still seen by many Europeans, and by some Americans, as being 'the only country in the world which has passed from barbary to decadence without ever having known civilisation'.[11]

This awareness, justified or imaginary, of American parochialism and cultural backwardness would send a few very wealthy Americans—from William Randolph Hearst to Peggy Guggenheim—criss-crossing the Atlantic in sometimes astute, sometimes misguided, and sometimes bizarre attempts to 'buy up' European high culture. If the United States was turning aside from the cultural manifestations of European high modernity, then it was only in the short term: too many Americans were fraternising with modernity's advance guard. No such hint of backwardness could realistically apply to Great Britain on the eve of the war. As Americans attempted to come to terms with the Armory Show, the British were already in the forefront of modernist art practice. 'In Britain, as on the continent,' Arthur Marwick wrote of that time:

the main characteristics of the modern movement were established . . . they were in a sense the product of the same restlessness and aspiration which led the peoples of Europe to welcome the war when it came. Britain had her futurists and her vorticists, her symbolists.[12]

The years 1913 and 1914 were high-water marks for British modernism; by 1919, except for literature, the tide was running out. The comparative political stability of a postwar United Kingdom meant that, if it was hardly a land 'fit for heroes,' neither was it unstable enough to be ready for a Grosz, a Dix, or a Heartfield. Instead of taking on bourgeois society, British postwar modernists took aim at bourgeois art, looking inwards to foster 'what was barest and grimmest in modernism'. It was also art for art's sake; an often sterile exercise satirising 'the canons of the older schools'.[13]

While Australia in 1913 may have begun to produce home-grown post-impressionists, there were still no futurists, vorticists or symbolists to carry on at even the level of the muted English response in the 1920s. The modernist forays of 1913 had been expressive of an outward-looking society yet to lose innocence on the Western Front; while artists like Cossington Smith continued to develop throughout the war, there was nothing like the patriotic fillip the Group of Seven war artists provided modernism in Canada. Not that this group influence went beyond employing post-impressionism's late-Edwardian techniques and colouring to ginger up a static landscape tradition, but it was clear progress of a kind unknown in Australia, where landscape seemed to have become too sacred and untouchable for any kind of modernistic change. By 1919 or at the latest 1920, if any advanced or advancing postwar ex-belligerent was in retreat from the cultural consequences of modernity, it was probably Australia.

Post-impressionism and the fragility of new society modernism

Because they were tame modernists by the standards prevailing in Europe, the Canadian ex-war artists could hardly be accused of cosmopolitanism, lack of patriotism, or of being a 'larrikin pack of degenerates out on a street-lamp-breaking foray'. Their patriotism was unassailable: they had painted for their country in war. Australia had employed no war artists remotely connected to the modern movement. Early postwar Australian modernists, conservative though their political ideas and aspirations might have been, were unable to cloak themselves in a similar mantle of patriotism which now seemed to cover only those who depicted the Australian landscape in a manner traceable to Streeton, or else exalted the 'Briton reborn' as an idealised, Aryanised, agrarian type in oils. Of course, there were artists and intellectuals who also saw themselves above mere nationalism, but Norman Lindsay's supra-nationalist Nietzschean cult—assuming they even wanted to join in—was no less off-limits to those infected with the modernist virus. By now, given their chronic lack of supportive advocates and patronage, Australian post-impressionists faced what represents, for artists, a terrible dilemma. Should they continue along their chosen paths and evolve as best they could in self-imposed isolation within an isolationist culture, or should they make accommodations towards work that was less demanding, but more likely to be exhibited, sold or even reviewed?[14]

As Wakelin has suggested, it was not simply a question of making accommodations for press attention or the possibility of a sale or two. Constant negative responses bred doubt, and that expressed itself in the compromises that can be seen in the uneven, sometimes timid, evolution of the Australian interwar post-impressionists. Yet, considering the circumstances they had to work in and the negativism too often prevailing, the achievement of the Cossington Smiths and the Wakelins merits the highest admiration. It is easy but unjust to dismiss theirs as a 'weak minority movement' confined to Sydney, or to write it off as an irrelevant blip in a laterally conceived art-historical chart that remorselessly connects up the male painters of the Heidelberg School with similarly bush-inspired male painters of the 1940s and 1950s—like Tucker, Nolan and Drysdale. But art is not just nationalistic landscape, though for much of the time in the interwar years it seemed almost as though it was.[15]

Jimmy's true art comes back

It was inevitable in the interests of balance that postmodern overviews would be critical about many previous modernist assumptions. But bringing into a more critical light the occasional inadequacies of modernist practice does not have to mean over-compensation in favour of practices which in their day were often considered old-fashioned, nor ascribing to their influence a kind of alternative progressiveness. By 1980, for example, it was possible to read the extraordinary claim that 'between the two World Wars, the imagery [of Australian landscape] again obliquely served a progressive end in the context of building up the local manufacturing base and a concomitant pride in locally made products'. This art now served 'to symbolize a national cultural independence and nationalist pride'.[16]

Even if nationalist pride could beget manufacturing—and there is nothing to suggest that it ought—then obliquely or otherwise it is not easy to imagine how an essentially anti-urban, anti-modern art, so often showing landscape devoid either of life or the agricultural machinery Australians had been designing and fabricating for about two generations, could have a positive connection with growth in local, mostly urban, manufacturing. Nor was it explained how this 'progressive end' was endorsed by J. S. MacDonald and Lionel Lindsay, both committed machine-haters and the arch-prophets of that landscape tradition. MacDonald and Lindsay were not the only ones who might have been perplexed. Any kind of 'progressive end' for the art of an Establishment endorsed by such notable 'progressives' as R. G. Menzies in his late-1930s form requires an almost quantum leap in faith.

A growth in nationalist pride and cultural independence is, on the surface at least, far more plausible, even if this art was, after all, the art of empire. In the late-1930s nationalism and imperialism ran in tandem, and men like Menzies, MacDonald and Lindsay would not have wanted it otherwise: landscape art was a national art, with 'national cultural independence' within an imperial context as its proudest aim. It could not be otherwise, for Arcadia could only exist if somebody else cleaned up or did the manufacturing work. It was then well-enough understood that Australia, like any other nation, could only exist as part of a world economy or, in more optimistic thinking, as part of a self-contained imperial one. In reality, it was no more possible to have an independent national economy than it was to have an imagined independent 'national' culture. Nor were either of these prospects, except as romantic visions, necessarily desirable.

The 'either/or' idea—either cosmopolitan modernism or nationalism— was and remains simplistic. Now it is of little consequence except as an art-historical interest, but then it dogged the cultural life of a generation. As Ian Burn has noted, given a 'predominance of modernist views' in favour of 'the writing of modernist art histories', it is right that historians should, from a postmodern perspective, wish to do justice to 'the more traditional work' which 'has been written out of the history of Australian art'. This should not be a matter of re-installing one set of once-fashionable values in place of another, or finding evidence for the 'progressive' in obscure, unexplained ways. And while it is desirable to recognise J. S. MacDonald's combativeness, courage, frankness, eloquence and—in consideration of old pictures—expertise in art, there was no justice then or now in depicting him merely as a misunderstood patriot who helped man the bulwarks against a modernist tide of cultural imperialism, even if MacDonald himself probably saw it rather like that.[17]

MacDonald wrote well about old and landscape art and, unlike many art writers at that time or since, tried to provide a cultural context for what he described. He can hardly be blamed for being better at his job than most. Nor can he be reproached for accepting art world positions offered him. What McQueen called his 'flawed talents as an artist, an author and an administrator' were, by the time he applied to the Victorian gallery, hardly well-kept secrets. But the qualities that made him a forceful and eloquent advocate for traditional landscape art—provided it was painted by men—could make him a vicious antagonist when confronted with what he disliked or failed to understand, which seemed to be most art made after about 1880. His two major career positions, as director of the National Gallery of New South Wales and then of the National Gallery of Victoria, called for tolerance, understanding and a broad appreciation not only of the art of the past and that which mimicked it but of art in step with the modern age, too. When he became director of the New South Wales gallery in the late 1920s, what was needed was a tactful constructor and bridge-builder rather than a gritty, pig-headed trench-fighting reactionary. Once warned by the experience of Sydney, Melbourne by 1935 should have known better. In most of the qualities needed by a director of Australia's two most influential art institutions between 1928 and 1938, MacDonald was singularly deficient.[18]

Yet MacDonald was employed, warts and all, by men who knew what he stood for and how he would respond. It can only be assumed that they endorsed his isolationism, his hostility to modernity, and his association of landscape with blood and soil nationalism, along with his élitism, distrust of democracy, and his belief that nation, culture and people were part of a racist whole. MacDonald is, thus, not so much a strange and somewhat eccentric aberration—lovable in a curious kind of postmodern way for his wit and willingness to call a spade a shovel when it came to putting modernists to rout—but an influential cultural leader and taste-maker chosen to represent the interests of a class and caste which saw him as their spokesman. If Australia and the landscape tradition that summed up its national soul were under threat from a modernist viral scourge that could only be kept out by vigilance and eternal hostility, then Jimmy MacDonald was a quarantine master par excellence.

Twin spectres of isolationism

By late-July 1929 Australians were used to warnings that the nation was 'experiencing a testing time of extreme severity'. Now they were told that they must take heed of the findings of the World Economic Conference held in Geneva two years previously. These had in part been critical of a 'great development of nationalistic spirit since the war' which had led to efforts by 'various countries to set up a "self-contained" and selfish policy of economic isolation'. Australia provided a flagrant example. It had 'shut itself up behind the walls of a high protective tariff' whose successive increases, 'followed by successive increases in the cost of living', had placed it 'in a vicious cycle'. A people hitherto 'too interested in football and races' were now warned of how for the past twenty years they had 'been following the wrong track':

> and now we must insist on a readjustment to our economic policy. We have been warned and advised. If we do not heed these warnings and follow the advice that has been given us after thorough and disinterested investigation we shall have only ourselves to blame.[19]

In recognising that this strange increase in postwar 'nationalistic spirit', the same spirit which had largely caused the Great War, was now largely responsible for the economic calamity facing the developed world, 'Mr. Mann, M.H.R.' was running ahead of the Australian pack. Nor was his blanket condemnation of high tariffs—even if backed up by the considered advice of some of the world's foremost economists—likely to find a receptive audience. By 1929 economic protectionism and cultural isolationism were part of the national psyche. Australia was barricaded behind an economic and cultural quarantine.

Isolationism is not exactly the mother of protectionism, more like the sister; either way, their relationship is patent: where isolationism exists, protectionism can not be far away. By the 1920s the desirability of isolation and the need to protect the emerging new race from potentially corrupting encounters was fairly ingrained into a culture whose 'beau ideal' had been the solitary bushman. Had not isolation also created the image of the resourceful and plucky character Australians were meant to admire? But, though culture is dependent upon economic and political decisions, the plausible enough argument that isolationism and protectionism can be essential to the proper growth and development of a young national economy hardly made the same kind of even debatable sense when it came to a national culture. Discriminating against the best or even the different both ran grave risks: those of accepting the inferior as first rate and, in the case of a small society, closing off legitimate areas of inquiry that could potentially enrich the local experience or even give it new form. But in the general mood of apathy that prevailed this hardly seemed to matter.

As far as Australia was concerned, the similarity between the protectionist and economic philosophy that dominated the interwar years and the dominant, high cultural attitudes is hardly unrelated; in fact, it may

Plate 18 Laurence Le Guay (Australia 1917–90) *The Progenitors* 1938 montage photograph on chloro bromide 38 × 37.6 cm Purchased 1979 Art Gallery of New South Wales.
   No longer fixed in 'useless admiration of the past', this is definitely not Jimmy MacDonald's true art.

serve to illustrate how much prevailing political or social ideologies inter-act to affect culture. Jimmy MacDonald's true art became the art that perfectly summed up this proposition: clean, representative, pleasant and uncontroversial, it was supposed to remind Australians constantly of where their national, imperial and racial roots lay. It was a polite art that made few demands and presented an idealised bush for the edification of those who, for the moment, could not go there. As such, it had abso-lutely nothing to do with the way the majority of Australians lived or perhaps wanted to live; as art, it was at a dead-end and had been for over a generation: without resorting to non-traditional devices how many ways are there to paint a gum tree or a landscape of rolling, cultivated fields?

But this art unquestionably was the expression of the culture and society that it represented. Protectionism, too, reached its dead end as an ideal in 1929, when it became obvious that the tariff and imperial preferences were no substitute for a living, vital economy. Jimmy's true art, referring back lovingly to imagery of the 1890s, was the perfect art to drift on repetitiously behind the barricades of a quarantine culture— a culture that men like MacDonald saw as having a future only in the past. As Australia began to emerge from the depression of the 1930s, this once-radical art of the 1890s, but now a reactionary art that upheld isolationism, was again becoming redundant. There could be no substitute in a living, vital culture for a living, vital art.

Appendix: The First AIF— a demographic sample

Nature of the sample

A sample of just under 1 per cent of men sent overseas has been used (some 3000 names, taken from the embarkation rolls held at the Australian War Memorial). To reflect changes in the nature of the force, groups of men were taken from six infantry battalions (two from the First Division and one each from the Second, Third, Fourth and Fifth Divisions) and the Light Horse, Engineers, Artillery, and so on, proportional to their numbers in the Australian Imperial Force (AIF) as a whole. The same procedure was adopted in taking groups from the successive waves of reinforcements and officers. The six infantry battalions reflect a natural weighting towards the larger mainland States, but ones from smaller States are included, and an attempt has been made to ensure that the area of original recruitment of these battalions does not reflect an overall urban or rural bias, though this consideration seemed to matter less as the war evolved. The age, religion, occupation, year of embarkation, nominated habitat, marital status and unit of each man selected were entered on a database, which offered rapid sorting and calculations.

The city or the bush?

As it transpired, the makeup of the group reflected the population balance of what was already one of the most urbanised societies on earth. To determine what was a metropolitan centre in 1914, the censuses of 1911 and 1921 have been used; only suburbs shown in the metropolitan maps for 1911 are accepted as being 'metropolitan'. From this a broad figure of 42.9 per cent of the AIF gave their place of residence as being in one of the State capitals or its suburbs, or in Newcastle or Geelong, and this accords closely with the censuses. City enlistments were possibly augmented to a slight degree by those moving into city accommodation to enlist from there, but this seems more likely to have affected the early days before country recruitment was made easier. For whatever reasons, however, city enlistments were lowest in 1914 (38.2 per cent).

Occupations

If the census-takers of 1911 and 1921 encountered difficulty in making sense of named occupations, there is no reason to believe it should be easier almost eighty years later. A natural human tendency to improve the stated status to one above the actual station in life is clear. For example a seventeen-year-old private calling himself an 'Engineer' from Redfern is possibly a fitter, more likely an apprentice fitter, but possibly also a semi-skilled, factory process worker. A forty-three-year old married Lieutenant-Colonel from Toorak calling himself an 'Engineer' is likely to be an engineer as the profession is understood. In the former case, the man has been given the benefit of the doubt and included among 'Tradesmen'; in the latter case, among 'Professionals'.

Figures for labourers should in real terms be much higher. Many of the job descriptions given, like battery feeder, reflect the old occupations of the late-nineteenth century and are virtually glorified labouring work. The category 'Country Callings' (Ernest Scott's term) is made up of men who describe themselves as farmers, graziers, orchardists, and so on, or farm-hands, farm-workers, stockmen, and the like. Two calling themselves 'bushman' appear in the sample. While the figures for most categorisations, as well as those for 'Professionals', accord closely with Scott's, those for 'Tradesmen' do not. In the case of the present sample many that Scott must have accepted as tradesmen—such as 'bakers' (who could be bread-carters), 'butchers' (who could be small shopkeepers), or 'handymen' (who could be anything)—have been included in a new category along with clerks, tailors, salesmen, and so on, called 'Commercial' (see Ernest Scott, *Official History* vol. XI, Appendix No. 5, p. 874).

The distribution of occupations in the sample group was as follows:

Labourers	27.3%
Commercial	21.3%
Tradesmen	20.2%
Country Callings	19.1%
Professionals	5.5%
Other	6.6%

Religion

The idea floated during the conscription campaigns that Catholics were slackers or even disloyal has little basis. Catholics joined in numbers commensurate with their numbers in society as a whole.

The distribution of religions in the sample group was as follows:

Church of England	51.1%
Roman Catholic	18.1%
Presbyterian	12.3%
Methodist	9.2%
Other	9.3%

It is also apparent that there were fewer Catholics in early drafts than came later (see figure A1), for Catholics continued to volunteer steadily throughout the conscription campaigns. This may be due to the changing perceptions of a war that began for them as an imperial undertaking and gradually came to be seen as an Australian one.

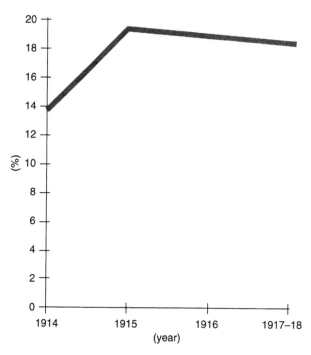

Figure A1 Roman Catholics as a proportion of total embarkations, in sample group: 1914–1918

In 1914 religion and class were closely interrelated. While nearly 37 per cent of enlisted Catholics came from the labouring class, only 16.3 per cent of 'Others'—Hebrews, Congregationalists, Free-Thinkers, Agnostics, Baptists, and so on—came from this class (see figure A2).

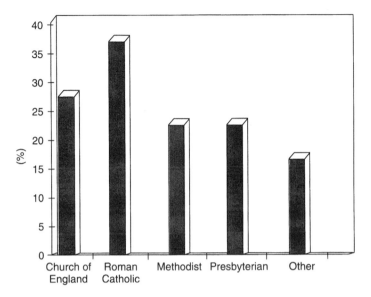

Figure A2 Proportions of labourers for each religious grouping, in sample group

A similar situation prevailed in respect of another signifier of class origins—the granting of the king's commission. For those described as 'Church of England', the proportion of officers correlates closely with overall enlistments in the force (approximately 50 per cent in both cases). In the case of 'Presbyterians', there are rather more officers (by about 3 per cent) than would be expected, all else being equal. With 'Catholics' and 'Others' the discrepancies are marked: Catholics make up just over 18 per cent of the sample group, but only 10.8 per cent of officers were Catholic; the 9.3 per cent of 'Others', however, provided almost 24 per cent of officers.

Age

One of the most vivid impressions that seems to linger around the image of the digger to this day in northern France is youthfulness. By comparison with the middle-aged conscripts that the French and Germans were forced to employ as the war dragged on, this memory is justified: if there was such a thing as an 'average' digger, this sample suggests he was single and under twenty-three years of age. Only 20 per cent of the sample group were over 30 years of age (figure A3).

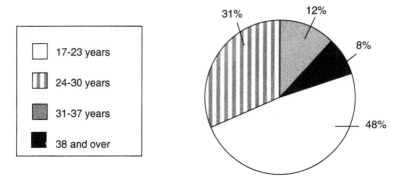

Figure A3 Age distribution, in sample group
(figures have been rounded for presentation)

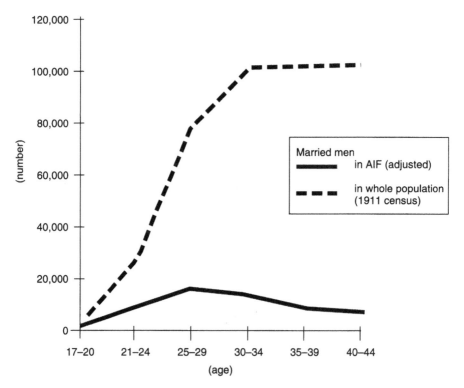

Figure A4 Married men in the AIF compared with married men in Australia as a whole

NOTE: The figures for total numbers of married men in Australia have been drawn from the 1911 census.

To arrive at the figures for married men in the AIF as a whole, the sample group has been extrapolated out, creating adjusted totals.

Marital Status

In those families that mourned the loss of a loved-one, it was far more likely that they would be grieving the loss of a brother or a son than either a father or a husband (see figure A4).

Summary

This survey is not intended as the definitive demographic statement of the AIF, rather as a guide to its make-up. Nonetheless, it is suggested that it is rather more than a rough guide; for in all vital respects it accords, within the bounds of normal sampling error, with information with which it can be directly compared, to be found in censuses or in Ernest Scott's *Official History*.

Notes

ABBREVIATIONS

Age	The *Age* (Melbourne)
AGNSW	Art Gallery of New South Wales
AIF	Australian Imperial Force
ANG	Australian National Gallery
ANL	Australian National Library
Argus	The *Argus* (Melbourne)
AWM	Australian War Memorial
SMH	*Sydney Morning Herald*
Telegraph	*Daily Telegraph* (Sydney)
Times	The *Times* (London)

CURRENCY TERMS

£1 Australian was converted to become $2 Australian in 1966. No other conversions have been applied in this text, and the original currency used for the time (US dollars, Pounds Sterling, etc.) is retained.

TRANSLATIONS

With some quotes of sensitivity, the original language may appear with the text or in the notes.

INTRODUCTION

1 P. G. Konody on Streeton, cited in 'The Art of Arthur Streeton', *SMH*, 22 November 1919; *Argus*, 7 June 1913; Streeton to Bean, AWM 3DRL 6673, item 322, 19 June 1933; *SMH*, 22 November 1919.
2 Cited by C. M. H. Clark, *A History of Australia VI: 'The Old Dead Tree and the Young Tree Green', 1916-1935*, Melbourne 1987, p. 139; *Sydney Mail*, 5 March 1913.
3 Marshall Berman, *All That Is Solid Melts Into Air*, New York 1982, p. 15.
4 Stuart Macintyre, *The Oxford history of Australia: The Succeeding Age, 1901-1942*, Melbourne (1986) 1993, p. 227.
5 Cited by Mary Eagle, *Australian modern painting between the wars 1914-1939*, Sydney 1989, p. 53.
6 Richard White, *Inventing Australia: Images and Identity 1688-1980*, Sydney 1988, p. 140; Clark, *History of Australia VI*, p. 130.
7 In February Australians had been advised that Bulgarian cavalry was 'attacking the Turkish outposts at Gallipoli, a town on the Dardanelles, 132 miles southwest of Constantinople', *SMH*, 6 February 1913. See, for example, 'Australia'

(supplement published by the High Commission for Australia) in *Times*, 30 July 1914.
8 *SMH*, 29 November 1919; Bean to Lloyd George, AWM 3DRL 606, item 82 [2], 15 July 1917.
9 C. E. Montague, Disenchantment, London 1922.
10 *Times*, 16 August 1918. See also Avner Offer, *The First World War: An Agrarian Interpretation*, Oxford 1989.
11 C. E. W. Bean, *The Official History of Australia in the War of 1914-18, Volume I, The Story of Anzac: The First Phase (From the Outbreak of War to the End of the First Phase of the Gallipoli Campaign, May 4, 1915)*, Sydney 1935, p. 4.
12 See also E. M. Andrews, *The Anzac Illusion: Anglo-Australian Relations during World War I*, Cambridge 1993.
13 J. S. MacDonald, 'Arthur Streeton', *Art in Australia*, October 1931, p. 23; Bean, *Anzac to Amiens: A Shorter History of the Australian Fighting Services in the First World War*, Canberra 1961, p. 19.
14 Egon Erwin Kisch, *Australian Landfall*, Melbourne (1937) 1969.
15 J. S. MacDonald, ANL MS 430 Box 2, Folder J.S. MacD—Corres, 20 October 1936; Roland Wakelin, 'The Modern Art Movement in Australia', *Art in Australia: The art of the year*, December 1928.

1 THE MAD *KERMESSE*

1 Cited by Berman, *All That Is Solid*, pp. 15 & 17; Hughes, *The Shock of the New: Art and the Century of Change*, London (1980) 1991, pp. 11-12.
2 Berman, *All That Is Solid*, p. 5; Sir Charles Lucas, cited in *Times*, 20 October 1914.
3 *Telegraph*, 23 April 1913; Robert Hughes, *Shock of the New*, p. 9.
4 *SMH*, 13 November 1913; *Telegraph*, 18 November 1913.
5 R. V. Jackson, *Australian Economic Development in the Nineteenth Century*, Canberra 1972, p. 106.
6 *Times*, 20 October 1914; *Telegraph*, 14 April 1913.
7 Pierre Assouline, *L'homme de l'art: D.H. Kahnweiler 1884-1979*, Paris 1988, pp. 43-44.
8 *Sydney Mail*, 3 September 1913; *Bulletin*, 20 November 1913, 15 May 1913.
9 *Bulletin*, 15 May 1913; *Age*, 4 April 1913.
10 *SMH*, 3 January 1913.
11 H. E. Egerton, 'The British Dominions and the War', *Oxford Pamphlets 1914*, No. 21, London 1914.
12 *Figaro*, 18 October 1914.
13 Camille Saint-Saëns, 'L'Allemagne exécrable' *Figaro*, 14 November 1914.
14 *Figaro*, 28 March 1917; *Berliner Tageblatt*, 2 November 1914.
15 *Berliner Tageblatt*, 2 November 1914, 9 October 1914.
16 *Figaro*, 27 October 1914; *Times*, 10 March 1915.
17 P. G. Konody, Catalogue Essay, *Introduction to Modern War: Paintings by C.R.W. Nevinson*, London 1917.
18 Philip Gibbs, *Realities of War*, London 1920, p. 191.

19 Cited in Dudley McCarthy, *Gallipoli to the Somme: the story of C.E.W. Bean*, Sydney 1983, p. 362. Cited in Phillip Knightley, *The First Casualty. From the Crimea to Vietnam: The War Correspondent as Hero, Propagandist, and Myth Maker*, London 1978, p. 99.
20 *Times*, 30 April 1915.
21 *L'Illustration*, 13 July 1918; Lionel Lindsay, Conrad Martens, his art: [revised typescript, with MS. corrections], copied from original text, Mitchell Library c860, 1920.
22 *Telegraph*, 26 April 1919. From Ashmead Bartlett's dispatch in 'The Gallipoli Landing—Valour of Dominion Troops', *Times*, 7 May 1918.
23 *Times*, 3 October 1914.
24 Edmonds to Bean, AWM 3DRL7953, item 34, 21 September 1927.
25 *SMH*, 29 November 1919.
26 *SMH*, 11 July 1919.
27 Sir Lawrence Weaver, *Catalogue of the Palace of Arts*, 1924.
28 Tom August, 'Art and Empire—Wembley, 1924', *History Today*, vol. 43, October 1993, pp. 38-44.
29 *Morning Post* (London), 5 May 1927; *Herald* (Melbourne), 25 June 1927.
30 *Herald* (Melbourne), 25 June 1927.
31 Lionel Lindsay, 'Australian Art', *The Exhibition of Australian Art in London 1923: A Record of the Exhibition Held at the Royal Academy and Organised by the Society of Artists Sydney*, Sydney 1923.
32 B. Nairn and G. Serle (eds), *Australian Dictionary of Biography* vol. 11: 1891-1939, Melbourne University Press 1988, pp. 644-45; L. Lindsay. Letter to L.H. Allen, ANL MS 1964, 20 April 1931; L. Lindsay, *SMH*, 15 September 1932.
33 *Australian Woman's Weekly*, 7 December 1935.
34 Adolf Hitler, at the opening of the House of German Art in Munich, 18 July 1937. In George L. Mosse, *Nazi Culture: Intellectual, Cultural and Social Life in the Third Reich*, New York 1981, pp. 11-12.
35 ibid.
36 R. G. Menzies, reply to letter from Norman Macgeorge, *Argus*, 3 May 1937. *Herald* (Melbourne), 4 May 1937; *Argus*, 28 April 1937; *Age*, 28 April 1937; *Argus*, 3 May 1937.
37 Lionel Lindsay, *Comedy of Life: An Autobiography*, Sydney 1967, p. 175; Jeffrey Herf, *Reactionary Modernism: Technology, culture, and politics in Weimar and the Third Reich*, Cambridge 1986, p. 2.

2   1913: A YEAR OF GOLDEN PLUMS

1 Modris Eksteins, *Rites of Spring: The Great War and the Birth of the Modern Age*, London 1989, p. xiv.
2 *SMH*, 15 March 1913.
3 Alexander Pentleton Stewart, *Argus*, 29 October 1919.
4 *Sydney Mail*, 1 January 1913; *SMH*, 12 November 1913.
5 *SMH*, 8 February 1913; *Argus*, 3 July 1913.
6 *Bulletin*, 20 February 1913.

7 *SMH*, 12 November 1913; *Sydney Mail*, 1 January 1913; *SMH*, 23 January 1913.
8 *SMH*, 4 January 1913.
9 Grace Watson in *SMH*, 20 September 1913. See also *SMH*, 13 March 1913, 15 November 1913, 10 December 1913; *Argus*, 9 June 1913, 11 July 1913; *Telegraph*, 2 September 1913; *Age*, 2 October 1913.
10 *Telegraph*, 26 April 1913; *SMH*, 15 June 1907. John Foster Fraser, *Australia: The Making of a Nation*, London 1910, p. 21; *SMH*, 18 January 1913.
11 Foster Fraser, *Australia*, p. 29; *SMH*, 14 November 1913; *Argus*, 16 July 1913.
12 Francis Adams, *The Australians: A Social Sketch*, London 1888, p. 166; *SMH*, 7 September 1870; Foster Fraser, *Australia*, p. 8; *SMH*, 21 May 1913. In the first four months of 1913 '133,000 British emigrants have left the United Kingdom . . . 66,911 went to Canada, 23,432 to Australia, 4881 to New Zealand, and 28,522 to the United States' *SMH*, 30 May 1913. *SMH*, 18 January 1913.
13 *Telegraph*, 6 May 1913; *SMH*, 4 March 1913; *SMH*, 15 November 1913; *Telegraph*, 31 December 1913.
14 *SMH*, 13 March 1913; *Telegraph*, 26 April 1913. The Empire Trade Commission is sometimes referred to as the 'Dominions Royal Commission' in press accounts; here the former version has been preferred.
15 *Telegraph*, 21 November 1913; *SMH*, 14 February 1913.
16 *Telegraph*, 17 June 1913; *SMH*, 28 October 1913; *Age*, 13 August 1913; *Telegraph*, 16 April 1913.
17 *Telegraph*, 23 April 1913.
18 *Telegraph*, 13 March 1913.
19 *SMH*, 10 February 1913; *Argus*, 2 July 1913.
20 On dry farming, see for example *Telegraph*, 13 May 1913, 23 April 1913. *SMH*, 15 May 1913.
21 *Telegraph*, 15 April 1913; 10 May 1913.
22 *Telegraph*, 27 December 1913.
23 ibid.
24 *SMH*, 15 November 1913; *Bulletin*, 6 November 1913; *SMH*, 14 February 1913.
25 *Telegraph*, 18 November 1913; *SMH*, 31 March 1913; *Telegraph*, 26 April 1913.
26 *SMH*, 12 November 1913.
27 *SMH*, 20 May 1913.
28 *Telegraph*, 18 November 1913.
29 *Telegraph*, 18 April 1913, 19 December 1913, 21 November 1913.
30 *SMH*, 13 & 28 November 1913.
31 *Bulletin*, 16 January 1913, 27 February 1913, 7 August 1913; *Age*, 8 August 1913.
32 *SMH*, 30 May 1913; *Telegraph*, 21 & 25 June 1913; *SMH*, 30 May 1913, 5 December 1913.
33 *Bulletin*, 16 January 1913; *SMH*, 9 December 1913.
34 'Shadow of Asia—[For The Bulletin.]', *Bulletin*, 6 March 1913.

35 *SMH*, 19 March 1913. See also *Bulletin*, 27 March 1913; *Telegraph*, 23 June 1913; *Argus*, 19 July 1913.
36 *SMH*, 10 February 1913, 17 March 1913.
37 Foster Fraser, *Australia*, p. 221; *Argus*, 9 July 1913.
38 *Telegraph*, 19 December 1913; *SMH*, 20 July 1907, 8 & 22 February 1913.
39 In 1953 Indians represented 0.38 per cent of Argentina's population, compared with 46.23 per cent in Peru, and about 50 per cent in Bolivia. Victor Alba, *Le mouvement ouvrier en Amérique latine*, Paris 1953, pp. 227-28; Germán Arciniegas, *The State of Latin America*, New York, pp. 27-46; John Gunther, *Inside Latin America*, London 1942, p. 236. *SMH*, 29 March 1913.
40 Gunther, *Inside Latin America*, p. 247; Foster Fraser, *The Amazing Argentine: A New Land of Enterprise*, London 1914, pp. 186-87 & pp. 271-72; *SMH*, 31 January 1913.
41 *SMH*, 1 February 1913; *Bulletin*, 6 February 1913.
42 *Telegraph*, 19 December 1913; *SMH*, 13 July 1907; *Telegraph*, 29 April 1913.
43 *Bulletin*, 24 April 1913, 6 February 1913; W. M. Hughes. Debate on the Federal Defence Bill, *Commonwealth Parliamentary Debates, vol. XLVII*, 7 October 1908, pp. 877-78; *Telegraph*, 3 May 1913.
44 *Bulletin*, 4 September 1913; *Sydney Mail Naval Number*, 1 October 1913.
45 *Age*, 6 October 1913.
46 Foster Fraser, *Australia*, p. 11; *Argus*, 12 July 1913.
47 *Census of the Commonwealth of Australia 1911*, pp. 145-47 and *1921*, pp. 60-62; *Argus*, 14 July 1913; *Age*, 4 October 1913; *Sydney Mail*, 12 February 1913; *Telegraph*, 17 June 1913.
48 *SMH*, 11 January 1913; *Bulletin*, 21 August 1913.
49 *SMH*, 1 April 1913.
50 *Telegraph*, 21 & 22 April 1913; *Sydney Mail*, 11 June 1913; *SMH*, 21 May 1913.
51 *SMH*, 15 May 1913.
52 *Sydney Mail*, 31 December 1913.

3   1913: NOWADAYS WE ARE MOST OF US NIETZSCHEANS

1 Jackson, *Australian Economic Development*, p. 98; *Royal Commission for the Improvement of Sydney and its Suburbs, Final Report*, Sydney 1909, pp. xxi, 127, 166, 136.
2 *Royal Commission for the Improvement of Sydney*, pp. xxiii, 127.
3 *Royal Commission for the Improvement of Sydney*, p. xxviii.
4 Eksteins, *Rites of Spring*, pp. xvi, 75.
5 *Technical Gazette of New South Wales*, vol. 2 part 1, February 1912, pp. 4, 5, 9.
6 Adelin Guyot and Patrick Restellini, *1933-1945 la mémoire du siècle: L'art nazi*, Brussels 1983, p. 129.
7 *SMH*, 19 May 1913, 9 January 1913; *Age*, 6 October 1913.
8 *SMH*, 15 November 1913, 28 August 1913.
9 *SMH*, 23 May 1913.
10 ibid.

11 *Telegraph*, 6 May 1913.
12 *Bulletin*, 31 July 1913, 4 September 1913.
13 *Age*, 11 October 1913.
14 E. J. Hobsbawm, *The Age of Empire 1875-1914*, London 1987, p. 20; *SMH*, 15 November 1913; *Argus*, 14 July 1913; *SMH*, 11 December 1913.
15 *SMH*, 15 June 1907; *Argus*, July 4 1913.
16 *Bulletin*, 9 January 1913, 27 February 1913, 30 October 1913.
17 Attributed to Karl Marx, in Roger Magraw, *France 1815-1914: The Bourgeois Century*, London 1987, p. 183.
18 The Armory Show was not the first American exhibition of modernist European art: Alfred Stieglitz exhibited Matisse at his '291' Gallery in New York in 1908. In 1911 a double issue of Stieglitz's *Camera Work* 'was devoted to reproductions of Rodin's drawings and analyses of his, Paul Cezanne's and Pablo Picasso's work.' Jonathon Green in Introduction to *Camera Work: A Critical Anthology*, New York 1973, pp. 14-15.
19 Hughes, *Shock of the New*, p. 44; *Technical Gazette of NSW*, February 1912, p. 3.
20 *SMH*, 30 October 1913; *L'Illustration*, 3 May 1913.
21 *L'Illustration*, 3 May 1913; *SMH*, 16 August 1913; *Argus*, 7 June 1913; *Telegraph*, 14 June 1913.
22 Raymond Bouyer, 'Les Salons de 1913: la Peinture', *Art et Décoration: Revue Mensuelle d'Art Moderne*, June 1913, p. 173.
23 Lionel Lindsay, *Addled Art*, Sydney 1942, p. 7.
24 *SMH*, 12 April 1913.
25 *SMH*, 5 April 1913; *Telegraph*, 22 November 1913.
26 *SMH*, 30 September 1913.
27 Milton W. Brown, *American Painting: from the Armory Show to the Depression*, Princeton 1955, p. 53. Roosevelt's taste in art revolved around the man whom he considered to be America's 'greatest living painter', his friend, the cowboy artist Frederic Remington. M. E. Shapiro and P. H. Hassrick, *Frederic Remington: the Masterworks. With essays by David McCullough, Doreen Bolger Burke and John Seelye*, New York 1988, p. 25.
28 William Moore, *The Story of Australian Art: From the Earliest Known Art of the Continent to the Art of Today*, volume two, Sydney 1980. Roland Wakelin, 'The Modern Art Movement in Australia,' *Art in Australia: The Art of the Year*, December 1928; *Sydney Mail*, 3 September 1913.
29 *SMH*, 11 January 1913.
30 *Sydney Mail*, 13 August 1913.
31 *Bulletin*, 15 May 1913, 20 November 1913; *Sydney Mail*, 3 September 1913.
32 *SMH*, 31 October 1913.
33 *SMH*, 15 March 1913.
34 ibid.
35 *SMH*, 15 March 1913; *Argus*, 6 June 1913.
36 *SMH*, 15 March 1913, 15 November 1913.
37 *SMH*, 1 March 1913.
38 *Sydney Mail*, 3 September 1913; *SMH*, 22 June 1907.
39 *SMH*, 30 September 1913.

40 *Age*, 9 August 1913.
41 *SMH*, 18 January 1913; *Sydney Mail*, 20 August 1913.
42 *Sydney Mail*, 20 August 1913; *SMH*, 8 February 1913, 29 September 1913, 10 February 1913; *Telegraph*, 21 April 1913; *Sydney Mail*, 5 March 1913.
43 *SMH*, 29 March 1913.
44 Foster Fraser, *Australia*, pp. 5, 43, 7.
45 *SMH*, 14 February 1913; *Sydney Mail*, 23 April 1913.
46 *Telegraph*, 21 April 1913; *SMH*, 29 March 1913.
47 Foster Fraser, *Australia*, p. xiii.
48 Foster Fraser, *Australia*, p. 11.

4   1914-19: THE GILDING OF BATTLEFIELD LILIES

1 Edmonds to Bean, AWM 3DRL7953 item 34, 16 November 1927.
2 Edmonds to Bean, AWM 3DRL7953 item 34, 24 January 1928, 7 February 1928.
3 Edmonds to Bean, AWM 3DRL7953 item 34, 2 September 1932.
4 Edmonds to Bean, AWM 3DRL7953 item 34, 19 September 1927.
5 *Figaro*, 6 August 1914.
6 L. L. Robson, *The First A.I.F.: A Study of its Recruitment 1914-1918*, Melbourne 1982, pp. 21, 23; Andrews, *The Anzac Illusion*, p. 45 (his emphasis).
7 *Berliner Tageblatt*, 16 October 1914.
8 *SMH*, 10 September 1914.
9 Gibbs, *Realities of War*, p. 7.
10 *Times*, 4 November 1914.
11 *Figaro*, 1 April 1918.
12 *Bulletin*, 17 March 1917; Robson, *The First A.I.F.*, pp. 77, 137.
13 Australia's proportion of deaths to mobilisations at 14.19 per cent is the highest in the British Empire, compared with New Zealand's 12.92 per cent, and Great Britain's 12.8 per cent. Of men mobilised, Germany lost 19.48 per cent and France 20.24 per cent. Malcolm Fraser, 'Let's not be confused by PM's sensible stand', *Sun-Herald* (Sydney), 8 March 1992.
14 Bean, *In Your Hands, Australians*, London 1918, p. 7; *Telegraph*, 3 May 1915.
15 *Technical Gazette of* NSW, vol. 6, part 2, 1916, p. 44; *SMH*, 14 November 1919.
16 W. D. Joynt V.C., *Saving the Channel Ports*, North Blackburn 1983, Preface.
17 *SMH*, 10 September 1914.
18 Count von Bernhardi cited in *Telegraph*, 3 May 1915; *Der Tag*, cited in *Times*, 26 April 1915.
19 *Berliner Tageblatt*, 11 & 1 May 1915; cited in *Times*, 3 May 1915; *Berliner Tageblatt*, 30 July, 1 August 1916.
20 *Berliner Tageblatt*, 28 July 1916; 7, 10, 14 & 16 August 1918.
21 *Figaro*, 2 July 1916.
22 *L'Illustration*, 7 April 1917, 23 March 1918.
23 *L'Illustration*, 26 June, 1915.
24 *Figaro*, 30 August, 1 & 2 September 1918.

25 *Berliner Tageblatt*, 22 August 1918; Campbell Jones of the *Sydney Sun*, cited in the *Times*, 17 August 1918.
26 Offer, *The First World War*, p. 206.
27 *SMH*, 29 & 30 April 1915; *Telegraph*, 30 April 1915; *SMH*, 1 May 1915.
28 *Telegraph*, 30 April 1915.
29 *Telegraph*, 1 & 7 May 1915.
30 Cited in *SMH*, 3 May 1915.
31 *Sydney Mail*, 31 March 1920; *Times*, 7 May 1915; cited by Kevin Fewster, 'Ellis Ashmead Bartlett and the Making of the Anzac Legend', *Journal of Australian Studies*, no. 10, 1982; *SMH*, 8 May 1915; D. A. Kent, 'The Anzac Book and the Anzac Legend: C.E.W. Bean as Editor and Image-Maker', *Historical Studies*, vol. 21, no. 84, April 1985.
32 *Times*, 7 & 8 May 1915.
33 *SMH*, 8 May 1915.
34 From the *Toronto Mail and Empire*, cited in the *Times*, 19 May 1915.
35 *Times*, 3 September 1915.
36 ibid.
37 *Telegraph*, 15 May 1915; McCarthy, *Gallipoli to the Somme*, p. 270.
38 *Telegraph*, 15 May 1915.
39 McCarthy, *Gallipoli to the Somme*, pp. 270-71.
40 *Times*, 24 July 1916.
41 We 'have abt 100 unwounded and 30 wd. (I ws told 250 but I believe this is wrong.)' Bean diary entry, 20 July 1916, AWM DRL 66 item 52, pp. 22-23.
42 *Times*, 26 July 1916.
43 McCarthy, *Gallipoli to the Somme*, p. 239; Bean Diaries, 13 August 1916, AWM 3DRL 606 item 54, p. 195.
44 *Australian Worker*, 28 June 1917; Bill Gammage, Introduction to 1982 edition of Bean, *The Official History of Australia in the War of 1914-1918, Volume IV: The A.I.F. in France 1917*, St Lucia 1982, p. xxvii; *Times*, 18 April 1917.
45 See Bean, *Official History IV*, pp. 285-354; McCarthy, *Gallipoli to the Somme*, p. 274.
46 *Times*, 20 April 1917.
47 E. M. Andrews, 'Bean and Bullecourt: Weaknesses and Strengths of the Official History of Australia in the First World War', *Revue Internationale d'Histoire Militaire*, no. 72—1990; *Times*, 11 May 1917. A paraphrase of this paragraph quoted from Bean's despatch can be found in John Laffin's *Digger*, but attributed to an 'Australian general'. Laffin, *Digger: The Legend of the Australian Soldier*, South Melbourne 1986, p. 92.
48 *Times*, 18 May, 5 June 1917.
49 *Times*, 8 August 1917.
50 *Times*, 6 October 1917.
51 *Times*, 7 November 1917.
52 *Times*, 6 October 1917.
53 *Times*, 7 October 1917.
54 *Times*, 30 October 1917.

55 *Times*, 2 April 1918.

56 *Times*, 20 April 1918.

57 Bean, *Letters From France*, London 1916, p. 230; McCarthy, *Gallipoli to the Somme*, p. 322.

58 *Times*, 27 April 1917; Cutlack, *The Australians: Their Final Campaign, 1918: An Account of the Concluding Operations of the Australian Divisions in France*, London 1919, p. 151.

59 *Times*, 30 April 1918.

60 *Times*, 19 August, 27 August 1918.

61 *Times*, 30 August, 2 & 5 September 1918.

5   1919-20: BLOWING THE NATIONAL TRUMPET

1 *Bulletin*, 10 July & 24 April 1919.

2 *SMH*, 9 July, 7 August, 7 July 1919; *Telegraph*, 1, 30, 21 January 1919.

3 *Sydney Mail*, 29 January 1919.

4 *SMH*, 5 July 1919; *Bulletin*, 20 November 1919; *Telegraph*, 31 December 1913; *SMH*, 21 July 1919; *Sydney Mail*, 3 September 1919; *SMH*, 4 July 1919.

5 *SMH*, 21 November 1919.

6 *Bulletin*, 13 November 1919.

7 *Sydney Mail*, 5 February 1919; *Bulletin*, 13 November, 24 April 1919.

8 *Telegraph*, 1 January 1919.

9 *Telegraph*, 4 & 11 January 1919.

10 *Sydney Mail*, 12 March 1919.

11 ibid.

12 Ernst Jünger, *The Storm of Steel: From the Diary of A German Storm-Troop Officer on the Western Front*, London 1929, p. 316.

13 *Sydney Mail*, 12 March 1919.

14 *Sydney Mail*, 23 April 1919.

15 ibid.

16 *Argus*, 25 April 1919.

17 *Age*, 25 April 1919.

18 *Telegraph*, 25 April 1915.

19 *Argus*, 26 April 1919.

20 *Telegraph*, 26 April 1919.

21 *Argus*, 28 April 1919.

22 *Telegraph*, 29 April 1919; *Sydney Mail*, 30 April 1919.

23 *Telegraph*, 26 May 1919; *Age*, 17 & 9 June 1919.

24 *Age*, 18 June 1919.

25 *Age*, 20 June 1919.

26 *Age*, 24 June 1919.

27 *Age*, 24, 30 June 1919.

28 *SMH*, 5, 7, 19 July 1919.

29 *Sydney Mail*, 16 July 1919; *Argus*, 18 July 1919; *SMH*, 18, 19 July 1919.

30 *SMH*, 19 July 1919.

31 ibid.

32 *Bulletin*, 31 July 1919.

33 *Sydney Mail, Victory Celebration Number*, 23 July 1919.
34 *SMH*, 8, 16 August 1919.
35 *Sydney Mail*, 1 October 1919; *Bulletin*, 6 November, 1919; *SMH*, 11 November 1919.
36 *SMH*, 14 November 1919.
37 *SMH*, 22 November 1919.
38 *SMH*, 27 November 1919 (emphasis added).
39 *SMH*, 29 November 1919.
40 ibid.
41 *Sydney Mail*, 10 December 1919.
42 *Sydney Mail*, 24 December 1919.
43 ibid.
44 *Sydney Mail*, 7 January, 25 February 1920.
45 *Sydney Mail*, 31 March 1920.
46 'Anzac Day, 1920.—By Edith Reddall', *Sydney Mail*, 20 April 1920.
47 *Sydney Mail*, 31 March 1920; *SMH*, 24 April 1920.
48 *SMH*, 24 April 1920.
49 *SMH*, 26, 27 April 1920.
50 *Sydney Mail*, 28 April 1920.
51 *SMH*, 3 May 1920.

6 THE RETURN OF THE CITY BUSHMEN

1 *SMH*, 9 September 1914.
2 *SMH*, 19, 10 September 1914.
3 *SMH*, 10 & 9 September 1914.
4 Robson, *The First A.I.F.*, p. 38; Andrews, *The Anzac Illusion*, p. 44.
5 R. Girardet, *Encyclopædia Universalus, vol. 11*, Paris 1971, p. 577; C. M. H. Clark, *A History of Australia V: The People Make Laws 1888-1915*, Melbourne 1987, p. 336; Henry Lawson, 'The Roaring Days', in Colin Roderick (ed.), *Henry Lawson—Collected Verse, Volume One 1885-1900*, Sydney 1967, pp. 56-57.
6 Henry Lawson, 'The Individualist', in Roderick (ed.), *Collected Verse, Volume Two*, Sydney 1967, p. 300; 'The Spirit of Sydney,' cited in Xavier Pons, *Out of Eden: Henry Lawson's Life and Works—A Psychoanalytic View*, North Ryde NSW 1984, p. 142.
7 Lawson, 'Coming Down', in Roderick (ed.), *Henry Lawson: Autobiographical and Other Works*, Sydney 1972, p. 178; Roderick, *Henry Lawson—The Master Story Teller: Commentaries on His Prose Writings*, Sydney 1985, p. 366.
8 McCarthy, *Gallipoli to the Somme*, p. 51.
9 Richard Hofstadter, *The Age of Reform: From Bryan to F.D.R.*, New York 1960, pp. 24-25.
10 Hobsbawm, *Age of Empire*, p. 152; *SMH*, 8 June 1907.
11 James Farrell, New South Wales Secretary for Lands, 7 November 1883, cited in J. M. Powell, *An Historical Geography of Modern Australia: The restive fringe*, Cambridge 1988, p. 56; Bean, *In Your Hands, Australians*, p. 53.

12 *SMH*, 15 June 1919. McCarthy, a sympathetic biographer, drew attention to Bean's lack of knowledge of bush life. 'How far he could have seen the squalor of a bushman ... in a state of alcoholic stupor in some wayside shanty for weeks on end until 'the horrors' seized him and his cheque was 'drunk out', as much a result of life 'out there' as the heroic virtues he so vividly discerned, is uncertain.' McCarthy, *Gallipoli to the Somme*, p. 67.

13 *Age*, 14 June 1919; *Bulletin*, 24 April 1919.

14 Hobsbawm, *Age of Empire*, pp. 39–40.

15 ibid.

16 Powell, *Historical Geography*, p. 75, and citing Lt-Col. Mersey-Thompson, *House of Commons Debates*, 5th series, vol. 109, col. 507.

17 Hobsbawm, *Age of Empire*, p. 47.

18 *SMH*, 8 June 1907.

19 *SMH*, 4 July 1919; *Age*, 17 June 1919.

20 W. J. Brown, 'Australia and the War', cited by Michael Roe, *Nine Australian Progressives: Vitalism in Bourgeois Social Thought 1890–1960*, St Lucia 1984, p. 45; *SMH*, 15 February 1913; Russel Ward, *The Australian Legend*, Melbourne 1988, p. 211; Judith Wright, *Preoccupations in Australian Poetry*, Melbourne 1966, p. 81.

21 *Athenæum*, 1876, p. 19.

22 Adams, *The Australians*, p. 165; Adams cited in W. K. Hancock, *Australia*, London 1930, pp. 246–47.

23 Spectator, 28 January 1888, p. 112. Cited by Powell, *Historical Geography*, p. 8.

24 Cited by Powell, *Historical Geography*, p. 131.

25 *Sydney Mail*, 4 June, 8 January, 23 April 1919.

26 *Argus*, 2 April 1919.

27 *Age*, 10, 14 June 1919.

28 Roe, *Nine Australian Progressives*, p. 19; Bean, *In Your Hands*, p. 11; *SMH*, 11 July 1919; Bean, 'The Old A.I.F. and the New', *Through Australian Eyes, Pamphlets on World Affairs*, Sydney 1940, p. 3.

29 *SMH*, 11 July 1919.

30 *SMH*, 12 July 1919.

31 *Bulletin*, 31 July, 24 April 1919.

32 *Argus*, 9 October 1919.

33 *Age*, 20 June 1919; *SMH*, 11 January 1913, 15 November 1919.

34 *Age*, 4 June 1919; *Bulletin*, 13 November 1919.

35 *Bulletin*, 13 November 1919.

36 *Telegraph*, 16 January 1919; *Sydney Mail*, 15 January, 2 April 1919.

37 *Sydney Mail*, 4 June 1919.

38 *Telegraph*, 28 April 1919.

39 *SMH*, 29 November 1919.

40 *Sydney Mail*, 26 November 1919, 11 February 1920.

7   ALIENS AMONG US

1 *SMH*, 26 July 1919; *Sydney Mail*, 29 January 1919.
2 *SMH*, 13 July 1907.
3 *SMH*, 27 May 1913.
4 *Argus*, 1 April 1919.
5 *Berliner Tageblatt*, 19, 22, 26 May 1919; *Bulletin*, 13 November 1919.
6 *SMH*, 30 July 1919.
7 *Figaro*, 17, 18 March 1917; *L'Illustration*, 24 March, 9 June, 22 September 1917.
8 *L'Illustration*, 29 December 1917.
9 *L'Illustration*, 5 January, 16 March, 13 July, 19 October 1918.
10 *Figaro*, 16 & 11 September 1918.
11 *L'Illustration*, 24 June 1916.
12 *Berliner Tageblatt*, 22 August 1918.
13 *Times*, 19 August 1918; *L'Illustration*, 21 September 1918.
14 *Times*, 27 August 1918.
15 ibid.
16 *Times*, 16 August 1918; *Figaro*, 10 September 1918.
17 *L'Illustration*, 14 September 1918.
18 ibid.
19 *Times*, 17 August 1918.
20 *Telegraph*, 8 January 1919.
21 *Telegraph*, 8, 10, 11 January 1919.
22 *Telegraph*, 17, 28 January 1919
23 *Sydney Mail*, 29 January 1919.
24 *Telegraph*, 30 January 1919.
25 *Argus*, 1, 2, 7 April 1919.
26 *Telegraph*, 29 April 1919.
27 *Argus*, 4 April 1919.
28 *Argus*, 1 April 1919.
29 *Argus*, 5 April 1919.
30 ibid.
31 *Argus*, 11 & 8 April 1919.
32 *Argus*, 19, 21 April 1919.
33 *Age*, 11 June 1919.
34 ibid.
35 *SMH*, 18 July 1919.
36 *SMH*, 30 July, 14 August 1919.
37 *SMH*, 11, 15 November 1919.
38 *Sydney Mail*, 21 December 1919.
39 *Sydney Mail*, 17 March 1920.
40 *SMH*, 24 April 1920.
41 *Telegraph*, 1 May 1919; *SMH*, 14 July 1919.
42 *Age*, 20 June 1919; *Argus*, 22 April 1919.
43 *Sydney Mail*, 29 January 1919; *Argus*, 4, 23 April 1919.
44 *Bulletin*, 24 April 1919; *SMH*, 9 July 1919.

45 *SMH*, 24 April 1920.
46 *SMH*, 27 April 1920.
47 Lionel Lindsay, Conrad Martens, his art: [revised typescript, with MS. corrections], Conrad Martens MS etc., Mitchell Library c 860, 1920.

8   BLUES IN THE JAZZ AGE

 1 *Figaro*, 29 March 1919.
 2 ibid.
 3 Assouline, *L'homme de l'art*, pp. 223-83; *Figaro*, 29 March 1919.
 4 Eagle, *Australian modern painting*, p. 53.
 5 Roland Wakelin, 'The Modern Art Movement in Australia', *Art in Australia: The art of the Year*, Third series, No. 26, December 1928; 'The Contemporary Group of Australian Artists, *Art in Australia: The Contemporary Group of Australian Artists*, Third Series, Number 29, September 1929. In 1943 Rubbo wrote to Lionel Lindsay complaining that 'for nearly nine years I have been ignored by the art critics of the Herald' while former 'pupils of mine, who failed to achieve something, are prominently claimed as rising genius!', Mitchell Library ML DOC 616, 30 August 1943.
 6 Wakelin, 'The Modern Art Movement'; Robert Hughes, *The Art of Australia*, Melbourne 1988, p. 120; Marjorie Barnard, 'Modern Art in Australia', *Art of Australia 1788-1941: An Exhibition of Australian Art Held in the United States of America and the Dominion of Canada Under the Auspices of the Carnegie Foundation*, New York 1941, p. 26. Roi de Mestre was his preferred version of his name until he left Australia in 1930, when he changed it to Roy de Maistre (*Australian Dictionary of Biography*, vol. 8, ed. Nairn and Serle, 1981).
 7 Geoffrey Serle, *The Creative Spirit in Australia: A Cultural History*, Richmond 1987, p. 159; P. G. Konody cited in 'The Art of Arthur Streeton', *SMH*, 22 November 1919.
 8 'Wenn ich Kultur höre . . . entsichere ich meinen Browning.' 'Whenever I hear the word culture, I release the safety catch on my revolver.' Hanns Johst, *Schlageter* (1934), Act 1, sc.1. Attributed to Hermann Goering in the form: 'When I hear anyone talk of culture I reach for my revolver.' *The Concise Oxford Dictionary of Quotations*, London 1975, p. 117; *Sydney Mail*, 25 June 1919. See, for example, 'January Quarterlies—Concerning Modernism—The Philosophy of Nietzsche', *SMH*, 1 March 1913; 'Art Study in London—(By Arthur Mason)—I-V incl.', *SMH*, 8 November to 6 December 1913.
 9 Bean, *War Aims of a Plain Australian*, Sydney 1943, p. 97.
10 Foreword. *Vision IV*, February 1924; Foreword. *Vision III*, November 1923.
11 P. R. Stephensen, *The Publicist*, November-December, 1936, pp. 10-11. Cited by Noel Macainsh, *Nietzsche in Australia: A Literary Inquiry into a Nationalist Ideology*, Munich 1975, p. 141.
12 Norman Lindsay, 'Elioth Gruner's "Morning Light" ', *Art in Australia*, Fifth Number, 1918.
13 Cited by J. S. MacDonald 'Lionel Lindsay', *Art in Australia: The Art of Lionel Lindsay*, Third series, No. 23, March 1928.

14 Lionel Lindsay, 'Australian Art', *The Exhibition of Australian Art in London 1923: A Record of the Exhibition Held at the Royal Academy and Organised by the Society of Artists Sydney*, Sydney 1923.
15 ibid.
16 Ernst Jünger from *Kampf als inneres Erlebnis*, p. 107, cited in Herf, *Reactionary Modernism*, p. 77.
17 Jünger cited in Herf, *Reactionary Modernism*, p. 79.
18 Eagle, *Australian modern painting*, p. 53; Ursula Prunstler, 'Norman Lindsay and the Australian Renaissance', in A. Bradley & T. Smith (eds), *Australian Art and Architecture: Essays Presented to Bernard Smith*, Melbourne 1980, p. 162; Lionel Lindsay, 'Australian Art'; 'Norman Lindsay's Etchings,' *Art in Australia*, Sixth Number, 1919; P. G. Konody, 'The Australian Exhibition in London,' *Art in Australia*, Third Series, Number Seven, March 1924.
19 'Australian Art and English Critics: Extracts from the English press relating to the recent Exhibition of Australian Art in London', *Art in Australia*, Third Series, Number Seven, March 1924.
20 P. G. Konody, 'Arthur Streeton's English Paintings,' *The Art of Arthur Streeton: Special Number of Art in Australia*, Sydney 1919; *Bulletin*, 4 December 1913; 'Report of a Committee Appointed to Select 7 Artists Required for Work in the Australian War Records Section', AWM 3DRL 6673 item 286, 10 April 1918; Bean to Treloar, AWM 3DRL 6673 item 286, 28 August 1918.
21 Foreword, *Vision: A Literary Quarterly, II*, August 1923.
22 Lionel Lindsay, 'Australian Art'.
23 ibid.
24 Lionel Lindsay, 'Australian Art'; Konody, 'The Australian Exhibition in London'.
25 Konody, 'The Australian Exhibition in London'; 'Australian Art and English Critics', *Art in Australia*, Third Series, Number Seven, March 1924.
26 *Advertiser* (Adelaide), 20 October 1923.
27 ibid.
28 Ken Stewart in J. Ritchie (ed.), *Australian Dictionary of Biography*, vol. 12: 1891-1939, Melbourne University Press 1990, p. 77.
29 Norman Lindsay, 'The Quick and the Dead', *Art in Australia*, Third Series, Number One, 1 August 1922.
30 L. Bernard Hall, 'Aesthetics and Present-day Tendencies,' *Art in Australia*, Third Series, Number Two, 1 November 1922.
31 Foreword, *Vision*, No.1, May 1923; Forward, *Vision, II*, August 1923.
32 Foreword & James Cunninghame, 'France The Abyss', *Vision, II*, August 1923.
33 Cunninghame, 'France The Abyss'.
34 Foreword, *Vision*, No.1, May 1923.
35 Lionel Lindsay, 'George Lambert—Our First Australian Master,' *Art in Australia*, 15 February 1931; Barry Pearce in B. Nairn and G. Serle (eds), *Australian Dictionary of Biography*, vol. 9: 1891-1939, Melbourne University Press 1983, p. 134.
36 August, 'Art and Empire—Wembley, 1924'.
37 Robert Rooney, *Weekend Australian*, 21-22 May 1994; *Daily Guardian* (Sydney), 28 April 1927.

38 *Morning Post* (London), 9 May 1927.
39 *Herald* (Melbourne), 25 June 1927.
40 ibid.
41 Lionel Lindsay, *Comedy of Life*, p. 259.
42 ibid.
43 *Daily News* (Perth), 10 October 1927; *Sun News Pictorial* (Melbourne), 15 October 1927.
44 *Telegraph*, 29 October 1927.
45 Michael Richards, *People, print & paper: A catalogue of a travelling exhibition celebrating the books of Australia, 1788–1988*, Canberra 1988, pp. 42, 45. 'Editorial,' *Art in Australia: The Art of the Year*, Third Series, No. 26, December 1928.
46 ibid.
47 'Editorial,' *Art in Australia: A Contemporary Group of Australian Artists*, Third Series, No. 29, September 1929.
48 Basil Burdett, 'Some Contemporary Australian Artists,' *Art in Australia*, No. 29, September 1929.
49 ibid.

9   FISSURES IN THE IMPERIAL LANDSCAPE

1 *SMH*, 17 May 1913; *Bulletin*, 9 January 1913.
2 Vance Palmer, 'The Labour Leader: Joseph Benedict Chifley', *National Portraits*, Sydney 1960, p. 207.
3 *SMH*, 27 April 1920; Bean, *In Your Hands, Australians*, pp. 40, 51; diary entries in AWM 3DRL 606 item 17 [2], 29 September 1915 and in AWM 3DRL 606 item 77 [2], 28 April 1917.
4 Bean, *In Your Hands, Australians*, p. 59.
5 N. G. Butlin, 'Australian National Accounts', in Wray Vamplew (ed.), *Australians Historical Statistics*, Sydney 1987, p. 127.
6 *Age*, 8 February 1927; Clark, *History of Australia VI*, p. 256.
7 Clark, *History of Australia VI*, p. 256.
8 Ian Burn, *National Life & Landscapes: Australian Painting 1900–1940*, Sydney 1990, p. 81.
9 Rose E. B. Coombs, MBE, *Before Endeavours Fade: A Guide to the Battlefields of the First World War*, London (1983) 1986, p. 29; Burn, *National Life*, pp. 80–81.
10 *Bulletin*, 6 February 1913.
11 Bean to Aspinall-Oglander, AWM 3DRL7953 item 27, 8 September 1927.
12 ibid. (Bean's emphasis).
13 Bean diary AWM 3DRL 606 item 6 [2], 8 May 1915.
14 Bean, *The Official History of Australia in the War of 1914–1918, Volume III, The A.I.F. in France 1916*, St Lucia 1982, pp. 288, 447; *Age*, 9 June 1919; White to J. Black Vict RSSILA, AWM DRL606 item 276 [1], 7 April 1937. Bean had also been with McCay when he'd acted similarly on 8 May 1915.
15 *SMH*, 7 October 1927; *Sydney Sun*, 7 October 1927.

16 Bean to Gellibrand, AWM 3DRL7953 item 27, 7 October 1927; *Daily Guardian* (Sydney), 8 October 1927.
17 *Telegraph*, 8 October 1927; Sydney *Sun*, 8 October 1927; *Observer* (London), 9 October 1927.
18 Bean to minister for Defence and Bean to Edmonds, AWM 3DRL7953 item 27, 11 October 1927.
19 From T. H. E. Heyes, Australian Representative at the British Historical Section to Director Australian War Memorial, AWM 3DRL7953 item 27, 13 October 1927.
20 *Smith's Weekly*, 15 October 1927.
21 *Argus*, 6 July 1929.
22 *Argus*, 11 July 1929.
23 ibid.
24 ibid.
25 ibid.
26 *Argus*, 12 July 1929.
27 *Argus*, 13 July 1929.
28 *Argus*, 5 July 1929.
29 *Daily Telegraph* (London), 12 July 1929.
30 *Sunday Times* (London), 14 July 1929; *Sunday Express* (London), 14 July 1929; *Daily Herald* (London), 14 July 1929.
31 Cited in *Argus*, 16 July 1929.
32 Douglas Copland cited in L. J. Louis and Ian Turner, *The Depression of the 1930s*, Melbourne 1968, p. 12; *Argus*, 16 July 1929.
33 *Argus*, 17 July 1929.
34 *Argus*, 23, 24, 25 July 1929.
35 *Argus*, 5 July 1929.
36 Bean, *In Your Hands, Australians*, p. 11; J. S. MacDonald, 'Arthur Streeton,' *Art in Australia*, 15 October 1931.
37 MacDonald, 'Arthur Streeton'.
38 Clark citing R. G. Menzies to R. G. Casey, in Clark, *History of Australia VI*, p. 485.
39 'Il y a beaucoup plus de cultures humaines que de races humaines, puisque les unes se comptent par milliers et les autres par unités: deux cultures élaborées par des hommes appartenant à la même race peuvent différer autant, ou davantage, que deux cultures relevant de groupes racialement éloignés.' Claude Lévi-Strauss, *Race et histoire*, Unesco [1952], Paris 1987, pp. 10-11.
40 Humphrey McQueen, 'Jimmy's Brief Lives', in Bradley & Smith (eds), *Australian Art and Architecture*, p. 177; Bernard Smith, *Australian Painting*, South Melbourne, (1962) 1992, p. 196.

10 CRASH AND AFTERMATH

1 *Australian Worker*, 16, 23 October 1929; Clark, *History of Australia VI*, p. 334.
2 Clark, *History of Australia VI*, p. 348; Cobbold, in Lord Blake and C. S. Nicholls, *The Dictionary of National Biography 1971-1980*, Oxford 1986, pp. 632-33.

3 Clark, *History of Australia VI*, pp. 352-53; David Clark, 'Fools and Madmen', in Judy Makinolty (ed.), *The Wasted Years? Australia's Great Depression*, Sydney 1981, p. 177.

4 *Labor Daily*, 23 August 1930; *Australian Worker*, 27 August 1930; *SMH*, 28 August 1930.

5 Clark, *History of Australia VI*, pp. 373, 380, 408.

6 *Sun and Guardian* (Sydney), 8 November 1930.

7 *SMH*, 24 April 1920; Cobbold, in Blake and Nicholls, *Dictionary of National Biography*, p. 633.

8 Henry Mayer, *The Press in Australia*, Melbourne 1968, p. 213.

9 Ronald Mason, *Ashes in the Mouth: The Story of the Body-Line Tour 1932-33*, Harmondsworth 1984, p. 22.

10 *Truth* (Melbourne), 9 April 1932.

11 Mason, *Ashes in the Mouth*, pp. 60, 68, 76.

12 Mason, *Ashes in the Mouth*, p. 91.

13 Keith Miller and R. S. Whitington cited in Mason, *Ashes in the Mouth*, p. 95.

14 Mason, *Ashes in the Mouth*, p. 106.

15 *Argus*, 22 August 1929; W. K. Hancock, *Australia*, London 1930, p. 264-65.

16 Richard Haese in B. Nairn and G. Serle (eds), *Australian Dictionary of Biography*, vol. 7: 1891-1939, Melbourne University Press 1979, p. 482; *SMH*, 15 September 1932.

17 Russel Ward, *A nation for a continent: the history of Australia 1901-1975*, Richmond, Vic. 1977, p. 127.

18 Eagle, *Australian modern painting*, pp. 69, 91.

19 Bishop G. M. Long, 'Country Problems', from papers of Melbourne Church Conference ML 283.901/A, 1925, pp. 180-89; *Sun News Pictorial* (Melbourne), 18 April 1932.

20 *Herald* (Melbourne), 10 February 1933.

21 *Australian Woman's Weekly*, 7 December 1935.

22 K. S. Murdoch to L. Lindsay, ANL MS2823/63, 4 January 1935.

23 Murdoch to L. Lindsay, ANL MS2823/63, 4 January 1935.

24 Streeton to *Herald* (Melbourne), ANL MS5823/63, 8 March 1935 (Streeton's emphasis).

25 Murdoch ANL MS2823/63, 18 December 1935.

26 Douglas Dundas, *Douglas Dundas remembers ...* , Sydney 1975, p. 75; MacDonald to G. Ross Thomas, ANL MS 430 Box 2. Folder J.S. MacD—Corres., 20 October 1936.

27 MacDonald to Prof. H. C. Richards, University of Qld, MS 430, Box 3, Folder: Collection of paintings and drawing to be sent to USA, 2 January 1941.

28 *Argus*, 11 March 1937; Christine Dixon and Dynah Dysart, *Counter Claims: Presenting Australian Art 1938-1941*, Sydney 1986, p. 12.

29 *Australian Woman's Weekly*, 28 January 1939.

30 ibid.

31 Cited by Leonard B. Cox, *The National Gallery of Victoria 1861 to 1968: A Search for a Collection*, Melbourne 1971, p. 164.

32 ibid.

33 Lionel to Daryl Lindsay, ANL MS 4864 Box 1 Folder 1, 9 October 1940.
34 Letter by Colin W. Wyatt, *SMH*, 15 October 1940.

11 WHATEVER HAPPENED TO THE 'LOST GENERATION'?

 1 Gregory Melleuish, *The Tradition of Cultural Liberalism in Australia c1880-c1960: A Study in Intellectual and Cultural History*, Cambridge 1995 (forthcoming).
 2 Bean, *War Aims*, pp. v, 3.
 3 John Rickard, *Australia: A Cultural History*, Melbourne 1988, p. 129; Bean, *War Aims*, pp. 3-4.
 4 Bean, *War Aims*, p. v, 97.
 5 Bean, *War Aims*, p. 160.
 6 Gordon Greenwood in Greenwood (ed.), *Australia: A Social and Political History*, Sydney (1955) 1978, pp. iii, 233, 203.
 7 Greenwood, *Australia*, p. 235.
 8 Greenwood, *Australia*, pp. 287-335.
 9 Ward, *Australian Legend*, pp. vi, vii, 1.
10 Ward, *Australian Legend*, pp. 229-30, 259.
11 Wright, *Preoccupations In Australian Poetry*, p. 82.
12 Heather Radi, '1920-29', in F. J. Crowley (ed.), *A New History of Australia*, Melbourne 1974, pp. 389-95.
13 Clark, *History of Australia V*, pp. 374, 425 and *History of Australia VI*, p. 16.
14 Clark, *History of Australia VI*, p. 317.
15 Clark, *History of Australia V*, p. 340; *History of Australia VI*, pp. 133, 7, 279, 403.
16 Bernard Smith, *The Death of the Artist as Hero: Essays in History and Culture*, Melbourne 1988, p. 70.
17 ibid.
18 Hughes, *Shock of the New*, p. 59; Alistair Horne, *Death of a Generation: Neuve Chapelle to Verdun and the Somme*, London 1970, p. 115.
19 Smith, *Death of the Artist*, p. 227.
20 Figures on German war dead taken from Paul Sethe, *Das Machte Geschichte: Von Königgrätz bis zum Ende in der Reichskanzlerei*, Frankfurt/M 1977, p. 273.
21 André Ducasse, Jacques Meyer and Gabriel Perreux, *Vie et mort des Français 1914-1918: Simple Histoire de la Grande Guerre*, Paris 1962, p. 469.
22 Stein cited by Ernest Hemingway in *A Moveable Feast*, London 1988, p. 28; Smith, *Death of the Artist*, p. 227. For critiques of Smith's claim see, for example, Caroline Ambrus, *Australian Women Artists: First Fleet to 1945: History, Hearsay and Her Say*, Canberra 1992, pp. 142-43 and Ian Burn, Nigel Lendon, Charles Merewether and Ann Stephen, *The Necessity of Australian Art: An Essay About Interpretation*, Sydney 1988, pp. 66-67.
23 Ambrus, *Australian Women Artists*; Smith, *Death of the Artist*, p. 227.
24 Figures for 1912 from unpublished student records collated by Ingeborg Tyssen, from work in progress on a PhD thesis on the Art Gallery of NSW. Figures from 1926 to 1945 from *Handbook Sydney Technical College*, Sydney

1946, pp. 159-160. In recent times the proportion of male art students has risen to 18 per cent in TAFE and 31 per cent in the former CAEs. Caroline Ambrus citing 1982 figures from the *Research Advisory Group of the Women and Arts Project*, in Ambrus, *Australian Women Artists*, p. 216.

25 *SMH*, 8 November 1913; Ure Smith cited in the *Sydney Mail*, 25 June 1919. Nettie Palmer letter to E. J. Brady, Vivian Smith (ed.), *Letters of Vance and Nettie Palmer*, Canberra 1977, p. 10.

26 'Le mythe prive l'objet dont il parle de toute Histoire. En lui, l'histoire s'évapore', Roland Barthes, 'Le mythe, aujourd'hui', from *Mythologies*, Paris (1957) 1970, p. 239.

CONCLUSION

1 *Bulletin*, 6 November 1919.

2 Keegan, *A History of Warfare*, London 1993, p. xvi; Bean, 'Australia.—IV.— The Australian.—(BY C.W.)', *SMH*, 22 June 1907.

3 Treloar to Bean, AWM 3DRL 6673 item 314, 5 May 1921; AWM 3DRL 6673 item 297, 31 May 1923; AWM 3DRL 6673 item 312, 4 June 1930.

4 Treloar to Bean, AWM 3DRL 6673 item 312, 4 June 1930; Bean to Treloar, AWM 3DRL 6673 item 312, 20 January 1930; Gullett to Bean, AWM 3DRL 6673 item 302, 13 February 1926; Bean to Treloar, AWM 3DRL 6673 item 302, 19 February 1926; Bean to Treloar, AWM 3DRL 6673 item 302, 30 July 1926.

5 Streeton to Bean, AWM 3DRL 6673 item 322 (emphasis added), 19 June 1933; Robin Gerster, 'War Literature, 1890-1980', in Laurie Hergenham (ed.), *The Penguin New Literary History of Australia*, Ringwood 1988, p. 339.

6 See, for example, 'Quebec Hostility to Conscription—Failure of Strike Move- ment—Disturbances at Montreal', *Times*, 1 September 1917; 'More Rioting in Quebec—Machine-Guns Used by Military—Opposition to Conscription', *Times*, 4 April 1918; 'Quebec Riots—Strong Measures to Preserve Order', *Times*, 8 April 1918 and 'Causes of Quebec Riots—German Agents at Work', *Times*, 10 April 1918.

7 For a detailed analysis, see Appendix: The First AIF, a demographic sample.

8 Bill Gammage, *The Broken Years*, Canberra 1974, p. 278; 'The A.I.F. Spirit— Its Value for Australia—The Diggers' Ideal—(By F.M. Cutlack)', *SMH*, 21 November 1919.

9 Rickard, *Australia: A Cultural History*, p. 128.

10 Max Ernst interviewed in a film by Peter Schamoni, *Max Ernst*, © Peter Scha- moni Film, München, 1991.

11 'L'Amérique est le seul pays au monde qui soit passé de la barbarie à la décadence sans avoir jamais connu la civilisation.' William Troy and William Carlos William cited in Serge Guilbaut, *Comment New York vola l'idée de l'art moderne*, Nîmes (1983) 1987, p. 26.

12 Arthur Marwick, *The Deluge: British Society and the First World War*, London and Basingstoke 1978, p. 220.

13 ibid.

14 J. S. MacDonald in ANL MS 430 Box 1 Notebook entitled 'Contemporary Art'. 1 January 1943.

15 Serle, *The Creative Spirit in Australia*, p. 159.
16 Ian Burn, 'Beating About the Bush', in Bradley & Smith (eds), *Australian Art and Architecture*, p. 98.
17 Burn, *National Life and Landscape*, p. 10.
18 McQueen, 'Jimmy's Brief Lives', in Bradley & Smith, *Australian Art and Architecture*, p. 182.
19 'Mr. Mann, M.H.R.' citing 'Two Almost Forgotten Reports', in *Argus*, 22 July 1929.

Select Bibliography

PRIMARY SOURCES

Archives & documents
C. E. W. Bean Diaries and Notebooks, Australian War Memorial
Daryl Lindsay Papers, Australian National Library
Lionel Lindsay Papers, Australian National Library
Lionel Lindsay Papers, State Library of NSW
J. S. MacDonald Papers, Australian National Library
Melbourne Church Conference Report 1925, private collection
K. S. Murdoch Papers, Australian National Library
Sir Arthur Streeton Papers, Australian National Library

Newspapers & periodicals
Advertiser (Adelaide)
Age (Melbourne)
Argus (Melbourne)
Art and Australia
Art in Australia
Australian Worker
Berliner Tageblatt (Berlin)
Daily Guardian (Sydney)
Daily News (Perth)
Daily Telegraph (Sydney)
Figaro (Paris)
Herald (Melbourne)
L'Illustration (Paris)
Illustrierte Kriegs-Chronik des Daheim

Labor Daily
Miroir (Paris)
Morning Post (London)
Observer (London)
Sun and Guardian (Sydney)
Sun News Pictorial (Melbourne)
Sydney Mail
Sydney Morning Herald
Technical Gazette of New South Wales
Times (London)
Vision: A Literary Quarterly
Weekend Australian
Weekly Telegraph (London)
Woman's Weekly

SECONDARY SOURCES

Achbar, Mark, and Wintoneck, Peter. *Manufacturing Consent: Noam Chomsky and the Media; Part One—Thought Control in a Democratic Society*, National Film Board of Canada, 1992.

Adams, Francis. *The Australians: A Social Sketch*, London 1888.

Alba, Victor. *Le mouvement ouvrier en Amérique latine*, Collection 'Masses et Militants', Paris 1953.

Ambrus, Caroline. *Australian Women Artists: First Fleet to 1945: History, Hearsay and Her Say*, Canberra 1992.

Andrews, E. M. 'Bean and Bullecourt: Weaknesses and Strengths of the Official History of Australia in the First World War', *Revue Internationale d'Histoire Militaire*, no. 72—1990.

——. *The Anzac Illusion: Anglo-Australian Relations during World War I*, Cambridge 1993.

Assouline, Pierre. *L'homme de l'art: D.H. Kahnweiler 1884-1979*, Paris 1988.

August, Tom. 'Art and Empire—Wembley, 1924', *History Today*, vol. 43, October 1993.

Banton, Michael (ed.). *Darwinism and the Study of Society: A Centenary Symposium. With an Introduction by J. Bronowski*, London 1961.

Barnard, Marjorie. 'Modern Art in Australia', *Art of Australia 1788-1941: An Exhibition of Australian Art Held in the United States of America and the Dominion of Canada Under the Auspices of the Carnegie Foundation*, New York 1941.

Barroso, Haydée M. Jofre. *La Política de los Argentinos: Reportaje a los aciertos, errores, dudas, certezas, intuiciones e interrogantes políticos de los argentinos*, Buenos Aires 1990.

Bean, C. E. W., *Letters From France*, London 1916.

——. *In Your Hands, Australians*, London 1918.

——. *The Official History of Australia in the War of 1914-18, Volume I, The Story of Anzac: The First Phase (From the Outbreak of War to the End of the First Phase of the Gallipoli Campaign, May 4, 1915)*, Sydney 1935.

——. *The Official History of Australia in the War of 1914-1918, Volume III: The A.I.F. in France 1916*, St Lucia Queensland (1929) 1982.

——. *The Official History of Australia in the War of 1914-1918, Volume IV: The A.I.F. in France 1917*, St Lucia (1933) 1982.

——. 'The Old A.I.F. and the New', *Through Australian Eyes, Pamphlets on World Affairs*, Sydney 1940.

——. *War Aims of a Plain Australian*, Sydney 1943.

——. *Anzac to Amiens: A Shorter History of the Australian Fighting Services in the First World War*, Canberra 1961.

Becker, Jean-Jacques. *The Great War and the French People*, Leamington Spa 1985.

Berger, John, Introduction to *Irony Curtain: Art and politics between the USSR and the USA*, A DIZVIZ Production for Channel Four UK 1990.

Berman, Marshall. *All That Is Solid Melts Into Air*, New York 1982.

Beumelburg, Werner (ed.). *Schlachten des Weltkrieges; In Einzeldarstellungen bearbeitet und Herausgegeben im Auftrage des Reichsarchivs: Flandern 1917*, Berlin 1928.

Boraston, J. H., C.B., O.B.E. (ed.). *Sir Douglas Haig's Despatches (December 1915-April 1919)*, London 1920.

Borges, Jorge Luis, *Discusión*, Madrid 1983.

Bradley, Anthony, and Smith, Terry (eds), *Australian Art and Architecture: Essays Presented to Bernard Smith*, Melbourne 1980.

Brandmayer, Balthasar mitgeteilt von Bayer, Heinz. *Meldegänger Hitler*, Munich-Holdermoor 1933.

Brown, Milton W. *American Painting: from the Armory Show to the Depression*, Princeton 1955.

——. *The Story of the Armory Show*, New York 1958.

Burn, Ian. *National Life & Landscapes: Australian Painting 1900-1940*, Sydney 1990.

Burn, Ian; Lendon, Nigel; Merewether, Charles; and Stephen, Ann. *The Necessity of Australian Art: An Essay About Interpretation*, Sydney 1988.

Cantrell, Leon (ed.). *Portable Australian Authors—The 1890s: Stories Verse and Essays*, St Lucia 1977.

Chilvers, Ian, and Osborne, Harold (eds). *The Oxford Dictionary of Art*, Oxford 1988.

Clark, C. M. H. *A History of Australia V: The People Make Laws 1888-1915*, Melbourne (1981) 1987.

——. *A History of Australia VI: 'The Old Dead Tree and the Young Tree Green' 1916-1935*, Melbourne 1987.

Commonwealth War Graves Commission. *The War Dead and War Memorials of the Commonwealth, V.C. Corner and Australian Cemetery, Fromelles, France*. Memorial Index Register No. 7. Commonwealth War Graves Commission (1925) 1987.

Conan Doyle, Arthur. *The British Campaign In France and Flanders 1915*, London 1917.

Cox, Leonard B. *The National Gallery of Victoria 1861 to 1968: A Search for a Collection*, Melbourne 1971.

Crowley F. J. (ed.). *A New History of Australia*, Melbourne 1974.

Cutlack, F. M. *The Australians: Their Final Campaign, 1918: An Account of the Concluding Operations of the Australian Divisions in France*, London 1919.

Cutlack, F. M. (ed.). *The War Letters of General Monash*, Sydney 1934.

Dixon, Christine, and Dysart, Dynah. *Counter Claims: Presenting Australian Art 1938-1941*, Sydney 1986.

Ducasse, André; Meyer, Jacques; and Perreux, Gabriel. *Vie et mort des Français 1914-1918: Simple histoire de la grande guerre*, Paris 1962.

Dundas, Douglas. *Douglas Dundas remembers . . .* , Sydney 1975.

Dutton, Geoffrey. *Famous Australian Art: Arthur Streeton 1867-1943*, Brisbane 1987.

Eagle, Mary. *Australian modern painting between the wars 1914-1939*, Sydney 1989.

Egerton, H. E. 'The British Dominions and the War', *Oxford Pamphlets 1914*, No. 21, London 1914.

Eksteins, Modris. *Rites of Spring: The Great War and the Birth of the Modern Age*, London 1989.

Ellis, Capt. A.D., M.C. *The Story of the Fifth Australian Division: Being an Authoritative Account of the Division's Doings in Egypt, France and Belgium*, London 1919.

Fewster, Kevin. 'Ellis Ashmead Bartlett and the Making of the Anzac Legend', *Journal of Australian Studies*, no. 10, 1982.

Foster Fraser, John. *Australia: The Making of a Nation*, London 1910.

——. *The Amazing Argentine: A New Land of Enterprise*, London 1914.

Gellert, Leon. *Songs of a campaign*, Sydney 1917.

Gerster, Robin. *Big-Noting: The Heroic Theme in Australian War Writing*, Melbourne 1987.

Gibbs, Philip. *Realities of War*, London 1920.

Girardet, R. *Encyclopædia Universalus vol. 11*, Paris 1971.

Golomstock, Igor. *Totalitarian Art: In the Soviet Union, the Third Reich, Fascist Italy and the People's Republic of China*, London 1990.

Graves, Robert. *Good-Bye to All That: An Autobiography*, London 1929.

Green, Jonathon. *Camera Work: A Critical Anthology*, New York 1973.

Greenwood, Gordon (ed.). *Australia: A Social and Political History*, Sydney (1955) 1978.

Grey, Jeffrey. *A Military History of Australia*, Cambridge 1990.

Gunther, John. *Inside Latin America*, London 1942.

Guyot, Adelin, and Restellini, Patrick. *1933-1945 la mémoire du siècle: L'art nazi*, Brussels 1983.

Haese, Richard. *Rebels and Precursors: The Revolutionary Years of Australian Art*, Ringwood Vic (1981) 1988.

Hancock, W. K. *Australia*, London 1930.

Hardach, Gerd. *The Pelican History of World Economy in the Twentieth Century; The First World War 1914-1918*, Harmondsworth, Middlesex (1977) 1987.

Hemingway, Ernest. *A Moveable Feast*, London 1988.

Herf, Jeffrey. *Reactionary Modernism: Technology, culture, and politics in Weimar and the Third Reich*, Cambridge (1984) 1986.

Hervier, Julien. *Entretiens avec Ernst Jünger*, Paris 1986.

Hinz, Bethold. *Art in the Third Reich*, New York 1979.

Hobsbawm, E. J. *The Age of Empire 1875-1914*, London 1987.

Hofstadter, Richard. *The Age of Reform: From Bryan to F.D.R.*, New York 1960.

Horne, Alistair. *Death of a Generation: Neuve Chapelle to Verdun and the Somme*, London 1970.

Hughes, Robert. *The Art of Australia*, Melbourne (1966) 1988.

——. *The Shock of the New: Art and the Century of Change*, London (1980) 1991.

Jackson, R. V. *Australian Economic Development in the Nineteenth Century*, Canberra 1972.

Joachimides, Christos M.; Rosenthall, Norman; and Schmeid, Wieland (eds). *German Art in the 20th Century: Painting and Sculpture 1905-1985*, London 1985.

Johnson, W. H. *The Right Reverend George Merrick Long M.A., D.D., LL.D., C.B.E., V.D. A Memoir*, by the Very Reverend W. H. Johnson, B.A., TH.L. Dean of Newcastle, Morpeth 1930.

Joynt, W. D. *Saving the Channel Ports*, North Blackburn 1983.

Jünger, Ernst. *The Storm of Steel: From the Diary of A German Storm-Troop Officer on the Western Front*, London (1920) 1929.

——. *Premier Journal Parisien 1941-1943*, Paris 1984.

——. *Le Boqueteau 125 (Das Wäldchen 125): Chronique des combats de tranchées 1918*, Paris (1932) 1986.

——. *Lieutenant Sturm*, Paris 1991.

Keegan, John. *A History of Warfare*, London 1993.

Kent, D. A. 'The Anzac Book and the Anzac Legend: C.E.W. Bean as Editor and Image-Maker', *Historical Studies*, vol. 21, no. 84, April 1985.

Knightley, Phillip. *The First Casualty: From the Crimea to Vietnam: The War Correspondent as Hero, Propagandist, and Myth Maker*, London (1975) 1978.

Konody, P. G. 'Arthur Streeton's English Paintings', *The Art of Arthur Streeton: Special Number of Art in Australia*, Sydney 1919.

Lacquer, Walter. *Weimar: A Cultural History 1918-1933*, New York 1980.

Laffin, John. *Digger: The Legend of the Australian Soldier*, South Melbourne 1986.

Lévi-Strauss, Claude. *Race et histoire*, Unesco [1952] Paris 1987.

Lindsay, Lionel. 'Australian Art', *The Exhibition of Australian Art in London 1923: A Record of the Exhibition Held at the Royal Academy and Organised by the Society of Artists Sydney*, Sydney 1923.

——. *Addled Art*, Sydney 1942.

—— (Sir). *Comedy of Life: An Autobiography*, Sydney 1967.

Louis, L. J. and Turner, Ian. *The Depression of the 1930s*, Melbourne 1968.

Luna, Félix. *Conflictos y armonías en la historia argentina*, Buenos Aires 1989.

Macainsh, Noel. *Nietzsche in Australia: A Literary Inquiry into a Nationalist Ideology*, Munich 1975.

McCarthy, Dudley. *Gallipoli to the Somme: the story of C.E.W. Bean*, Sydney 1983.

McQueen, Humphrey. *The Black Swan of Trespass: The Emergence of Modernist Painting in Australia to 1944*, Victoria 1987.

Madelin, Louis. *Le Chemin de la Victoire II: De la Somme au Rhin (1916-1918)*, Paris *ca.*1920.

Magraw, Roger. *France 1815-1914: The Bourgeois Century*, London (1983) 1987.

Makinolty, Judy (ed.). *The Wasted Years? Australia's Great Depression*, Sydney 1981.

Marwick, Arthur. *War and Social Change in the Twentieth Century: A comparative study of Britain, France, Germany, Russia and the United States*, London 1974.

——. *The Deluge: British Society and the First World War*, London and Basingstoke 1978.

Masefield, John. *Gallipoli*, London 1926.

Mason, Ronald. *Ashes in the Mouth: The Story of the Body-Line Tour 1932-33*, Harmondsworth (1982) 1984.

Mayer, Henry. *The Press in Australia*, Melbourne (1964) 1968.

Mendelssohn, Joanna. *Lionel Lindsay: An Artist and His Family*, London 1988.

Montague, C. E. *Disenchantment*, London 1922.

Moore, William. *The Story of Australian Art: From the Earliest Known Art of the Continent to the Art of Today*, 2 vols, Sydney (1934) 1980.

Mosse, George L. *Nazi Culture: Intellectual, Cultural and Social Life in the Third Reich*, New York (1966) 1981.

Offer, Avner. *The First World War: An Agrarian Interpretation*, Oxford 1989.

Palmer, Vance. 'The Labour Leader: Joseph Benedict Chifley', *National Portraits*, Sydney (1940) 1960.

Pons, Xavier. *Out of Eden: Henry Lawson's Life and Works—A Psychoanalytic View*, North Ryde NSW 1984.

Powell, J. M. *An Historical Geography of Modern Australia: The restive fringe*, Cambridge 1988.

Proudfoot, Peter R. 'Canberra: the triumph of the Garden City', *Journal of the Royal Australian Historical Society*, vol. 77, part 1, June 1991.

Radi, Heather. *'1920-29'*. In F. J. Crowley (ed.), *A New History of Australia*, Melbourne 1974.

Richards, Michael. *People, print & paper: A catalogue of a travelling exhibition celebrating the books of Australia, 1788-1988*, Canberra 1988.

Rickard, John. *Australia: A Cultural History*, Melbourne 1988.

Robson, L. L. *Australia in the Nineteen Twenties: Commentary and Documents*, Topics in Australian History Series, Melbourne 1980.

——. *The First A.I.F.: A Study of its Recruitment 1914-1918*, Melbourne (1970) 1982.

Roderick, Colin. *Henry Lawson—The Master Story Teller: Commentaries on His Prose Writings*, Sydney 1985.

——. *Henry Lawson—Collected Verse, Volume One 1885-1900*, Sydney 1967.

——. *Henry Lawson—Collected Verse, Volume Two*, Sydney 1967.

——. *Henry Lawson: Autobiographical and Other Works*, Sydney 1972.

Roe, Michael, *Nine Australian Progressives: Vitalism in Bourgeois Social Thought 1890-1960*, St Lucia 1984.

Rule, E. J. M.C. *Jacka's Mob, With a foreword by John Masefield, Poet Laureate, Author of "Gallipoli", "The Everlasting Mercy,"* etc., Sydney 1933.

Schamoni, Peter. *Max Ernst*, Co-production by Peter Schamoni Film, RM Arts, Inter Nationes, ZDF, © Peter Schamoni Film, München 1991.

Schwarte, M. (ed.). *Der große Krieg 1914-1918: Der deutsche Landkrieg. Erster Teil. Vom Kriegsbeginn bis zum Frühjahr 1915*, Leipzig, 1921.

Scott, Ernest. *The Official History of Australia in the War of 1914-18, Volume XI, Australia During the War*, St Lucia (1936) 1989.

Serle, Geoffrey. *The Creative Spirit in Australia: A Cultural History*, Richmond Vic. 1987.

Shapiro, Michael Edward, and Hassrick, Peter H. *Frederic Remington: the Masterworks. With essays by David McCullough, Doreen Bolger Burke and John Seelye*, New York 1988.

Smart, Judith, and Wood, Tony (eds). *An Anzac Muster: War and Society in Australia and New Zealand 1914-18 and 1939-45, Selected Papers*, Monash Publications in History, Clayton, Vic. 1992.

Smith, Bernard. *Australian Painting*, South Melbourne (1962) 1992.

——. *The Death of the Artist as Hero: Essays in History and Culture*, Melbourne 1988.

Smith, Vivian (ed.). *Letters of Vance and Nettie Palmer*, Canberra 1977.

Solleder, Dr Fridolin (ed.). *Vier Jahre Westfront: Geschichte des Regiments List R.I.R. 16*, München 1932.

Staniforth Smith, Lieut. The Hon. M.B.E., F.R.G.S., F.Z.S. (44th Battalion A.I.F.). *Australian Campaigns in the Great War: Being a Concise History of the Australian Naval and Military Forces 1914 to 1918*, London 1919.

Tillyard, S. K. *The Impact of Modernism 1900-1920: Early Modernism and the Arts and Crafts Movement in Edwardian England*, London 1988.

Ure Smith, Sydney. 'Foreword,' *The Exhibition of Australian Art in London 1923: A Record of the Exhibition Held at the Royal Academy and Organised by the Society of Artists Sydney*, Sydney 1923.

Vamplew, Wray (ed.). *Australians Historical Statistics*, Sydney 1987.

Virilio, Paul. *Guerre et cinéma I: Logistique de la perception*, Paris (1984) 1991.

Ward, Russel. *A nation for a continent: the history of Australia 1901-1975*, Richmond, Vic. 1977.

——. *The Australian Legend*, Melbourne (1958) 1988.

White, Richard. *Inventing Australia: Images and Identity 1688-1980*, Sydney (1981) 1988.

Willett, John. *The New Sobriety: Art and Politics in the Weimar Period 1917-33*, London 1978.

Williams, E. T., and Palmer, Helen M. *The Dictionary of National Biography: 1951-1960*, Oxford 1972.

Williams, J. F. 'Modernism & the Lost Generation', *Art and Australia*, vol. 29, No. 1, Spring 1991.

——. 'Art, War and agrarian Myths: Australian Reactions to Modernism: 1913-1931'. In Smart and Wood (eds), *An Anzac Muster: War and Society in Australia and New Zealand 1914-18 and 1939-45, Selected Papers*, Monash Publications in History, Clayton, Vic. 1992.

——. 'Eight Battles', *Journal of Australian Studies*, September 1993.

Winter, Denis. *Haig's Command: A Reassessment*, London 1991.

Wright, Judith. *Preoccupations in Australian Poetry*, Melbourne (1965) 1966.

Index